THE AUTOBIOGRAPHY OF

# MAJOR TAYLOR

## THE FASTEST BICYCLE RIDER IN THE WORLD

# Note from Publisher,

We are thrilled beyond measure to take part in re-printing a book that is a breath taking example of Black excellence. Major Taylor and other titans somehow shattered barriers and established new records in many arenas in spite of racist beliefs and behaviors. Under almost impossible circumstances which in Major Taylor's case included threats to his life, foul play, being choked until unconscious for 15 minutes, and,

STILL. WE. RISE.

This story of adventure, stamina and inner strength of the first world recognized Black athlete is sure to inspire every generation. Stories of Victory, Success and Accomplishment abound in history. We are duty bound to share them to all who will listen.

# Afriware Books, Co

COVER/QUOTE PAGE PHOTO CREDITS : GALLICA/WIKEMEDIA COMMONS
DESIGNED BY: AFRIWARE BOOKS, CO

# The  Fastest
# Bicycle Rider
# in the World

I am writing my memoirs,
however, in the spirit
calculated to solicit
simple justice, equal
rights, and a square deal
for the posterity of my
down-trodden but brave
people, not only in
athletic games and sports,
but in every honorable
game of human endeavor.

- Marshall "Major"

# The Fastest Bicycle Rider in the World

## Major Taylor

First published in 1928
reprint in 2022 in the U.S.A. by:

Afriware Books, Co
1701 S. 1st Ave., Suite 400
Maywood, IL 60153
www.afriwarebooks.com

# THE FASTEST BICYCLE RIDER IN THE WORLD

Major Taylor

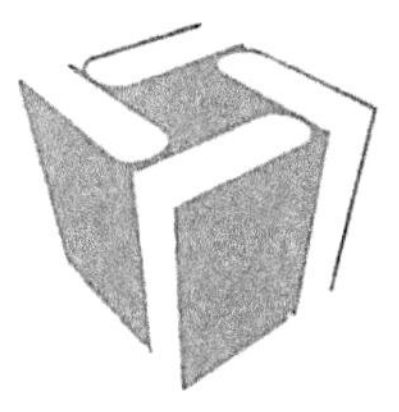

Major Taylor

# *The* Fastest Bicycle Rider In the World

## THE STORY OF A COLORED BOY'S INDOMITABLE COURAGE AND SUCCESS AGAINST GREAT ODDS

AN AUTOBIOGRAPHY BY
MARSHALL W. "MAJOR" TAYLOR

WORMLEY PUBLISHING COMPANY
14 BLOSSOM STREET
WORCESTER, MASSACHUSETTS

## DEDICATION

# TABLE OF CONTENTS

# FOREWORD

These reminiscences, covering the most colorful chapter in all the history of bicycle racing, among other remarkable facts, brings out very clearly many of the outstanding qualities characteristic of my race, such as perseverance, courage, and that marvelous spirit of forgiveness.

It also proves to the world literally, that there are positively no mental, physical, moral or other attainments too lofty for a Negro to accomplish if granted a fair and equal opportunity. The records and success that I achieved in my chosen line of athletic sports, certainly the greatest of all if played fair, and the brilliant performances of other colored athletes in various branches of the sports where permitted to compete will verify this somewhat emphatic assertion.

The primary object of this narrative, however, is not for any personal glory, or self praise but rather to perpetuate my achievements on the bicycle tracks of the world, for the benefit of all youths aspiring to an athletic career, and especially boys of my own group as they strive for fame and glory in the athletic world.

A perusal of the following autobiography and chronologically arranged news clippings will reveal many of the secrets of my great success, notwithstanding the tremendous odds and almost tragic hardships that I was forced to do extra battle against owing to color prejudice and jealousy of the bitterest form. With the aid of the press, however, the strict application to the rules of training, and the help of God, I was able to overcome that bitter intensity of feeling to some extent, or sufficiently at least to accomplish my life's greatest objective, namely, "The Fastest Bicycle Rider in the World."

Judging by the manner in which colored athletes have repeatedly demonstrated their skill and prowess in the athletic world, it is quite obvious what might well be accomplished on a whole as a race in other pursuits of life if granted a square deal and a fair field. We ask no special favor or advantage over other groups in the great game of life; we only ask for an even break.

I am writing my memoirs, however, in the spirit calculated to solicit simple justice, equal rights, and a square deal for the posterity of my down-trodden but brave people, not only in athletic games and sports, but in every honorable game of human endeavor.

# INTRODUCTION

As I look back over my eventful career of seventeen years bicycle racing, replete with unique experiences, thrills and hardships, and the interesting part I played in the history of the great game, after having gained all the triumphs, gold, and glory possible to obtain in that line of the sport, I find that my name is now and then mentioned among that steadily increasing list of notables, placed in the immortal cycle hall of fame, commonly known as "Old Timers." I was finally beaten fairly and squarely once at least by one who is destined eventually to trim even the best of us. I refer to the mightiest champion of them all, and one who needs no introduction—"Father Time."

During my turn as champion cyclist I out-gamed and out-sprinted him over and over again, and occasionally after handing him a very bad beating I was even conceited enough to give him the laugh, but somehow he didn't seem to mind it at all. I fancy I can see him even now just plugging along steadily, with that grim expression on his face, trying to overtake me. But alas, however, the scene is changed, the table is turned, not only has he overtaken me, but has actually passed me by, and is still gaining upon me at every revolution of the pedals, for "Time Eventually Wins."

One thing, however, he was at least decent about it, and just like the good old sport that he is, he didn't give me the laugh as he speeded past me, or stop to remind me of how I used to poke fun at him. No, "Father Time" was more considerate, he let me down easy.

I tried to take my licking gracefully however, because after all is said, done, and written, I rather consider it an honor to be defeated by him and by no means a disgrace; as a matter of choice I would much prefer defeat at his hands than by "Kid Nicotine," or flattened by that other frightful bogy—old "John Barleycorn," who has the reputation of having floored more great athletes, world-beaters, and in fact people in all walks of life than perhaps any other adversary in the world.

However, I can boast of having had at least the most "colorful" if not the most unique career of any person that ever won a World's Championship title, and now I have a wonderful message for any youth aspiring to an athletic career if he will only accept it, which is a message growing out of my many years of racing and trying experiences.

*A fair field and no favor, now as we begin*
*A square deal for all, and may the best man win;*
*A fair field and no favor is our appeal,*
*A square deal will conquer in every field.*

## CHAPTER I

### HOW I STARTED RIDING

A freak of fate started me on what was destined to be my racing career which was climaxed by my becoming champion of the world when I was only twenty-two years of age. Born in Indianapolis, November 26, 1878, I was one of eight children, five girls and three boys. When I was eight years old my father was employed by a wealthy family in that city named Southard, as a coachman. Occasionally my father would take me to work with him when the horses needed exercising, and in time I became acquainted with the rich young son Daniel, who was just my age.

We soon became the best of friends, so much so in fact, that I was eventually employed as his playmate and companion. My clothing was furnished and we were kept dressed just alike all the time. "Dan" had a wonderful play room stacked with every kind of toy imaginable, but his work shop was to me the one best room in the whole house, and when there I was the happiest boy in the world.

The rest of "Dan's" playmates were of wealthy families too, and I was not in the neighborhood long before I learned to ride a bicycle just as they did. All the boys owned bicycles excepting myself, but "Dan" saw to it that I had one too. I soon became a big favorite among them, perhaps because of my ability to hold up my end in all the different games we played, such as baseball, tennis, football, roller-skating, running and cycling, trick riding, and all the rest.

There was only one thing, though, that I could not beat them at, and that was when we went down to the Young Men's Christian Association gymnasium. It was there that I was first introduced to that dreadful monster prejudice, which became my bitterest foe from that very same day, and one which I have never as yet been able to defeat. Owing to my color, I was not allowed to join the Y. M. C. A., and in consequence was not permitted to go on the gymnasium floor with my companions. The boys protested to their parents about it, but they, even with their powerful influence, were unable to do anything about it, consequently I could only watch the other boys from the gallery go through their callisthenics, and how my poor little heart would ache to think that I was denied an opportunity to exercise and develop my muscles in the same manner as they, and for really no reason that I was responsible for. However, I made the best of matters knowing that I could beat them on the campus.

Some time later the Southard family moved to Chicago, and because my mother could not bear the idea of parting with me, I

( 1 )

dropped from the happy life of a "millionaire kid" to that of a common errand boy, all within a few weeks.

Not satisfied with having this bicycle all to myself I decided to become a trick rider. It will be well to remember at this point that in those days bicycles held the same relative position that the automobile occupied a generation ago. That meant that in reality I was a pioneer in this trick-riding field, and had to teach myself. However, the same perseverance that later played such a prominent part in my successful career on the bicycle track evidenced itself while I was a barefoot boy. After long hours practicing I became a pretty fair trick rider and to my skill along this line I attribute my initial appearance in a bicycle race when I was thirteen years old.

It came about in this way. I went to the bicycle store owned by Hay & Willits in Indianapolis, to get a minor repair made on my machine. After the repair had been made I made a fancy mount on my bicycle in the middle of the store and immediately drew the attention of Mr. Hay. He asked me who taught me that trick, and when I replied myself he smiled doubtfully. I told Mr. Hay that that was one of my easiest tricks and that I had a number of others that I would like to show him if he was interested. He was, and he ordered the store cleared to a certain extent and I did a number of my homemade tricks for him and his guests of the occasion that made them fairly gasp. In fact the exhibition was so good that Mr. Hay, his mind ever alert for good advertising for his store, invited me to repeat them in the street in front of his place of business. In a short time there was so much congestion on the spot that the police were called to open it up for traffic.

Going into the store later on Mr. Hay's invitation he asked me how I would like to go to work for the firm. I told him I was peddling a paper route and earning $5.00 a week at it, and that, of course, I would expect a little more for my services if my mother would allow me to work for him. My eyes nearly popped out of my head when he said, "I will give you that $35.00 bicycle and $6.00 a week if you will come to work for me. I told him I would consult my mother and let him know shortly. I went to work for him in the course of a few days.

My first duty in the store every morning was to sweep and dust, but every afternoon at four I was booked to give an exhibition of trick and fancy riding in my nice new uniform out in the street in front of the store. At the time there was a gold medal on exhibition in one of our show windows, the first prize for the annual ten-mile road race which was promoted by my employers, and which was one of the outstanding sporting events of Indianapolis. I spent more time daily fondling that medal than I did wielding the duster. It seemed to me like that would probably be the only chance that I would have to be near such a valuable prize.  I recall clearly being so bold one day as to pin the medal on the lapel of my coat and strut with it for five minutes in front of the mirror.

However, it was in the books that within a comparatively short time that medal was to be all my own—the reward of my first victory in a bicycle race.  My entry into this event was an accident pure and simple.  I had gone out to witness the event, which attracted the cream of the amateur riders of Indiana, and had taken a vantage point near the start when Mr. Hay spotted me.  Thinking to inject a laugh into the race for the benefit of the thousands that lined the course, Mr. Hay insisted that I take my place on the starting line.  I rebelled, but he fairly dragged me and my bicycle across the road saying, "Come on here, young man, you have got to start in this race."  I was badly scared at the thought as one may well imagine since I had never seen a bicycle race before.

Although the band was playing a lively tune and the crowd was cheering wildly I was crying.  When Mr. Hay saw that he started to lift me from my wheel, but stopped and whispered in my ear, "I know you can't go the full distance, but just ride up the road a little way, it will please the crowd, and you can come back as soon as you get tired."

Crack! went the pistol, and with tears in my eyes I was off with a fifteen minute handicap on the scratch man.  There were hundreds of cyclists stretched along the route, and it seemed to be a friendly sort of cheer and one that encouraged me and inspired me to keep on going even after I had begun to feel very tired.  Those words telling me that I could turn back after going a short distance inspired me on when it seemed like fatigue was about to overtake me.  They made me all the more determined to show my employer that I could go the distance.  As I pedalled along the seemingly endless route I felt sure my knees had been torn out of their sockets by my pedals, but I was determined to cover the entire distance no matter how long it took.

After I had ridden some distance I noticed a group of riders coming to meet me.  As they drew closer I recognized Mr. Hay among them. He had the gold medal that was hung up for first prize and dangled it in front of my eyes as we rode along.  As he did so he informed me that I was a mile ahead of the field and had half of the distance left to go.  The thought flashed through my mind that I had a chance to own that medal which I had so many times pinned on myself in the store.  The sight of it seemed to give me a fresh start, and I felt as though I had only just begun the race.  The thought of that gold medal becoming my property spurred me on to my greatest efforts.

The act on Mr. Hay's part was the psychological turning point of the race for me. From then on I rode like mad and wobbled across the tape more dead than alive in first place about six seconds ahead of the scratch man, Walter Marmon. Incidentally this same Walter Marmon is president of the Marmon Automobile Co. today.

Once across the finishing line I collapsed and fell in a heap in the roadway. Kind hands revived me shortly and I recall clearly that the first thing I saw on regaining consciousness was that big gold medal pinned on my chest. I had been through a nerve-racking, heart-breaking race, my legs pained me terribly, but I felt amply repaid for my efforts as I scanned that medal. My first thought was to take it home and show it to my mother. Fast as I had ridden that race I rode with greater speed to my home. My mother laughed and cried in turn as I related the incident of my first race. And one may well imagine my enthusiasm as I told her about the race, as I was but thirteen years old at the time.

# CHAPTER II



My next race was in Peoria, Illinois, in the summer of 1892, an event for boys under sixteen. I was fourteen at the time. Although I did not win the race, I was third, but the kindly manner of the public toward me created a lasting impression in my mind. Little did I imagine then that the next time I appeared on this track that I would be greeted as the Champion of America and it is a safe bet that nobody else imagined so. Thanks to the encouragement given me on that occasion I continued striving towards championship honors, and was elated several years later to be able to return to Peoria as champion sprinter of America.

Peoria was the Mecca of bicycle racing in those days. On its historical track all of the fastest riders in the world struggled for fame and glory. Among the most noted of them were: Zimmerman, Windle, Van Sicklen, Lumsden, Munger, Spooner, Githens, Stone, Temple, Davis, Thorne, Dernberger, Barrett, Kinsley and Hollinsworth, in fact that galaxy of stars participated in the feature event of the program which included the race for boys under sixteen in which I rode.

I clearly recall seeing one of the racers in that meet, William Laurie, participating on his racing machine which was equipped with the first pneumatic tires ever ridden in a bicycle race in this country. Hitherto all racers had their wheels equipped with solid rubber tires as pneumatics had not been perfected up to that time. Hoots and jeers greeted Laurie throughout the afternoon as he blazed the trail for the use of pneumatic tires, which revolutionized bicycle racing, and the manufacture of bicycles simultaneously. Shortly came the cushion tires and soon thereafter the self same pneumatic tires that Laurie demonstrated so well that day came into common use on the bicycle tracks in the country.

The following spring I went to work for H. T. Hearsey, a bicycle dealer in Indianapolis. My principle occupation was giving bicycle lessons, although I also did general work about the store.

While in the employ of Mr. Hearsey I won a number of races, the most important one being a 75-mile road race from Indianapolis to Matthews, Indiana. It was promoted by Mr. George Catterson, a very wealthy sportsman who made his home in Indianapolis. Because of a growing feeling against me on the part of the crack bicycle riders of the day, due wholly to the fact that I was colored, the greatest secrecy surrounded the arrangements for this big event.

It may be well at this time for me to outline just how this race prejudice feeling against me came to a head. A few months before the 75-mile road race was held, Walter Sanger, one of the greatest bicycle riders of the day, made an attempt to establish a new track record for 1-mile on the Capital City race track in Indianapolis. Before an immense throng he established a mark of 2.18 and was paid a handsome bonus for his stunt.

A number of my friends secretly arranged to have me make an attempt on Sanger's record shortly after he left the track. Because of the color prejudice that my previous success had earned for me I had to be taken into a dressing room secretly. Hardly had the cheers of the immense throng which greeted the announcement of Sanger's time died away before I made my appearance on the track ready to endeavor to lower Sanger's record. Quickly the news flashed through the crowd that I was to make an attack on his recently established mark, and the crowd held their seats as I took a few preliminary trips around the track, which measured one-fifth of a mile to a lap.

One could hear a pin fall as I made my way up the track for a flying start against Sanger's record. I was paced by a number of my friends who were mounted on tandems. The first one paced me on the first three laps, and a second tandem took me over the balance of the distance going as fast as the track would permit. Those pacemakers were spurred on in their efforts by the thought that they were fighting for a principle as well as for my personal success. They were all white men, and had stacked their all in the belief that I was capable of breaking Sanger's newly established record. Because of the feeling that was stirred up against me among the bicycle riders in general simply because of my color, my pacemakers stood a chance of being scoffed at had I failed to break his record.

I made my last great effort and pulled up alongside the tandem in the last fifty yards, beating them about two lengths across the tape, and finishing the mile in 2:11, seven seconds under the highly paid Sanger.

Just to show what I could do, I came out on the track later in the evening and did a fifth of a mile unpaced. I rode around the track twice to get going properly, and then took the word. The crowd grew enthusiastic, for it was seen that the way I was riding I would come close to the fifth of a mile record on a five-lap track. The time-keepers compared watches, and I was surprised to learn that I had made a record of :23 3/5, beating the record made in Europe that spring by Macdonald, on the famous Paris track 2/5 of a second.

When the time for my ride was announced I received one of my most flattering ovations. The white riders attracted by the cheering of the spectators, crowded on to the track to see what was going on.

As I passed through them to my dressing room I heard several threatening remarks aimed at me.  They were not only angry at me for having broken the records, but also at the track manager as well for having allowed me to race on the track, even though I had no white men opposing me.  Incidentally my track records stood as long as the track remained.

My friends had put over a clever little trick in smuggling me on the track for my record-breaking ride, but in so doing they incurred the enmity of a group of narrow-minded people.  I received no pay for my record-breaking mile, other than the satisfaction that it gave me, that feeling being enjoyed also by my good friends who were pleased that they had a part in my demonstration to the public of my riding ability provided I got a square deal.  Down in my heart I felt that if I could get an even break I could make good as a sprinter on the bicycle tracks of the country.  That was ample pay for me.

Thereafter I was barred from ever competing again on any track in Indianapolis.  However, my being debarred from those tracks fortunately paved the way for one of the greatest races I ever participated in.

Several weeks after I had established the record for the Capital City track in Indianapolis, the See-Saw Circle Club which was composed of more than 100 colored riders, held a ten-mile road race.  It was announced in advance of the event that the rider who won from scratch would represent the club in a big ten-mile road race in Chicago, all expenses being paid for by the club, including a trainer.  This event was open only to Negro riders, and they came from all parts of the country.

Henry Stewart, who was known the country over as the "St. Louis Flyer," was easily the outstanding star of the event.  Just before the race started one of the club officials accompanied Stewart into my tent and introduced him to me.  Stewart and I were the scratch men of the occasion.  He was a man of powerful physique, having well-developed legs and muscular arms and shoulders.  He smiled at me cynically, being evidently bent on unnerving me.  For a time it had the desired effect on me as I grew weak and nervous.  It was the first time in my life that I had experienced such a reaction.  As I lay trembling on my cot I heard Stewart talking, evidently for my benefit just outside.  He ridiculed me and requested the secretary of the race to give me the limit handicap, as he said he felt I looked as though I needed it.  His sarcastic remarks proved to be his undoing, however, as they stirred me as I never had been stirred before.  Instantly all my fighting spirit rushed back to me, and I jumped into my racing togs determined to beat Stewart at any cost.

As he strutted to the starting line in his bright bath robe, I became more determined than ever to defeat him.  He got a wonderful reception from the immense gathering, but I don't recall whether there was any applause for me or not—that's how worked up I was.

When the starter sent us away Stewart promptly jumped into the front and started to sprint right from the very outset, riding as if he was in a quarter of a mile race instead of a ten-mile grind. He set a heartbreaking pace in an effort to shake me off in the first half-mile, but finding me right up even with him he decided that he had better settle down and let me do a share of the pacemaking. However, I had an advantage over him as his big frame served as a fine wind-shield for me while I was so small that he did not get a similar advantage while riding at my rear wheel.

After alternating in the pacemaking positions for several miles, and with half the distance gone Stewart's rear tire blew out. Another rider turned his wheel over to Stewart and the latter promptly took up the race again. As soon as I saw Stewart in trouble I slowed down. Soon we were at our task again, and I noticed after we had reeled off several very hot miles that the grind was beginning to have its effect on Stewart. My first thought was that it was a ruse on Stewart's part to save himself for the final dash to the tape, as I knew him to be a very tricky rider. Shortly, however, with less than a mile to go, I could plainly see that Stewart was in distress. I held my sprint for the last quarter of a mile,.and then bolted for the tape. Stewart fought gamely as I passed him, but I led him over the line by ten lengths.

I was carried about on the shoulders of a number of Indianapolis men and received a flattering ovation from the packed stands.

Stewart claimed that he lost the race to me through having to use a strange bicycle. He challenged me to a match race for five miles, and I promptly accepted. We raced at Rushville, Indiana, and again I made Stewart trail me over the line. Thereafter I won three other races on the same program.

Upon my return to Indianapolis I was accorded a splendid reception, but I honestly believe that the greatest benefit that came out of my victory over Stewart was the fact that it gave me confidence and as-surance. After I had disposed of Stewart in those two races I felt very certain that no rider, regardless of his size or physique could ever shake me off his rear wheel, and no man ever did.

I wound up that very colorful racing season by winning three races, quarter, half and mile, that were held at the Lexington, Kentucky Fair in that city, under the auspices of the colored citizens. Those were the only bicycle races on the program, but they attracted the fastest riders from Louisville, St. Louis, Chicago and Cincinnati.

As word spread about my being barred from the tracks in Indian-apolis, because of color, Mr. George Catterson gave me a chance to again demonstrate my ability as a bicycle rider. He decided that from Indianapolis to the town of Matthews would be the course. Keeping the fact that I was to be a competitor secret Mr. Catterson offered prizes that were sufficiently attractive to interest the best bicycle riders in the state. Had they known I was to start, none of them would have entered. However, they did not share Mr. Catterson's secret, and all of them were on hand when the starter took up his position.

Shortly after his pistol shot sent the bunch away on the 75-mile grind, I jumped from my hiding place and started in hot pursuit of the fifty-odd riders who were pedalling for all they were worth down the roadway. I trailed along in the rear for several miles and was resting up in good shape before they were aware that I was in the race. They made things disagreeable for me by calling me vile names, and trying to put me down, and they even threatened to do me bodily harm if I did not turn back. I decided that if my time had come I might just as well die trying to keep ahead of the bunch of riders, so I jumped through the first opening and went out front, never to be overtaken in the feverish dash for the finish line.

When I took the lead we had covered about half the distance and were on a weird stretch of road that was thinly inhabited, with weeping willows on one side and a cemetery opposite. The thought ran through my mind that this would make an ideal spot for my competitors to carry out their dire threats. Spurred on by such thoughts I opened up the distance between my wheel and the balance of the field to make doubly sure that none of them caught up to me and got a chance to do me bodily injury.

As we neared Marion, Indiana, I noticed a number of local riders waiting for us to pace the leaders through that city. At first I was afraid they were out to do harm and rode cautiously towards them. I was agreeably surprised, however, when I found out they were friendly to me and very anxious to pace me the final twenty miles of the race. I finished fairly fresh, considering that the last 25-miles were ridden in a hard rainstorm. I finished more than an hour ahead of the second man and happy as I was over my victory, Mr. Catterson was even more pleased. He had proven that with a square deal I was one of the fastest riders in the state.

First prize was a house lot which was located in the center of the town of Matthews, Indiana. As soon as I had tucked the deed therefor into my pocket I rushed home, and presented it to my mother, explaining how it had come into my possession. I had not previously told her of my plans to enter the race because I felt she would worry about me until I returned home. Of course she was elated over my success, but she made me promise that I would never ride such a long race again. I was only sixteen years old at the time.

Louis D. "Birdie" Munger

# CHAPTER III



Shortly after this I entered the employ of Louis D. (Birdie) Munger, one of the greatest riders that ever sat in a saddle and who had but recently retired from the track to engage in the manufacture of bicycles in Indianapolis. I was employed in practically every department of his plant.

Mr. Munger's bachelor quarters in Indianapolis had long since become famous among the bicycle racers and bicycle salesmen throughout the country. Many of them made their home with Mr. Munger while in the city on business. When I was not tied up with tasks in the factory I served as a helper around the house. In this capacity I came to know all of the leading bicycle racers of the country, but what is more I won the admiration of Mr. Munger and he became one of my staunchest supporters and advisers.

I clearly recall meeting Arthur A. Zimmerman, the champion bicycle rider of America, on one occasion that he came to Indianapolis to race. It had been arranged that he would be the guest of Mr. Munger and I was delegated to meet Mr. Zimmerman and conduct him to the Munger home. I recognized my hero from pictures of him that had been printed in the newspapers. While hundreds surged about the train to welcome Mr. Zimmerman to Indianapolis where he was a prime favorite, and a brass band rent the air, while a welcoming committee stood by, I worked my way to the great cyclist's side. Quickly I gave him my message and Zimmerman smiled as he grasped my hand and asked me my name. He insisted that I ride in the carriage with him to Mr. Munger's home and he talked with me continuously en route.

His attention centered on the gold medal that I had won in my first race—the ten-mile road race in Indianapolis when I was thirteen years old. He was surprised when I told him of that feat, and even more so as I told him of many other boys' races since winning that gold medal.

Once in Mr. Munger's home, Mr. Zimmerman asked his host about me. Shortly Mr. Munger confirmed all that I had told Mr. Zimmerman about my races and a lot besides. "I am going to make a champion out of that boy some day," said Mr. Munger. At Mr. Zimmerman's request I sat down to the dinner table with them—a great honor indeed.

While on my way out to the race track on an errand the next day I found myself sitting alongside one of the other big champions of the day, Willie Windle of Millbury, Mass.  That gold medal of mine arrested his attention and Mr. Windle inquired as to its history. I was the proudest boy in the world as it became noised about that I had shaken the hand of the two outstanding bicycle greats of the bicycle circles of the country—Zimmerman and Windle.  I was

A. A. ZIMMERMAN—Champion of the World, 1893–1894

especially impressed with the friendliness of the two of them, especially towards me, a colored boy.  In my youthful mind the thought flashed that men can be champions and still be broad-minded in strange contrast with the young would-be champions that I had met in and about Indianapolis.  There was no race prejudice in the make-ups of Zimmerman and Windle,—they were too big for that.  And that expression has been fresh in my mind ever since that day.

Strangely enough I was destined not only to equal the best performances of Zimmerman and Windle, but to actually exceed them. Meantime I remembered their sterling qualities and did my best to live up to them, endeavoring to measure up to the high standards or sportsmanship set by them.  I take no little pride in the fact that throughout my racing career covering sixteen years I was never charged with an unsportsmanlike action.

Meanwhile Mr. Munger became closer and closer attached to me as time went on. Had I been his own son he could not have acted more kindly toward me. One day a member of the firm asked Mr. Munger why he bothered with that little darkey, meaning myself. He answered that I was an unusual boy and that he felt sure I had in me the makings of a champion bicycle rider. "I am going to make him the fastest bicycle rider in the world," said Mr. Munger. "He has fine habits, is quick to learn, is as game a youngster as I have ever seen, and can be relied upon to do whatever he is told. He has excellent judgment and has a remarkably cool head. Although he is only sixteen he can beat any boy in the city right now. He is improving every day, I notice it every time I go out with him."

That I might get the maximum speed in my races Mr. Munger built me the very lightest and best bicycle that could be produced. It weighed only fourteen pounds.

In those days high school and college games featured bicycle races on every athletic program they conducted. Just prior to many of the meets a number of athletes would borrow racing wheels from Mr. Munger for the games and I was assigned to instruct them on the track. Before I started to instruct the youths Mr. Munger would inform them that he would permit every one of them who led me over the tape to use the racing wheels in the meet. The young athletes realized they had little or no chance of beating me, and some of them tried to bribe me to let them nose me out. After their training preparations Mr. Munger would ask me to name the athletes who were in my opinion the best riders. They got the use of the wheels.

Incidentally, the weekly workouts with the high school boys helped mightily into rounding me into championship form. I am firmly convinced that the best way to gain experience in racing tactics is by actual participation with the various riders.

But there was a dark lining to my silver cloud. Members of the firm objected strenuously to Mr. Munger's befriending me simply because of my color, and I was inadvertently the cause of Mr. Munger's severing relations with the firm and his decision to establish a bicycle factory in Worcester, Massachusetts. At Mr. Munger's proposal I came with him and have since made my home in that city. Before our train pulled out of Indianapolis Mr. Munger informed a group of his friends that some day I would return to that city as champion bicycle rider of America.

# CHAPTER IV



I was in Worcester only a very short time before I realized that there was no such race prejudice existing among the bicycle riders there as I had experienced in Indianapolis. When I realized I would have a fair chance to compete against them in races I took on a new lease of life, and when I learned that I could join the Y. M. C. A. in Worcester, I was pleased beyond expression. I recall that as a small boy I tried to join the Y. M. C. A. in Indianapolis, but was turned down on account of color, despite all the influence that some of the most influential families of the city could exert on my behalf.

It did not take me very long to get acquainted in Worcester, especially when its riders discovered that I owned a fine, light, racing wheel on which I could ride with the best of them. I shall always be grateful to Worcester as I am firmly convinced that I would shortly have dropped riding, owing to the disagreeable incidents that befell my lot while riding in and around Indianapolis, were it not for the cordial manner in which the people received me. Incidentally I was striving my utmost to make good on Mr. Munger's promise to his Indianapolis friends to have me a champion when I returned to their city. Three years later I did return a full-fledged champion, and I cannot say whether Mr. Munger or myself was the happiest, since I had previously been excluded from all racing in that city because of my color.

I wish to pay my respects at this time to Mr. Edward W. Wilder, director of Athletics in Worcester schools, who was then physical director of the Worcester Y. M. C. A. when I arrived in that city. Not long after I arrived Mr. Munger took me to the Y. M. C. A. After examining me carefully, Mr. Wilder outlined some exercises that he felt would keep me in trim throughout the winter season. He found my legs quite naturally well-developed while the upper portions of my body were sorely in need of exercise. Following his instructions to the letter I succeeded in building the upper part of my body in excellent physical form, but not until I had put in two or three winter's work in a gymnasium.

I used light dumb-bells, indian clubs and a Whitley exerciser in my room regularly, even while travelling, and became an adept at deep breathing through long and patient practice. At the height of my racing career many expert trainers declared that I was the best developed rider on the bicycle track.

There was a saying at that time that any bicyclist who could climb George Street hill, one of the steepest inclines in Worcester, had the makings of a high grade bicycle racer. Appraised of that tradition I decided to try my skill on the hill. There was a big crowd on hand to see me make my initial attempt. It was a tough assignment that I had wished on myself, but I made it on the first attempt and within fifteen minutes I repeated the stunt riding down on both occasions. That was the first time a bicycle rider ever turned this trick—and very few have accomplished it in the intervening thirty-two years.

# CHAPTER V



In the fall of 1895 I rode my first bicycle race in Worcester, Mass. I had joined the Albion Cycle Club which was composed of colored riders. Later I was one of the club's team selected to ride in the annual ten-mile road race that attracted hundreds of entries. My old hero, Willie Windle of Millbury, Mass., was the donor of the trophy offered the winner of first place. I won this event and repeated it the following year that I might obtain permanent possession of the cup.

When Mr. Munger's factory moved to Middletown, Conn., the following year, I had my first real test against the best amateur sprinters in the East. I went along with the firm elated at the prospect of being able to compete against the pick of the amateur bicycle sprinters of the East.

I made my début at a State meet sanctioned by The League of American Wheelmen at New Haven, Conn. I decided to start in the one-mile open race, the feature event of the day. Having qualified in the preliminary heats I lined up at the tape with eleven of the fastest amateurs in this part of the country. Naturally I was nervous in this, my first tryout, but was all primed to go. However, instead of jumping out front at the crack of the pistol I was obliged to change my tactics and rode in last place until we were three-eighths of a mile from the tape. At that point I made my spurt and passed the entire group, gaining six lengths on them before they realized what had happened. I won by six lengths and received a wonderful ovation and a gold watch which I promptly presented to my friend Mr. Munger in appreciation for some of the many kindnesses he had extended to me.

Shortly afterwards I participated in the half-mile open race at Meriden, Conn. This time I was unable to come out of a very bad pocket which I found myself in half way down the home stretch and I had to content myself with second place. The winner leading me home by a matter of inches. My prize, a beautiful dinner set, I shipped to my mother for a birthday present.

Then came one of the greatest tests of my racing ability—the famous Irvington-Milbourne, N. J., 25-mile road race. Oscar Hedstrom and I trained for a couple of weeks over the course, under the watchful eye of Robert Ellingham. As the starting hour arrived I was in excellent fettle to measure speed with over 140 of the best road racers of America.  In this classic were some of the most coveted distinctions in the bicycle world.

Monte Scott, the best road-race rider in the country at the time and myself were the scratch men.  Throughout the race I was never off his rear wheel, and we were having a beautiful duel until we came to within one-half mile of the tape, then somebody threw a pail full of ice water in my face, and before I recovered from the shock Scott had crossed the line a winner, while I was forced to take second place.  I might say that the water throwing episode was due to accident rather than design as many of the riders arranged for such a stunt, and some trainer evidently miscalculated when he showered the ice water on me.

Itching for an opportunity to show my speed as a road-race rider, I jumped at the opportunity to enter the Tatum 25-mile road race which was scheduled to be held at Jamaica, L. I.  Two other riders and myself were the scratch men, there being about 60 in the field. The other scratch men framed it up against me with the two one-minute men to have the latter stall along until the scratch men came up, and within a certain distance of them, the two scratch men were to suddenly jump away from me, catch the two minute-men, and by alternating pace make it physically impossible for me to overtake them alone.  However, their plan failed.  They used every trick in the calendar against me but without success.

Five miles from the finishing line I decided to try one of my own tricks to throw off my rivals.  I pretended to be exhausted and made difficult work of holding on to the leaders.  The field fell for my stall and immediately dropped their foul riding tactics and set sail for the tape.  In reality they were playing right into my hands when they were doing that, and I held my sprint in reserve until we only had a half-mile to go.  Then I shot past the bunch and won out by six lengths, George Hicks second, Wallie Owens third, and Bill Loosie fourth.

Since this was my first victory in a race of this distance I was overjoyed at winning, and particularly since I was able to overcome the foul tactics of the strong combination that was lined up against me throughout the event.

# CHAPTER VI



Shortly after my success in the Tatum road race I decided to cast my fortunes with the professional riders. It was in the books that I was to make my professional bow on the historic Madison Square Garden track in the winter of 1896. I entered the half-mile open handicap race which was the curtain raiser for the annual six-day bicycle race that has long been staged at that famous track.

In the half-mile handicap race I started from the 35-yard mark with such stars as Eddie (Cannon) Bald, Tom Cooper, Earl Kiser, and Arthur Gardiner, as scratch men. At the crack of the pistol I shot out for the lead and gained the front position in the first three laps. Not satisfied with this I continued my wild sprint, and almost lapped the field when I won the event, and the $200 that was hung up for first prize. The Garden which was taxed to capacity on that Saturday night went wild when they noticed that I had failed to hear the bell for the last lap, and continued tearing off lap after lap until I had ridden three laps more than the required distance. I immediately wired the $200 to my mother. This was my first money prize.

A few hours later I took my place at the starting line for the six-day race. Upwards of fifty of the greatest long distance riders in the world took to the gun at one minute past midnight Sunday morning in the long grind. This was my first attempt at such a long distance and I was very anxious for the test, as I felt that if I could stay up near the front I could certainly give a good account of myself when the final sprint came. In those days this event was run off under different conditions than apply today. It was commonly termed a go-as-you-please affair. Being an individual race, each man having to ride single-handed, no partners, and with no restrictions as to when a rider could leave the track to eat, sleep, bathe or for any other purpose. Time lost in dismounting was strictly up to him.

Being the only sprinter in the race, I had no difficulty in regaining many of the laps lost in leaving the track. My greatest difficulty being to keep awake. I found the older riders, who were fully matured and thoroughly developed, could stand the strain of loss of sleep better than I. However, I managed to stick to my wheel for a stretch of eighteen hours of continuous riding, much to their amazement. I was only eighteen years old at the time.

About three o'clock one morning I complained to my trainers that I was sleepy, hungry, thirsty and fatigued, and begged them to allow me to dismount.  However, they urged me to continue riding just a few more laps until the doctor arrived.  Later I found this was only a ruse to keep me going.  I rode for three miles and four laps more, and then stepped off my wheel and went to my dressing room to eat, bathe and sleep.  My nap was of short duration as I was rushed out on to the track after fifteen minutes, my trainers explaining that I had slept fifteen minutes over my schedule.  On the way to the track one of my trainers gave me a glass of water into which he had dumped a powder which he claimed cost $65.00 an ounce, and which would allow me to ride without any sleep until the race was over.  This was only the third day of the race.  Later I found out also that this powder was nothing more than bicarbonate of soda, but it kept me going for the next eighteen hours without a wink of sleep.

Somehow or other I stuck in the race and finished in eighth place with 1,787 miles to my credit.  The race was won by Teddy Hale, an Englishman.

My trainers and many of the star bicycle racers declared that this long distance race would kill my fine sprint.  I returned to Worcester immediately after the race and spent the winter in the Y. M. C. A. preparing myself for the next season, determined to show the experts that the six-day grind had not put an end to my sprinting ability.

The following spring I competed in the League of American Wheelmen's opening race meet at the Charles River track, Boston, against some of the leading professional riders of the country. Among them were Tom, Nat and Frank Butler, who were widely known in racing circles as the famous Butler brothers.  I won the feature event, the one-mile open race and proved to myself, at least, that the six-day grind had not killed off my sprinting ability, defeating the Butlers, Watson Coleman, Eddie McDuffee and others.

My next success was at the Providence, R. I., meet which was also staged by the League of American Wheelmen, and I ran away with the one-mile open, the feature race of that program, again defeating the famous Butler brothers and a field of the greatest professional riders.  Flushed with that victory I competed in the half-mile open and was beaten for first prize by Orlando Stevens.

In those days the three Butler boys were looked upon in the bicycle world as practically invincible.  When word reached the western riding circles in the spring that I had taken their measure at the Charles River Meet there was much nodding of heads.  Included among the starters at the Providence Meet were Floyd MacFarland, Orlando Stevens and other star western riders.  Here again I demonstrated my superiority over the Butler brothers, Stevens and MacFarland, and even the experts thereupon agreed that my experience in the six-day race had not finished my career as a sprinter, but enhanced it instead.

Despite the fact that I was at the top of my form that summer I was not able to make a fight for the championship that season because the circuit extended into the South and my entry had been refused by all southern promoters. They claimed it would be folly for me to compete with white riders in that section of the country.

I found that the color prejudice was not confined to the South entirely, in fact it had asserted itself against me even in and around Boston. It would be difficult for me to narrate all the unpleasant experiences which I underwent in my long racing career, and also to call to mind all the vicious attempts that were made in vain to eliminate me from bicycle racing. I was the only colored rider ever permitted to compete in the professional class, and one may well surmise the obstacles I had to overcome against prejudiced and narrow-minded opponents. Incidentally, there were a few stars who matched skill with me that never tried to do an underhanded trick to me whether on or off the track.

But to get back to the unpleasant experiences I had in Boston. So apparent was the ill-will of the white riders against me that the press of the city took them to task and demanded that I receive a square deal in all future races. A deliberate foul on me at Waltham on Memorial Day when I was pushed off the track, and another foul committed against me at the Charles River track were the beginning of my racing difficulties. The officials and members of the press were unanimous in their demand that I be accorded the same treatment given the white riders.

One of the Boston newspapers carried a story the day after one of my races in which it took a rider named W. E. Becker to task for choking me into a state of insensibility. This incident followed the close of the one-mile open event which was won by Tom Butler with myself second, and Becker third.

Just after we had crossed the tape Becker wheeled up and hurled me to the ground. He then started to choke me, but the police interfered. It was fifteen minutes before I regained consciousness. The crowd threatened Becker who claimed that I had crowded him into the fence. However, the judges disqualified Becker, and ordered the race re-run, but I was too badly injured to start.

I quote the following from a clipping in the Boston *Post:* "At the opening of the Southern Circuit last fall Taylor's entry was refused at Louisville, Ky., and throughout the South, on account of his color, and opposition against him has become so marked that he was compelled to give up the circuit. The League of American Wheelmen, which professes to control bicycle racing, draws the color line, and only white riders are allowed to compete in professional races. This is a violation of good sense, but if the L. A. W. permits Major Taylor to start in professional races, it should certainly protect him.

"The L. A. W. must keep the dirty professionals off the track. During the National Circuit Races here it was commented that in every professional race that Major Taylor entered he had more than his share of trouble. There appeared to be a deliberate effort by certain riders to throw him. He was tossed once successfully, and the man who did the job was loudly hissed, and Major Taylor was roundly cheered in front of the grand stand. He was very badly scraped and bruised. The same dirty tactics have followed the plucky little colored rider all around the circuit, and it is to the everlasting discredit of the men who are in on the schemes.

"It does not appear to be the big riders so much as the cheap riders who are out for a fraction of the purses that they can steal from the big riders who may have an off day now and then. If a referee now and then saw these offenses and ruled off a rider it would add much to the interest of the sport. Major Taylor's last episode at Newark, when he had won the one-mile open in a great finish was openly threatened. He asked to be excused in the next race, but the referee compelled him to get up and take the chances. He did, but kept out of the bunch and did not try for a place.

"Attention was recently called in the New York *Sun* to the fact that Major Taylor in all his big races is in deadly fear of his racing companions. He was recently thrown at Worcester and badly injured, and it was charged that the accident was the result of a conspiracy.

"At the Circuit meet at Waverly, N. J., on September 20, Taylor captured the one-mile open event handily, and qualified for his heat in the mile handicap, but when the final race of the latter event was called, Taylor did not show up, and investigation by the referee disclosed that Taylor had been threatened and was afraid to start. The referee refused to excuse Taylor and the colored boy started reluctantly but made no effort to win.

"The situation calls for prompt action on the part of the Racing Board. Major Taylor now ranks with the fastest men in this country, but the racing men are envious of the success, and prejudiced against his color, and aim to injure him whenever he competes. This conduct robs Major Taylor of many chances to secure many large purses and endangers his life besides."

About this same time the New York *Journal* carried this article: "Fears of Major Taylor. Much talk is going the rounds about the unfairness on the part of the other riders toward Major Taylor, the colored boy, and he is said to be in fear of bodily danger if he continues to keep in the front.  Possibly there may be little ground for complaint by Taylor, but in the Metropolitan district in which he has competed he has not been sinned against.  The colored rider has a very dangerous habit of crowding in on the pole, no matter how narrow the opening is in the finish down the home stretch, and on a couple of occasions the holder of the third desirable position has upheld his rights with a bit of elbow work that was provoked by the offender.

"In the record race at Springfield there was a stiff fight between Tom Butler and Taylor, but Tommy was not in any combine to do up the other, but was simply having it out with him on a personal score.  They both come from Boston.  The success of the colored boy (and he has done some excellent riding) was sure to arouse bitter opposition and feeling among the other riders, but officials of the meets have been particularly vigilant in seeing to it that Taylor got all that was coming to him.  In baseball and fistic circles the color line has caused any amount of trouble, and the same difficulty is now being experienced in bicycle racing.

"One prominent rider declined a match race with Taylor for a substantial share of the gate receipts, and it was not because he was afraid, but simply through his unwillingness to be singled out in a match race with one he considered his social inferior.  But for Major Taylor it must be said, however, that he is the most modest and retiring youngster with which his race was ever favored."

## CHAPTER VII

### THE NATIONAL CHAMPIONSHIP

Aside from the unpleasant experiences which I encountered from time to time because of color prejudice, my success of my first year's work as a professional was very satisfactory indeed, not only from a point of speed but financially as well. I won several thousand dollars and gained valuable experiences, besides making many new friends, by riding all my races entirely unassisted, and doing my utmost to win every time I got up. I was especially determined to go after the Championship of America in the season of 1898.

There was a plan on foot to bar me, as a colored racing cyclist, from future racing on all tracks under the jurisdiction of the L. A. W. It was grounded on the fact that the League had refused to admit professional membership, but placed a tax of $2 on them and compelled them to register, also it did not admit Negroes to membership.

Naturally I was somewhat disturbed by these conditions until I signed up with the American Cycle Racing Association which was headed by Wm. A. Brady, James Kennedy and Patrick Powers, to ride as a member of a racing team with Fred Titus, "French" Edward Taylore, and under this management I was sent South to engage in about two months of training, but owing to the racial prejudice my stay in Savannah was somewhat brief, as this New York newspaper will show.

"The Cyclists of Savannah, Ga., are congratulating themselves on the fact that Major Taylor, Champion Cyclist was driven out through a White-cap letter sent him during his recent brief stay there, but such is not the case. Taylor left Savannah by order of the American Cyclist Racing Association with whom he is under contract as told in the *Evening Journal* last week.

"Major Taylor did receive a letter supposed to be written or rather printed, as an effort was made to conceal the identity of the writer, by the city's crack triplet team with whom he had some words while training on the road. The letter which bears the postmark of Savannah under date of March 2nd, is now made public for the first time. It is as follows: 'Mister Taylor, If you do not leave here before forty-eight hours you will be sorry. We mean business. Clear out if you value your life. Signed, White Riders.'

"This letter concludes with a very poor attempt on the part of the writers to portray a skull and cross bones."

In 1897 the L. A. W. decided to permit me to register for races under their sanction. But this by no means ended my racial difficulties for I was barred from several tracks in the North on account of my color. I quote the following from a newspaper.

"The announcement made by Tom Eck to the effect that all colored riders including Major Taylor, The Dusky Champion, would not be allowed to race on the Woodside track, Philadelphia, has stirred up a big row, in which the National Racing Board may play a prominent part. While Eck says he has no personal objection to the colored champion's arrangements the owners of the track give him the right to say who or who shall not race on their tracks, and they are against permitting colored men to compete, and so entry blanks will be marked 'For White Riders Only.'

"The peculiar racing rules this year may be the means of causing considerable trouble for the gray haired manager for he cannot very well bar Major Taylor from racing without the risk of being heavily fined by the racing board and also having his track blacklisted. The question is fully covered in Sec. 13, Clause C of the racing rules which are as follows: 'A legal entry is one which cannot be rejected by the promoter, one which complies with the racing rules, and is accompanied by the required fee for all entries of the meet.'

"Major Taylor is in good standing with the L. A. W. and has a perfect right to enter races as the League, while it does not admit Negroes to membership, does permit them to enter races to be held under their jurisdiction. Billy Brady who looks after Major Taylor's interest, has expressed himself in no measured terms as to what he calls unjust discrimination and he has issued a sweeping defy on behalf of the colored lad for any style of racing in sight, and with Eck's best foreign stars preferred. Eck's partner, Senator Morgan, stated yesterday that he had no desire whatever to bar Major Taylor from any of his tracks and he will see if matters cannot be adjusted to the satisfaction of all parties concerned.

"He accepted Brady's challenge on behalf of Jaap Eden, Sissac or Boulay. The fight for public favor between the Morgan-Eck combination and Brady, Kennedy and Powers interest, promises to develop plenty of enthusiasm before the season is over."

I somehow used to imagine that if I won my first race of the season I was due for a big year. So in the spring of 1898, the year in which I won the Championship of America for the first time, I bent all my energy to win my initial start in the Asbury Park, N. J., one-mile open event. I won that race and continued on my winning way right through the season winning the Championship that I had longed for since my boyhood days. This Asbury Park event was the opening of the Grand Circuit races, it being stipulated that the rider scoring the highest average throughout the season would be declared the Champion of America. During the year, however, much jealousy and dissension cropped up in the racing of the professionals and some of the leading riders in the Grand Circuit seceded from the L. A. W. under whose control all riders and tracks had come for years. This step caused a bitter fight for the Championship honors, five of the leading riders including myself claiming the title, Eddie Bald, Arthur Gardiner, Tom Butler and Owen Kimble.

When I began racing in the 1898 season, my one great ambition was to win the National Championship of America on my merits. After making a hard fight for it against great odds, I was within 14 points of Eddie Bald, who was leading, and had a splendid chance of defeating him in St. Louis when my entry was rejected, thus giving him a decided advantage, but I still had hopes of evening up the score at Baltimore. However, the promoters there also refused my entry which practically shut me out of all possibility of winning the title, which I believe was the object of their conspiracy.

If the L. A. W. accepted my entry for the Championship races I could not understand how it could be lawfully rejected.

I then offered to make a match with Eddie Bald, the possible National Champion, for a purse and a side bet of $500, winner to take all. However, Bald refused to compete against me. He also declined to participate in a race with Jimmie Michaels, the famous diminutive Welshman and myself on the Manhattan Beach track.

Commenting on my being barred from the Baltimore races, John Barnett, the Baltimore representative of the L. A. W. racing board, had this to say. "No race promoter holding a National Circuit sanction from the L. A. W. has the right to bar out any competitor who is in good standing and a regular competitor on the National Circuit, unless for some flagrant breach of the rules. When promoters accept L. A. W. sanction they accept L. A. W. rules and as the L. A. W. draws no color line in racing circles they cannot refuse the entry of a colored rider who has qualified to compete, even though they may have ground rules to the contrary. Major Taylor is a regular follower of the Circuit and is a recognized competitor for the Championship, and he has as much right to compete in the Championship races at St. Louis and Baltimore as Bald, Cooper, and Gardiner, or any of the rest of them."

The Philadelphia Press in speaking of conspiracy aimed at me said that the fact that my rivals on the National Circuit had entered into a conspiracy to prevent me from winning the National Championship was not without foundation.

"Of course," read the Press, "it will be a hard matter to prove but, nevertheless, Chairman Mott would be doing something for the benefit of a great sport if he begins an investigation at once. Major Taylor is the greatest sprint rider in America and his white rivals all know it. Personally they all speak well of the little colored boy,

but there is not one of them who has not at one time or another
expressed the hope that Major Taylor will be kept from winning the
Championship honors.  They have pocketed him at every opportunity
and ran him wide on the turns, and used other foul tactics in order
to defeat him, but as yet not one of them has been punished.  The
L. A. W. recognized Taylor when Chairman Mott accepted his
registration fee and the League should give him all the protection
necessary.

MAJOR TAYLOR—Champion of America, 1898

"St. Louis cannot have the Circuit sanction until it promises to
accept the entry of Major Taylor, and the National Circuit date of
October 9th, originally granted to Berkeley Oval, N. Y. C., has been
transferred to this city.  The sanction covers the National Five-Mile
Championship and 60-point score. Bearing in mind the fact that the
race-meet promoters have refused Major Taylor's entry for the last
Circuit meeting, Chairman Mott granted the sanction on the con-
dition that Major Taylor's entry should be accepted."

With the closing days of the cycle racing season of 1898 rapidly
drawing near the newspapers of the East gave a lot of space to the
discussion as to who should be declared the National Champion. Some
of them frankly declared it was a case of black or white.  It was
pointed out that two men stood out head and shoulders above the field
for the honors—Eddie Bald, the three times winner of the title, and
myself.

I quote from a Metropolitan newspaper: "There is a grave question as to who is champion cyclist of America for the season of 1898. Is it Eddie Bald, who from the League tables was leading when the professionals seceded from the League practically as a walk-over, or Arthur Gardiner who won more firsts at National Circuit Meets than any other rider, or Owen Kimble, whose points under the L. A. W. and other outlaw organizations makes the largest total, or is it Major Taylor who in all classes or races throughout the season scored the greatest number of victories?

"A table has been compiled by Charles M. Mears, the Ohio State Handicap official, showing the net results of the efforts of all the riders, and according to it Major Taylor is the most logical one to have the honor of being called the Champion of America for the year of 1898. This table shows the number of times that each rider has won first, second and third place in any race either on the National Circuit or under the outlaw jurisdiction. This table simply counts firsts, seconds and thirds, figuring four points, two points, and one point respectively for the place, which is the system which is mathematically just.

"According to this calculation Major Taylor heads the list, and thereby wins the title of Champion of America after the table:

|  | 1sts | 2nds | 3rds | Points |
|---|---|---|---|---|
| Taylor, Major | 21 | 13 | 11 | 121 |
| Gardiner, Arthur | 21 | 12 | 5 | 113 |
| MacFarland, Floyd | 16 | 15 | 13 | 107 |
| Bald, Eddie | 19 | 17 | 8 | 98 |
| Fisher, Johnnie | 18 | 11 | 0 | 94 |
| Simms, Fred | 16 | 10 | 5 | 89 |
| Eaton, Jay | 16 | 9 | 4 | 86 |
| Walthour, Bobbie | 12 | 11 | 7 | 87 |
| Stevens, Orlando | 14 | 5 | 10 | 76 |
| Titus, Fred | 13 | 11 | 1 | 75 |
| Freeman, Howard | 8 | 17 | 6 | 72 |
| Cooper, Tom | 10 | 11 | 7 | 69 |
| Lawson, Iver | 9 | 12 | 4 | 64 |
| Johnson, Johnnie | 14 | 3 | 1 | 63 |
| McDuffee, Eddie | 15 | 0 | 0 | 60 |
| Bowler, Jimmie | 10 | 4 | 6 | 54 |
| Butler, Tom | 10 | 2 | 5 | 49 |
| Kimble, Owen | 7 | 7 | 7 | 49 |
| Martin, Bill | 8 | 5 | 7 | 49 |
| Elks, Harry | 11 | 2 | 0 | 49 |
| Butler, Nat | 7 | 8 | 3 | 47"

# CHAPTER VIII



In the spring of 1898 war was formerly declared against the League of American Wheelmen by the cycling champions who fol‑lowed the National Circuit. Fifty or more famous racing men formed an association to further and protect their interest at the same time. This meeting was held at Trenton, N. J., and was one of the most interesting events in the history of cycle racing in America.

Eddie Bald, the great Buffalo (N. Y.) rider who won three American championships in as many seasons, was among those present. Another at the meeting was Tom Cooper, also champion of America, Floyd MacFarland, Orlando Stevens, Arthur Gardiner and every other bicycle racer of note in this country.

Champion Bald was named chairman, F. Ed. Spooner, circuit correspondent, was chosen secretary. The executive committee comprised A. G. Batchelder, former New York state handicapper, F. Ed. Spooner, E. C. Bald and Arthur Gardiner. This group was appointed to meet track promoters and track owners of the country. At their sessions it was voted to organize an American Racing Cyclists Union.

While this meeting was in progress the L. A. W. officials kept the wires hot as they posted each other on the developments at Trenton. While the new organization was deliberating a telegram was received from the L. A. W. officials imposing a ten-dollar fine on Bald, MacFarland, Stevens and all the riders who had been suspended for training on a blacklisted track in New York. The officials were instructed to permit the riders to race after the fines were paid, thus raising the suspension which had been placed upon them. The riders considered this action a backdown on the part of L. A. W. and a clean-cut victory for them. However, Bald and the other riders refused to pay their fines, but Secretary Muirhead of the L. A. W. did so for them. Next day all of the riders competed in a big bicycle meet in Trenton.

Although practically all of the star riders of the country were in favor of a change of government for the sport not all were ready to jump from the L. A. W. Fred Titus, Fred Simms, "Doc" Brown, Nat Butler, Owen Kimble, Howard Freeman, Tom Butler and several others, including myself, wished to continue to ride under the auspices of the L. A. W. until we were sure that the control of bicycle racing was to be turned over to competent men.

Due to the revolt against the L. A. W. and the formation of the

American Racing Cyclists Union came the organization of the N. C. A.—National Cycling Association—which body is still in control of bicycle racing in this country. With the N. C. A. in control of the bicycle racing events in the country that year, 1898, the L. A. W. practically passed out of the picture. However, there was a fly in my championship ointment through no fault of my own. While I was winning the N. C. A. title the L. A. W. circuit continued its championship races and Tom Butler was declared champion of that season under the auspices of that organization.

Prior to my signing up to race under the N. C. A. auspices I entered into a gentleman's agreement with all of the riders in that group, whereby we promised to do no racing on Sunday. However, I was doomed to keen disappointment when I was informed that that agreement was to be considered a scrap of paper and the very first race that I was to ride in under the N. C. A. colors was scheduled for Sunday in St. Louis. At the time, Eddie (Cannon) Bald was leading me by a very narrow margin for the championship honors; therefore, the race at St. Louis was all important to me. Had I won in the Mound City, Bald and I would have an equal rating in the standing. It was my intention to then bend every effort to beat Bald in the final championship race of the year (1898) at Cape Girardeau, Mo., but a rainstorm in St. Louis on the Saturday on which the race was to have been held, caused a postponement. I insisted that the race be held any day but Sunday but my fellow riders, forgetting our agreement, favored its being held on the Sabbath, as did the promoters and it was held on Sunday. I had won my heat on Saturday, thereby assuring myself of a place in the starting line when the final event was called, but I steadfastly refused to ride on Sunday as it was against my religious scruples.

Within a few days all of the riders moved along to Cape Girardeau which was to stage the final championship races of the year. Naturally, they were all bent on doing their very best on this occasion, as between Bald and I lay the distinction of being the champion of the country for the season under the N. C. A. auspices. However, I was doomed to another keen disappointment.

While we were still in St. Louis one of the promoters of the Cape Girardeau race meet came to me to secure my entry for that event. He knew that the color line had been drawn on me so tightly in St. Louis that I was unable to get hotel accommodations, which placed me at a great disadvantage, as any athlete in strict training may well appreciate. It forced me to secure lodgings with a colored family and even though I was on a very strict diet I did not feel free to ask my hostess to rearrange menus in my favor. Instead I made a long trip three times a day for my meals which I secured for several days in a restaurant at Union Station. After several meals at this location the restaurant manager very rudely informed me that I would not be welcome henceforth and so instructed the head waiter who was one of my own color. This, however, the waiter refused to do and was promptly discharged for that reason.

Smarting under this shameful treatment I had about made up my mind to pack my racing bicycle and make tracks for my home in Worcester, Mass. It was while I was pondering the question that Mr. Dunlop, the bicycle race promoter from Cape Girardeau, appeared on the scene. He stated he sympathized with me in the rough treatment that I had received in St. Louis at the hands of the hotel and restaurant men. He told me he was proprietor of a hotel in Cape Girardeau and he promised me faithfully that I would receive the same treatment and attentions in his hotel as the rest of my fellow racers. Spurred on by that offer and still bent upon winning the championship, which I felt was at stake in the Cape Girardeau meet, I reluctantly signed an entry blank for that fixture, but upon arriving in Cape Girardeau, I found Mr. Dunlop had made a complete turnabout toward me. All of the racers went to his hotel, signed the register and were alloted rooms. When it came my turn to affix mv signature Mr. Dunlop stated he was sorry, but had to inform me that he had made arrangements for me to stay elsewhere. He had arranged that I would stay with a colored family in the neighborhood during my stay at Cape Girardeau. When I informed him that this was not in accordance wth our gentleman's agreement he again stated he was sorry but the new arrangement would have to stand. With recollections of the inconveniences that I suffered at St. Louis a few days prior still fresh in my mind I did not welcome a second encounter with the color line. In order to avoid any argument at the hotel I made my way to the house designated by Mr. Dunlop and was most royally entertained by my colored host and hostess. However, I felt that since Mr. Dunlop had broken faith with me first that I was under no further obligation to participate in his championship races the next day. Early that morning I made my way to Union Station and purchased a ticket for Worcester, Mass. As I waited on the platform for the train to start, Mr. Dunlop, several of the racers and one of the N. C. A. officials approached me. They told me that if I failed to ride in the races that afternoon they would see to it that I was barred forever from the racing tracks of the country. I replied I was not interested in the future but was deeply concerned with the present, and since Mr. Dunlop had not lived up to his agreement with me I felt free to absent myself from the championship meet that afternoon and was going to do so regardless of consequences.

As time went on I became convinced that the color line was drawn against me in St. Louis and Cape Girardeau by hotel proprietors when in reality the strings were pulled by my co-racers. They evidently felt that I was a good enough rider to land the championship out on the track and that the best way to insure one of their number corralling the honors was to have me kept off the race course through some ruse. I was suspicious that this plan was afoot following my experience in St. Louis. When the brazen Cape Girardeau trick was pulled on me I became convinced of their diabolical plan and had made up my mind that I would never ride in another race.

True to their word the group of officials and bicycle racers who saw me off at the Cape Girardeau Union Station did their utmost to have me barred for life from the tracks of the country. They put every pressure they could muster into service at the N. C. A. meeting that winter with but one thought in mind—to bar Major Taylor for life from all the tracks. I had been automatically suspended for my failure to ride in the Cape Girardeau championship meet, and this well-developed plan to have the sentence carry life suspension against me followed my application for reinstatement.

Meantime the facts of the case had been thoroughly presented to the public through the press. I had always received the fairest treatment at the hands of the newspapers of the country, regardless of the unfair tactics that I was almost continuously facing at the hands of most of the racers on the track. Now the press again came to my rescue and when I sorely needed assistance. News items and editorials in most of the leading papers in the country, from both above and below the Mason-Dixon line, crystallized public sentiment in my favor.

The fact that I refused to desert the L. A. W. arrayed a large number of riders against me. The case was stated thus by the Philadelphia Press: "Major Taylor was the last professional to desert the L. A. W. and join the outlaw movement. It required a considerable amount of argument to move him, and he was never satisfied with himself after he flopped. He rode the outlaw races in the fall of 1898, and his failure to win a clear title doubtless added to his discomfiture, and when the riders reached Cape Girardeau, Mo., he was thoroughly disheartened. His failure to secure desirable accommodations was the straw that broke the camel's back, and he packed his grip and returned east. Therefore the riders' independent movement knew him no more.

"He went back to the L. A. W. and remained there until the League abandoned cycle racing and left him without a guardian. Now he wishes to ride under the N. C. A., but before the N. C. A. will register him he must make his peace with the riders, or fail in this appeal to the N. C. A. Board of Appeals, and abide by its decision. Treason is the charge against him, and life suspension is the threatened verdict.

"The riders have drawn the color line, which is, unconstitutional, un-American and unsportsmanlike. It is wrong in the abstract, unrighteous in the concrete, and undefensible, particularly at a time when dealing with something other than a theory, and all the more so since the color line will not be accepted by the American public as a valid cause for the ruling off of a champion.

"Major Taylor is a stern reality. He is here in flesh and blood, and must be dealt with as a human being, and he is entitled to every human right. His case cannot be settled on the color question, but on its actual merits, and this we believe the riders so agree. That being the case, the question arises, what punishment does he deserve? In answering this query, the judges must be unprejudiced, to gain for themselves the hearty esteem of the public. It is required that they make due allowances for the unique and trying position Major Taylor has always held, and take into consideration the admitted shortcomings of his race. If they (the judges) would win golden praise, they should temper justice with mercy, and then turn in and prove, if they can, his inferiority as a racing man, by defeating him fairly and squarely in the championship competition.

"Major Taylor is no angel, his faults are no fewer than those of any racing man, but he has always been the subject of a natural prejudice, and at all times due perhaps to his good work. He has always thought himself an unwelcome competitor. Had he felt at home among the Governors themselves, the professionals, he never would have deserted them, a fact not to be overlooked.

"Then also when Taylor displayed weakness in deserting the riders because of malice on his part, had it been proven? This, too, must be considered, furthermore he should have been dealt with in a spirit of consideration for his inborn shortcomings. We might go on still deeper into this matter, but feel there is little necessity for it. The racing men have triumphed and as victors they can afford to be merciful. Not one of them wants it said next fall that he won the championship because Major Taylor was barred or prohibitally fined. Nor will the riders' committee give anyone the opportunity to cause aspersion of the champion of 1900.

"The committee will, we believe, even be more lenient to Major Taylor than its members would, were he a white man, if for no other reason than to disprove the public suspicions of unfair play, and to prove their manhood and their confidence in their ability as racing men, and their right to govern themselves to the degree vouchsafed them."

More to the same effect was echoed by many other fair-minded newspapers, for the case excited widespread comment. The Syracuse *Journal* goes after them in an editorial. It says, "If a colored man can ride a bicycle as well as a white man he should not be denied the privilege of displaying his ability." The Syracuse *Journal* further goes after the outlaws with a big editorial stick, under the caption: "The Negro should be made to know that He is a Man." The *Journal* prints the following strong editorial, founded in the decision of the American Racing Cyclists' Union, not to allow colored men in its competitive events:

"Ordinarily little interest is taken in the action of bicycle racing associations. They are usually formed and controlled by those who have not yet reached a period in life to treat things seriously. The young and frivolous are the moving spirits and the indulgent parents pay for the moving, but when a cycle association makes a rule denying a colored man the right to ride on the track it behooves the indulgent parents to be less indulgent.

"Such an act as performed by the American Racing Cyclists' Union is a dangerous thing. It would be, of course, better if the colored man spent his time on the school primer instead of on a bicycle track, but that is not the intent of the act. It is an evidence of antipathy, and the condition of the colored man in America is one of the greatest questions for us to handle. All intelligent people know that we do not benefit the condition of the colored man by denying him the privileges that we enjoy, he has been treated like a beast too long, and we must make him know that he is a man before we educate him.

"The colored man has always been denied the rights to share the fruit of civilization with the white man. The school doors have been closed against him for generations, and he has been allowed to propagate in ignorance. He has been forced to toil, and not to study, and that is the reason why the ordinary Negro lacks the mental power of a white man.

"Education is the remedy that the Negro needs, and the remedy cannot be obtained by him if he is deprived of the opportunities of receiving it that his white brothers enjoy. The practice has been pursued for years with the result that makes us wince so often at the shocking news from the South.

"Uncle Sam allows the Negroes to serve him, and if he can pass the civil service examinations he can handle our mails, and if he is qualified he should have the same position a white man can have, and if he can fulfill all the requirements, his color should have no weight against him. If he can ride a bicycle or a horse or play baseball as well as a white man, why should he be denied the privilege of demonstrating his ability?

"The public sentiment is with Taylor, but its sympathy is not pronounced enough to have much weight with a body of riders who are jealous of Major Taylor's successes, and are determined to keep him out at all costs. Track owners would unquestionably like to see Major Taylor riding again, and in every cycle racing center of the country there are many who go to the races simply to see Major."

The *Cycling Gazette* had this to say:

"Boycotting against Major Taylor too long delayed. The white bicycle racers have drawn the color line. They assert they will no longer compete against Major Taylor, the black whirlwind of the cycle tracks. It is all very well for these speedy white gentlemen to insist upon the proper respect for their color, and the *Morning Telegraph* is pleased to see this much delayed but emphatic assertion of the superiority of the Caucasian over the Ethiopian. Still, in the interests of the L. A. W. and to the end that there might be no invidious criticism on the action of the white riders, we could have wished that they had boycotted Major Taylor before he had defeated them all. It looks now as if the ease with which this ebony wonder cut down records and carried away first money in all the big contests in which he entered had as much to do with the action of the white flyers as their active self-love.

"It is, of course, a degradation for a white man to contest any point with a Negro. It is even worse than that, and becomes an absolute grief and social disaster when the Negro persistently wins out in the competitions."

I cannot begin to quote the newspaper opinions on both sides, but at last the matter came to an issue, when the Executive Committee of the American Racing Cyclists' Union met, the organization being affiliated with the N. C. A., at Newark, New Jersey. These officials took notice of this sweep of sentiment in my favor and instead of life sentence, which was sought by several of my fellow riders and a number of officials of the parent organization, I was ordered to pay a fine of $500. Since I felt this was a very unjust verdict, I made up my mind that rather than pay the fine I would hang up my racing togs forever. It was the principle of the thing that I was fighting, and it would have made no difference to me whether the fine was $5 or $5,000, I would refuse to pay it. To me the payment of any fine under the circumstances would be an admission of guilt on my part for doing something which I felt in my heart I had never done.

About this time Mr. Fred Johnson of Fitchburg, Massachusetts, President of the Iver Johnson Arms & Cycle Company, made me an offer to ride his company's bicycle in the coming season.   When I agreed he promptly sent a check to the N. C. A. to wipe out the unjust fine which had been imposed upon me.

It gave me no little pleasure, however, to note that the members of the executive committee of the A. R. C. U., Earl Kiser, Tom Cooper, Orlando Stevens, Howard Freeman, Johnnie Fisher, and Jay Eaton, voted unanimously in favor of my reinstatement.   I felt that was a complete vindication for me.

A newspaper of the day printed this paragraph which I believe is pertinent to the case in hand:  "All the racing men agree that Major Taylor should be barred out, but the Eastern riders have come to believe it is in the best interest of the racing game that he should be reinstated.   Track associations, clubs and promoters everywhere feel that Major Taylor is a big attraction, and really demanded his reinstatement."

# CHAPTER IX



While the moguls of bicycle racing in this country were determining my fate in the winter of 1898–1899, I kept in the pink of physical condition.  Naturally, I was somewhat worried as they maneuvered back and forth in an effort to stall my case, but I felt that the scales of justice would eventually swing my way so I kept hard at work at the gymnasium preparing for a busy season in 1899.

No sooner had I been fined $500 for my failure to participate in the Cape Girardeau, Mo., race meet, which wound up the 1898 championship season, than I started to work in earnest for the ensuing campaign.  I made up my mind that 1899 would be my banner year, and that I would extend myself more than usual, if that were possible, to pick up any extra prize money, and the excessive amount that I still claim was unjustly levied against me in the guise of a fine.

I also determined to vindicate myself in the estimation of those good friends who had stood by me, and who had done everything possible to assist me in regaining my standing once more, and also to justify the good opinion of the press that had come to my rescue, and forced my opponents to let down the bars and reinstate me, as well as that of the public, whose sentiment was with me from the start.

Down in my heart I felt disappointed at the way the championship season terminated in 1898.  Although I was declared the champion there were claims advanced for the honors by Eddie (Cannon) Bald, Tom Cooper, Arthur Gardiner and Tom Butler.

So as the 1899 championship season dawned I redoubled my efforts to establish myself as champion of America, and to make the margin wide enough between myself and my competitors to leave no room for doubt.  Since such sterling riders as Bald, Cooper, Kiser and Gardiner, who were considered the four fastest riders in the country, and such other good men as Kramer, Eaton, Freeman, Kimble, Stevens, the Butler brothers, MacFarland, Bowler, Fisher, Simms, Terrill, Newhouse, Cutler, Wilson, Taylore, Jaap Eden, Mertins, Weinig, Collette, and Bobby Walthour were all competing for the championship title that season, I felt I had in that field foemen worthy of my steel.  Incidentally the fact that I was competing against such a galaxy of racing stars as these, spurred me on to my greatest efforts, and 1899 will always live in my memory as one of my greatest seasons because I won the championship that season beyond a shadow of a doubt—my keenest competitors conceding me the laurels.

(36)

Before I won the American championship I competed in the world's championship meet at Montreal, and there won the world's one-mile sprint championship title. In Chicago I established a world's record for one mile.

My first race that season for the championship honors came at the King's County Wheelmen's Meet at Manhattan Beach (L. I.), June 23. The quarter-mile national championship event was the feature of the program. It attracted more star riders than had ever competed before in a race at this distance. Among them were Bald, Cooper, Gardiner, Taylore, Kiser and Tom Butler, the "big-six" of the racing world, together with Jaap Eden, Mertins, MacFarland, Stevens, Newhouse, Eaton, Weinig, Terill, and Kiser.

The final heat found Jaap Eden, champion of Holland, Fred, Howard Freeman, Arthur Gardiner, and myself lined up at the starting line. I have never seen a group of crack riders that seemed more fit than the five of us, and each was keenly anxious for the pistol to send us away. After I had gotten away with a very bad start, things seemed to be breaking exceedingly bad for me, each of my opponents having a whack at me as they passed, and I found myself in a bad rut and was the last man to enter the home stretch, Eden leading at a furious clip.

After being bumped, jostled, and elbowed until I was sorely tried, I felt sure that as we entered the last straightaway, I must have looked like a 1,000 to 1 shot. However, I quickly found myself and went after the bunch with every bit of vitality that was in me. I pedalled down the home stretch at two kicks to every one, slipped in between Eaton and Simms, despite their efforts to close in on me and won by a scant foot with Eaton second, Simms third, Freeman fourth and Gardiner fifth. The entire field with the exception of Gardiner went over the tape within a half wheel's length of each other.

This was one of the most sensational sprints I had ever made and the crowd was not slow to appreciate it. My trip about the track immediately upon the close of the race became a triumphal march as the enthusiasts in the grandstand gave me one of the greatest ovations that had ever fallen my lot.

Shortly after this event I participated in a one-mile championship race at the Quill Club meet at the Manhattan Beach track.

Tom Cooper, Gardiner, Butler and myself won our trial heats and faced the starter's gun in the final. Butler led me over the line while Cooper trailed me, and Gardiner finished fourth. In this race I was again on the receiving end of some of the foulest tactics that I ever encountered in my more than sixteen years of racing. While I was able to offset them in the one-quarter mile championship event, which I won, I found the odds were all strong against me in this second race at the Manhattan Beach track, and considered myself very fortunate to finish in second place.

A week later I went to Philadelphia to take part in the Castle Wheelmen's event on the Tioga four-lap cinder track which was remarkably fast. Following the rough treatment I received in my race a few weeks previous at the Manhattan Beach track, in my race against Eden, Simms, Freeman and Gardiner, and later on the same track against Tom Butler, Cooper and Gardiner, I decided on a plan of action to offset any rough tactics that my opponents might attempt to pull on me in future races. My trainer bitterly opposed my putting the plan into practice, but I insisted and it so happened that they were to be tried out in this Philadelphia meet. In the first race referred to above I was the object of some clever pocketing. My strategy now was to avoid both in my future starts by beginning my sprint from the front of the field. Hitherto I had always started my sprint from the rear of the field, and naturally in doing so had to sprint past all my rivals giving them an opportunity to elbow me or force me into a pocket, or otherwise make me the victim of rough riding tactics.

"In this Philadelphia meet," said the Philadelphia Press, "besides Eddie Bald, three times winner of the cycling championship of America, there were 25 of the fastest racing men in the world, including the pick of America's best sprinters and the recognized champions of Europe." I won the third of a mile championship event from that field and was mighty proud of my conquest, but I believe I was more pleased at the way my new tactics worked out for me in this hectic dash.

Now to explain my new tactics. In the finish of the quarter-mile championship race at Manhattan Beach, a short time before, the riders, including myself, covered the last 200 yards in faster time than we covered the same distance in this Philadelphia event. The Manhattan Beach race was a much more difficult one to win than that in Philadelphia. The reason was that up to and including the one-quarter-mile championship event, all of my races had been ridden and won in the most difficult manner possible—namely by trailing along in the rear of the field in order to avoid pockets or a fall until the last lap, by which time the riders would be sprinting for all they were worth for the tape. Then I would undertake to ride outside the field in my dash to the finish line. Even if I was successful my victory would be only by a very narrow margin, and in many close finishes I saw a well-earned victory wrest from me by the officials. It is a fact that the verdict rendered against me in one of these so-called blanket finishes, caused me to adopt my new riding tactics.

My plan of action henceforth was to start my sprint from the front of the field rather than from its rear.  In a word I was to maneuver into the front of the field (in second or third position) as we came into the home stretch on the last lap.   I reasoned that in my hard sprint, which won me the one-quarter-mile event at the Manhattan Beach track a few weeks previous, had I started my dash for the tape from the front of the field, instead of the rear, I would have won by between eight and ten wheel lengths instead of the ten-inch margin that separated me from Eaton who was in second position.

As I made my way to the starting line for the big race I heard my trainer urge me not to try out my new tactics that afternoon.  I rode in my customary style until the bell rang announcing the start of the final lap, and then I forgot the good advice of my trainer and started riding on my own initiative.  At the sound of the bell all of the racers started to maneuver for what are generally considered the choice positions, known to riders as the winning positions.  As we entered the back stretch I slipped into second position being on Arthur Gardiner's rear wheel.

Let me quote from the Philadelphia Press:—"As the bunch took the turn into the home stretch at terrific speed, Bald jumped from the middle of the bunch and plowed into the lead like a shot, for he was coming like a champion never came before, and the spectators were yelling like mad for the boy from Buffalo, but in the midst of the excitement in the grand rush for the big purse which was to be the winner's end, the little black form of the colored boy was seen to forge rapidly to the front.  He overtook Champion Bald halfway down the home stretch, passing Eaton like a flash, beating him out by 10 lengths.  In an instant the crowd was on its feet and the cheering for Bald was quickly changed to wild cries for 'Taylor, Taylor,' and Taylor it was for sure.

"The colored boy just flew past the champion while the band played, and the crowd cheered and cheered.  Long after the race was over the applause kept up, and Major Taylor was obliged to ride around the track several times bowing his acknowledgment of the cheers of the spectators."

Naturally I was elated at having won such a great race, but I was even more proud because of the fact that my strategy had worked out so well.

While I was heartily congratulated by many of the riders and officials, not one of the racers that I had defeated, however, saw their way clear to shake my hand.  That some of them at least were peeved because of my victory became apparent while they were racing for the honors in the one-mile handicap event which was held shortly after the championship number.

Again I quote from the Philadelphia Press—"Hon. Albert Mott, Chairman of the L. A. W. racing board and generally considered the outstanding figure among the bicycle racing officials of the country, who refereed the races, saw something in this one-mile handicap event which was not just right, but was not in a position to see who should be punished for it. Major Taylor, the colored boy whose wonderful riding made him the idol of the meet, and who caused the crowd for once to forsake Champion Bald, and applaud the efforts of a hated rival, was crowded from his position in the center of the track until he was nearly run into the press box occupied by the reporters.

"Mr. Mott demanded to know who was responsible for it, but was unable to learn, although the judges admitted that Taylor was crowded out of his course. This was one of the unfortunate events of the day, but one for which the Castle Wheelmen were in no way to blame, as the officials of the meet were carefully selected from the best known wheelmen in the country through whose mistakes Major Taylor must suffer."

As a matter of fact, my position on the track as a result of this foul was so precarious that I had to back pedal for all I was worth over the tape, whereas, were it not for the rough tactics employed against me, my pathway would have been cleared to the tape, and I would have pedalled to a well-earned victory, as is indicated by the fact that I finished in second place, despite my back pedalling.

Incidentally, the Philadelphia Press conceded that I was in the best position of the field to win up to the moment that the foul occurred.

## CHAPTER X

### RACE AGAINST JIMMY MICHAELS MY GREATEST

I have been asked thousands of questions relative to my career on the bicycle track that range from how I happened to start riding a bicycle to what I considered my hardest race. What was my fastest time for a mile, and how I got the name Major, how I managed to get out of pockets. Since every heat leading up to every final that I figured in during my almost 17 years of racing was desperately fought every inch of the way, because of that color business, it is no easy matter for me to answer that last question. However, my special match race against Jimmie Michaels at the Manhattan Beach track in the summer of 1898 was perhaps my greatest achievement. Incidentally, I believe it was also my most spectacular victory.

As I delved into my records and scrap-books to get data on which to base my answer to that greatest question, I came across a number of entries including the following:—"Major Taylor easily won the championship" and "Major Taylor easily breaks world's records." I might say at this time that the impression that I won my races easily was perhaps due in a great measure to my own peculiar position on my wheel. It was distinct from that of any other rider on the track—in fact, it was my own invention which was made necessary when I adopted extension handle bars for my sprint races. I was a pioneer among the sprint riders to adopt the extension handle bars. Today the extension handle bars and the position I perfected for myself on my racing wheel, are accepted as the standard by bicycle sprinters the world over.

My racing position was made conspicuous because of the absence of any unnecessary motion of the head or body, awkward or otherwise, which was so noticeable in some riders. I reasoned that any unnecessary motions only tended to impede the rider's efforts, whereas, if the same amount of exertion were employed in the only motion necessary, from the hips down, with a light, quick motion of the ankle, it would not only produce a maximum of efficiency, but by constant practice it would produce an easy, graceful celerity of motion that is pleasing to the eye. It would also conserve the rider's energy for the final lap where it is most needed. So carefully had I worked out my racing style that newspaper men in general always conceded that I was the most graceful rider on the track.

But to get back to what I consider was undoubtedly my hardest race. Jimmie Michaels, the famous little Welshman, and myself were in excellent physical trim for this race of races on the historic

Manhattan Beach track on a mid-summer afternoon 28 years ago.

We found the three-lap cement track at Manhattan Beach lightning fast on that torrid afternoon, because of the absence of the usual gale which swept the track. In the grandstand and strewn out along the rail that bordered the track was one of the greatest throngs that ever witnessed a sporting event in this country. Newspapers had

JIMMY MICHAELS—Champion Middle-distance
Rider of the World, 1901, and
Floyd MacFarland

devoted considerable space to the event because of the spectacular way in which this special match race was brought about. Mr. William A. Brady, of New York, who was manager of James J. Corbett when he was the heavyweight champion boxer of the world, was looking after my interest at the time. His challenges on my behalf fell on deaf ears as regarded the other crack sprinters of the day. The great Eddie (Cannon) Bald refusing to be matched against me on grounds that it would affect him socially. In desperation he assembled the sporting editors of the New York daily papers and requested them to broadcast his willingness to wager $1,000 on a winner-take-all basis, and that I could defeat any one of them in a one-mile paced sprint race. Jimmie Michaels was the only one of the bunch that accepted the defy. It was agreed between Michaels and myself that the prize would go to the rider winning two out of three races from a standing start with pace.

I daresay no bicycle race that was ever conducted in this country received the amount of space in the daily sporting pages that this one did. The outstanding reason for this keen interest was the fact that Michaels was at the moment the King of the paced riders of the world while the experts generally conceded that I held the same position among the sprinters. As a matter of prestige, however, the victory meant far more to me than to my worthy opponent, as the event in which we were to participate was classed as a sprint race even though it was to be paced. Michaels stepped out of his class when he consented to ride a short distance while I did likewise by undertaking to ride behind pace. Michaels through his long experience riding behind pace entered this match race with a decided advantage over me, inasmuch as following pace was an innovation for me at that time.

The inside story of Mr. Brady's anxiety to arrange a match race between myself and the cream of the sprinters of the country, including Eddie Bald, Tom Cooper, Earl Kiser and Arthur Gardiner, widely known as the "big-four," centered about the rough treatment accorded me on the Brooklyn track one week before my race with Jimmie Michaels. I quote the following paragraph from one of the New York papers to explain Mr. Brady's attitude on the race referred to and his determination to match me against those who would have prevented my winning any of the prize money at the Brooklyn event:

"On Saturday last the bicycle racers seemed determined to prevent Major Taylor, the colored youth, from winning any prize money in the Brooklyn track meet. However, Major Taylor was equal to the occasion, wiggled in and out of pockets set for him and won the one-mile handicap event in addition to finishing second in the one-mile national championship event.

"Mr. Brady was indignant at the show of race prejudice against the colored cyclist in the Brooklyn events. He claims that under his handling Major Taylor will develop into a world-beater. He has been riding very fast this season and is now up in fourth place in the percentage table, and only a few points behind the leader. Brady claims that if the rest of the racers give Taylor a fair shake he will win every sprint race in which he starts. 'Unhampered, Major Taylor is the fastest man on the track today. Just think of the great odds he has to ride under and then give a thought to the great number of races he wins year in and year out against the cream of the world. Of course it is humiliating to have a colored boy win over them, but Taylor turns the trick honestly and carefully and in racing parlance

there is not a whiter man on the track, he is game to the core, and
you never hear him complain or protest about his ill treatment,' said
Mr. Brady."

It was due to the observations Mr. Brady made at those races in
Brooklyn that he challenged the sprinters to meet me in a match race
for $1,000.  He told the newspaper men that he had implicit con-
fidence in my ability and that if he had not he would never put up
$1,000 on me.

Now to get back to this all important race between Jimmie
Michaels and myself on the Manhattan Beach track.  The press con-
ceded that the rider who got away in front in our race would have a
slight edge on his opponent in the dash for the tape.  Again I quote
further from the same clipping referred to above:—"But this does
not mean to say that he will necessarily win the race which will be
the best second and third heat struggle with quintet pacing.  It will be
a wild rush on the part of the two contestants to locate themselves
behind their big pacing machines at the getaway and the same sort of
a wild scramble will ensue in the concluding few yards when they
leave the protection of their multicycles to sprint for the tape."

"The colored rider gets away very fast and the Welsh boy is not
negligent in this respect.  The battle between the two will be the
first of its kind ever staged in this country, and should prove to be a
heartbreaker."

The following article appeared in the New York *Journal* the
morning after our race:—Major Taylor a winner.  Phenomenal
performances in Special Match Race.  Major Taylor runs away from
Jimmie Michaels and establishes a new World's Record of 1:41
which will, no doubt, stand for years."

"The Welsh Rider was hissed while the Colored Rider was
cheered."

"Major Taylor, the colored cyclist, met and defeated Jimmie
Michaels in the special match race yesterday afternoon at Manhattan
Beach.  Michaels winning the first heat easily.  Major Taylor's
pacing quintet going wrong in the final lap. Major Taylor's riding
was wonderful both from a racing and a time standpoint, having
established a new world's record, which was absolutely phenomenal.
For the first time in his racing career Michaels was hissed by the
spectators as he passed in front of the grandstand deserted and dejected
by Major Taylor's overwhelming victory.

"Immediately after the third heat was finished, and before the
time was announced, William A. Brady, who championed the colored
boy during the entire season, quickly issued a sweeping challenge to
match Taylor against Michaels for any distance up to 100 miles, for
from $5,000.00 to $10,000.00 a side.  The challenge was received

with tumultuous shouts, yelling and continued applause from the large assembly, and the colored rider was lionized when his time was announced.

"Edward Taylore, the French rider, had held the world's competition record of 1.45 for that distance in a contest paced from a standing start.  The world's record against time was made by Platt Betts, of England, which was 1.43-3.  Michaels broke Edward Taylore's record by four-fifths of a second.  Major Taylor wiped out this new mark and tied Betts' record against time.  In the second heat Taylor rode on the outside for nearly two and one half laps, it can be easily seen that he rode more than a mile in the time, and shrewd judges who watched the race said that Major Taylor would do even better in his third attempt.

"That he justified this belief goes without saying.  After taking up his position on the pole, Taylor jumped away at a hair-raising clip and opened up a gap of 10 lengths.  In the first lap of the last heat Michaels never had a 'look-in' after his adversary entered the second lap, as Taylor skimmed along as swiftly as the flight of a swallow, and on the back stretch of the last lap Michaels sat upright and pedalled leisurely to the tape, for he saw it was useless to attempt to catch his speedy rival.  The Welsh rider was as pale as a corpse as he jumped from his wheel, he had no excuse to offer for his defeat, for at no time could he keep up with the terrible pace set by Taylor.

"Major Taylor's wonderful performance undoubtedly stamped him as the premier sprinter of the world and judging from the staying qualities that he exhibited in the six-day race, the middle distance championship may yet be his also before the season is over."

After having lost the first heat because of a mishap to my pacing machine, I went to the tape for the second heat fairly bubbling over with confidence that I could take my opponent's measure this time, providing my pacing machine gave me no further trouble.  I felt this way even after Michaels had again won the toss for the pole position which gave him the advantage.

After two or three false attempts to get away, due to the snapping of chains on our pacing machines, which was caused by over anxiety on the part of our pacemakers, we finally got off to a perfect start.

I will now relate the most amazing part of this widely advertised match race which the press did not get, and which is told here for the first time.

I was always credited with being the fastest man in the world, off the mark, among the sprinters, while my opponent enjoyed the same distinction among the paced riders. Michaels, having won the favored position on the pole in this heat, the second, experienced little difficulty in getting away first, well in the lead, but my pacers dashed after them with a vengeance.  As we turned into the back stretch they were confident that I could hang on to them regardless of their speed and with this thought in their minds they tore down the back stretch and around the turn at a rate of speed that must have given the crowd a rare thrill.

After the most furious efforts ever seen in pace-racing, we succeeded in closing the big gap gained by Michaels at the getaway.  We were on even terms crossing the tape at the end of the first torrid lap, when fresh teams picked us up with desperate though marvelous accuracy, because in changing pace from one machine to another the slightest possible miscue means certain defeat.  Michaels and I were both struggling for dear life to hold on to our big machines as the pace was waxing hotter and hotter with every turn of the pedals.  Being obliged to fight around on the outside of the track for the entire distance, the heart-breaking speed was now beginning to have its affect on me.

Immediately after I had changed over to my fastest pacing team steered by Austin Crooks with Allie Newhouse coaching on the rear seat, this team having been held in reserve to cover that last feverish lap, I felt my strength ebbing very fast.  It was just as I was turning into the last lap and despite my utmost effort the rear wheel of my big quintet was getting away from me, inch by inch.  My pacemakers were straining every muscle and fiber in their well-trained legs and were pedalling with perfect rhythm, apparently satisfied that I could take all the speed that they could give me.  At this tense moment when we were in the back stretch of the last lap, Michaels was slightly ahead, although our elbows were almost touching, and we were racing neck and neck.

Our coachers on the rear seats of the big pacing machines were shrieking frantically, "C'mon, C'mon."  It now seemed only a question of which of us would be shaken off first, and it really seemed that it would be me, for at this point in the race I was more than a yard off the rear wheel of my quintet after having failed in my last super-effort to regain it.  In another fraction of a second I would have been defeated and badly crushed, but at this point the unexpected happened.

Michaels, who was now leading by more than two yards, could withstand the great strain no longer.  He yelled frantically to his coach, "Steady, Steady" which was synonymous for "Slow, Slow."  When I heard Michaels' cry "Steady, Steady" to his pacemakers I could scarcely believe my ears.  That proved to be the psychological turning point of that race, the one I now consider my greatest achievement.

Michaels' urgent plea of "Steady, Steady" sounded his death knell and simultaneously inspired me to my supreme efforts which were shortly culminated by a remarkable victory.  Up to the moment that I heard Michaels direct his pacemakers to slacken their speed I felt certain he would defeat me.  I was absolutely burned out.

Just how I ever managed to kick up to the rear wheel of my pacing machine will always remain a mystery to me, but in a flash I got it and was yelling like mad, "Go, Go," and go they did, with every ounce of energy they had left in them.  They were delighted to hear me call for a faster pace and on they dashed as we rounded into the home stretch.  It was a glorious sensation to see victory now within my grasp, when only a few seconds before inevitable defeat stared me in the face.  As we made for the finishing line I was even bold enough to jump from the rear of my pacing machine and beat it across the tape, breaking the record established by Michaels in the preceding heat, and leading him over the line by 200 feet.

Both my pacing-team and that of Michaels were pedalling desperately in that heat for supremacy of speed and low score.  For that reason Michaels' pacers disregarded his distressful cry of "Steady, Steady"—their one thought being to lead my boys over the finishing line.  This they did but only because my pacers had to fight hard all the way around on the outside of the track.  However, it gave my pacing quintet no little satisfaction to know that they had finished the race with me hanging onto them while the rival quintet had left their star away back on the track.

I never heard such applause as that which greeted me when I dismounted and started for my dressing room.  I was pretty well "baked," and nearly dropped twice, but the cheers of the crowd did much to revive and stimulate me and by the time I reached my cot I was in pretty good condition.  At this point I resorted to some strategy which I always regarded as one of my best cards.  It was in effect to have the third and final heat of the race run off as quickly as possible.  I always felt that since I was in such perfect physical condition throughout the racing year that I could recuperate more quickly after a gruelling race than any of my competitors.  Therefore, my anxiety was to get Michaels out for the final heat at the earliest possible moment.  Mr. Brady, my manager, saw to it that we were called out again in short order.  Excitement was at a high pitch as Michaels and I took up our positions to start the final heat.  Interest in this final sprint for the $1,000 prize, was at fever heat since each of us had won a heat with a record attached to each whirl around the track.  I have seen enthusiastic gatherings at bicycle race tracks all over the country but I never saw one more on edge than the assembly that witnessed the final heat in this great race with

Michaels. Incidentally thousands of dollars were waged on the outcome with the odds being two to one on me.

I noticed that as Michaels came to the tape for the final test his face was colorless. His countenance plainly showed that he had been through a trying ordeal in the last heat. When I won the toss for the pole position Michaels seemed to grow even paler. That position gave me a slight advantage such as he had over me in the other two heats. As he stood over on the track it was apparent that Michaels realized that all the breaks were in my favor, and he seemed especially conscious of the bad defeat he had received in the last heat. The mental suffering and physical strain under which Michaels was laboring at the moment seemed to bewilder him. I felt I had him beaten even before the race started.

I jumped to the front at the crack of the gun, taking the lead by 10 or 12 wheel lengths, which I steadily increased as the race continued. The pace in this heat was terrific and I could tell from the outset that we were travelling in record time. Still it did not seem to have the same strenuous effect on me that I had experienced in the second heat and several times I called for more pace.

After the start I did not see my opponent again until the race was concluded. Michaels quit somewhere on the last lap, and for the first time in his life he was roundly hissed as he rode past the grand stand. I felt sorry for him, because Michaels was the best man in the world at middle-distance racing. But he had made the mistake of his life by going out of his class just as I did sometime later when he defeated me in the 20-mile paced race which was his favorite distance. As I made my way to the dressing room it dawned upon me, as never before, that the public is always with the winner, regardless of color.

It was a well-known fact among trainers, managers, riders and newspaper men that Jimmie Michaels was practically unbeatable as long as he could maintain the lead. However, it was agreed among them that if for any reason he lost the front position he was at that moment a beaten man. In a word he could not fight an up-hill battle to win a race. I knew this before we started that epoch-making race referred to above.

As a result of this extraordinary match race with Jimmie Michaels I gained a distinction that never befell the lot of any other racing cyclist in the world, and created a precedent in bicycle racing that has never been equalled, let alone excelled in the history of any athletic sport as far as I have been able to learn.

In all three heats the world's record for the one-mile competition, standing start, 1.45, which was established by Edward Taylore, the famous French rider, was broken. In the first heat Michaels turned the trick in 1:44-1; in the second heat I set the new mark at 1:43-3, and in the final heat I lowered that mark to 1:41-2, a world's record which has not been bettered in the 29 intervening years. Incidentally in the second heat I set up a mark of 1:43-3 equalling the world's record established by Platt Betts in a mile race with a flying start behind human pace several years before. In the final heat I not only lowered the world's record for the standing start competition to its present figure, 1:41-2, but I also shaved 2:1-5 from Betts' world's record. Therefore, I had the honor of having tied the world's record and beating it in successive heats.

So highly elated was Mr. Brady, my manager, that he made me a present of $1,000 for defeating Michaels. Of course, I was delighted with such a material token of his appreciation for my efforts, or as he so generously put it, "Just a little present from one good sport to another."

Deeply mindful of the important part played by my pacemakers leading up to my victory over Michaels, I decided to split Mr. Brady's thousand dollars with them. At first they were reluctant to do this claiming that they were amply repaid for their efforts by the sincere thanks that I had bestowed upon them as soon as we had entered our dressing room. They also took no little pride in the fact that in that furious second heat they were able to furnish me speed and more speed when I really needed it in my mad dash for the tape and victory. Nevertheless, I insisted and Mr. Brady's generous gift was split among them.

Incidentally, no man was ever more grateful to a group of co-workers than I was to those pacemakers who served me so loyally and well in my defeat of the great Jimmie Michaels. Had any one of them so desired he could have brought about my defeat absolutely without one of his team mates even suspecting a plot. I will always be grateful to my pacemakers on that occasion as they played no small part in what is considered the greatest paced race in the history of the sport in this country.

All of my pacemakers in my race against Michaels were white while I was black, but color evidently was neither a burden, handicap or drawback in this instance. Those fine sportsmen, who paced me in that epoch-making race against Michaels, admired me as an athlete, respected me as a man, and gave their utmost in as trying a race as has ever been ridden, that I might achieve victory over the remarkable Jimmie Michaels.

The following paragraph is quoted from a New York newspaper:

"Major Taylor's victory over Jimmie Michaels, coming as it did just after the unsuccessful efforts of certain race meet managers to debar him from their tracks on account of his color, and for no other reason, has established fortune for him. Now the colored boy's services will have to be sought after by the race track promoters as he is among the very best, if not the very best drawing card among the racing men of the country.

"In view of his newly acquired standing, Major Taylor will doubtless know how to deal with those who have sought to retard his progress and injure his prospects as a National Circuit rider. As for those circuit riders who have heretofore given Taylor the cold shoulder, and sought by unfair and unsportsmanlike methods to compass his defeat in past races, they will now do well if they entertain the slightest hope of defeating or making a creditable showing against this new star, to get a match with him without delay. Their mere suggestions in arranging a match with the colored boy will bring most of them greater prestige than they have ever enjoyed in their careers, while to defeat Major Taylor would make them famous."

# CHAPTER XI



### ZIMMERMAN'S TIP BROUGHT ME VICTORY

One of my first tests on the Grand Circuit in 1898 came at the Asbury Park (N. J.) track. The final heat found the five following riders who were the leaders in the battle for the championship crown:—Tom Cooper, Eddie Bald, Orlando Stevens, Arthur Gardiner and myself, opposing each other in this championship event. I won the final heat but great as that victory was in itself, it remains in my memory merely as an accident to one of my greatest achievements on the track.

As I stepped from the train at Asbury Park the afternoon preceding this race I was met by appointment by Arthur A. Zimmerman, the ex-champion of the bicycling world, the hero of all boyhood, as well as my own ever since I was able to read the newspaper. Five years had elapsed since I saw the great Zimmerman. In my capacity of errand boy for "Birdie" Munger in his Indianapolis home in 1893, I was privileged with a personal introduction to Zimmerman who at the moment was riding on the top wave of his wonderful career. He praised me for my having won a road race in Indianapolis as a boy of 13, tidings of which I later learned were furnished him by my good friend, Mr. Munger, who in after years became my manager.

At dinner that night my joy knew no bounds when Mr. Zimmerman requested that I share the guest's place at the dinner table with him. I wore the gold medal which I had won in the above mentioned road race of my boyhood days and it frequently evoked compliments from Mr. Zimmerman. In the course of the dinner Mr. Zimmerman questioned Mr. Munger closely on my bicycling achievements. Mr. Munger said, "I have told Major Taylor that if he refrained from using liquor and cigarettes, and continued to live a clean life I would make him the fastest bicycle rider in the world." Mr. Zimmerman replied that I had a long way to go before I could hope to acquire those laurels, but he added, "Mr. Munger is an excellent advisor and if he tells me you have the makings of a champion in you, I feel sure you will scale the heights some day."

Through the intervening years Mr. Zimmerman's path and mine had never crossed. However, he kept close tabs on my race track activities and invited me to be his house guest as soon as he learned of my entry in the Asbury Park mile championship race. Incidentally, Mr. Zimmerman was to be starter of the title race.

While the riders were limbering up on the track on the forenoon of the race day, Mr. Zimmerman approached me. He told me again and again how pleased he was at my success on the race tracks. Several times he mentioned what an excellent prophet Mr. Munger proved to be when he forecasted my becoming a champion. "I am very anxious to see you win the championship event this afternoon, Major," said Mr. Zimmerman, "and I feel sure you will, even without a suggestion from me, however, I have one to offer, which aided me greatly in my heyday, and I trust you will give it consideration." Mr. Zimmerman then pointed out the spot on the track at which he advised me to make my "jump," and it was on the back stretch halfway to the last turn. "If you can lead the field into this turn, nobody can pass you before you cross the tape. I made all of my successful sprints from this identical spot." This suggestion on the part of Mr. Zimmerman was to govern my racing tactics in the final heat, the arrangement being that I was to use my own judgment in the qualifying heats.

I thanked Mr. Zimmerman for his kindness in offering this suggestion and assured him I would employ his strategy at all costs in the final heat. I kept my word and won the race which stands out even today as one of my greatest. Hardly had the cheering of the immense throng died away before Mr. Zimmerman and myself repaired to a telegraph office and wired the particulars of the race to our mutual friend and admirer, Mr. Munger.

No group of racing horses ever faced the barrier in a more nervous state than the five riders who were on edge for this championship mile event. Cooper, Bald, Stevens, Gardiner and myself were straining every muscle in an effort to win this classic and thereby get an early edge on the rest of the field for the season's honors. As an indication of how fast the qualifying heats were for our race I might mention that such sterling sprinters as Howard Freeman, "Doc" Brown and Bob Terrill were eliminated, and the speedy Gardiner only won his place in the final heat by winning the extra heat for second man.

The first three laps of that mile race were as hotly contested as any I ever rode in. The pace was terrific. As the bell rang announcing the start of the last lap, and the pacemaker slid out of the picture, there was a mad scramble for final positions. Halfway down the back stretch I made my jump and was leading the field when the turn was made into the home stretch. Bald nearly closed up the gap in a wild sprint but he was not quite equal to the task, falling short by less than a length. Cooper finished at Bald's wheel while Gardner finished fourth, Stevens bringing up the rear. I had kept faith with Mr. Zimmerman and started my sprint at the exact spot he had pointed out to me as he gave me some wonderful advice that forenoon.

Of all the ovations that I ever received the one that crowned my efforts at the Asbury Park track on this memorable occasion will remain fresh in my memory forever.  I can hear it now.  I honestly believe that Mr. Zimmerman got as much pleasure out of the ovation as I did myself.  I have never seen a more happy man in my life than Arthur A. Zimmerman as he shook my hand warmly at the conclusion of the race.  Our friend "Birdie" Munger was right, he kept saying.

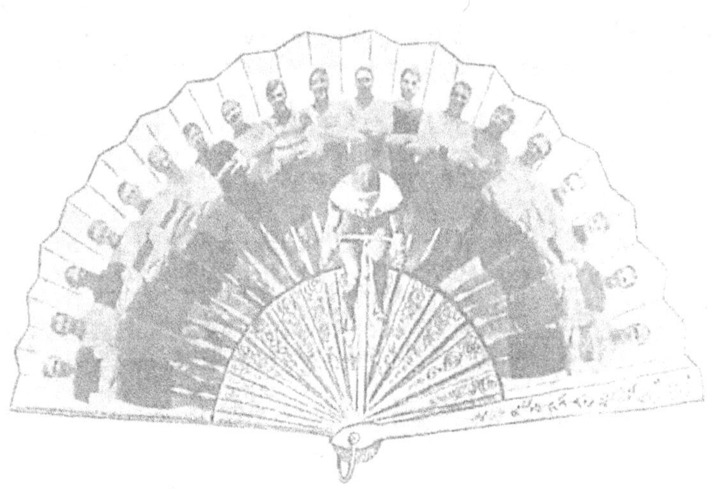

The Bicycle Fan

# CHAPTER XII



I had always considered my physical condition my greatest asset and simultaneously my one and only real weapon of defense. Throughout my racing career I was so fine that a matter of ounces over or under my normal weight would have put me out of the running for the honors.

So when I arrived at the Tioga track in Philadelphia on that summer's afternoon in 1898 I was as near physically perfect as an athlete could be. On top of my excellent physical trim I was bubbling over with confidence with the memory of my victory of the previous week over Bald, Cooper, Gardiner and Stevens.

However, I had no idea that before the sun would set that afternoon I was to make race track history by winning two national championship events on the same program.

When I won those two championship events that afternoon I established a record that has never been equalled on any bicycle race track in this country. During my long period of racing I frequently won two first places on the same program and on numerous occasions I won three firsts in a single day's racing which was the equivalent of winning nine races when one considers the qualifying heats which in many cases were even harder and faster than the finals. Of course, such strenuous racing meant that a man had to be in excellent physical condition at all times and nobody knew this better than myself. I was known as one of the most consistent performers on the track and this was due in a large measure to the excellent care I took of myself.

But to get to my record-breaking performance of winning two championship races in the same program. Let me quote the following paragraphs from the Philadelphia Press:

"Two Victories. Major Taylor rode in front in Circuit Meet. Worcester Boy beat Bald in clever style. Major Taylor, the unbeatable colored boy, took both National Championship events, the one-third mile and the two-mile, at Tioga track today. He won out over the best fields of the season, not excepting the National Meet at Indianapolis, and his excellent work placed him 10 points nearer in the race for the championship fight.

"Major Taylor won his heats and finals under the greatest difficulties, he was third and fourth place in the bunch as they rounded the last turn into the home stretch, and again and again managed to win out in spite of the fact that the very best men in the country were ahead of him on entering the stretch.

(54)

"Major Taylor was superior to his fields today, as was Zimmerman superior in the days of long ago on the same track.

"For the one-third mile championship battle, Eddie Bald, Major Taylor, Tom Cooper, Arthur Gardiner and Howard Freeman were the most excellent line-up. Gardiner rushed off in the lead with Taylor and Bald just back of him, side by side, Taylor on the pole and Freeman and Cooper following, with Freeman on the pole directly behind Taylor. It was the Detroit man, Cooper, however, who made the jump for the tape and shot to the front, gaining two clear lengths. Taylor jumped from the side of Bald, then Freeman came up from the rear, Taylor quickly catching Cooper and gaining his side. At this point Freeman came to the front making the battle a three-cornered one to the tape, with Taylor winning out by inches over Freeman while Cooper was third. The three finished within half a length, Gardiner was fourth and Champion Bald last."

I was given such a splendid ovation at the conclusion of that race that I determined to enter the two-mile championship event. However, some of my opponents were not anxious to have me start in that event and as I made my way to the dressing rooms one of them openly threatened me with bodily harm if I dared to start in that event. His objection was not based on anything that I had done to him because he did not even ride in the final of the one-third mile championship. Had there been any question in my mind about riding in that two-mile championship it would have been cast aside when I heard that threat. I decided on the spot that I would participate in that race, come what may, and it gave me no little pleasure to lead the field across the finish line for my second championship win of the afternoon, the time owing to excitement was not taken.

Again I quote from the Press account of the meet:

"For the two-mile championship Eddie Bald, Orlando Stevens, Major Taylor, Arthur Gardiner, and 'Plugger' Bill Martin formed the second block of five and a most excellent field. Bald jumped the gun but Taylor beat him in a good race for the pacemaker. Taylor was followed by Bald, Stevens, Gardiner and Martin.

"The pace was so fast that there was no change in positions until the bell lap, when Gardiner came from the rear with Martin on his rear wheel. The pair rounded Taylor and took the lead. Then Bald gained the side of Taylor, placing him in a bad pocket. Stevens made a hot sprint from the rear but was stalled off by Martin, who broke for the tape, which gave Taylor his liberty, the latter being in fourth place on entering the home stretch.

"With a clear field, Taylor jumped with a most wonderful burst of speed, but it was not before the tape was reached that he snatched the lead and won by two feet with Gardiner, Martin, Stevens and Bald close up in that order."

Just before this two-mile race was started a spectator came to me and asked if he could say a few words in private. He was highly excited but I granted his request and we moved off a few feet. He told me he had overheard the other riders planning to throw me. He

Eddie "Cannon" Bald—Champion of America,
1895–1896–1897

implored me not to ride in this race, but I thanked him and told him I was determined to participate regardless of what might happen. However, the information together with the threat one of the riders had made to me personally, had its affect on me and I became nervous. I went to the officials and asked if they would put in double pacemakers for this final and place a very low time limit on the race that we might attempt to establish a world's record for the distance. "I am feeling tip-top today," I told the officials, "and if you will grant this request I assure you that you will see the greatest race you have ever witnessed on this track, or ever will witness on it, and this, regardless of who wins."

Reluctantly they agreed to my plan. However, I had to explain to them my reason for making these unusual requests. I explained to them that the other riders were out to injure me and the only chance

I had to prevent their doing so was to set such a hot pace from the crack of the pistol that they would have their hands full trying to hang on, let alone endeavor to throw me down.

After hearing my extraordinary plea the officials were intensely interested to see how my plan would work out and picked the best and strongest riders for pacing that were at the track. They were instructed to set as fast a pace as possible—and they certainly did. One of the requests that I had made was to have the first pacemaker placed out on the 50-yard mark. When my opponents saw him at that mark they complained that he was out too far but the referee waved aside their protests. They knew all too well that this was a point in my favor because I could jump away from the mark faster than they.

Since there was considerable more than usual at stake in this race I beat the gun a little. So did Eddie Bald, the champion, but in the scramble between us for the pacemaker I gained the advantage and we were off at a terrific rate of speed. Bald was out to redeem himself for having suffered defeat at my hands in the preceding race and he was putting forth his greatest efforts in an endeavor to square himself.

The pace was a scorcher but the race was going exactly the way I had figured it would. The positions were unchanged right up to the bell lap. With the sounding of the bell the monster crowd was in an uproar. There was a mad scramble for the tape but in it the riders had to be very careful in their tactics as the slightest miscue meant certain defeat for them.

As we tore into the back stretch, each rider straining every nerve and muscle in an effort to get the advantage, I was in fourth position and I held that place as we fairly flew into the last turn and rounded into the home stretch. With the most frantic effort I had ever made I fought my way through that bunch of madly sprinting riders and took the front position just as we burst across the tape. My margin of victory was narrow but there was no question about my having won and I received the most thundering ovation that has ever been my lot as I rode an extra lap around the track. The band played "Dixie" and there was a shower of straw hats, fans and programs on the track before I could dismount and make my way to the dressing room.

Every one of the officials of the meet congratulated me warmly on the great race I had just turned in. They all reminded me that I had kept my promise to show them the best race they had ever witnessed. However, down in my heart my greatest thrill centered not so much in having won the race, and I prized the victory highly, but in the fact that I had thwarted the "frame-up" planned by my fellow riders.

Shortly after I had reached my dressing room and was being rubbed down by my trainer, all of the riders who participated in the program that afternoon came rushing into my quarters. Naturally I was frightened, having in mind the threat I overheard, and the warning given me by one of the spectators just before the two-mile race started. However, I was due for a very pleasant surprise when every one of the riders shook my hand in turn, and congratulated me on my two championship victories during the afternoon.

It was the first time in my career that any of my so-called "big" competitors had ever congratulated me for any of my achievements on the track. I was elated, naturally, at this turn of affairs and the satisfaction that I had in having my rivals congratulate me for my successes that day was worth considerably more to me than the prize money I took home. It was the first manifestation of good sportsmanship on the part of my opponents. I felt that their action was a demonstration of their admiration and respect for me as a man and that meant far more to me than even the special purse which was offered the winner of this two-mile race. Incidentally, their action proved my contention that the spirit of true sportsmanship will bring out, or at least should bring out the highest qualities and very best motives that a man can possibly possess. I also beat the field out at a night meet on the Woodside track, Philadelphia, in a hard run mile open event, making a total of three first places in the same day.

# CHAPTER XIII



Disgusted by the foul tactics employed to bring about my defeat at the Philadelphia meet a few weeks prior, when I won the one-third mile and two-mile championship races, Howard Freeman, one of my fairest and speediest opponents, wrote the following article for a Philadelphia newspaper:

"How they elbowed the Major. Written by Howard Freeman. Major Taylor's Great Sprint as seen by one who raced with him. Having had the good fortune to finish in front on several occasions, and the misfortune to finish in the rear on numerous occasions, I am in a good position to comment on the relative amount of speed possessed by Eddie Bald, who has won the cycling Championship honors of America for the past three years, (1895-1896-1897), and Major Taylor, the prospective champion and the most dangerous opponent the Bison has had since 1896 when Tom Butler came so near wresting the laurels away from him.

"The season of 1898 has developed several second raters into the Championship class which has made the struggle for the Championship harder and a more even fight than ever before in the history of American cycle racing. Floyd MacFarland, and Owen Kimble are the most prominent of this class, and they are close upon the heels of Bald and Taylor in the Championship race, but the Championship honors are without a doubt between Bald and Taylor.

"Many people are under the impression that it simply requires speed alone to win bicycle races, but such is not the case. It requires a combination of both speed and track generalship, but Bald and Taylor possess a greater amount of these required qualities than their opponents which accounts for their being at the top of the ladder.

"At one time Major Taylor was a very clever trick rider which now serves him greatly when being elbowed or when racing on a poorly banked track. He is the most daring rider on the track and his diminutive size is a great advantage to him when going through a small opening. He is also a hard rider to elbow as he rides very low, his nose almost touching his handle bars, and he is also very clever at giving others the elbow.

"At Philadelphia on September 17, a little elbow work won the one-third mile Championship for him. In this race Arthur Gardiner was leading in the last 200 yards with Major Taylor on his back wheel, and Bald on the right of the latter, which placed Taylor in a very bad pocket, and his only chance was to get by on the pole which he succeeded in doing. In passing the last twelfth, Gardiner swerved out about a foot off the pole, quick as a flash the 'Major' jumped through and won the race. I was in the same final, and was trailing Taylor, but I would not take the same chances he took under any circumstances.

"Major Taylor has a wonderfully quick jump and when he finds an opening he manages to jump through it so quickly that it is impossible to close in on him. He has won a number of races this season in this manner but the majority of his races have been won in the cleanest possible manner, apparently without effort and by a pure burst of speed.

"The fact that most of the racing men hate him is anything but encouraging. Eddie Bald threatened to thrash him several times this season, but owing to interference he did not get a chance to disfigure the Major's black countenance.

"On August 16, at Green Bay, Wis., Taylor won all the professional races on the entire program and in a most decisive manner. During the entire season he has shown that he is blessed with an almost superhuman burst of speed. The Major cannot stand a race paced fast and jerky as well as Eddie Bald, who excels in this kind of a race, and the majority of defeats that Bald has administered to the Major has been in races of this class.

"Major Taylor however, deserves a great amount of credit for the splendid manner in which he has ridden this season, as it has been done under the most discouraging circumstances. All the boys willingly acknowledge him to be the fastest rider on the track and also as a splendid fellow personally, but on account of his color they cannot stand to see him win over them. If it were possible to make him white all of the boys would gladly assist in the job, but try as they may I think it will be almost impossible to keep this little Negro boy, who came into the cycling world entirely unheralded, from winning the cycle championship of America for the season of 1898." After reading this comment of Howard Freeman's I composed the following verses:

## BLACK VERSUS WHITE

As white as you are, and black as I be
Speed is quite natural to me,
For black as I am and white as you be
My color is "fast" black you see.

As white as you are, and black as I be
Still I'd rather be me.
For black as I be and white as you are
I may be whiter inside by far.

As white as you are, and black as I be
Still it was nature's decree
For black as I be, and white as you are
I can be white though blacker than tar.

As white as you are, and black as I be
God created us both, and He
Can best judge though black as I be,
Who's the whiter inside, you or me?

## CHAPTER XIV

### HOW MY STRATEGY FOILED "POCKETS"

A few weeks after I had won the one-third and two-mile championship races in the same afternoon at Philadelphia, I practically repeated those performances at the Green Bay, Wis., track. On this occasion I won the one-third mile event and the one-mile national championship race. Prize money amounting to $2,500 was offered for this meet and it attracted the crack riders of the country.

A short time before the final heat of the one-mile championship race the trainer for another rider informed me that there was a plot afoot among my opponents to pocket me. I made my way to the officials and told them of this plan. They asked for a suggestion as to how they could overcome that conspiracy and I replied by ordering double pacemaking for the event. They readily agreed.

The following clipping from a Green Bay newspaper will show how my strategy allowed me to again lead the field across the tape in two finals:

"Major Taylor, the colored boy from Worcester, Mass., easily proved himself to be the king of the pedal-pushers at the local track today. By his magnificent riding he gained second place in the championship struggle for points and finished his day's work only 14 points behind Bald, who failed to qualify, as did MacFarland and Kimble, who failed to gain recognition in their respective heats.

"In the final of the one-mile professional championship race a field of seven as good men as could be found in America today qualified, and double pacemaking was employed. The contestants caught on behind them in this order: Eddie Bald, Orlando Stevens, Major Taylor, Arthur Gardiner, Johnnie Fisher, Howard Freeman and Owen Kimble.

"There was no change of positions until the pacemakers dropped out, at the last quarter, when Taylor made a jump for the front. Fisher then made a dash past him for the lead which he immediately lost again to Taylor. Freeman watched for the rear wheel of Taylor, who finally made his jump for home winning again by two open lengths, with Freeman second, Gardiner third, Kimble fourth and Bald last.

"In the final of the one-third mile race Freeman, Gardiner, Cooper, Fisher and Taylor lined up in that order from the pole. Taylor with Fisher at his side, jumped to the lead right from the start. Cooper tried to come around them, but failed. Then Gardiner also tried but with no better success.

(62)

"At the quarter, Taylor made his famous jump but Fisher went after him hot-foot while Gardiner dropped back in single line and shot down the home stretch. It was too late, however, as Taylor finished, an open winner, by two lengths with Fisher second, and Gardiner and Cooper at his rear wheel, only inches apart with Freeman last. The time was 42 seconds which was close to the record despite the poor condition of the track."

Realizing that the entire field was out to pocket me in the one-mile championship race, which was the feature of the program, I decided to employ my so-called Philadelphia strategy to nip their plot in the bud. My tactics centered about having the officials put in double pacemakers.

They had little chance to deal with me in the one-third mile race because the distance was so short. A race of this distance calls for a mad scramble from the crack of the pistol to the tape with no opportunity in between to jockey for positions.

Although I told the officials of the race track that I desired the double pacemakers in an effort to forestall pocketing and other rough tactics on the part of my competitors in the one-mile championship race I really had something else in mind. My thought was to have the pacemakers set such a terrific pace from the outset that the scheming riders would be so busy holding the pace that they would not have time to carry through their foul plans. As the officials seemed a bit skeptical about my reason for making this unique request, I played my trump card. It was, in effect, that I was feeling in exceptionally fine form that afternoon and felt that with the proper pace a world's record might be established. They swallowed my line of reasoning, hook, line and sinker. That's just what the crowd wanted—and the officials also. I received a wonderful ovation.

Despite the fact that I had number "13" wished on me by the racing officials in that season of 1898, and notwithstanding the foul tactics of my opponents, the press of the country was almost unanimous in declaring me the sprint champion of the country. My record for the season, covering 49 starts, included 29 first places, nine second places, and 11 third places.

The official standing of the leading sprinters of the country that year credited me with 121 points to 113 for Arthur Gardiner, 107 for Floyd MacFarland, and 98 for Eddie Bald, who was Champion in 1895-6-7.

# CHAPTER XV

After having participated in about 50 regularly scheduled bicycle racing events in 1898, there was an insistent demand that I try to reduce the one-mile record behind human pace. It had been established a short time previously by Edward Taylore, the famous French flier, at 1:32-3 as against the 1:35 mark created by J. Platt Betts in England some time previous. It is a coincidence that three Taylors figure prominently in the assaults on Betts' record as the following newspaper story will indicate:

"Three Taylors have figured in reduction of the One-mile World's Record. It is an interesting fact that since the days of Willie Windle, when that wonderful record breaker from Millbury, Mass., brought the world's bicycle (ordinary) record for one-mile across the Atlantic wresting it from Fred J. Osmond, the English Champion in 1892, whose best time was 2:15, the one-mile has been held by no less than three Taylors. Windle's record was 2:25 3/5.

"The first of these Taylors was George F. Taylor of Ipswich, Mass., a Harvard University graduate. He made two trials; and when he finished the record was 2:14, behind human pace. Later he went out to lower this 2:14 mark and succeeded in 1894, setting up as his final record 2:11. He was satisfied with having lowered the mile mark and after devoting some time to competitive racing he retired to private life in 1894 and is now a prosperous dentist.

One of the first things of vital importance that I learned after joining the big pros, which gave me a world of confidence was that no rider on the track could handle his machine with greater dexterity than I, which was due to the fact that I had formally been an expert trick and fancy rider. Another thing equally important to me was that all of the top-notchers were extremely afraid of a fall, and if forced into a pocket, or suddenly bumped or elbowed, many of them would actually sit up, or quit cold rather than risk bumping the track.

I was not so much in fear of a toss from the big riders as by the second and third class men, who were in the pay of the big riders for a cut of the purse, and they would stop at nothing. Knowing these vulnerable spots in the big sprinters was a great advantage to me, and now that I had mastered the scientific and technic of bicycle racing, "pockets" and "elbows" no longer had any terrors for me. I have been asked numerous times how I got out of a pocket.

In order to be able to get out of a pocket successfully, is to do it without interfering with or bringing any one down. To pull this stunt a rider must have a lightning like "jump," and he should also develop a wonderful bunch of nerve to put it over.  I actually had the trick down so fine at certain times that I have often really invited a pocket as a matter of tactics, when I had a dangerous man on my rear wheel I would slip right into a pocket, making no effort to get out until just nearing the tape then timing my jump perfectly I would suddenly hop through leaving my rival in the lurch.  The chances were a thousand to one that he would make no attempt to follow me through, and in case he did get through successfully it would be too late, as I would invariably be over the tape yards ahead.

In the middle of a turn I always found the most favorable spot on the track to get out of a "pocket" because it is almost impossible for a rider to tear off a dead sprint at top speed without swerving, or wobbling more or less, and therefore even more difficult and dangerous for three or more riders to engage in a furious sprint on the steep banking and ride steady, and at the same time carry out their part of the plot, then crouching very low, I have often started through with scarcely space enough for my front wheel to pass, and having been so well protected from wind resistance, since the pocket formed a sort of a vacuum I was able to kick through like a cork out of a champagne bottle as I have often heard remarked.  As a matter of fact I consider this the most skillful bit of tactics in bicycle racing.

As a rule it requires at least three good men to form an effective pocket, for example, one man leading on the pole, with the pocketed rider on his rear wheel, when the second man comes with a rush and suddenly eases up when slightly in advance of the pocketed rider, the third man quickly comes around from the rear of the pocketed man and dashes for the tape, defeating all the others, the two men forming the pocket sacrificing their chances by holding their victim in the pocket. The winner would of course be expected to split the spoils with the riders who formed the pocket.

What I considered the most vicious practice in the way of foul riding on a bicycle track was often staged by two riders, while we were entering home stretch, or on the back stretch at a break-neck speed, with one leading on the pole, the other close on his right, at this point the man on the right would swerve out just enough to tempt the rider following to pass between them, they would suddenly then close in on him, causing him to bump the track with a terrible crash.  If he came through the experience alive it's a safe bet he would never try it again.

These treacherous tactics were nothing less than an attempt to kill, and riders guilty of such fiendish practices should be dealt with severely, or at least permanently eliminated from the sport.  I have often been criticised for going through a pocket on the pole, and it was a strict violation of the racing rules, but my answer was this: I was always on the defensive, they were the first to violate the rules by forcing me into a pocket, in the next place it was also an infraction of the rules for a rider, or a number of riders to interfere with another rider. Without such unfair tactics it would not be necessary for me to undertake such dangerous risks, I only took such daring chances as a last resort; they were teaming, which was strictly against the rules, while I was playing the game single-handed in the big majority of my races, so under the circumstances the odds were so overwhelming that I always felt perfectly justified in getting out of a pocket in any manner possible, so long of course as I could do so without bringing anyone down; besides, my own neck was in jeopardy.

In extricating myself from these perilous positions I did not rely entirely on my quick jump but it was also a matter of perfect judgment, skill and daring required in timing a jump, and be able to flash through at the critical moment. At times it might be necessary to force matters by giving the riders' rear wheel directly ahead of me, a side slap with my front wheel by a quick jerk of my handle bar, this would frighten him and invariably cause him to swerve out a trifle, instantaniously I would kick through, and win the race. Incidentally I never once brought any rider down, which was remarkable, considering the hundreds of times I worked it. And I openly challenge and defy any track official to say that I ever willfully, accidentally, or otherwise threw another rider, or in any way did commit a dishonorable act in bicycle racing as long as I was connected with the game. I admit I was no angel, I had my faults, but in my honest opinion a real honest to goodness champion can always win on his merits.

On more than one occasion during my career it was my good fortune to enjoy many rare thrills, such as I imagine comparatively few people have ever been privileged to enjoy. It was the climax that followed a bitterly fought out victory over a vast field of competitors, who with their managers and trainers had concentrated both their mental and physical forces in figuring out and practicing certain tricks, and schemes for weeks, in order to trim the "nigger."

On the day set for the big race every rider trained to the minute and chock full of confidence, and keyed up to the highest pitch of nervous energy, and rareing to go. The stage all set, the final words of instructions whispered by their anxious trainers, the crack of the pistol sounded, and we were off with a wild dash tearing off speed they had never shown before.

I could only figure out the frame up as the race progressed, but instantly I detected their schemes, by a clever bit of jockeying or maneuvering I could invarably upset their crooked plans, and once their moral was destroyed they were thrown in a state of confusion, the rest was easy, I had only to rely on a well-timed jump in the home stretch to complete the job, and sail across the tape a winner amid the roaring cheers of the spectators.

With this victory, came the sublime thrill that was beyond the power of words to express, and the fact of having defeated single-handed the whole crooked outfit, the riders, their trainers and managers, as well, made it a victory fit for the kings.  Having won over them in a clean-cut decisive manner I considered it ample compensation for

Quintet Pacing Teams.  Before the Days of Motor Pacing

all their unfair and cunning schemes.  It was as sweet a revenge as one could wish for.

"The next Taylor to set the one-mile human-paced record was Edward Taylore, the French rider.  He spells his name with a final "e," simply to distinguish himself from Major Taylor. Edward Taylore won the honors at Philadelphia in 1898 when he lowered J. Platt Betts' record of 1:35 and set a new mark of 1:32-3.  It was thought that these figures would stand for a long time but within a few months Major Taylor had whittled the record down to 1:31-4 and insisted he could lower it to better than 1:30.  With that end in view the maker of the bicycle Taylor was riding at the time offered his pacemakers a bonus of $10,000 if they succeeded in aiding Taylor to turn the mile inside of 1:30.

"In the past 20 years the world's record for one mile has been reduced nearly one half.  In all, it has witnessed 48 reductions in which no less than 25 riders have taken part.  America and England are the only two countries represented in the table and of course this country takes the lead."

Anxious as I was to establish the one-mile human-paced record, I had something else in mind as I turned my sails to lower Taylore's phenomenal mark.  I felt that if I could establish a new world's record for the mile that such a performance would go far to dispel any doubts about my right to the American sprint championship honors.

So intent was I upon establishing a new world record for the one-mile that in preparation for my race against time, I hung up new marks for the quarter, one-third, half and three-quarter mile distances.  I made these four records on the Woodside Park track in Philadelphia which was also scheduled to stage my race against time in the one-mile event.

I quote from an article printed at the time in the New York *Sun* as follows:

"It is a serious fact that last week, when the horse was monarch in New York, its silent steel-framed contemporary, the wheel, was monarch in Philadelphia, and succeeded in establishing some records for time that throw all past performances of trotters and runners into total eclipse.  Indeed, the surprising exhibitions of Major Taylor, the crack colored cyclist, at Philadelphia, have opened the eyes of all wheelmen and horsemen as well.  During the week, Major Taylor lowered the paced records for the quarter-mile and one-mile and some of his feats were accomplished under circumstances which would probably have discouraged almost all other riders with reputations for high speed.

"But none of Taylor's remarkable performances equalled the efforts of Wednesday when compelled to exert himself to the utmost because of faulty pacing, he smashed his own record of 1:32, shortening the time for the distance by one-fifth of a second and thus establishing his new one-mile mark of 1:31 4/5.  Soon after this achievement Major Taylor sought to lower the figures for the three-quarters of a mile and succeeded in clipping one-fifth of a second from his own record, making the new one read 1:08 2/5.  In the same trial he covered the half-mile in :45 1/5 which was one-fifth of a second under the best previous time and :02 2/5 under the record held by Windle.  It is worthy of note that Major Taylor's achievements were made in almost continuous riding, very little time being devoted to rest.

"In that respect, as in regard to the number of excellent records established, his performances will doubtless arouse the admiration of all racing men the world over, but it will doubtless startle the cycling fraternity.  However, more than anything else, is the fact that four-fifths of a second has been slashed from the old record of the one-mile mark, and further evidence has been given that ere long the 1:30 mark will be easily within the possibilities of the wheel.

"It can scarcely be expected that the one-mile figures will show some drop correspondingly in the next 14 months, as has been shown since September, 1897. In that month J. S. Stocks rode a mile at Crystal Palace, London, in 1:35 2/5. It was that performance which exhibited the bicycle as speedier by one-tenth of a second than the horse. When two or three years previous, W. W. Hamilton of Denver, rode a mile at Coranado, California, in 1:39, it was thought that the bicycle had attained an astonishing speed, but a little over a year after Hamilton's record was lowered almost a second by Eddie McDuffee of Boston, and in about a week after the latter's record ride, J. Platt Betts, the English champion, rode the mile in 1:37 2/5.

"It was thought by many when Stocks knocked two seconds from the previous record that it might remain for some time on the other side of the water, but now our English fliers will have to bestir themselves if they hope to regain past honors."

Another New York newspaper carried the following story on the same day:

"Major Taylor a Cycling Wonder. His Riding at Philadelphia stamps him as the Fastest Bicycle Rider in the World. Colored Marvel will make an Effort to cover the Mile in less than 1:30. No man knows what speed possibilities are concealed in those lithe limbs of the colored boy, Major Taylor, who today is being deluged with telegrams from all parts of the country congratulating him on the annexation of the world's one-mile and half-mile bicycle records, but Taylor smiles and is not satisfied. He is certain of 1:30 for the mile or better, and 44 seconds or better for the half mile is possible.

"Taylor has shown himself a wonder. Other record breakers have again and again tried for the coveted record. Hamilton tried 16 times before he turned the trick in 1:39 1/5 which stood as a record for 17 months. Earl Kiser followed Hamilton in 16 trials, in a great majority of which he lost his pace, and made it in 1:40, and could not come lower. Johnnie Johnson went 12 times for the record of Hamilton, but came no nearer than 1:40.

"While it is true that attempts since that time have been more uniformly successful, as in the case of Eddie McDuffee and Edward Taylore, these have been made at the very height of the racing season when pacemaking teams were at their very best, and after months and months of training and not during the early winter when the cold winds made the teeth chatter, and when officials and spectators would rather have been at the side of a warm stove than at the track side.

"Major Taylor went up against great odds and succeeded. He made his attempts when others would not have done so, and succeeded. He failed but once, and that was the mile which he did in 1:33 3/5, very near the record. He twice cut the two miles and finally lopped 13 seconds off the mark, and that within a few minutes after establishing the mile record. He did quarters, and thirds in these rides that were records again and again, and he is confident that no record so far made, will stand if he goes again. His pacemakers have been unable to shake him and they, too, are confident."

In that campaign of 1899, covering six weeks of very strenuous work I established seven world's records, viz.:—the quarter, third, half,

Establishing World's One-mile Record behind Multicycles

two-thirds, three-quarters, one mile and two miles. However, I got the most satisfaction out of my one-mile accomplishment as it is generally regarded as the standard distance for all kinds of speed tests.

While I was delighted with these records I felt in my heart that I could have broken 1:20 for the mile if my pacemakers could hit up that clip. My reason for being so confident was that in all my racing career I never was in better fettle than when I was making those successful onslaughts against the long standing records for almost all distances up to two miles, in the teeth of those November gales. However, I kept my belief to myself as I knew full well that were I to mention covering the mile in 1:20 I would have been made the laughing stock of the racing-track world.

One day just before making my successful try for the new one-mile record I became convinced that I could never do a faster mile behind human pace. The reason for this was that I knew my pacemakers, who were among the very best in the world, gave me everything they had in that race against time, and the best they were able to do was :01 4/5 over the goal I aimed at—1:30. I am confident that they could have ridden several seconds faster on a hot day, but on that cold bleak November day when I lowered the mile record, my pacemakers were absolutely going at their utmost speed when I established the record of 1:31 4/5.

I might mention an incident that occurred shortly before I made my record-breaking ride to establish the mile record to show just how fast I was riding. In my record trials every day I was continuously calling to my pacemakers for more speed. My requests in themselves annoying my pacemakers somewhat and doubly so as some newspaper men overheard me as I called for more speed. The pacemakers unknown to me, got together and decided to shake me off at the next day's trial against time. They purposely held the fastest pacing quintet on the track, all picked men, to take me on the last lap, one-third of a mile, in my record-breaking one-mile race. I had a fresh quintet for each lap in that record-breaking attempt. As a matter of fact, I had another spare quintet take me around the track for the bell lap just prior to the start of the race. This combination giving me a much desired warming up sprint before picking up the team that would take me around the initial lap to my record-making mile.

However, on the last lap I called again and again for more speed from my pacemaking quintet and failing to get the desired results I set out on my own hook, and actually passed that crack combination on the home stretch, leading them over the tape. It was long after that that I was told about the "frame-up" arranged by my pacemakers in their efforts to shake me off in this record-breaking mile sprint. The laugh was certainly on the pacemakers and the newspaper men took good care that it was widely heralded.

# CHAPTER XVI



Throughout the winter of 1898 I kept in fine physical trim at the Y. M. C. A. gymnasium in my home town, Worcester, Mass. My trainer outlined a course of light exercises for me which I followed to the letter and when the spring rolled around I was in excellent condition for what was destined to be my greatest season on the American tracks. To make sure that I did not get down too fine I carried about six pounds extra weight the same being my reserve in case my opponents started crowding me.

All through that winter season I had four objectives before me. One was the championship of the world, the second was to again win the American championship, the third was to reduce the one-mile world's record to 1:20 or lower, and the fourth was to secure a match race with Tom Cooper or Eddie Bald, leading claimants for the championship of America at the moment and formerly undisputed champions of America. I knew that it was an heroic-sized order and never for the moment did I let up in my training stunts.

I started the ball rolling that season by winning my very first race at Philadelphia. One of my most spectacular victories of the year was winning the big $500 two-mile handicap sweepstake on the Charles River track in Boston on Memorial Day.

I started from scratch with Nat Butler, that great old war-horse who was widely known as the "Handicap King." A last-minute accident deprived me of my sprint bicycle and I was forced to ride a wheel that I only used behind pace. It was geared to 114 inchees which was a tremendous jump from the 92-inch sprinting gear which I had planned to use in this event. Any bicycle racer will appreciate the handicap that that difference of 22 inches means to a rider in a sprint competition race. It is considered an insurmountable handicap. However, I had become so used to doing what seemed to be impossible stunts on a bicycle that I decided to take another chance in this race with my big gear. Again I was relying mainly in this emergency upon my fine physical condition to carry me through.

I left the mark with a jump with Nat Butler on my wheel and we were soon in hot pursuit of his brother, Tom Butler, who had been given a handicap of 50 yards on us. Another brother, Frank Butler, and Watson Coleman started from the 80-yard mark but by alternating pace at half-lap intervals Nat Butler and I managed to overtake the leaders just as the bell clanged for the beginning of the final lap.

Frank Butler was leading at that moment. Then Nat Butler shot

"

to the front of the bunch with brother Tom on his wheel.  I made a quick play and nailed Tom's rear wheel as I could see they were relying upon him to defeat me for the big stakes.  It was known far and wide that the three Butler Brothers were just about the cleverest combination in regards to team work in the racing world.  Thanks to my track generalship I was able to hold my position with that fast field right into the home stretch, and then I cut loose with a great burst of speed that let me break the tape first with several lengths to spare.

There was a tremendous crowd on hand for this special event, the three Butler Brothers being especially popular with the racing fans of their native Boston.  Residents of the Hub were well posted in the finer points of the racing game and appreciated full well just how tricky the Butler Brothers were.  They were noted throughout the country for their speed and cleverness.  With those facts in mind one may well appreciate the ovation that was accorded me for outgeneralling and outsprinting the great trio and the rest of the field in that hectic two-mile race which I won in 4:34.

After a short rest I returned to the track and won the final of the one-mile open race thereby repeating my former successes at Philadelphia and Green Bay when I made bicycle race track history by winning two events on each of those programs, one championship race in each of those meets and the other victories being in open events.  Incidentally, I took home $875 as my day's winnings on the Charles River track on May 30, 1899.

The following is an excerpt from the Boston *Post*, printed the day after the Charles River meet.

"Major Taylor Triumphs.  Proved a Star.  Colored Rider Wins Twice in dashing sprints.  Wins Two-mile Sweepstake and One-mile Open.  Tom Butler easily beaten.  Major Taylor proved to be the star of the A. C. C. meet at Charles River Park yesterday afternoon and succeeded in winning every race in which he competed, his winnings amounting to $875.  The Butler Brothers, Nat, Tom and Frank took about everything the Major left on the list. A large crowd witnessed the races which were good and lively with exceptionally fine finishes in the two professional events.  The weather was perfect and conditions were never better for fast racing except for a heavy wind on the back stretch.

"In both the one-mile open professional and the two-mile A. C. C. sweepstake Major Taylor was on scratch with Nat Butler and won both his heats and finals leaving the other scratch men behind.  James J. Casey of Worcester was out on the 120-yard mark in the sweepstakes and ran fourth in the final.  The Major raced under difficulties by being compelled to ride a machine geared up to 114 inches.

This is the first time a sprinter ever used such a high geared wheel in a sprint race, and manage to win out in a sprint with it.

"Tom Butler, who is to ride Taylor a match race at Westboro on June 10, ran second in the sweepstakes, he having 50 yards on the man whom he is to ride from scratch with. Butler rode well, however. Major rode a splendid race in the two-mile sweepstake. He started from scratch with Nat Butler and the pair caught the bunch on the sixth lap and the Major set the crowd wild by a magnificent sprint down the home stretch which carried him in first. The time was 4:34. Tom Butler on the 50-yard line was second, Frank Butler on the 80-yard line was third, and James J. Casey, 120 yards, fourth. Watson Coleman and Eddie McDuffee also ran."

On June 10 I lost the match race to my great rival Tom Butler at Westboro, Mass. Naturally, Butler was elated at this victory over me and especially since it was by a very wide margin, thereby removing considerable of the sting attached to my victory over him at the Charles River Park meet 10 days previous. I always considered my loss of that race due to the fact that I was obliged to ride my wheel with the big gear, which I had used in the sweepstakes race in Boston, only a short time before and partly to the fact that the Westboro race was run on a four-lap dirt track making it impossible for me to jump as fast as Butler. He was at his best in that race and as a result he led me over the line for the first time in his life.

In addition to the purse offered for the race at Westboro, which was divided 75 percent to the winner and 25 percent to the loser, the winner also was to get 25 percent of the gate receipts. On top of that Butler and I placed a side bet of $200 all of which was to go to the victor.

Three weeks later, July 2, I more than atoned for this defeat at the hands of Tom Butler. This match race was held on the Charles River Park track, Boston, and in it I had the use of my sprint wheel which was geared to 92 inches.

# CHAPTER XVII



On July 2, 1899, I participated in one of the greatest match races of my career when I defeated my old rival Tom Butler in straight heats on the Charles River Park track, Boston, for a purse of $1,000. Coming three weeks after his defeat of me on the Westboro, Massachusetts track for a purse that aggregated $500, this victory was especially pleasing to me. I felt that the fact that I was obliged to ride a wheel with a big gear brought about my downfall at Westboro,

Tom Butler—One of the Famous Butler Brothers

as it was impossible for me to jump as fast as Butler on the four-lap dirt track there. An accident to my 92-inch sprint wheel caused me to shift to the big gear at the last moment.

My match race with Tom Butler at the Boston track was the feature of the L. A. W. meet on that occasion. It was arranged that we would ride one-mile heats, the winner of two of them to have the purse of $1,000. I won the first two heats but had to ride the second one over again as the spectators were not educated to the French method of riding the unpaced mile heat, and insisted that the second heat be re-run. I readily consented to do this and the newspaper men present agreed that I showed Tom Butler as fast a sprint, in that re-run heat, as he had ever seen.

In the first heat Frank Gately furnished the pace and when he dropped out at the last quarter Butler and I sprinted for ourselves. We flew into the home stretch about even but I quickly jumped, and shot across the tape, winning by a half wheel length. No pace-makers were used in the second heat, as is the custom in France, the riders loafing along until within 200 yards of the tape. At this point the pair of us made a gallant effort for first place. I won by a wheel's length. I received a wonderful ovation.

My next race, which marked the opening of the Grand Circuit, was held in St. Louis, in July 1899. No rider ever received a greater ovation than I when I won that championship.

I quote this account of it from a St. Louis newspaper:

"Major Taylor a Champion. Beats Them All In One-Mile Championship. Major Taylor won the one-mile national champion-ship this afternoon. A large crowd was present to witness the post-poned races.

"Tom Butler was a favorite with many of the spectators, who looked to him to win, but he disappointed their expectations by fin-ishing fourth in what was a comparatively slow race. But the real race of the day was between Jerry Woodard, Major Taylor and Charles McCarthy. All three stayed together all through the race until the colored rider by a plucky jump managed to leave them at the finish line by a wheel's length. The crowd cheered the Major heartily and he evidently has many friends in this city.

"The final of the one-mile national championship was won by Major Taylor first, Woodard second, and McCarthy third. St. Louis has for years been a great cycling town, and has turned out many famous riders, such as, Charles McCarthy, Jerry Woodard, Dute Cabanne, the famous Coburn brothers, and many other fast riders." I received a most flattering ovation from the spectators, and officials.

Next I went to Chicago for the L. A. W. meet. In those days Chicago was a hotbed of racing. The city had turned out such famous sprinters as, Bliss, Githens, Diernberger, Lumsden, Was Sicklin, Spooner, Munger, Barrett, Tuttle, Rhodes, Gardiner, Bowler, Leander, Peabody, the wonderful amateur champion, and a host of other star riders. It was my first appearance in Chicago since I won the 10-mile road race against Henry Stewart, "the St. Louis Flyer," back in 1894. I was anxious to show the bicycle fans of that city how much I had improved in the meantime.

The one-mile professional championship event was the feature of the card and it was one of the greatest bicycle races that Chicago had ever seen.  The starters included Tom Butler, Nat Butler, Jimmie Bowler, Charlie McCarthy, and myself, all having qualified in the four preliminary heats.  In the final Bowler and myself were so close together at the finish line that the judges declared it a dead heat although a number of the newspaper men declared positively that I had won.

It took two starts to get us away for the final heat and it was nip and tuck all the way.  Bowler had the lead on the last lap and kept it into the stretch.  "Fifty yards from the tape," read a Chicago newspaper account of the race, "Major Taylor began a magnificent spurt.  It looked as if Bowler was a sure winner, but the colored rider came with a great rush and passed him at the tape.  The crowd yelled for both Bowler and Taylor, and some for a dead heat, according as the finish impressed them, but a dead heat was declared although it looked to many as if Major Taylor had fairly won the decision.  The riders divided the purse, and tossed up for first place, which was won by Major Taylor, Nat Butler was third."

I believe I won that race, but Chicago was Bowler's home town.  On top of that I had never received the benefit of a close decision.  I offered to ride the race over again right on the spot, the winner to take both first and second money, and also the championship points, but Bowler refused.  Much to the disappointment of the public.

Janesville, Wisconsin, was the scene of the next National Circuit Championship event in which I figured.  Tom Butler defeated me in the one-mile title event, that being the first time I trailed anybody in a national championship race that year.  Nat Butler was third in this championship, while Bowler, the Chicago man, who rode a dead heat with me the preceding week in Chicago, finished fourth, with Eddie Llewellyn fifth.  However, I made up for that loss by winning the one-mile open and the five-mile handicap events, Tom Butler being second to me in the five-mile race, in which he startd from the 25-yard mark, with Barney Oldfield, who later won undying fame as an automobile racer, third, and Dunbar fourth.

That made still another occasion in which I won two races on the same program, tossing in a second place for full measure.

# CHAPTER XVIII



I decided to give up riding on the National Circuit for a week or two, following the Janesville program, so that I might go to Chicago to make an attempt to once more lower the one-mile world's record. That meant I would skip the Circuit races which were scheduled to be held at Ottumwa, Iowa, July 26 and 27.

Arriving in Chicago, I met "Birdie" Munger who was to take charge of my record trials. My objective was the world record for the mile, which was held by Eddie McDuffee, who was the first bicycle rider to ride the distance under 1:30. As I trained for this trial against the world record something went wrong with my big steam pacing tandem which had been specially built for me for this occasion.

Since it would take several days to make repairs to my pacing machine I decided to jump to Ottumwa and participate in the Circuit races there. I had been working out on the Chicago track for two weeks with a big gear, it measured 114 inches. Shifting from that 114-inch gear back to my usual sprint gear, 92 inches, would, I felt certain, prove too much of a handicap for me against the fast field that were entered in the Ottumwa Races. Followers of bicycle racing will readily appreciate what it means to have a rider drop from a 114-inch gear to one of 92 inches, after having practiced for a fortnight exclusively on the higher gear.

Nevertheless, I won two first places and one second place in the Ottumwa two-day program, using the 114-inch gear. One of the events that I won was the one-mile national championship. I also won the one-mile open and finished second to Nat Butler in the two-mile championship race.

I quote from an Ottumwa newspaper as follows:

"Major Taylor Wins National Championship of the Iowa State Meet on the Ottumwa Track. Major Taylor, the far-famed Negro, was a great surprise to the crowd that attended the National Championship races of the Iowa state meet on the new Ottumwa track yesterday. He is a perfect wonder on the wheel, which he rides much easier than any other rider on the track, and yet he always seems to have a reserve force that would land him a winner. Although the people could not help but admire his riding he was given a marble heart at the start. The crowd did not like him and did not want to see him win, but in spite of this he carried off his share of the honors.

"When that doughty old warrior, Nat Butler, undoubtedly one of

the finest men on the circuit, won the prettiest race of the entire
program putting Major Taylor down to second place, winning the
two-mile professional championship, the crowd demonstrated its ap-
proval by a roar of enthusiasm.    The two Butlers, McCarthy and
Gibson all qualified for this event and from the very outset the race

NAT BUTLER—The "Handicap King." One
of the Famous Butler Brothers

was hotly contested.    The final heat was paced by Davidson and
Lavin, alternating two laps each.    Tom Butler took the lead in the
second lap.    His brother, Nat, caught his rear wheel immediately with
Taylor following, McCarthy and Gibson hanging on in that order.
Gibson looked like a possible winner until Taylor arrogantly swung
ahead and took the lead, even trying to lead the pacemaker.    This

caused his defeat as the two Butlers crowded him so closely he was exhausted.

"On his last lap-and-a-half Nat Butler suddenly jumped ahead of his brother Tom with Taylor closely following. Tom Butler held the lead for the first half of the final lap but dropped out and finished fifth. The cleverness of the sacrifice was apparent at a glance. Taylor exhausted by his long lead, could not catch Nat Butler while that clever rider sprinted over the tape as fresh as a daisy with a full wheel to spare with McCarthy third."

In the one-mile open race, Tom Butler won the first heat and Llewellyn was second with Phillips third, the time being 2:40 4/5. I won the second heat in 2:41 3/5 with Dunbar second, Harley Davison third. Nat Butler won the third heat with McLeod second the time being 2:08 2/5. The fourth heat was won by McCarthy in 2:08 2/5 with Gibson second. I won the final heat in 2:06 3/5 with Tom Butler second and Charlie McCarthy third. This was an especially closely contested race, as the fast time will indicate. There were no pacemakers used but there was plenty of team work. I believe that my good judgment rather than my speed, enabled me to win this race. From the outset I was determined that the other riders would slip nothing over on me as I had a very vivid recollection of the pocket they had driven me into in the two-mile championship race just finished.

Close as were the two-mile championship and one-mile open events, the national one-mile championship race excelled them. It was arranged in advance that only the winners of each heat would ride in the final. I was fortunate enough to land my heat and then in that hair-raising final I led the field across the tape winning by a wheel's length from Nat Butler with Harry Gibson third. The time was 2:00 2/5, the last quarter being clocked in 26 2/5 seconds which was the fastest quarter ever ridden on the Ottumwa track.

Tom Butler won the first heat, George Llewellyn second with Dunbar third, the time being 2:43 2/5. The second heat was won by Nat Butler with Wood second, time being 2:26 4/5. I won the third heat with McLeod second, and Phillips third, time being 2:26 4/5. Gibson won the fourth heat with McLeod second and Shook third, time 2:29. Harley Davison led the field home in the fifth heat with Lavin second and the time was 2:57.

"Dunbar paced the final heat," reads a clipping from an Ottumwa daily. "Tom Butler jumped away at a hair-raising clip. He held the pace, which was hot from the start for eight laps, after which the race was between Major Taylor and Nat Butler, the Major making a great jump at the last lap."

In commenting on my showing at this meet the same Ottumwa paper printed the following:

"Major Taylor demonstrated that he is a wonderful rider in this event. He has tremendous power and his ebony legs seem to fairly fly around the short circuit made by the pedals. He rides with apparent ease, and a lack of exertion that brands him as a true athlete. He seems to have a reserve force behind him at all times and can put forth an effort at the very last moment when it seems as though he must be completely exhausted.

"Major Taylor is a queer specimen. He is supremely arrogant and egotistical and does not readily make friends. He imagines that he is the whole performance. The sympathies of the crowd were naturally with the white riders, yet they could not help admiring Taylor's wonderful speed, his marvelous endurance and his doggedness, which makes him cling on in a race as long as there is any hope to win."

In passing I might say that the above attack was the only one ever launched against me in my career. I feel that in justice to myself I should explain the motive behind that charge of egotism and arrogance. The writer was connected with the Ottumwa track and in common with the other officials thereof, he was peeved somewhat because I had not sent my entry for the meet several days in advance. This I was unable to do as I had tried to make my attack on the world's record for the paced mile at Chicago on the very day that the Ottumwa meet opened. This writer-official was keenly perturbed because, had he known of my plan to participate in the Ottumwa program, an advertising campaign would have been launched to center about my participation therein. Therefore, my eleventh hour entry did not give the track officials an opportunity to advertise my entry as they would have had I arrived with the rest of the riders. The inference was that my failure to reach Ottumwa with the other riders caused the track hundreds of dollars loss as it was felt that many more would have attended the program had I been advertised as a starter.

The riders were also surprised by my sudden appearance and greeted me very coolly. Something on the order of that lawn-party and the skunk business. Thinking I would not be on hand they imagined that they were going to have everything their own way, but much to their chagrin I spoiled their little party, and just about cleaned up the program.

This same writer declared that the sympathies of the crowd were with the white riders. Still I recall receiving one of my greatest ovations the moment I set foot on the track to take a warming up spin about its surface. This was the first time that I had ever been in

Ottumwa. The reception accorded me as I won the one-mile open event fairly swept me off my feet.

This victory in the one-mile open event came after Nat Butler had defeated me in the two-mile championship race. It was so apparent to the spectators that I was beaten because of a pocket the riders forced me into that they fairly howled with glee as I led the galaxy of stars home in the mile event, so far in front of my competitors that they were unable to attempt to box me or otherwise bring about my defeat by unfair tactics of any kind. I was delighted with the treatment accorded me by the public of Ottumwa despite the belief expressed by the writer quoted above.

# CHAPTER XIX

I went direct from Ottumwa back to Chicago to resume my attempts to lower the world's motor-paced record for the one-mile. This mark, 1:28, was made by Eddie McDuffee on the New Bedford, Mass., three-lap board track one week before I established the new record.

In my first two attempts to lower McDuffee's record I was balked by the failure of my pacing machine to function properly. But let the following clipping tell the story of my efforts to establish new figures for the mile. I quote from one of the Chicago newspapers as follows:

"Major Taylor Fails in Record Attempt but Wins One-mile National Championship Race. Major Taylor in his trial against the world's record for one-mile proved to be a disappointment at the Ravenwood Park track, Illinois, last night. Three attempts were made but the machine broke down each time. However, the other events on the program were run off in fine style.

"Major Taylor, was, of course, the center of attraction, although Jimmie Bowler came in for a good share of applause. Aside from the attempts at the record the race that aroused the greatest enthusiasm was the one-mile national championship which went to Major Taylor with Tom Butler second and Nat Butler, third, the time being 2:02. A great race was looked for between Bowler and Taylor. The Chicago boy won his heat but was not fast enough in taking up the sprint and did not get a place in the final."

Undaunted by the failure of my first attempt to establish a new world record for the mile, I was more determined than ever to lower McDuffee's mark. In the preceding November I broke the old record, human pace, for the mile, establishing the figures of 1:31. A few weeks before my unusual attempt to still further lower the record for the mile, machine pace, Eddie McDuffee shaved three seconds off my 1:31 mark which I established at Philadelphia.

In my 1899 attempts for a new record I was much better equipped than I was at Philadelphia. I had a specially constructed steam motor tandem, whereas in my Philadelphia race against time I had to depend upon 30 men to furnish the pace for me. I felt that with my pacing machine operating properly I could put the record below the 1:20 mark. In addition to my confidence I knew I was in the very best physical condition, so much so that I was very anxious for this all-important record-seeking test.

No sooner had repairs been made to my pacing machine than I went after the one-mile record again. A Chicago newspaper gave the following account of my second attack on McDuffee's record:

"Major Taylor fails again. Pacing Machine gives out before Half the Distance is Covered. Plucky Colored Boy will go out after Mark once more. After six unsuccessful attempts to lower the one-mile world's record at the Ravenwood Park (Ill.) track yesterday, Major Taylor shifted his affections to the Garfield Park track (Ill.) which is a half-mile cement surface. His manager, "Birdie" Munger, thought that the fewer turns on the half-mile track might possibly benefit the pacing machine. However, this made no difference and Taylor failed again. Everybody who has seen Major Taylor in action declares that the colored rider is capable of sticking to almost any kind of pace, for even when the machine is going at its very best he keeps up to it with the greatest ease. Both Munger and Taylor are anxious to get the job off their hands, so the machine may be sent east where some alterations are to be made in its construction. Major Taylor will join the circuit chasers as soon as possible and try to get in shape for the Montreal World's Championship Meet."

A few days later, August 3, 1899, to be exact, I made my third and successful attempt to establish a new world's record for the one-mile motor-paced event. Again I quote from the above mentioned Chicago newspaper:

"Major Taylor's Fast Ride breaks One-mile World's Record. Made Mile in extraordinary Time of 1:22 2/5. Major Taylor today at Garfield Park clipped 5 3/5 seconds from the record made by Eddie McDuffee last Saturday at New Bedford, Mass. The steam pacing machine was taken to the track early this afternoon and in a couple of trials it worked admirably. Then it went wrong again and the crowd prepared to leave, but at six-thirty the officials announced the machine was repaired and that Major Taylor would make another attempt at once.

"Taylor was sent around the track for a preliminary warming up behind a triplet team steered by Jimmie Bowler. Major rode a fast mile behind the triplet, then the motor picked up the colored rider with him sticking to the rear wheel.

"The speed was gradually increased until the three-quarter mark was reached when Munger who was operating the steam pacer, turned her wide open. The jump was made so quickly that for a moment Taylor dropped back and when the machine and rider crossed the starting line he was a yard behind it. With a final great effort he shoved his front wheel up close to the rear wheel of the big motor a few seconds after the officials' watches had been snapped. The eye of every timer rested on the quarter mark and as the machine flew by it, one of them shouted, 'Twenty and one-fifth.'

This was at the rate of 1:20 4/5. The second quarter was 19 1/5 seconds. This was a 1:16 4/5 clip, or just 2/5 of a second slower than the time made by Joe Downey on the straightaway course. The third quarter was made in the same time as the first. The tripler was in readiness to pick up the Major in the last quarter, but as it turned towards the pole, the pacing machine with Taylor swerved aside and shot by the triplet as if it had been standing still.

" 'Now jump!' Munger yelled to Taylor, who immediately made a greater effort and his wheel crept up beside the pacing machine and they crossed the line almost together, this breaking the record in the remarkable time of 1:22 2/5 much to the pleasure and shouting of the hundreds of enthusiastic spectators who had remained to see this successful trial."

Naturally I was pleased at my performance and was delighted that this series of nerve-racking time trials was over with. However, I had no time to celebrate the establishment of the new record as I was scheduled to participate in the world's championship races at Montreal within only nine days after I broke the world's record for the mile. I was anxious to get to Montreal so that I might engage in practice on the track on which the world meet was to be held on August 12, most of my competitors having been there already for several weeks. Entries were received from practically every country in Europe, the United States, Canada and Australia.

## CHAPTER XX

### REALIZING A LIFETIME AMBITION

Upon my arrival in Montreal for this international meet I read in one of the local papers that I was looked upon as the most likely winner from this country in the short distance events, while McLeod, McDuffee, and McCarthy were named as the likely winners in the long distance events. When I made my first trip to the Queen's Park track I found more than 100 professionals and amateurs from all parts of the world training on it.

As I was now in my very best physical condition it required the best judgment of my trainer and myself to keep me in trim for the big championship race. I knew that if I overtrained or undertrained the least bit it might cause a reversal of form at the last moment and, of course, that would undoubtedly throw me off my championship form. By dint of hard work we happily struck the right combination and I finished up by light sprint practice for several days before the championships on my 88-inch sprinting gear which I changed to my regular 92-inch gear on the day of the big championship event.

I won the world's one-mile championship at this meet shortly after I had been "jockeyed" out of a well earned victory in the half-mile open event for professionals the day before. All through my racing career my one outstanding motive was to win the world's championship—and the same desire inspires every rider to his greatest efforts at all times.

This country furnished about 60 percent of the contestants at this international meet. England, France and Australia sent the cream of their cyclists to participate in this, the greatest bicycle program of the year. So keen was the interest of the public in the meet that thousands of enthusiasts gathered at the track daily to watch their favorites going through their training preparations. In the breast of every one of that contingent of riders, amateurs and professionals, burned the desire to win the world's championship title in his chosen distance, and take the crown back to the country under whose colors he rode.

The first race in which I participated was the half-mile open for professionals. The starters were Nat, Tom and Frank Butler, Charlie McCarthy, of this country, Angus McLeod, D'Outreion, Harley Davison, Blaney, Clarence Carman, Tom McCarthy the Canadian, Harry Gibson, Calgar, Watson Coleman, Jimmie Bowler, James J. Casey and Church.

Through a weird ruling of the judges I was forced to take second money despite the fact that the rank and file in the crowded grand stand insisted that I had won. But let the following clipping from a Montreal daily tell the story as a disinterested reporter saw it.

"The World A'Wheel. Greatest Gathering in the Records of Bicycling. The world's record in a racing way, and the world's attendance in an attendance way—that tells the story in a small kind of way. There were more than 5,000 people who could not get in at the Queen's Park track yesterday for the International Races. Inside were gathered 18,000 bicycle race enthusiasts.

"There was only one mistake and it is extremely difficult to account for. That was, why Major Taylor was deprived of a race that he had won. Just what the judges could have been thinking about no one seems to know. That Major Taylor won his race seemed clear to all the spectators who arose in a mass and cheered the colored rider every time he appeared on the track. This was the only difficulty of the first day's meeting. It was unfortunate, however, for the man who won the race was not credited with his winning. It was 'Taylorian Day.' Color cut no ice at any stage in the game.

"The largest crowd ever seen in Montreal was gathered inside Queen's Park track for the races and the program was worthy of the gathering. Chief interest centered in the half-mile open race for professionals in which the most prominent speed merchants were entered. The leaders were Major Taylor, Nat Butler, Frank Butler, Charlie McCarthy, Angus McLeod, D'Outreion, Harley Davison, as well as a host of other fast riders who gave promise of being heard of in cycle circles in the future.

"The final of this race had a most unsatisfactory termination in that the majority of spectators were of the opinion that the Worcester, Mass., boy had won the race in which he made such a spectacular finish by crossing the tape not less than a foot ahead of McCarthy and Nat Butler.

"The first heat was won by Nat Butler with McCarthy second and Blaney of Toronto, third. The second heat went to Carman, T. B. McCarthy second, and Gibson third in a terrific finish.

"There was a broad smile on Major Taylor's face when he lined up for the third heat. Frank Butler cut out the pace; behind him riding leisurely came Major Taylor who was greeted with cheers at every turn. Woodward and McLean trailed Taylor. There was little interest from a strictly racing standpoint until the last quarter of the lap when the black wonder straightened out his limbs and fairly lifted himself into the lead. He ran away from the Cambridge rider in the sprint and finished easy. The Detroiter, Woodward was second while Butler had to be content with third place. The trailers were Murray and McLean.

"Angus McLeod won the fourth heat, D'Outreion was second, Watson Coleman third with Bowler, Casey, and Church bringing up the rear.

"McCarthy set the pace in the final with Taylor in second place and Nat Butler bringing up the rear. The race was a pretty one until entering the home stretch when Taylor was caught in a bad pocket formed by the other riders.

"Major Taylor saw the trick about as quickly as it was sprung and held himself in reserve, but when he saw an opening he fairly lifted his machine through. McCarthy was leading until within a few feet of the tape when the Major shot in ahead and it was the opinion of 18,000 people in the grandstand that Taylor was the winner by at least a foot. The judges, however, ruled otherwise and awarded the race to McCarthy, giving Taylor second place and Nat Butler third. The time was 1:00 2/5.

"When the foregoing announcement was made on the bulletin board the people in the grandstand set up a vigorous protest, calling upon the Board to reconsider its decision and award the race where it rightfully belonged. Major Taylor also thought that he was the victor and expressed some surprise when he walked up to the Board. He asked one of the judges if that was their honest decision that McCarthy had won. When informed that such was the result of their deliberation, the Major said, 'Well, all right, if that is your verdict, gentlemen, I shall have to abide by it, but I know I won.'"

Still another newspaper clipping reads as follows:

"No More Pockets. Major Taylor runs right away from the Field. Wins World's One mile Championship Title. The Two-mile Open was easy. The last day of the World's Championship Meet was attended by fair weather. Major Taylor of the United States had little difficulty in adding the one-mile world's professional championship title to his laurels. All of the preliminary heats were marked by good finishes save the one won by Major Taylor who easily rode down his field.

"In the final of the one-mile world's professional championship race Nat Butler took the lead at the start, Major Taylor dropping into last position. The pace was slow. On the back stretch of the second lap there was some pretty maneuvering for positions and when it was all over Taylor had gotten the position he was jockeying for —second place on the pole with Nat Butler leading. The others were well bunched behind them. McLeod went to the front with a great rush and attempted to make a runaway of it but the others were not to be denied. They rounded the turn into the home stretch, McLeod still leading; but half way down the home stretch Taylor had the race well in hand and there was a great fight on between Nat Butler, Taylor, D'Outreion and McLeod.  They finished in that order.

"Major Taylor was too much for his associates and landed the world's championship by a wheel's length.  He was cheered and cheered by an enthusiastic crowd of 18,000 people who loyally greeted the new world's champion, Major Taylor, U. S. A."

Still another Montreal newspaper printed this account of the the world's championship meet:  "The most really exciting incident of the world meeting was the final of the half-mile open professional.  Major Taylor, the colored rider, for some reason or other, took the fancy of the spectators right from the beginning.  He did some marvelous riding in the trial heats and the applause that greeted him was insistent and continuous.  He is a very pleasing looking boy when he smiles and his skin, though dark, looks soft and smooth as velvet.  Though rather small he is finely proportioned and taken all around, is probably the best developed man on the track.

"In the final referred to McCarthy and Taylor crossed the tape so nearly in a dead heat that it was very difficult to decide who should be awarded the decision.  Referee Ingles announced McCarthy the winner and when this finally dawned upon the spectators in the grand stand they went frantic at what they believed was an injustice done to their protege.  Some people began to shout for Taylor and it was taken up everywhere.  They kept at this for nearly half an hour varying the monotony with some name and yelling scathing remarks to the judges and doing other things to create diversion but always with the idea in view of expressing their disapproval of the decision.

"Finally someone suggested that all those who were against the decision should stand up and in a flash every man, woman and child had arisen.  The entire stand was on its feet and Mayor Prefountain, Aldermen Stevenson and Larry Wilson, who occupied a box just opposite the tape, vigorously joined in the protest.

"The referee, however, stuck to his decision and met the remarks of the angry crowd with a look of perfect indifference. It might be well to understand that in the case of so close a finish only the very few that can be actually on the starting line and on the track are in a fit position to judge who wins.  In this case there was considerable difference in opinion among the officials, but as the referee decided against Taylor, and the judges, who represented Canada, United States and France, backed up the decision it can hardly be seriously questioned."

While waiting to start in the final of the greatest race that I had ever been called upon to contest, the one-mile world's championship at Montreal in 1899, I was a trifle nervous, perhaps, because I knew full well that I was going to be up against the most formidable racing combination known in the cycle racing world, the famous Butler brothers whose superlative tactics and skill in team work really were perfect. They were noted for their ability to outgeneral and out-sprint any combination of riders or tandem team in the racing game.

They worked with clock-like precision, and understood each other so perfectly that no signals or secret codes were necessary. If they had pre-arranged to pull off a certain tactic and their plans miscarried they were each fast enough sprinters to overcome the miscue, and invariably win out down the home stretch. I am frank to admit they were the fairest on the track where I was concerned.

I was confident that the other contestants, big Angus McLeod and D'Outreion, would be riding on their "own." In other words I figured that they would not be in any combination with the Butlers. I was in wonderfully fine form, however, and was never in doubt as to the outcome, my only bogey was being caught in a pocket.

A most dramatic solemnity seemed to settle over that vast audience as we took up our positions at the starting line. The officials and trainers went about their respective duties in a reserved silence. The pistol was the first to speak out loud, however, which signified that within only a few moments more that terrible nervous suspense would surely be over. Then all would know who was really the fastest bicycle rider in the world.

In winning this long-sought title, the highest honor to be obtained in the cycling world, I had at last accomplished my life's greatest ambition. I felt amply repaid for my strenuous efforts in that great race when I was awarded the gold medal which was symbolic of the world's one-mile championship, to say nothing of prestige.

My success in this memorable event was won in precisely the same manner in which I figured it would be. It proved to be more a matter of tactics and track generalship than speed. I had my first test in competing under the French style of competition in which victory and victory only counted. The time occupied in the race being no factor, except that the timers always clocked the last 200 meters.

This type of race puts a premium on the rider's strategy, skill and power.

In the half-mile open race on the preceding day I was caught in a very bad pocket as we entered the last turn into the home stretch, causing me to finish second to Charlie McCarthy according to the decision of the officials. Despite the fact that a reporter at the finish line, who was quoted above, wrote that the grand stand rose en masse and yelled its disapproval of the unfair decision. They believed I won and so do I, even to this day. However, I learned my lesson in that race and I decided henceforth never to be caught in a pocket again, especially in the one-mile championship race which came the next day.

Now for the inside story of how I won the world's one-mile championship at the same meet, and it is being told here for the first time.

I was positive that I could win the race as far as speed alone was concerned. But in spite of my very best judgment and after using every precaution I avoided being caught in a pocket only by the narrowest margin. Just coming into the back stretch on the second lap there was considerable finessing and jockeying for positions.

Dashing into the home stretch on the last lap, Nat Butler was leading at a very fast clip. I was following him with Tom Butler on my rear wheel, D'Outreion next, with McLeod bringing up the rear. We crossed the tape in that order as the crowd cheered wildly and were going great guns as we swept around the turn into the back stretch. Everything was going along nicely up to this point when suddenly the positions changed, as we swept into the back stretch.

I quickly saw a pocket opening up for me, but thanks to the big Canadian Champion, Angus McLeod, who at the same instant made a mighty dash for the finish line at about 250 yards from home, I avoided the pocket.

I had an abundance of reserve power, in fact, I did not dare risk putting my full force into my jump for fear of damaging my trusty machine. According to the track rules, if an accident happened on the last lap the race could not be re-run unless the winner agreed to such a procedure as a matter of sportsmanship in case an opponent was put out of the race through a mishap. So I simply unwound a lively sprint and quickly brought the canny Scot, McLeod, back. I instantly realized that the only obstacles in my way at this critical point to the world's championship were the two Butler brothers, Nat and Tom, and I also realized that they were two tough hurdles to take.

I adopted new tactics the moment I overtook McLeod. I knew that McLeod was no longer a factor so I but kept a very close watch on the Butlers from under my arm until they started their last desperate struggle as we flew into the last turn. It was now a thrilling fight with victory almost within my grasp. As we swung into the home stretch our three front wheels were almost abreast. At a glance I realized that for the first time in my life I was going to be able to make that last supreme effort to break the tape first without interference of any kind. In a word, the four of us came down that home stretch much the same as sprinters are confined to their lanes in a 100-yard dash. It was a fair field—there was no crowding or elbowing, it was a case of winning or losing the world's championship on merit alone.

That style of racing suited me to perfection, so with a great burst of speed I bolted for the tape, and flashed across it more than a full length ahead of Tom Butler.  In the meantime there was a great fight on between Nat Butler and McLeod and the French rider, D'Outrion, who by a mighty effort in the home stretch nosed out Nat Butler and Angus McLeod for third position. But I had actually won.  How the great throng did roar.  I was elated with my victory and especially because it was a clean cut and decisive triumph with a margin wide enough to forestall any cause for complaint on the part of my opponents whom I had turned back.  They were the cream of the cycling world.  It was indeed a glorious thrill.

I shall never forget the thunderous applause that greeted me as I rode my victorious lap of honor around the track with a huge bouquet of roses.  It was the first time that I had triumphed on foreign soil, and I thrilled as I heard the band strike up the "Star Spangled Banner."  My national anthem took on a new meaning for me from that moment.  I never felt so proud to be an American before, and indeed, I felt even more American at that moment than I had ever felt in America.  This was the most impressive moment of my young life, and I was a mighty happy boy when I saw my trainer crate my bicycles that evening for I was still three months under twenty-one years of age when I won that world's championship and gold medal.

During that joyous demonstration there was but one regret in my mind—that my manager, Mr. Munger, could not be present to actually witness his remarkable prophecy, "the fastest bicycle rider in the world," become a wonderful reality in such a spectacular manner. I considered my great championship success a big victory for him as well, not only for his confidence in me as a rider, but also on account of his high ideals and true sportsmanship for which he stood.

In my successes at the International Meet in Montreal I once more performed what among bicycle riders is considered a remarkable feat— winning two firsts on the same day, after having been "gypped" out of a first place in a race on the preceding day at the same track.  That made two first places and one second place for me in the same program, an unusual feat particularly in view of the fact that one of my victories was a world's one-mile professional championship.  The second victory was in the two-mile open event while the much discussed first place I lost at Montreal was in the half-mile open event in which the judges ruled I finished second, whereas the crowd of 18,000 figured I had won first place in this race also.

# CHAPTER XXI



### I REFUSE TO RIDE THE WORLD'S AMATEUR CHAMPION

After I had won the world's one-mile professional championship title I centered my thoughts on the next race, the two-mile open event. I had in mind winning this race in order to give me two first places for the day, which would have been the 10th time in my career, up to that moment, that I had won two first places on the same program. Incidentally, on four occasions I turned in three victories in as many meets, a feat seldom accomplished.

As I was preparing for the two-mile open event one of the track officials called me to the starting line to race Thomas Summersgill of London, England, who, on the preceding day had won the world's amateur one-mile championship. I agreed until I found there was no purse hung up for the event. The officials told me that since Summersgill was an amateur he could not compete for a money prize. However, I reminded them that there was no rule in the professional riders' code that provided for a professional riding a match with no purse attached to it, and that in a race between an amateur and a professional they could not very well be guided by amateur rules.

In the end I agreed that I would be delighted to ride Mr. Summersgill provided the management would put up a prize of $200 in addition to a side bet of $150 each, the winner to take all. I insisted that I would not ride for the mere glory of it, and no amount of persuasion could change my stand. I felt that it was a matter of principle with me, and on top of that I was somewhat peeved over the way that I had been "gypped" out of first place in the half-mile open race the preceding day, and the fact that the prizes for such important races were exceedingly low. Winning the world's professional title at this meet netted me a paltry $200, despite the fact that there was a capacity attendance of 18,000 at the event.

I remained steadfast in my position and as a result there was no race between Summersgill and myself. Naturally considerable discussion centered about my decision there being a feeling of keen disappointment throughout the throng that attended the races as well as among the officials. One sporting writer on an American newspaper who was prejudiced against me on account of my color even went so far as to say that I was "yellow." However, I discounted his attack because of the fact that on the preceding day he had aided to have me out of first place in the half-mile open event, therefore, he eagerly grasped this opportunity in an attempt to belittle me in the estimation of the sporting public because I had "side-stepped the engagement."

His article read as follows:

"Major Taylor Backed Down. Colored Cycling Star refused to Ride an Amateur for Championship. Demanded big purse. Declined to Compete unless big Purse of $150. Major Taylor refused to fulfill his obligation as a sportsman today. He developed a grand streak of yellow, and refused to meet the amateur champion, Thomas Summersgill of London, in a championship match race of one-mile. Taylor, it is stated, demanded a purse of $150, and would listen to no requests of the L. A. W. officials that he represent his country like a sportsman and meet the amateur champion.

"Secretary Henry Strummey of the I. C. A. stated tonight that hereafter there would be provided a penalty of one vear's suspension for a rider who refused to go up against a champion of the amateur class, which suspension would be enforced the world over.

"However, Major Taylor suffers nothing for his action, but an absolute loss of reputation for true sportsmanship."

I felt that I was well within my rights when I declined to race for nothing. Had the track officials been in the driver's seat I would have been forced to ride Summersgill regardless of my personal feelings in the matter.

My real outstanding reason for not riding against Summersgill was the fact that the very next race on the program was the two-mile open which I was extremely anxious to win. Naturally, I felt that if I extended myself in a race against Summersgill I would not be in the best of condition for the two-mile event. It was well within the pale of possibility that I would have to ride three heats against Summersgill to determine that one-mile championship, so-called, unless I were strong enough to win the first two. Winning the first two would mean that I would have to extend myself to the utmost, therefore, minimizing my chances materially in the two-mile event which called for my participating in three heats, the first heat, semifinal and the final—providing I won in my heats.

Meantime Summersgill won his championship race on the day previous and, therefore, had a full day's rest before he was called out to oppose me. If that race between Summersgill and myself was held, my opponents in the two-mile open event would have been taking it leisurely in their dressing rooms as Summersgill and I pedalled like mad for the honor that meant little or nothing to me.

That I showed good judgment in this matter was proven when I won my heat in the two-mile open, and later led the field home in the final of that event. Charlie McCarthy of St. Louis, won the first heat defeating his namesake from Toronto by a wheel, Nat Butler being shut out. I won the second heat from Frank Butler, Tom Butler winning the third heat handily from Jimmie Bowler.

One of the Montreal sports writers made the following comment in his paper about the two-mile race the next day:

"In the final it looked as if an attempt was being made to get

Taylor into a pocket, and in the back stretch he was obliged to pick his way through the field as they went into the home stretch. Taylor gave up trying to get through on the pole and bolted for the outside. Once around the bunch he jumped with a terrific sprint defeating Tom Butler quite easily, who in turn had a half wheel on McCarthy who finished third.

"Taylor received a flattering ovation at the closing of this race, the 18,000 people present apparently fully appreciating the wonderful work done by this colored star in winning the world's one-mile championship honors and the two-mile open event in the same afternoon. Incidentally, the writer believes Major Taylor also won the half-mile open professional race yesterday with Charlie McCarthy second, but the officials gave Taylor a shabby deal, and decided that McCarthy won with Taylor in second place, although the crowd shouted its disapproval of the award in no uncertain way."

The following compliment paid me by the Secretary of the International Cyclist Association seems to offset that bitter attack of the sporting writer who criticized me so unjustly for refusing to ride a match race without a purse. From a Montreal daily:

"He is A Good Man. Major Taylor is appreciated by Henry Strummey. Among the thousands of friends he has made during his career, Major Taylor, the World's Professional Champion Cyclist, has no more enthusiastic admirer than Mr. Henry Strummey, the honorable secretary of the I. C. A. In a recent article upon the famous cyclist at the L. A. W. International Championship races at Montreal last month, Secretary Strummey paid this splendid tribute to the Worcester boy.

" 'He is a non-smoker, a teetotaller, and a clean-living fellow. He is right at home on any kind of a track and clever at trick riding. Major Taylor, of the United States, is a most dangerous opponent at any stage of bicycle racing. Many of the American cracks soon become jealous of him, and did all in their power to have him barred from all racing, but the Major was a hard man to fight against, and despite the deal set against him, he trained on and appeared where possible, and thanks to his great perseverance, he has now gained the proud title of the One-Mile World's Professional Champion.

" 'His specialty, like Burrillion, is in his marvelous jump, and he is from three to four seconds faster off the mark than any other American rider. He has met and defeated every rider of note in the United States, and can be backed to ride any rider in the world, but he does not care to visit Europe, as all the principal races there are held on Sunday. There is no doubt that the secret of his great success is due to the careful manner in which he trains, and the careful manner in which he lives when not in training.' "

# CHAPTER XXII



At the close of the world's championship meet in Montreal, where the most colorful page was added to the history of bicycle racing, I competed at the A. C. C. in Boston, on August 16, 1899, four short days since I won the World's One-mile Professional Championship honors, I received a most remarkable ovation as I made my first appearance on the Charles River Park track, under my newly acquired title, World's Champion, and I was a mighty proud one too.

I tried in vain to qualify for the final, but the entire field violated every rule of the track at my expense as the fans howled their disapproval of the underhanded methods adopted by my rivals. The officials did not so much as reprimand those who had fouled me in such a daring manner.

Later in the day I tried to qualify for the final of the one-mile handicap event but I was so badly roughed by the field that I failed to win a place. I was a pretty sorely mussed up World's Champion when my rivals had finished with me at the end of the first day's racing.

One of the Boston dailies had the following to say about the meet: "Major Taylor is shut out of every heat. Riders pocket and otherwise prevent him from winning. In the expressive language of the training quarters, they hung it on to Major Taylor today in every race he started in. The first trick was turned in the five-mile professional championship.

"Two men in each of the fastest heats, and only the winner of the slowest heat, were to qualify for the final. In Major Taylor's heat, owing to scratches, there were but five starters besides Major Taylor. In the other two heats there were eight and eleven respectively, and although the Major did his share of pacing in the fifteen laps of his heat, Watson Coleman beat him for first place by inches only. But in the other two heats the men rode like fiends in order to make their time faster than Taylor's heat, and as they were successful, the Major could not start in the final of the championship event. But had he not been 'pocketed' in his heat until the tape was reached, Coleman's win might not have been a fact."

My troubles began in the first heat of the five-mile championship race and even before the pistol was fired I surmised what the frame-up was going to be. In vain I asked the referee to have pacemakers put in telling him that I felt certain there were some underhanded tactics planned for the race. My suspicions were aroused when half of the men scheduled to ride in my heat had allowed their names to be scratched, or withdrawn, incidentally, which was a trick to make my heat the slowest in order that the winners of the other two heats and the second in the fastest heat might be eligible for the final. Besides, with only six starters in my heat, including myself, and no pacemakers, they would have a much better chance to deal with me.

The bunch were slow getting away from the starting line. Then, as prearranged, one of the riders came from the rear with a wild rush, riding as if he were sprinting the last lap instead of the first. As no one else offered to go after him I volunteered and after chasing him a full lap I then swung out so as to allow the next man to go out and do his bit. He refused as did the rest of them, so I went out strong this time and brought him back after chasing him two laps and a half, with the rest of the field hanging on to me.

By this time I was pretty well winded, when lo! another rider repeated the same trick, shooting out from the rear after having been passed by the other riders up to that moment. Again the other men refused to alternate with me in an effort to bring him back. If I failed to go after him he would, undoubtedly, have won the heat, shutting me out entirely—which was their scheme to keep me from qualifying. The crowd was quick to sense the tactics of the other riders and registered their disapproval of them by hissing and hooting them every time they passed the stand. In the meantime the rider out front was gaining all the time and I was just about worn out because of the unsportsmanlike tactics adopted by the other riders.

Riding the entire race single-handed I was able to give this lone rider the battle of his life before he won. However, I rode most of the last lap on my nerve as I was almost completely exhausted by their foul methods used against me. They had worked me into the worst pocket that had ever balked the efforts of a rider and the storm of hisses that greeted the winner indicated the big crowd on hand for the races was fully aware of the underhanded methods to bring about my defeat.

Nat Butler won the first heat in the one-mile professional handicap race and his brother Tom was the victor in the second. I was scratch man in my heat but the best I could do, in the event of the unfair tactics adopted by the riders against me, was to finish second being thereby eliminated from the finals.

This race was practically a repetition of the heat I figured in in the five-mile championship event. In both races the other riders refused to do their share of pacing which allowed the high handicap man to win. Come what might, I decided not to do all the donkey work in this race. The crowded stands again showed their disapproval of the tactics adopted by my competitors but to no avail.

In these two races I received the worst deal that was ever handed me by the riders but they were not even censored by the officials for their unsportsmanlike tactics.  I felt it was the price of being the world's champion and also because at the moment I was leading in the race for the American championship.  In this latter competition the season was fast nearing its close and my nearest opponent had but a single chance of beating me out.  The entire field in the Boston races was evidently in sympathy with my rival, and they were out to stop me at any cost in order that he might possibly beat me out and the officials seemed to be working hand in hand with them.

On the next day, however, I regained whatever prestige I may have lost in the preceding afternoon's races.  I quote from a Boston daily concerning the second day's program:

"Major Taylor Turns Tables On the Butlers.  Shows His Rear Wheel to the Butler Boys in the Half-Mile L. A. W. Championship.  Major Taylor is the Champion half-mile rider.  It was a field day for Major Taylor as he turned the tables very neatly on the Butler boys with his wonderful, fast jump when within a few yards of the tape, which demonstrated again, that, with fair treatment, he can ride rings around any of the professionals enrolled at present in the L. A. W.

"Although the program said that the first three men in each heat of the half-mile professional championship were to qualify for the final, they made it three in the fastest heat, and two in the slowest heat, but Major Taylor made good this time by winning his heat, in which there were four other contestants.  Hugh McLean started to cut out a hot pace from the pistol, but Colgan accepted his challenge.  Major Taylor hit up a sharp sprint and led Colgan by three open lengths at the tape.

"In another heat Frank Butler and Coleman rode at the front of the bunch watching each other.  Urquhart started to shake the whole bunch but Colgan would not have it and took first by inches only, Frank Butler being third.  Nat Butler was shut out in his heat by McCarthy with Carman second.

"The starters in the final heat were Colgan, Urquhart, Coleman, McLeod, Bowler, McCarthy, Carman and Major Taylor.  Bowler jumped to the front and started to sprint, and Taylor worked his way ahead also, then went out in the final sprint, fighting it out with McCarthy and Jimmie Bowler.  Major Taylor won out by a length at the tape with the other two finishing in the order named."

Notwithstanding my hard luck on the first day, I did manage to win one of the two championship events, and made many new friends because of the unfairness of the other riders.  I was fortunate to finish up without a scratch or serious injury, and was in wonderfully fine physical condition for the last championship race of the season which terminated in Brockton, Mass.

# CHAPTER XXIII



Of all the gruelling races that I figured in in that season of 1899, the one-mile championship at Brockton was the hardest. It was fiercely contested every inch of the way. The first three riders being so closely bunched at the finish line that it took the judges some time to determine the place winners. Some of them decided it was a dead heat but in the end I was awarded first place, James Bowler of Chicago, second, and Watson Coleman of Springfield, Mass., third.

I quote from an article in a Brockton newspaper of the following day as follows:

"Major Taylor wins National Championship. The first national championship races at the new Brockton track were run off yesterday. The events were all hotly contested and the meet was a huge success. The features of the program were the capture of the two-mile paced record by Harry Gibson of Cincinnati, and the winning of the one-mile national championship by Major Taylor. The first event was remarkable for the time of the second mile. The time of the first mile was 1:38 and then Gibson got down to business. All through the second mile he kept calling for more pace and reeled it off in 1:31 4/5 making the time for the two miles 3:09 4/5. The previous record for two miles was 3:13 held by Major Taylor, and the Major was there to see it done.

"The final of the one-mile professional championship was the hardest fought since the opening of the National Circuit, and the verdict of a dead heat or the placing of any one of the first three men to the front, would not have been much doubted. Major Taylor was given the decision, however, with James Bowler of Chicago, second, and Watson Coleman of Springfield, third.

"There was not eight inches between the three. Coleman had a good lead two yards from the tape, but Taylor and Bowler came up fast and it took a good eye to see which brushed the tape first, Coleman or Taylor. Bowler was also caught for first place on the outside of Taylor. The crowd and the riders near the tape shouted for Coleman, but the announcement later in favor of Major Taylor seemed to please the audience. Coleman's third, however, was a sticker. No time was taken, owing to the excitement."

In this race the riders succeeded in getting me into a tight pocket that I could not very well get out of without bringing someone down with a crash, and possibly two or three of them, because every man in the race had a hand in the job. I was obliged to use every trick I knew in extricating myself from my dangerous position. With but 250 yards to go, and the field sprinting like mad, I managed to wiggle my way out of my bad position without interfering with any other rider. It was the tightest box I was ever in.

In the end I was forced to pick up and come around on the outside of the entire field. Once clear, I made a last desperate plunge for the tape and got across the line a few inches ahead of Bowler with Coleman in third place.

As the three of us bolted across the line a crowd of riders sitting near the tape immediately started shouting for Coleman. It was an old trick, the object of it being to influence the officials and the spectators to favor Coleman for his place. This was one of the most sensational races I had ever figured in and it was extremely difficult to judge. Realizing the shabby deals that had been given me under similar circumstances in other races, I fully expected to be awarded second or even third place. But I was pleasantly surprised when the judges rendered the verdict in my favor—the first close decision that had ever been given me.

It was a strange freak of fate that Bowler and myself figured in another very close race only a short time previous. It happened in Chicago, Bowler's home town. In that race the judges decided Bowler and I had ridden a dead heat although the grand stand hissed the decision and yelled wildly for the verdict for me.

The officials who rendered the decision in my favor on this eventful occasion unfortunately became involved in a dispute which became bitter, and did not end with the closing of the races, but almost resulted in a feud. It went so far as to break up friendships of years' standing in Brockton.

# CHAPTER XXIV



I received a fine ovation when I appeared on the historic Lake View Oval track in my native city, Worcester, Mass., on September 8, 1899, to participate in my first track race there. Four years before I arrived in that city from my old home in Indianapolis and a month later I won a 10-mile road race that was an annual fixture in that Bay State city. Although I trained every winter and early spring in Worcester, for my campaign on the tracks of the country I had never ridden in that city except in that road race, until I went there on the occasion in mention.

I was scheduled to ride in the half-mile open, the one-mile handicap, and the five-mile pursuit race with James J. Casey, who is now head of the detectives of the Worcester police department.

I had long since been recognized as an adopted son of Worcester and had even been given a place with her most illustrious sons in the hall of athletic fame, that included Edward Hanlon Ten Eyck, winner of the world's greatest rowing laurels, the Diamond Sculls; J. Fred Powers, the all-round champion amateur athlete of the country; Harry Worcester Smith, internationally famous gentleman jockey and steeplechase winner; Jay Clark, Jr., national champion trap shooter and Willie W. Windle, although a native of Millbury, Mass., but claimed by Worcester, who stills holds the world's record for the high wheel one-mile event, made on October 7, 1891, and who was second only to the great Arthur Zimmerman, when he was in his prime as the champion sprinter of this country.

Jesse Burket was a former New York Giant star batter and one of the greatest Major League batters of all time. Burkett produced some of the greatest baseball teams that Holy Cross College ever put on the field. He managed the Worcester Baseball Team of the New England League in the early 1900 series and won four successful pennants. Billie Hamilton, baseball's champion base stealer and batsman; Joe Higgins, holder of the one-mile world's record for foot-running; J. J. Munsey, world's champion candle-pin bowler.

Jack Barry, present coach for the famous Holy Cross baseball team, was for eight years a short stop for the Philadelphia American League Team and a member of the famous million dollar "Infield" that won four consecutive world series. He was later traded to the Boston American League team and was second baseman and manager when that team won the World Series in 1916. The latest stars to be added to this list of celebrities, however, is the now famous Albina Osipo wich, the one hundred meter free style Olympic champion swimmer and Harry Devine, American bantam-weight prize fighter.

I was given an honored position in that group of celebrities by reason of being the world's one-mile professional champion and by virtue of the fact that I held the world's one-mile paced record. Also the championship of America title.

The Worcester program was sanctioned by the L. A. W. and included my five-mile pursuit race with Casey, the one-mile professional handicap, one-half mile open and two one-mile amateur events. The match pursuit race between Casey and myself was advertised as the feature of the meet and the purse of $200, winner take all, was hung up for the victor. Casey rode that day under the colors of the Vernon Bicycle Club, one of the most famous organizations in Worcester. Since I had never ridden on the flat oval track nor won in a pursuit race, Casey was the favorite to win.

However, I won the pursuit race and the half-mile open and was well up with the leaders in the mile handicap race when a spill in the last lap put me out of the racing. Incidentally, I assumed a new rôle on that afternoon when I appeared in racing togs to race Charlie Raymond, a widely known Worcester bicycle rider and 100-yard dash man, at 50 yards, best two heats in three to determine the winner. I won in straight heats the time for each being 5 4/5 seconds.

Frank Butler of the famous trio of brothers from Boston was the heaviest money winner among the six professionals who competed at this meet. He took second prize in the half-mile and won the mile handicap from the 20-yard mark. Casey was second in the mile handicap and third in the half-mile open.

In the half-mile open the starters were Frank Butler, Watson Coleman, Hugh McLean, James Urquhart, Nat Butler, Jimmie Casey, Charlie Bly, Alec McLean and myself.

I quote from a Worcester newspaper of the following day:

"At the sound of the pistol the men left the tape with a rush, Jimmie Casey taking the lead and Major Taylor following closely. These positions were held throughout the first lap and around the second on the back stretch with the bunch following the leaders. At the 220-yard mark Casey cut out a hot clip for the tape. Taylor had the best position, next to Casey, who was doing all the donkey work, and when the field turned into the home stretch Taylor jumped Casey, closely followed by Frank Butler who had never left his rear tire. He tried hard to pass Taylor on the home stretch but the latter was sprinting like a fiend and passed Casey without any trouble, winning by two lengths with Butler second by inches only. The time was 1:11 4/5 which is very fast for the Oval.

"But for the spill in the mile handicap that race would have been a hair-raiser, but Major Taylor and Hugh McLean went down on the last lap at the 220-yard post. As it was the time was a record for the Oval. The spill allowed Frank Butler to capture this event with Jimmie Casey 10 yards in his rear and 'Nellie' Bly third. In this race Nat Butler and Major Taylor were on scratch, Watson Coleman and Frank Butler had a 20-yard handicap, James J. Casey 35 yards, Hugh McLean 40 yards, A. A. McClean 50 yards, James Urquhart, 60 yards, and 'Nellie' Bly 75 yards.

"Major Taylor rode a clever race against Casey in the five-mile pursuit number. The track did not seem to bother him in the least and he took the turns with ease. He rode the first two miles slower than Casey, being seven seconds slower in the first mile but gained during the progress of the second mile and was but 1 4/5 seconds slower than Casey, whose time was five minutes flat. Both rode pretty evenly in the third mile, Casey having an edge of 3/5 of a second on Taylor in this mile.

"From the third mile on it was Taylor's race as it could be plainly seen that Casey was not moving along as fast as he had been; he looked tired. He clung gamely to his task, however, and was but 3 4/5 seconds behind Taylor at the fourth mile. Taylor was riding strong and hit up a fast clip on the last mile, winning the race by a quarter of a lap. Taylor's time for the five miles was 12:52." Major Taylor received a splendid ovation from his Worcester admirers.

# CHAPTER XXV



After a week's serious training at the Charles River Park track, following my appearance at Worcester, I participated in a one-mile open event at Taunton, Mass., on September 20. Although this was not a championship meet the prize money was very attractive and a galaxy of star riders was attracted to the event. After the race, which was marked by roughhouse tactics on the part of my opponents, despite which I won, I immediately entered all of the events scheduled for the Peoria, Illinois track to mark the close of the racing season. In fact, I participated in the Taunton events simply to keep in shape for this Peoria program, which was one of the biggest of the entire year.

The Peoria races were scheduled to be held on October 12, which was three weeks removed from the Taunton meet. As I was in top-notch physical condition for the Taunton event my most difficult problem as I pointed for the Peoria program, was to keep from training down too fine. I was especially anxious to be at my best for the meet in Peoria, as I was desirous of closing the season in a blaze of color. I was just as careful about my training and diet for those races as I had been for the world's championship events at Montreal, two months previous. The last time I appeared in Peoria was as a contestant in a race for boys under 16. I was 14 years old at the time and finished in third place on that famous fast and beautiful dirt track. Now after a period of careful training, struggle and perseverance, covering seven years I returned to perform on the same track. I received a splendid ovation as I took my place at the starting line for the first race. It reminded me of the reception accorded me when I stepped on to the track as a boy several years before.

On that Peoria track as a boy of 14 I got my first glimpse of the great stars of the bicycle track. As I waited for the boys' race on that occasion, I saw several champions deposed in thrilling finishes down that wonderful home stretch. I marveled at the cheering of the thousands of people in the grandstand as those mighty stars whirled around that famous half-mile dirt track. Little did I imagine that I would ever set foot on that track again, let alone ride there as the World's Champion Professional sprinter.

No doubt there were hundreds in the stand that day who had seen me bolting my weary way around that same track as a boy. Imagine their surprise when I was announced as the world's professional sprinter champion, champion American sprinter and the holder of the fastest mile ever ridden on a bicycle track. Then picture their amazement when the announcer also reminded them that I was the same boy who in 1892 had finished third in the race for boys.

After I had received one of the most flattering ovations, I set about my afternoon's work. Incidentally it was won before I had even hit the measure. Before the sun set I had won three races—the one-mile invitation, the two-mile open and the five-mile lap race. All the finals were paced by motor and despite the fact that the track was very heavy because of recent rains the time was exceptionally fast.

In the one-mile invitation race Harry Gibson of Cincinnati rode second to me and Charles Porter of Chicago was third. Tom Butler of Boston was second to me in the one-mile open event; Charles Porter of Chicago was third and Gus Phillips of Chicago was fourth. In the five-mile lap race Tom Butler followed me over the tape with Gus Phillips third, the time being 11:35.

Newspaper men who were present for the program were a unit in declaring had the track been dry that several new world records would have been established in each of the races because all of the final heats were motor paced. This was without a doubt the hardest racing program that I had ever undertaken and but for my wonderfully fine physical condition I would never have been able to accomplish this strenuous task. The Peoria track was one of the fastest in the country. It was not a trotting track but was built especially for bicycle races. The management for selfish reasons decided to have all of the final heats motor-paced which was an innovation for sprint racing.

Although I was "dog tired" after having won the first two finals, I decided at the last minute to start in the five-mile event. A plot aimed against me by the other riders in the race was responsible for my starting in this last-named race. As the cyclists discussed their plans to put me down in the five-mile race, my trainer overheard them and reported the fact to me. That settled it. I was out on the track in a few minutes gritting my teeth and tugging at the leash to get another crack at the field. This specially arranged program attracted an all-star entry list. One of the finest that had ever graced any meet of the entire season. I figured that since this was the last meet of the year I could well afford to risk being thrown from my wheel by the other riders as I would have several months in which to recuperate before the next season's races started.

At the crack of the pistol Butler jumped and beat me to the pace-maker. He had the pole while I was on the outside, his position providing him with a good footing, while out where I was it was quite soft and heavy. Shortly, however, by quick maneuvering I got the position I desired—right at Butler's rear wheel. There I stuck.

Butler kept calling to the pacemaker to increase the speed while I was shouting to him to take it easy. Since Butler was riding directly behind the motor, he had the advantage over the rest of us as the pacing machine was breaking the wind for him. The rest of the field, including myself, were riding at a disadvantage as compared with Butler because we were absolutely unable to take advantage of the wind break caused by the fast moving pacing machine. So hot was the pace that not one of the riders was able to change his position throughout the first nine and one half laps. As we dashed into the last quarter mile of the race the pacing machine withdrew and the riders rushed out on their own in a wild scramble for the finishing tape.

Butler and I started our desperate fight for the tape the minute the motor dropped out of the race. We had a terrible fight for the honors as I challenged him for the lead when we entered the long home stretch. It must have been a wonderful finish to witness with the crowd on its feet shouting frantically as we struggled nip and tuck for the honors. Butler and I had in some unaccountable way mis-calculated the laps that were left for us to travel before the finishing line was reached, and as we peddled for the finishing line it was my advantage, being first across the tape by a wheel's diameter. The bell clanged, indicating another lap to go. The crowd screaming wildly.

Bewildered at the turn of events, Butler and I were astonished to see the rest of the field fly past us, some of them gaining more than a dozen lengths on us. Gasping for breath I struggled fiercely to regain my stride, Butler and I were in a very trying predicament. Butler either could not or would not make any attempt to go after the bunch, so I undertook the task with Butler hanging on my rear wheel.

As we were rounding into the home stretch I overtook the leaders. At this moment I glanced at the finishing line and it seemed miles and miles away. The sprint was not fast, but it was decidedly feverish. I bolted across the finishing line in lead, but to this day I cannot tell how I ever turned the trick. Every rider in the race was completely knocked out by the strenuous grind, Butler and I collapsing.

Even now I consider that five-mile race the climax of the most gruelling day's work I ever put in on the bicycle track during my whole racing career covering almost seventeen years on both sides of the Atlantic.

As I mentioned before, this race, being the final event of the sea-son, attracted the speediest of the bicycle racers of the country. It was no easy job winning a place in the heats for the three events which I won that day, as every one of them was fought tooth and nail. Never in my life was I so completely exhausted as when I streaked home in the five-mile lap race which was the last event on the

Peoria track on that memorable occasion.  I had sprinted home a winner in what I thought was the last lap of the five-mile race using everything I had at my command to defeat my worthy rival, Tom Butler, out by inches, when the bell sent us away on another heart-breaking trip around the track.  On top of that I had to catch the field which had slipped by the two of us as we sat up following our crossing of the finishing line.  It took a desperate effort to overtake the field and just as I had succeeded, the bunch rounded in to the home stretch, and I was forced to ride on the outside of the track from this point to the tape as the balance of the field had taken places on the pole where the track was hard, thus giving them a very good footing, while mine was exceptionally poor, since it was soft.  However, I stuck to my task and fought for the finish line and won with Tom Butler trailing me.

Imagine my feelings when I was informed in my dressing room a few minutes after the finish of that wicked five-mile race that the manager of the track had disappeared, in the meantime, with the entire gate receipts.  That meant I was to receive nothing for my efforts on that afternoon—the most trying of my career.  It gave me little consolation to know that my fellow racers shared a similar fate, and we were a sorely disappointed lot as we made our way to the railroad station bound for home.

Incidentally, that was the last race held on that famous track in good old Peoria.  It was known throughout the cycling world as one of the finest that ever staged a bicycle race.  As a matter of fact the Peoria track, and those in Springfield, Massachusetts, Waltham, Massachusetts, and Asbury Park, New Jersey were four of the most famous bicycle tracks in the earlier days of cycle racing in this country.

From Peoria I made tracks for my old home in Indianapolis.  A few days after I arrived there I received formal word of my having been declared champion of America by the L. A. W. for the second consecutive season.

# CHAPTER XXVI



As I settled down to what I thought was going to be six months of rest after my strenuous season on the bicycle tracks of the country I received a wire to come to Chicago forthwith to attempt to lower my world's record of 1:22 2/5 behind motor pace. It came from Mr. Harry Sager the inventor of the Sager gear, which was used on the bicycle I was riding at the time. He informed me that one of my great rivals, Eddie McDuffee of Boston, was camping at Garfield Park, Chicago, with the avowed intention of breaking my world's record which I had established on the self-same track a few months previous.

McDuffee was provided with a steam motor pacing machine which he had designed himself and which had been built by the Stanley Steamer Company of Newton, Massachusetts. It was constructed especially for this assault by McDuffee on my record. After weeks of effort McDuffee clipped 1 2/5 seconds off my world's record of 1:22 2/5.

Meantime, my motor pacing machine, which was an exact duplicate of McDuffee's, arrived at Garfield Park, and I set out to lower McDuffee's newly established record for the mile. Incidentally, I had set my mind upon turning the mile under 1:20, which feat had never before been accomplished. Since McDuffee was bent upon doing the same thing, the rivalry between us grew to white heat.

After many trials and tribulations extending for a period of six weeks I reached the climax of my fondest ambition—riding the mile behind motor pace under 1:20. I was just one second lower than that mark and the newspapers of the country heralded the feat with first page stories. My mark of 1:19 clipped 2 seconds off McDuffee's time which was but a few days old when I cracked it.

Extract from a Chicago newspaper:

"Major Taylor in Chicago, Champion Cyclist comes here to lower the World's One-mile Motor Pace Record. Major Taylor, champion cyclist of the world, arrived in Chicago today to defend his one-mile pace record of 1:22 2/5 which is threatened by Eddie McDuffee, who came here a week ago for the express purpose of putting the mark well inside 1:20. Major Taylor brought with him his famous steam motor tandem, which is working 50 per cent better than when he lowered the record several months ago on the same track. The fault of this slowing down in the last quarter mile has been remedied.

"Two mechanics will man the big machine so it is hardly possible there will be a slip up this time. McDuffee is credited with having recently done 1:21 for the mile, but he used windshields in his attempt which is against the L. A. W. rules. Taylor feels that he can lower his present record of 1:22 2/5 without the use of windshields. In fact he is of the opinion that he can turn the trick in 1:18 or better, although he is not in the same condition now as when he established the present world's record, having increased his weight from 148 to 160 pounds.

"McDuffee is still in the city anxiously waiting for his motor which was shipped east to be repaired. He will continue his trial as soon as it has returned, so that Chicago will be the scene of the greatest dual that has ever been staged for the one-mile pace record which is the blue-ribbon distance on the cycle track. There has always been great rivalry between these two men and to add fuel to the flame is the fact that they are riding rival chainless machines, Taylor using the Sager gear while McDuffee rides the Columbia chainless gear."

Another Chicago daily printed the following article:

"Major Taylor is ready for the Mile Record. Major Taylor is all ready to make the trial for a new world's record for the mile at Garfield Park track and is awaiting until parts for his machine arrive from Boston. On the other hand Eddie McDuffee declared yesterday he is now ready to go after the record despite the fact that his pacing machine tuned up well and turned the trick in 1:17 2/5 in a practice sprint. This is the fastest time made by McDuffee's device and it is also faster than Taylor's machine has ever covered the mile in. That makes it look as if McDuffee has the best chance for the record unless Taylor's machine picks up a bit."

On the following day a Chicago paper printed the following story:

"Major Taylor Rides the Mile in 1:19. Smashing the World's Record. Major Taylor smashed the world's record for the paced mile at Garfield Park yesterday, being two seconds under the figure made by Eddie McDuffee a few days ago. Taylor's mile was 1:19. Aided by windshields, the colored boy kept the fast pace his motor tandem set for him for two circuits of the track and crossed the tape on time well under the fastest ever before clocked under similar conditions.

"Early in the afternoon Taylor's motor was working badly and the fastest mile was made in 1:30, and again it was tried and considerable improvement was made, the time was 1:26-2. An ordinary racing cyclist would have considered these two trials at such intense speed quite enough for one day, but Taylor was hoping for greater things and being assured that the motor could now be made to go 1:20 or better he essayed one more trial. After a vigorous rubdown in his training quarters, Taylor announced himself prepared for the great test, with only one circuit of the track as a preliminary warm up and the race was on.

"Motor and rider crossed the tape at a terrific clip, the start having been made with the wind in their favor, the first quarter of the ride being into it. From the start it was evident that the ride would be close to McDuffee's mark of 1:21, or better, providing the motor held out. Taylor stuck like a Trojan to his pace, pedalling away like mad. The half was caught by some in :39-1, others in :40, and when they flashed for the tape one of the timers caught Taylor in 1:18-4, another in 1:19-1 and a third in 1:22-2. As several watches held unofficially registered between 1:18 and 1:19, the time was officially set at 1:19 flat."

Still another Chicago daily quoted the following item the next day:

"Will Ride No More. Eddie McDuffee knows Major Taylor is his superior. Quits Track forever. Major Taylor's claim to sprint record remains undisputed. Eddie McDuffee, who spent several weeks trying to lower the mark which the Worcester Flyer put up, has given up the task and will ride no more. He announced his retirement from the bicycle race track.

"Major Taylor's supremacy is unquestioned, regardless of McDuffee's retirement, for the Worcester Whirlwind proved beyond a word of a doubt that he can push a wheel faster than McDuffee, who had every opportunity that a rider could have to beat Taylor's mark, or to set a mark which Taylor could not reach, but he was not equal to the task. Everything was in his favor while Taylor rode in a handicap. McDuffee had the fastest pacing machine, and he had it provided with windshields. The speed of his machine was shown in one of the trials when it covered the mile in 1:17-2, which time Taylor's machine never made. Had it gone in that time, Taylor would have been in ahead of it, as he was when his machine turned the mile in 1:19.

"Taylor first went after the records without windshields and made the quarter-mile mark in twenty seconds without them. McDuffee went in 3/5 of a second better by using them. Shortly McDuffee announced he would not use windshields but altogether his trials showed he could never touch Taylor's mark which he has stuck to. As Major Taylor never got any credit for his marks without windshields he put them on and went so fast that McDuffee gave up his task in disgust. Taylor had a big following at the track and despite the repeated failure of his motor to function properly, there were several thousand on hand to witness the successful trial. In addition to getting the mile mark, yesterday, Taylor tried for the half-mile and the third mile marks but his pace failed and the best he could do for the half-mile was :41-4."

# CHAPTER XXVII

## A REPORTER'S PRAISE

"Major Taylor is Champion. Colored Youth won L. A. W. and International Championships and set many new records, capturing 22 firsts in 29 races. Has enviable record. If he never had it before Major Taylor this year has gained the title of Champion Cyclist of the World. It would be presumptuous for anyone to question his standing. This is the story of the colored boy who has astonished the world of cycling by his great feats of speed on the cycle tracks, 'Major Taylor, National Champion of the L. A. W., One-Mile International Champion, and Holder of the Quarter, Three-Quarter

MAJOR TAYLOR—Champion of America,
1899

and One-Mile Paced Record,' is the subject. Major Taylor's record this year is one to be proud of.

"Physically, Major Taylor is admirably put together. He has never been sick a day in his life. He has a well knit form, and is agile and supple in all his movements. He has continued to put on flesh since

1895 at which time he weighed 118 pounds.   At present he weighs 160 pounds.

"In racing Taylor rides very low, his back arched over his handle-bars which offers but little chance for the wind to impede his progress. Major Taylor's father, Gilbert Taylor, a veteran of the Civil War, having served with the Union Army, is still living in Indianapolis. Taylor finds the racing and record-breaking business profitable, and has cleared several thousand dollars out of it.

"Despite the pleas of the race track managers and the bicycle riders Major Taylor has refused for years to compete on Sunday, as he has felt that all should rest on the Lord's Day.   He has held strictly to that theory and in 1898 his decision to refrain from riding on Sunday almost cost him the American championship title.

"Major Taylor has never ridden on Sunday and says he does not intend to.   When the International Cyclists' Association was formed in September 1898, Major Taylor went with the other riders in order to finish out the championship series in which he had been competing with the other fast men.   Taylor claimed the N. C. A. promised not to hold any races on Sunday if he went with them, but this agreement was not kept, and later the colored boy sought reinstatement in the League of American Wheelmen.   The colored champion does not say in so many words that the N. C. A. took this action in order to force him out of taking a big slice of the honors, but that he believes as much cannot be doubted."

The Official Bicycle Record Book gives the following chronolog-ical order of my achievements in the year of 1899:

| Date | | Race | City | Place |
|---|---|---|---|---|
| May | 27 | One-third-mile open | Philadelphia | First |
| " | 30 | One-mile open | Boston | First |
| " | 30 | Two-mile handicap (scratch) | Boston | First |
| June | 10 | One-mile match (vs. Tom Butler) | Boston | Lost |
| June | 16 | One-third-mile open | Boston | First |
| " | 16 | Twenty-five-mile match (paced vs. Eddie McDuffee) | Boston | Won |
| July | 1 | One-mile match (vs. Tom Butler) | Boston | Won |
| " | 8 | One-mile Championship | Chicago | First |
| " | 12 | One-mile Championship | Janesville | Second |
| " | 12 | Two-mile handicap (scratch) | Janesville | First |
| " | 16 | One-mile Championship | St. Louis | First |
| " | 26 | Two-mile Championship | Ottumwa | Second |
| " | 26 | One-mile open | Ottumwa | First |

| | | | | |
|---|---|---|---|---|
| " | 26 | One-mile Championship | Ottumwa | First |
| " | 29 | One-mile Championship | Chicago | First |
| Aug. | 12 | Half-mile open | Montreal | Second |
| " | 12 | One-mile World's Championship | Montreal | First |
| " | 12 | Two-mile open | Montreal | First |
| " | 16 | Five-mile Championship | Boston | Lost |
| " | 16 | Half-mile Championship | Boston | First |
| " | 23 | One-mile Championship | Brockton | First |
| Sept. | 3 | Half-mile open | Worcester | First |
| " | 3 | Five-mile match (pursuit) (vs. James Casey) | Worcester | First |
| " | 3 | | | |
| " | 3 | Fifty-yard match (foot) (vs. Charles Raymond) | Worcester | First |
| " | 20 | One-mile open | Taunton | First |
| Oct. | 12 | One-mile invitation | Peoria | First |
| " | 12 | Two-mile open | Peoria | First |
| " | 12 | Five-mile lap | Peoria | First |

## CHAPTER XXVIII

### CHAMPIONSHIP HONORS FOR 1900

"Who will be the Cycle Champion of 1900? Racing Season begins Thursday and struggle for Title promises to be unusually keen. Experts pick Frank Kramer. American cycle racing season will open next Thursday in Louisville, where at Mountain Ferry track the stars will meet for the first time. One week later Vailsberg will open and several other New England tracks will open about this time. There will be a vast increase in the number of competitors this season which has been apparent in the request for both amateur and professional registrations at the office of the board of control of the N. C. A.

"Big match races will be the feature of the season, but the sprint race field includes more prominent men than ever before. The professional champions of both the N. C. A. and the L. A. W. of last year, and the amateur champions of both organizations will come together in professional ranks this year. The sprinters who planned European trips have decided with one exception to remain at home, but one prominent rider, and one coming champion, Elks and Ross will be missed from the paced ranks. Just at this time there is a lot of talk regarding the probable champion of the season among the professional and amateur sprint riders.

"The decision of Tom Cooper, the champion of last season, and Earl Kiser, his closest competitor, to remain on this side has added great interest to the problem. The entry of the stars in the amateur ranks, and the probability of Major Taylor's name being added to the list of competitors, and Eddie Bald's decision to go out again for the championship has complicated matters and made the discussion even more interesting. Cooper was the N. C. A. champion last season, and the year Arthur Gardiner was considered one of the champions and for three years previous to that Eddie Bald held the honors. Major Taylor was champion last season under the L. A. W. For the past several seasons Orlando Stevens has been a prominent factor in the championship race. Frank Kramer, amateur champion the past season, and Jimmie Moran, who held the same honors under the L. A. W. have both become professionals with the opening of the season. Floyd MacFarland promises to figure more prominently in the race this year, as does Al Newhouse. In addition to these men Howard Freeman is liberally touted and Hardy Downing, the Californian, may give the best of them a rub. These men are all sprinters of the first rank. Among many who have watched the development with

(114)

interest, Frank Kramer is expected to clean up the whole bunch. Jay Eaton, the board track king, is a close observer and has ridden with many of these stars for years, and speaks by the book on cycle racing matters, and he gives as his best opinion that Frank Kramer will surely win the sprint championship of America, this year, 1900."

Despite the fact that most of the sports editors of the country picked Frank Kramer to win the American sprint championship in 1900, I made up my mind that he would not. As the season opened I felt physically fit and was confident that I would once more top the field of the sprint stars of the country before the 1900 season closed.

The field was one of the greatest that ever set out to win the championship as the 1900 season dawned. There was Tom Cooper, who won the N. C. A. championship in 1899, myself, who won the L. A. W. title the same year, Earl Kiser, Cooper's closest competitor, Eddie Bald, the former champion for three years, Orlando Stevens, Frank Kramer, former amateur L. A. W. champion, Jimmie Moran, who also held the amateur honors under the L. A. W.; Floyd MacFarland, Al Newhouse, Howard Freeman, Hardy Downing, Tom Butler, Nat Butler and Frank Butler, the famous trio of brothers from Boston, Watson Coleman, Arthur Gardiner and Owen Kimble, and a host of other good men.

No less an authority than Jay Eaton, the board-track king, who was one of the closest observers of bicycle riders, picked Frank Kramer to win the laurels that season. Eaton's opinion in this case was highly regarded especially since he had ridden with many of the stars who were to participate in the mad scramble for the sprinting honors that season.

When I failed to win the first race of the 1900 season some of my closest followers started nodding their heads. They knew the controversy surrounding my being dropped by the L. A. W., and my subsequent reinstatement by the N. C. A. upon my payment of a fine of $500 had not only worried me but also caused me to let up in my off season training. This inactivity caused my weight to increase eight pounds, and that was the reason I was unable to finish better than third in the premier race of that season, June 23, 1900, on the historic Manhattan Beach track. I won my preliminary heat and also placed in the semi-final heat. I led the way in the final heat and was well down the home stretch before I started to fade. Jay Eaton was at my rear wheel and we were pushing like mad for the finish line when Johnnie Fisher of Chicago burst into first place about twenty yards from the tape to win by a length over Eaton who beat me by half a wheel.

That was the first time in my career that I had failed to win the opening race of the season. I knew that my poor showing at the Manhattan Beach track was due to the excess weight I was carrying so I set about taking off the extra poundage that I might be in the best possible condition for the remaining races in that campaign.

Since Frank Kramer had recently defeated Tom Cooper his name was on the tongues of all followers of the bicycle racing game. He was looking for new worlds to conquer and on several occasions suggested that he would like to take me on for a sprint or two. Before long Kramer and I were signed up for a match race for a purse of $500, the winner thereof to take all. This race was held on the Manhattan Beach track on June 30, 1900.

I trained hard and faithfully for this race with Kramer and on the eve of it felt I was riding fast enough to give him my dust. Incidentally, I had an additional motive. I felt that if I defeated Kramer and won the $500 purse it would just offset the fine that bicycle moguls had imposed upon me in what I have always considered an unfair manner in the preceding season. So faithfully had I trained for this race that a few hours before I went to the track I weighed but three pounds above my best sprinting weight, indicating that I had taken off five pounds in one week's training.

I quote from a New York newspaper of July 1, 1900, concerning that race:

"Major Taylor Defeats Frank Kramer. Negro takes two straight Heats in decisive Style. The great special match race between Major Taylor and Frank Kramer at Manhattan Beach track yesterday afternoon, was a treat of the first water. Last Sunday Kramer, who has been riding like the wind, administered a crushing defeat to Tom Cooper, the N. C. A. professional champion at Newark.

"Kramer defeated Cooper in two straight heats. but yesterday Major Taylor served the same medicine to Frank Kramer and he turned the trick so easily that his position in the very foremost ranks of the sprinters must be acknowledged.

"The race was single paced. Bob Miller was put in front and he cut out a good fast clip. In the first heat Taylor lost the toss for position and took the place on the rear wheel of the pacemaker. When the last turn was reached Kramer tried to jump by, but Taylor beat him to it and pulled away from him up to the home stretch until there was only a peck of daylight between them as they flew past the tape.

"In the second heat Kramer was obliged to take the pace, and he was outgeneraled by the colored boy in every way. Even as they reached the last turn Kramer made the least bit of a bluff to jump and then tried to get the Major past him, but no, Taylor just simply rode along in second position until they were nearing the home stretch and well out of gale; suddenly there was a dusky streak and Frank Kramer got second place. Major Taylor won by two lengths and he was moving faster when he crossed the tape than he was down the home stretch. The reason—tremendous applause.

"On the whole Major Taylor is King-Pin among the sprinters. There is only one other man now who appears to have a chance of defeating Taylor, and it will take all of the great Eddie (Cannon) Bald's very best speed and tactics to do it."

Immediately after my match race with Kramer I signed up for another with Jay Eaton, famous champion of another era, who was widely known as "Indoor King." I was fully aware that I had my work cut out for me with the clever and speedy Eaton. I knew that a loss to him would offset even my fine performance against Kramer. However, I had no fear of him so far as speed was concerned and I figured that I was as clever otherwise as he, although he was a very tricky rider. On top of that Eaton had worlds of experience and realizing all these things I admit I was a little anxious on the eve of the race. Nevertheless, I tore after Eaton and felt like a new man when I led him over the tape and satisfied myself that he was more tricky than speedy.

This race was held on the famous Vailsburg (N. J.) track. As was the case in my match race with Frank Kramer the purse in my match with Eaton was $500, winner take all. My race with Eaton followed his sweeping defy to all the professional riders of the country. It was inserted in all of the papers over the signature of Fred W. Voigt, Eaton's manager and read as follows:

"Jay Eaton's Defy to All Professional Riders. I will match Jay Eaton, 'The Indoor King' against any rider in the world with or without single paced, one-mile heats, best two in three heats. The match to take place on the Vailsburg track upon receipt of two weeks' notice from challenger. No one is barred, and the challengers will be taken in order of acceptance of this defy, and the winner of the match to receive $500. The only stipulation I make is that the challengers post $100 in the hands of the official referee which shall serve as a forfeit that the match shall take place and subject to the conditions named above. Signed: Fred W. Voigt, Manager Jay Eaton, 'Indoor King.' "

A New York newspaper carried the following story about my race with Jay Eaton on the day following the event:

"Major Taylor Easily Defeats Jay Eaton 'Indoor King' in Special Match Race. Major Taylor, the champion colored rider, is the fastest bicycle rider in the world, which was again demonstrated yesterday on the Vailsburg Track when he defeated Jay Eaton, the 'Indoor King' in two straight heats in a mile special match race for a purse of $500. The fight between these two great riders had been counted upon as being likely to produce some gilt-edge sport, but the dusky-hued champion defeated the Jersey man in two successive heats in neither one of which did the finish measure in inches. The 'Indoor King' was simply outclassed both times.

"In the first mile heat Taylor followed Eaton to the last lap, until the turn into the home stretch when he came from behind with a perfect jump and beat his rival to the finishing line, the greater part of a length.  In the second heat Eaton sat upright on his wheel about half way down on the home stretch when the dark streak flashed along side of him, the Major again crossing the tape two yards to the good, mid the storm of applause from the big crowd."

After these two victories over Frank Kramer and Jay Eaton, I was now in my very best sprinting form, and, if anything, I was perhaps a shade better than usual because I felt stronger than ever, and therefore, could hold a sprint longer.  I next went after a matched race with one of my greatest rivals of the day, Tom Cooper, whom I had long been anxious to meet in a match race.  In fact I longed for a match with Cooper ever since I witnessed the great race between he and Eddie Bald two years previous at the League of American Wheelmen's meet in Indianapolis, which Bald won.

Immediately after that Indianapolis match race between Cooper and Bald I challenged either of them in a match or that I would take on both of them in a three-cornered race.  However, I was promptly turned down by Bald who still insisted on drawing the color line.  He made no bones of stating that if he raced me it would hurt his social standing.

Cooper tried to evade meeting me in a match race using the color line as a dodge.  However, the fact that he was champion under the N. C. A. auspices put him in an awkward position as I insisted on his meeting me.  On top of that the purse of $1000 which was to go to the winner of our match race, proved to be very tempting to him.  No doubt, my defy to Cooper would not have borne fruit were it not for the fact that the newspapers of the country got solidly behind me and demanded that Cooper race me or forfeit his title forthwith. That pressure caused Cooper to lower the bars he had set up against the color line and accept my defy.

When we met to make the final arrangements for the match I offered to put a side bet of $1000 with Cooper that we might make a real race of it but his manager refused to cover my money.

Down in my heart I knew that Cooper had taken a leading part in having me fined $500 for my alleged infraction of the racing code in 1899.  Cooper was treasurer of the American Cyclists' Racing Union at that time and he was one of the principal instigators who aimed to debar me for life from bicycle racing tracks of the world.

With these facts in mind one can readily appreciate how I felt as I walked on to the track at Milwaukee on July 13, 1900, to race Cooper for the purse of $1000. I felt that after months of waiting I was about to realize one of my most cherished ambitions—that of getting a chance to show one of the men who would have ruled me off the bicycle tracks of the world in an unfair manner, the way to the tape. If ever I was anxious to win a race I most certainly was on this occasion. I felt it was the most important race that I had prepared for up to this time—that is how much there was at stake in it.

However, the fates had decreed that Cooper and I were not to hold that all important match race on the Milwaukee track that day. After both of us had jogged about the track a few times there was a conference of officials concerning the construction of it. This was brought about in no small degree by a fall sustained by Cooper during his workout. The upshot of the confab was that the track was condemned as being unfit to ride upon. The officials of the track asked me, in view of this fact, if I still desired to ride against Cooper. I replied in the affirmative and said I was ready to start to if Cooper was, but the race was declared off.

# CHAPTER XXIX

### MY RETURN TO MY NATIVE CITY, INDIANAPOLIS

Knowing that my next appearance on the track was scheduled for Newby Oval, Indianapolis I trained hard that I might make a good showing before the people in my native city. In that event which was held on July 18, 1900, were entered most of the star riders of the country.

Racing in one's home town is incentive enough for anyone to do his utmost to win. Imagine then my anxiety to lead the pack home in the two races in which I was entered, the two-mile handicap and the half-mile professional championship, as I realized that my father was to occupy one of the boxes at the track. It marked the first time that he had ever consented to see me race and that made me doubly desirous of giving one of my best performances in the track. My father who was a veteran of the Civil War, had as his guests on the occasion a number of his comrades in the Union Army.

Try as I might, however, I was unable to win my heat in the half-mile professional championship race. Fate was kinder to me in the two-mile handicap event and I picked my way through a big field to win first money in a most spectacular manner.

I quote as follows from an Indianapolis newspaper clipping concerning that race meet:

"Major Taylor and Owen Kimble Capture Professional Races at Newby Oval. Major Taylor is still the best of them all. Once in a while he fails to win, as instanced in the third heat of the half-mile professional championship last night, but all in all the black streak comes through first in a big majority of his races, and it matters but little who is competing against him.

"Major Taylor showed all his old time form in his race last night and made such a wonderful finish in the final of the two-mile handicap that he was cheered time and again by the immense crowd at Newby Oval. This was the greatest race of the evening. Major Taylor, Newhouse, Rutz, Maya, and Jimmie Bowler qualified for the first heat. Owen Kimble, Pease, Stone, Barney Oldfield, Stinemetz in the second heat.

"'Now watch for the race between Major Taylor and Owen Kimble' was the word that went around, and the crowd did watch for it with great excitement. For seven laps all Taylor did was keep his eyes open watching the other riders like a hawk to see that he was not pocketed. On the bell lap he was well in front of the bunch and riding on the outside. Then, quick as a flash, he shot up the banking and on the famous northeast turn of the oval he dashed down on the pole again which gave him the lead and he pedalled like a fiend for the last two hundred yards.

"Kimble, the speedy Kentuckian, set sail after him, but there were not revolutions enough in his wheel to bring him anywhere near Taylor, who had gotten in that famous jump of his and he was never headed. Major Taylor finished by three open lengths, with Al Newhouse second, and Owen Kimble third. The time was 4:28 3/5.

Owen S. Kimble—"Old Kentucky"

"Major Taylor was scratch man in the first of the two-mile handicap event, and also first in the final. In the first heat he caught the foremost rider, Lew Gorden, who had a handicap of one hundred yards before the first lap was completed. Taylor, however, failed to qualify in the half-mile championship, by Kimble getting the jump on him in the last eighth of a mile and finishing a length ahead. Kimble made a runaway of the final of this event winning by a dozen lengths."

My set-back in the half-mile championship race made me more determined to win the two-mile handicap in which I started from scratch. I won this race after one of the most sensational rides I ever made; that was immensely pleasing to the public, and I received a splendid ovation.

My father who had never seen me race before came into my dressing room after the races were over to congratulate me. He had a rather surprised look on his face when he said, "Well, son, there is one thing I don't understand, that is, if you are the fastest bicycle rider in the world, as the newspapers say you are, why in time don't you beat those white boys out further at the finish line?" "Well," I said, "I won by a couple of lengths, didn't I?" "Yes," he said, "but I expected to see you leave them so far behind that you could get dressed and come out and see the rest of them fight it out for second, and third money." The innocence of old age.

I tried to explain to him that I was perhaps not quite as fast as the papers proclaimed me to be, and he readily agreed. Then he wanted to know as to why it was they made me start way back in the last place in the two-mile handicap race, and place all the white boys away out ahead of me. I again tried to blame it on to the newspapers, but he couldn't see it that way; he insisted that I was being picked on again because of my color.

This was my father's idea how fast his boy could ride a bicycle, and also his idea of what I was up against because of my color.

# CHAPTER XXX



Keenly disappointed because of my defeat in the half-mile professional championship at the Indianapolis meet on July 18, 1900, I determined to show the same riders, if possible, the way home in the next race at that distance. My opportunity came on the famous Buffalo Athletic Field track on August 2, 1900. This meet attracted the cream of the country's bicycle stars including Owen Kimble, Frank Kramer, Earl Kiser, Johnnie Fisher, Al Newhouse, Otto Maya and Charles Kunkle.

So intent was I upon winning the half-mile professional championship race at the Buffalo meet that I decided to spend some time on the track there preparing for the event.

A Buffalo newspaper carried the following item a few days before the race was held:

"Major Taylor Comes to Buffalo and Astonishes Cycle Fans. Major Taylor who is credited with being the speediest cyclist now before the public, accompanied by his trainer, arrived in Buffalo yesterday from Indianapolis. He went to the athletic field at once to do a little work in preparation for the big race meet that is to be held here next week. Otto Maya, one of the fastest riders in the country, arrived at the same time and the men worked out together. They alternated pace for a number of laps after which they wound up by reeling off a mile in the remarkable time of 2:02. That Major Taylor is capable of even better efforts was demonstrated later in the day when he covered a mile in 1:59."

On the day following the meet this item appeared in one of the Buffalo newspapers:

"Major Taylor Still Fast. Kramer and Kiser Unable to Hold Dusky Streak Who Won the Championship Race. Defeat of the Leading White Professional Riders. Major Taylor, the sprinting cyclist, still rides fast. At the Buffalo field last night the Major proved conclusively to the large assemblage of cycle fans that despite his enforced absence from the track and being blacklisted by the riders' association he has not lost any of his old-time speed. The feature of the National Circuit Meet was the half-mile professional event with increased points to count in the records for the championship, which was captured by the dusky whirlwind.

"The riders were divided into two heats, four men in each heat, the winners and second men in the fastest heat to meet in the three-cornered final provided for by the rules of the N. C. A. Board of

Control.  Major found Kimble, Stone, and Kunkle in his heat, and although at one time it seemed as if the Black Streak was safely pocketed, on the back stretch Stone swung a trifle wide just entering the last turn and like a flash Taylor jumped through on the pole and was yards away from danger.  Kimble was out after him like mad, but not dangerously close.  The heat was a loaf and the time was so slow that the riders in the second heat put up a stiff argument for the two coveted places, which meant the winners thereof were certain of competing in the final.  Kramer outsprinted Kiser, who was too much for Newhouse and Maya.

"The management put in Johnnie Fisher to pace the final.  Kiser declined the pacemaker's rear wheel but Taylor accepted it with the two white boys trailing.  On the last lap Major Taylor swung wide up the bank carrying the other two with him.  Frank Kramer shot out in front with a dash for the tape, but Taylor began a terrible sprint that carried him right past the others and landed him a winner by yards; Earl Kiser finished in second place with Frank Kramer third, the time being 1:04.

"The victory was so impressive that spectators were convinced that if America is to have a white champion this year Major Taylor is the man they will have to defeat for the honor.  Major Taylor received a thunderous ovation.

"Otto Maya won the two-mile handicap event from the 150-yard mark.  Frank Kramer barely beat out Major Taylor for second place, who in turn was a nose in front of Newhouse, who was hard pressed by Kiser.  The time was 4:09.  In this event Major Taylor and Frank Kramer rode from scratch.  Newhouse had a handicap of 90 yards, while Kiser started from the 25-yard line, and Owen Kimble, who failed to place, had a handicap of 30 yards."

# CHAPTER XXXI



On the day following the race this article appeared in a Hartford newspaper:

"Major Taylor Wins Again at the New Veledrome Track. Thousands Enjoy the Exciting Sport. Major Taylor, the colored cyclone, easily proved himself to be the cycling crack of the country by defeating the fastest representative gathering of professional riders seen this season on the new Veledrome Track last night.

"Thousands of lovers of the silent steed crowded the stands to witness the sport, and the colored wonder was given a rousing reception. At no time was the colored rider forced to let out an extra link in his speed, except in the final of the one-mile handicap, when the long-mark men including the Kreamers of Chicago and Aronson of Pittsburg set out at a terrific pace from the very start, and by alternating pace kept Taylor worried until the last lap. Then the colored boy came like a streak on the outside of the track and passed the bunch on the very last turn into the home stretch, winning by a length. His time was 1:59, only a quarter of a second slower than the world's competitive record made by Tom Cooper at Manhattan Beach.

"Major Taylor was also winner of the one-mile open event, the contest being a pretty one right up to the tape between the three aspirants for the championship honors, Bobby Walthour, Johnnie Fisher and the Bay State Wonder.

"Walthour appeared on the track swathed in bandages as the result of a spill in Baltimore, but he put up a plucky race. For the first four laps the six men who were qualified loafed until Rutz started out to set the pace in the fifth lap, and then the real fight began. Around the track the men flew with Fisher in the lead, and Walthour close up with Taylor on his wheel. The two riders hugged the pole closely and Taylor was forced to ease up for a fraction of a second and swing out on the last turn, but he had the speed, and with a tremendous jump he beat the Chicago man out almost at the tape. It was a sensational race and the winner was greeted with a storm of applause.

"In the one-mile open professional event the starters were Bowler, Jacobson, Maya, Fisher, Rutz, Downing, Walthour, Stone, Titus, Newhouse, and Butler. The time for this event was 2:05.

"Starters in the one-mile professional handicap were Aronson, 125 yards; G. Kreamer, 90 yards; Williams, 110 yards; T. Butler, 30 yards; Collette, 15 yards; Taylor, scratch; Miller, 50 yards; D. Kreamer, 100 yards; Downing, 50 yards; Stone, 75 yards; Jacobson, 75 yards. Major Taylor won the final heat, Aronson was second, and Kreamer third. Major Taylor also established an unpaced record of :59 for the half-mile."

# CHAPTER XXXII



One week later I participated in the N. C. A. Grand Circuit Meet, in connection with the L. A. W. midsummer gathering. It attracted all of the star professional riders of the country.

The following item appeared in a New Bedford newspaper the day following the meet:

"Major Taylor in Fine Form. Wins One-Mile Championship in Best Sprint Races Ever Witnessed in New Bedford. The cream of bicycle riders in the country raced at the Buttonwood track yesterday afternoon at the N. C. A. Grand Circuit Meet which was held in connection with the L. A. W. midsummer gathering. Among them was Major Taylor, the great colored rider, who is without question the neatest rider who sits in a saddle today, as well as being the fastest sprinter in the short distances. The meet produced the best sprint races that have ever been seen on the local track.

"One very fast mile was ridden and it was thought that the track had another low mark. It was the second heat of the semi-final of the one-mile championship. Major Taylor won the heat in the splendid time of 1:56 2/5 which is the fastest mile that has been ridden in this year's circuit races. The national championship event was a very interesting contest, although in each preliminary heat for three laps the riders loafed as only professionals can, the last lap, however, made up for their laziness.

"After the first half dozen sprints the spectators were wrought up to a high pitch of excitement. They were prepared for the semi-finals and the last heat which was more exciting than the ones which weeded out the slower ones. Major Taylor won the championship and also the five points that went with it. Frank Kramer was second and Al Newhouse was third. Major Taylor now leads in the 1900 championship races with thirteen points to his credit. Frank Kramer is second with eleven, Freeman and Kiser have eight each, Kimble four, Walthour and Bowler two, and Fisher one.

"The first heat of the mile championship race was won by George Collette who defeated Kiser and Walthour. Bennie Monroe beat Miller who had the rear place when it came time to sprint, but Monroe watched him closely and kept his lead to the finish. Frank Kramer one of the fastest of the bunch rode rings around Jimmy Moran who was in his first professional contest. Major Taylor won his heat in which Freeman was second. Freeman defeated the Major in a championship meet only the night before at New Haven. Newhouse beat Frank Butler easily and Bowler won over Rutz.

(126)

"When it came to the semi-final, Kramer defeated Collette and Monroe. Major Taylor and Newhouse left their pacemakers and Bowler behind in their race, Taylor being in front at the tape. This was the fast mile which has been alluded to. The heat which was to decide who should get the most points and the choice slice of the prize money was the prettiest finish of the day. Major Taylor, Frank Kramer and Al Newhouse all came down the stretch together, and the finish was as close as it could be and not be a dead heat. Taylor had the outside and was a few inches ahead of Kramer and Newhouse was almost even with Kramer."

Another New Bedford newspaper printed the following item the day after the meet:

"New Track Record Made by Major Taylor Who Also Wins the Half-Mile Professional Championship Race. Major Taylor was easily the favorite at the race meet on the Buttonwood track yesterday afternoon. He did some wonderful sprinting during his preliminary work-out which immediately caught the fancy of the crowd. Howard Freeman of Portland, Oregon, won the first heat in the half-mile professional championship race with George Collette second, Hardy Downing third and Bill Tensler bringing up the rear. The time was 1:05 1/5.

"In the second heat there were only two starters. Tom Butler was on the pole while Alex McLean was on the outside. It was a cinch that both men would qualify for the final as they could alternate the pace and make it the fastest heat which they did. On the back stretch Butler cut loose and went past McLean like an express train winning by ten yards. The time was 1:02 4/5.

"There were three starters in the third heat. Major Taylor had the pole. Jimmie Moran, the Chelsea milkman, got away in the lead which he played for. He played a shrewd game. On the turns he carried Taylor far up the bank. Taylor could not ride long and could not get any more speed from the slope of the track than Moran could, but on the last lap Taylor shot past him like a thoroughbred race horse going past a truck horse. He put on a tremendous burst of speed. The time was 1:11 which was slow due to Moran's tricky riding. Moran finished second but was shut out of the final as the heat was the slowest of the three.

"The starters who lined up for the final were Freeman on the pole, Tom Butler next, Major Taylor, Alex McLean, and George Collette in that order. Big Bill Tensler was placed out on the ten-yard mark as pacemaker, but according to instructions he only went two laps. Major Taylor caught the pacemaker and they flew around for two laps with Taylor hanging tight to Tensler's rear wheel, Freeman being in second place and Collette in third.

"The first lap was covered in :24 and the second in :43. There was no change in the order until entering the back stretch on the third lap when Taylor made his famous jump and opened a wide gap at once. Freeman was not quite ready for the jump though he got going as quickly as possible and around the turn he gained a little, but the jump made by Taylor was too much. Freeman could not make it up and finished several yards back at the tape. Tom Butler and Alex McLean made a pretty race for third place. Butler landed the position in a mad sprint from the last turn, beating the Chelsea man by a foot, while Collette was a poor last. The time was 1:25.

"Austin Stone and Oscar Hedstrom came on the track with the Hedstrom motor which is considered the fastest in the business. This team was selected to pace Major Taylor in his trial for a record. The crowd had never seen a motorcycle before and went wild over its speed. Major Taylor came out while the motor was circling the track and began riding. He made a pick-up on the lower turn and did it very cleverly. He followed the machine around for a number of laps, the audience marveling at his ability to stick to it so closely. When he passed the officials the second time, he signalled that he would start the next time around and the word was given.

"He rode finely and the half was made in :46 1/5 which was close to a 1:32 clip and the speed did not diminish for the next two laps. On the last lap the speed was increased a trifle but Taylor hung right on to it, and around the turn through the back stretch they tore into the home stretch across the tape in the remarkable time of 1:37. Taylor was given a great ovation."

# CHAPTER XXXIII



In the three weeks interval between the race meet on the new Bedford track and the next championship race which was scheduled for the Vailsburg track at Newark, New Jersey, on September 3, I spent my time training on the Colosseum track in my home town, Worcester. This track which was on the site which later housed the Worcester Professional Baseball Club attracted some of the greatest bicycle riders in the world to Worcester some thirty years ago. It has long since passed out of the picture but will ever remain a pleasant memory to hundreds of the country's greatest riders and thousands of loyal bicycle fans.

It was heralded far and wide that the quarter-mile championship event would be the outstanding feature of the Vailsburg meet. Knowing that, I set to work in a determined way in an effort to win this event. I knew the field that would start for the laurels in this race would represent the greatest bicycle racers in the United States. With this fact in mind I trained faithfully on the old Worcester track for hours at a time.

A Worcester newspaper commented as follows after one of its reporters had clocked me in practice sprints at the old Colosseum track:—"Major Taylor is doing his preliminary training at the Worcester Colosseum for his next championship race at Newark on September 3, and if faithful and consistent training will win, Major Taylor has the quarter-mile championship already won. In practice sprints at the local Colosseum yesterday afternoon Major Taylor showed wonderful form, he covered a sixth of a mile (or one lap of the track) unpaced in the remarkable time of :16 flat, or at a 1:36 clip for a mile. From a standing start unpaced he finished a lap in :20 1/5."

On the day following the holding of the meet on the Vailsburg track one of the Newark dailies carried the following article:

"Major Taylor Unbeatable. Wins Quarter-Mile Championship Showing Positive Superiority Over All Competitors. The Vailsburg track furnished an afternoon of rare sport yesterday for 10,000 people. The principal event of the day was a quarter-mile dash for the championship of America. This race was won by Major Taylor, the ebony complexioned record breaker, from a field of clever sprinters including Owen Kimble, Frank Kramer, Tom Butler, George Collette, Howard Freeman, and Al Newhouse, the pick of the fastest sprint riders known in this country with the single exception of Earl Kiser who did not appear.  The time was :33.

"Major Taylor as usual in such races had everything his own way and won the final easily.  Johnnie Fisher took the lead followed closely by Taylor with Frank Kramer bringing up the rear.  Major was offered the pole on the back stretch but refused it, he made no effort to begin his wonderful winning jump until the last turn was

FRANK L. KRAMER

reached.  Kramer then cut down to the pole behind Fisher and Taylor and rounding into the home stretch set sail for the tape unhindered. Fisher was beaten at the head of the stretch and Kramer did not have enough left in him to overtake and pass the dusky whirlwind, though he made a strenuous effort.  The Major was never headed and won by a clean open length, Frank Kramer was second and Johnnie Fisher was third."

The final of this quarter-mile championship race was one of the most popular victories I ever won.  This was due in considerable measure to the fact that I considered the Vailsburg bicycle fans far better educated upon the fine points of bicycle racing than any other similar group in the country, and as far as I can learn the same holds true today.  The Vailsburg fans liked my style of riding from the very first time I competed there.  They seemed to appreciate my efforts, were always very fair to me and gave me very generously of their applause.

I realized these facts very well as I trained faithfully for this quarter-mile championship race, incidentally, I knew I had a man-sized job on my hands if I were to win this big event and anticipated the

A Smile of "Fair Play"

bitterest battle of my life down that home stretch if I were to lead the pack home.  I was trained to the minute for this big classic and was never in better fettle than on the afternoon of the race, the weather being well nigh perfect and the fans giving me a tremendous ovation as I came onto the track.

The manner in which the heats were run placed only the three best men in the final, which in a short race of this kind gave each man a good chance, providing there was no frame-up—that is none of that "two-against-one" business.

I was a little nervous when we were called to the starting line for the deciding heat of this big race.  However, when I noticed that I was pitted against Frank Kramer and Johnnie Fisher for the laurels I gave a sigh of relief.  This was not due to the fact that I underrated these two stars, not by a long shot, as they were two great riders and very smart in tactics.  I had the utmost respect for them as sprinters but I knew that they were not on friendly terms with one another and that convinced me that each of them would be out to win on his "own," and that fact gave me a tremendous psychological advantage at the start of the race.

Before we had covered fifty yards, however, I knew the race was being ridden strictly "according to Hoyle," meaning that each man in the race was riding his own race with but one thought in mind —to win, or every man for himself, and the devil grab the hind-most across the tape. My mind was at ease as I realized that for once in my life I would not have to contend with pockets or combinations against me. With that fact in mind I felt I had a big advantage over my opponents especially in view of my fine physical condition. I actually smiled as I realized that this race was to be won by the best man, on merit alone, with nothing to count but speed and good judgment. It was a "fair field and no favor." Incidentally this was the first and only smile of the kind I ever enjoyed of all my many successes.

So confident of victory was I that I actually allowed my opponents to lead me right into the home stretch at top speed before making my jump, when I came from third position and won out by about three lengths. Had I failed to win this race under such unusually favorable conditions I should have felt that the end of my racing days were in sight.

Incidentally this race was the first one I had ever contested in which I was not hampered by pockets or other foul tactics. In a word it was the first race I had ever ridden that was settled on merit, speed and good judgment.

## CHAPTER XXXIV

### PREJUDICE ROBBED ME OF A CHAMPIONSHIP VICTORY— INDIANAPOLIS

Immediately after the Vailsburg meet I went to Indianapolis to compete in a big event on the famous Newby Oval in that city. I was very anxious to win all of my starts in my native Indianapolis for several reasons. First of all, it was the scene of my very first race; secondly, because at one time I had previously been barred from the self-same track there because of my color, and thirdly, to show my hosts of good friends in that city that their faith in me and my riding skill had not been misplaced. And also to further make good Mr. Mungers' proud boast.

I was in fine physical condition as we stepped on to the track for the final heat of the third of a mile championship race, and well I might be as there was a galaxy of racing stars entered in the event, the outstanding race of the program. Among them were Owen Kimble, Frank Kramer, Earl Kiser, Jimmie Bowler, Stinemetz, Gordon, Watson, Pease and Newhouse.

In the final heat of this event the judges decided that Owen Kimble and myself had raced a dead heat although I am convinced to this day that I beat him to the tape by a safe margin. It developed later, however, that one of the three judges who made the dead heat decision was swayed to that verdict by his prejudice to my color. The dead heat decision stood, nevertheless, and indirectly caused Kimble and myself to be matched to race the same distance on the same track a week later for a purse of $300, winner take all.

I quote the following item from an Indianapolis newspaper published the day following the first meet on Newby Oval:

"Two Dead Heats at the Night Meet. Major Taylor and Owen Kimble ride dead heat in Championship Race. Two Judges favor Major Taylor for first place. A big crowd witnessed the races of the N. C. A. meet at Newby Oval last night in which Major Taylor, Owen Kimble and Frank Kramer were declared in a dead heat. Kimble and Taylor being tied for first place. The N. C. A. Board of Control will be obliged to pass on the matter.

"Major Taylor made his famous jump on the home stretch, having previously passed Kramer. The front wheels of Kimble and Taylor were so nearly even when the tape was reached that the judges, Sterns, Fisher and Kane, declared the race a tie, while Hay and Hunter decided that Major Taylor won. The majority ruled, however, and the race was decided a dead heat. No time was announced due to excitement. Both men refused to ride the heat over, Taylor claiming he won and Kimble alleging that Taylor fouled him by elbowing him in the home stretch.

"The third of a mile championship race: First heat won by Howard Freeman, Pease second; second heat won by Frank Kramer, Earl Kiser second; third heat won by Major Taylor, Jimmie Bowler second; fourth heat won by Owen Kimble, Stinemetz second; fifth heat won by Gordon, Watson second. First semi-final heat won by Kramer, Kimble second; second semi-final heat won by Taylor, Freeman second. Final heat Major Taylor and Owen Kimble dead heat, Frank Kramer third. The time was not caught owing to excitement."

Another Indianapolis newspaper published the following item on the eve of the running over of the championship race between Owen Kimble and myself on the local track:

"Championship Run Over. Major Taylor and Owen Kimble, who rode a dead heat at Newby Oval last Thursday night have consented to ride the tie off at next Tuesday evening's meet. They have agreed to race for a purse of $300, winner take all, and the winner to be credited with eight points and the loser four. This is expected to be the most exciting race of any on the circuit this season.

"The judges who officiated last Thursday night will not be asked to serve next Tuesday evening, for it has been reported that one of the judges who decided the race a dead heat afterward declared he believed Major Taylor had won the race, but because he disliked the colored rider personally he decided against him."

I have mentioned several times previously how I was more than once most shamefully dealt with at the hands of unscrupulous track officials. On this memorable occasion, at Newby Oval, Indianapolis, however, it was one of the judges who used his official position of trust and honor in order to take an unfair advantage of me, simply because nature had decreed that the color of my skin should be black.

More than once when I have heard or read one of the dominant race boasting over some unfair advantage he has taken of a down-trodden Negro, simply because of his color, or perhaps his inferior position in life, I have recalled a remarkable utterance by the famous late Colonel Robert G. Ingersoll, who, perhaps actuated by a feeling of remorse, said: "Every time I meet a Negro I feel like getting down upon my knees to ask his pardon for crimes my race has inflicted upon his."

This cowardly judge boasted among some of his friends after the above mentioned tie race between Kimble and myself how he had trimmed the "nigger." However, the unsportsmanlike conduct of this judge gained many friends for me and his bitter prejudice only caused me to fight all the harder in my next race on the Indianapolis track. It nettled me, however, to think that this low piece of business robbed me of one of the hardest earned victories of my life. It was a man-sized task at best to beat Kramer and Kimble to the finish line and to turn the trick with those two riders combined against me was nothing short of a Herculean task. On top of the team work of Kramer and Kimble, who were out to best me at all costs, I had this unscrupulous judge to contend with and although I defeated Kramer and Kimble on the track on that eventful night I was unable to compete with the underhand methods adopted by the aforementioned track official. That three-way combination was simply unbeatable.

# CHAPTER XXXV

TWO THRILLING CHAMPIONSHIP VICTORIES—INDIANAPOLIS

I decided to make the best of matters in the meantime, however, and assured myself that the best way to assuage my feelings would be to defeat Kimble on the same Indianapolis track. By some clever maneuvering my trainer and myself drew my great rival into a championship match to decide the dispute over the dead heat business between us. We agreed to ride for a purse of $300, winner take all, and I tried in vain to persuade Kimble to add a side bet of $100 tc make an even $500 purse.

I knew that Owen Kimble being a southerner did not like me because of my color. He was naturally imbued with all of the old traditions relative to that perpetual color prejudice and race hatred that are so typical of that section of the country. Kimble felt that in order to uphold those inherited ideals of his forefathers he was obliged to hate me with a genuine bitterness and to do his utmost to defeat me every time we met. Because of this intensity of color hatred for me, Kimble always seemed to be able to develop an extra degree of speed when battling it out with me that he never displayed against any other rider in the world. In fairness to Kimble, however, I wish to state that he took a decent stand against me in all of our races inasmuch as he had never actually put me down by unfair means.

He made a claim, however, that I elbowed him in the championship event the week before, which was declared a dead heat. His claim was not allowed as he was generally known to be very unsteady in sprinting, and was very wobbly even in practice, but he was a very dangerous rider at any stage of the sprint game and I had the utmost respect for his somewhat awkward though powerful sprinting ability.

No sooner had the agreement for the special match race between Kimble and myself been drawn than I set about training as I never had before. I sought to be in my best sprinting form for this big event which was already creating great interest and promised to draw a tremendous crowd. I was now at a point where too much training might prove disastrous by causing me to go "stale." On the other hand if I were insufficiently trained, of course, I could not expect to be at the height of my form. In a word my chief concern at this time centered about my fear of being a little "off color" so to speak, so I trained very carefully and cautiously.

My rival was equally vigilant in his training and was in wonderful condition also. However, I was confident of being able to bring the big Kentuckian into camp again, single-handed and without the

(136)

assistance of any of the officials. It was while I was training for this championship match that I was credited with tearing off the fastest mile ever recorded on any track under the same conditions, the mark of 1:45 standing to this day.

I quote as follows from an article printed in an Indianapolis newspaper concerning that record mile:

"Major Taylor's Fast Mile. Colored Champion Paced by Other

Major Taylor and Trainer, R. W. "Bob" Ellingham

Cracks Does Stunt in Remarkable Time of 1:45. This is the fastest time ever clocked for the distance on any track. The record-ride was made in a work-out, and does not stand as an official mark. R. W. Ellingham held the watch on Taylor as did Earl Kiser, the great sprinter, and several others. They were dumbfounded as they realized what Taylor had done and so were the other riders who were assembled at the track to watch the work-out. None of them seemed to be able to realize that Taylor was capable of such a marvelous performance. Taylor made this mark on a wheel geared to ninety-two inches and Palmer tires.

"Major Taylor was pulled out by the cracks who are in training at Newby Oval. Lew Gordon paced him to the tape with a flying start, and George Leander took him to the first quarter in :26 flat. Owen Kimble paced him for the second quarter in :26 3/5, the half by Taylor being :52 3/5. Jimmie Bowler pulled Taylor to the third quarter in :26 3/5.  Taylor rode the last quarter alone in :26 3/5 completing the mile in 1:45.  The best previous time for the distance was 1:51 by Orlando Stevens, at Louisville.

"On Friday afternoon Taylor rode a quarter of a mile in the unheard of time of :22 3/5, which stunt startled the riders training at Newby Oval especially when they learned a close tab was kept on the watch while the colored marvel took his work-out."

On the eve of my special championship match race with Owen Kimble, the strong boy from Louisville, I was at the peak of physical condition ready and anxious for the starters gun to send us on our way.

The following article is quoted from the columns of an Indianapolis newspaper the day after my race with Kimble:

"Major Taylor Champion.  Takes Both Big Races From the Aggregation of Eastern Racing Talent.  $500 in the coin of the realm, the National Professional Championship of 1900, and a permanent place in the estimation of the bicycle race loving public of Indianapolis is what Major Taylor has gained during his present sojourn in this city. One week ago last night he and Owen Kimble demonstrated that they were in a class by themselves, so far as sprint racing is concerned.  Last night Major Taylor proved that he is the best man in this class and had he not been pocketed in the half-mile handicap he undoubtedly would have earned $100 more.

"Major Taylor was the prime favorite of the meet.  When starter Allison's pistol announced the start of the first race there were thousands of cycle enthusiasts at the track and before the fight for the third of a mile national championship was started the crowd was even larger.

"The first event of importance was the match race between Major Taylor and 'Old Kentuck' Owen Kimble.  Pacemaker Watson was placed ten yards in advance of the two men.  Hardly had the report of the revolver died away when Taylor tacked on to Watson's rear wheel.  When the gong in the official's box announced the beginning of the final lap, the riders were tearing off speed that would make a locomotive envious.

"Around on the back stretch Watson dropped out so as to give the contestants an opportunity for the final spurt to the tape.  Down the back stretch they tore, each man straining for himself.  Kimble's wheel seemed to fairly leave the track as he made the effort of his life but it was to no avail.  He could not shove his front wheel past the colored boy's handle bars.  When they flashed over the tape both men were well nigh exhausted.  Major Taylor won by a fraction of a wheel's length in :39 3/5.  He was cheered loud and long by the great crowd.  It was a beautiful race.

"Then came the two-mile national championship. Frank Kramer was an important factor in this event. He defeated Major Taylor in the preliminary heat but the colored boy got in on the final. The second and third men in the two heats rode another heat to decide who should be entitled to start in the final. The starters in this heat were Taylor, Howard Freeman, and Jimmie Bowler. Both gave Taylor something of an argument but he won out hands down. In the final of this event Taylor led Kramer and Owen Kimble over the tape."

The following item is quoted from an Indianapolis newspaper:

"Major Taylor's Early Sprint. Taylor, Kimble and Kramer lined up for the final of this great two-mile national championship race. In the last lap of this event Taylor gave one of the most remarkable exhibitions of sprinting ever seen in this decade. All three were following single pace furnished by the Stinemetz boys and allowing things to take their own course. As they passed the press box Major Taylor was seen beginning to edge to the outside, as he was the last man in the vanguard.

"With a sudden jump on the first turn Taylor passed the other two men as though they were stationary. Usually the fate of a rider who starts a sprint that early is to finish in about the lowest possible position, but it was not so with Taylor, who gained about two wheel's lengths before the other two men were aware that there was anything doing and he kept right on sprinting. They tore after him like mad, Kramer leaving Kimble in the rear as he pushed after the Negro. It was to no avail, however, and Taylor won by over a wheel's length in 4:43." The applause was again thunderous.

Of all the incentives that spur athletes to their best efforts, I believe the most outstanding is the desire to dethrone a champion in his home town before a host of admiring friends. I realize a handsome purse, a diamond-studded medal, a gold or silver trophy and even a champion's best girl seated in the grandstand are wonderful inspirations for any competitor. However, that almost fiendish desire on the part of a field to humble a champion in his native city outdoes them all by a wide margin. I speak from experience as I'm frank to say that no rider ever exerted himself more than I did to beat the great Eddie "Cannon" Bald on the Buffalo Athletic Field Track. Bald lived in Buffalo. I never defeated Bald in Buffalo.

For this and other reasons Kimble and Kramer, my bitter rivals, combined against me in both the championship races on this occasion particularly in the two-mile event. Their tactics in this race were the more noticeable because, the distance being longer, they had better opportunities to pull something.

After his stinging defeat in the third of a mile championship match only a few moments before, the stalwart Kimble's hot southern blood was at the boiling point.  He was furious when called out to start in the two-mile championship race final and was counting upon squaring himself in this event.  Kramer was also nursing a grudge because of his defeat in the championship the week before.  He was out to retrieve his laurels.  Besides the purse, championship points and prestige that were at stake, just enough of that "color business" was injected into it to rouse one's sporting blood, giving the race just the right "pep" and the public an extra run for their money.  I figured that Kimble and Kramer were out to get me.  The big Kentuckian looked grim as we came out to do our "stuff" in the two-mile race.  Kramer looked somewhat worried as if a little uneasy about the part he was to play.  I must have looked rather serious myself because I was trying to figure out what new joker they had up their sleeves.  As I could not foresee this, my best bet was to ride on the defensive, keeping alert to beat them at whatever they tried.

Before we reached the first half I realized what their plans were. To beat them required a burst of speed that seemed almost suicidal. But I knew my "stuff."  I timed them perfectly, and threw every ounce of strength into a jump when about 270 yards remained to go. The confidence I felt because of my never failing physical fitness enabled me to gain a lead of two lengths and I gained a third on the way to the tape.  It was a furious sprint with a glorious thrill at the end, which was increased by the excited cheering of that frantic crowd. Had I allowed Kimble and Kramer to pocket me I might have had no chance at all.

Neither Kimble nor Kramer offered to congratulate me as such an act of sportsmanship was not in their code.  The wonderful ovation given me by the sports lovers of Indianapolis when I scored my second victory on that program again demonstrated that the public always likes to see the best man win.

Once in their dressing room my rivals immediately became involved in a heated argument that almost ended in fist-a-cuffs over the collapse of their plan.  That quarrel resulted in a complete split between them which worked out very much to my advantage as it meant just one less combination to battle against.

It was not always the mere excitement of out-generaling, and outracing my opponents around the track and across the tape first that gave me the greatest thrill, but the real climax was the glory of vindication and the joy of retribution following each success, which was always indeed a personal triumph, because of their prejudice and unsportsmanlike methods.

# CHAPTER XXXVI



## WINNING THE NAME MAJOR

Hardly had the cheers of the throng that saw me win the third of a mile championship special match race from Owen Kimble and the two-mile championship race from Kimble and Frank Kramer died away before I recalled an objection raised by a prominent Indianapolis merchant over my riding under the name of Major Taylor.

Shortly after I had won my very first race, that ten-mile event on the Indianapolis highways as a boy of thirteen, I received a letter from this merchant asking me to call around and see him. Strangely enough his name was Major Taylor. I knew Mr. Taylor by sight.

For several minutes after I called at Mr. Taylor's office I was grilled by him. Among forty and one other things, he asked me what my christian name was, but he did not give me an opportunity to answer. This third degree business made me very nervous and I was very anxious to get out in the open air. Mr. Taylor accused me, among other things, of appropriating his name, which he led me to believe was a very serious offense. Likewise he alleged that I was receiving his mail, which charge to me was second only to one of murder. As our talk, if it could be called such, came to an end this merchant said to me: "Now I warn you, young man, never to use my name again. If you do I will send you straight to Plainfield (the location of the boys' reformatory) until you are twenty-one just to start with, and after that I am not sure just what will happen to you."

I began to cry. His reformatory talk struck terror into my heart. I was all fed up on that Plainfield business, for years, before I was old enough to know what it was all about. The mere mention of its name caused me to quiver. After I had promised never to use his old name again he then handed me a letter addressd to "Major Taylor." It was mine but he had opened it. I figured he wanted to frighten me out of doing what he thought I might do about this letter, because it was what he would have done under the same circumstances.

Shortly after that interview in Mr. Taylor's office I received a letter from a big law firm there asking me to drop in to see them at my earliest opportunity. In the meantime I had won a number of bicycle races in and about Indianapolis and my name was appearing more or less frequently in the daily papers. These lawyers accused me of using the name of Major Taylor, their client, the merchant referred to above, illegally. They asked me what my correct first name was and I told them "Marshall." They told me to use my right name henceforth or they would land me in Michigan City (penitentiary). I promised them I would but added, "But I can't stop all the kids in town from calling me 'Major,' but I'll try."

Not long after that I left Indianapolis. The next time I returned to the city I was a big "champ," and no longer a little "chump." The name, Major Taylor, was appearing frequently in big headlines in the newspapers throughout the country and on billboards as well.

The day after my success on the Newby Oval track, when I won the third of a Mile Special Championship match race and the Two-mile Championship race, I received another letter. Imagine my surprise when I learned it was from Mr. Major Taylor, the local merchant. Again he asked me to call to see him, I figured that I was a big champion now and couldn't be bluffed any more, so down I went to see him with blood in my eye. However, I found that Mr. Taylor had evidently experienced a change of heart. He told me that I had performed on the race tracks of the country in such a sportsmanlike manner that I was now free to adopt the name "Major." He also told me that my work on the track had won the honor for me. "I want to congratulate you as champion and wish you every success," said Mr. Taylor as he shook my hand warmly.

When I recovered from my surprise I thanked Mr. Taylor for the privilege of using his name Major, and assured the venerable gentleman that I would always do my very best to uphold with dignity and pride the proud old family name of "Major Taylor," even though the "Major" part of it had been wished on me.

An Indianapolis paper got wind of this meeting of Major Taylor and Major Taylor and ran the following item concerning it in their next issue:

"Major Taylor and Major Taylor. Major Taylor the business man, and Major Taylor the bicycle racer are both of Indianapolis, yet they are two distinct individuals. This could be easily seen if the two were brought face to face.

"The racing man is young and black, while the business man is past the racing age and white, but unfortunately, so Major Taylor the business man says, thousands of people are not aware of this fact and confuse the two. He also says that the use of his name in connection with bicycle racing is causing him no end of trouble, and that he has been obliged to explain to hundreds of his friends that he has not deserted his business and gone into the bicycle racing game.

"Major the racing man, so he asserts, is masquerading around under an assumed name, and that the racing man's correct name is Marshall Walter Taylor. This the racing man admits but claims the right to answer to the name of Major if he likes, although he does not sign his name Major.

"Major is a name in both cases and not a title. Major Taylor the racing man will be in the city next week and promises not to interfere in any way with the business pursuits of Major Taylor the business man. Major Taylor the racing man has made a great reputation this season. No one knows of Marshall Taylor on the National Circuit, but thousands are watching the clever riding of Major Taylor and the clever little colored rider is determined to stick to the name which he has made famous. Meanwhile Major Taylor the business man will continue to send out notices that he is still doing business at the same old stand."

Numerous titles were hung on me by the sports writers of the country when I was in my heyday. Some of them referred to me as the "Black Zimmerman," "the Black Streak," "the Ebony Streak," and the "Black Cyclone." However, I believe the most popular one was "the Worcester Whirlwind."

Some of the riders also had a few choice "pet" names for me occasionally when I flew over the tape ahead of them. These outbursts, of course, were true indications of poor sportsmanship and also showed what hard losers they were.

# CHAPTER XXXVII



The last race of the 1900 championship season was scheduled for the Montreal track on September 24. I was entered in three events on that program, the third-mile, the one-mile and two-mile handicap events. Although I had what was generally conceded to be a safe margin to insure my winning the championship title for the season, there was an outside chance that my closest rival, Frank Kramer, by winning the mile championship race at Montreal and the five-mile championship event on the Hartford, Connecticut, track a week later, could tie me for the laurels.

With those facts in mind I determined to put everything I had into my races at Montreal that I might start in the Hartford events with a margin over Kramer that he would be unable to wipe out as we sprinted like mad for the laurel wreath. This marked my first appearance in Montreal since I won the world's championship title the year previous. When I first came on to the Queen's Park track for my warming up sprints I received a tremendous ovation indicating that the crowd had not forgotten my riding to the International honors on the same boards in 1899.

Despite the fact that I was in excellent condition on this occasion Owen Kimble defeated me in the one-mile championship event, the feature number on the all-star program, this being the only championship event I lost that season. However, I won the third of a mile handicap event from scratch, and was very anxious to test my speed in the two-mile handicap event when some water I had drank made me so ill that I was unable to start in that race.

Among the star riders who participated in the Grand National Circuit Meet in Montreal on this occasion were Owen Kimble of Louisville, Kentucky, Frank L. Kramer of Newark, New Jersey, Floyd Krebs of Newark, New Jersey, Saxon Williams of Buffalo, New York, George Collette of New Haven, Connecticut, and C. T. Boisvert of Montreal.

In the one-mile International professional championship race I won the first heat with Saxon Williams second, the time being 2:30 2/5. In the second heat Frank Kramer was the winner with George Collette second, the time was 3:13. Owen Kimble won the third heat in 2:40. I won the first heat in the semi-final in 2:22 1/5. Kimble was first in the second heat of the semi-final with Collette second, the time being 2:14 4/5. Kimble won the final heat with myself second in 3:48.

I won the third of a mile handicap race for professionals, Boisvert being second and Williams third. The time was :40.

Commenting on the meet one of the Montreal dailies printed the following: "There was a monstrous crowd at the Queen's Park track yesterday to witness the cream of the bicycle riders of this country and the United States as they strove for the laurels in the Grand National Circuit Meet. All of the races were hotly contested, in one or two instances the heats nearly resulted in ties. Included in the field of starters was the old favorite, Major Taylor of Worcester, Massachusetts. The appearance of the 'Major' on the track was a signal for a hearty round of applause, which the crack rider politely acknowledged by doffing his cap.

"Several surprises were sprung on the audience during the afternoon, the most notable one being the winning by Owen Kimble of the one-mile championship event with Major Taylor second. It was generally conceded by the knowing ones that the Major had a 'cinch,' but it seems that on the finish Taylor misjudged his sprint with the result that before he was aware of the fact Kimble darted past taking the lead and flying over the line a safe winner. It was a great spurt and although the true merits of the race were challenged by the many, nevertheless, the winner deserved the victory, not only for his plucky fight throughout the race, but the manner in which he grasped the opportunity to turn a certain defeat into a triumphant win when only a few yards from the finish.

"This seemed to act as a tonic on the 'Major,' for in the one-third of a mile handicap which followed, Taylor, who had practically the same men against him as he had in the former race, set a terrific pace from the crack of the pistol and after one of the most exciting and keenly contested bicycle races ever witnessed at Montreal, and probably not surpassed by any other in America for the same distance, flew over the line a winner by ten yards, making the remarkably fast time of :40. Taylor is remarkably popular with Montreal audiences and it seems they have not forgotten the little incident that happened at the World's Meet last year when he was 'gyped' out of a hard earned victory in the half-mile open event through a ruling of an unscrupulous judge.

"When the two mile handicap professional race was announced it was learned with deep regret that the 'Major' was in no condition to contest it as he had become suddenly indisposed, no doubt as a result of the terrible pace he had set in the third of a mile event. This was very disappointing as it seemed to take the interest out of this particular contest."

Following my victorious riding in Indianapolis, and prior to the Montreal races mentioned above I took part in two other programs.

On September 10 I raced at Terre Haute, Indiana winning the one-mile professional open event in the fastest time ever made in competition on the new track there, 2:04. In my second start on that occasion, the two-mile professional handicap, I was unable to place.

In my preliminary heat in the one-mile professional open event I won over Howard Freeman, the time being 2:29. In the final of that race Jimmie Bowler of Chicago was second and Lew Gordon third. Pease won the two-mile professional handicap with Gordon second and Bowler third. I was slowed up in my heat by Freeman for three laps but sprinted the next two laps and caught the bunch. Stinemetz thwarted my efforts thereafter and I was too exhausted to overtake the bunch again. The time for this two-mile event was 4:38.

On September 17, at Erie, Pennsylvania, I was scheduled to meet the three fastest sprinters in America, Frank Kramer, Owen Kimble, and Otto Maya, in a special four-cornered race. It developed to be a case of three against one in this event, however. I knew in advance that the odds were decidedly against me but decided to do my utmost to win especially as I recalled it was one of the last events of the season and my initial appearance in Erie. Fortune smiled on me that day and I led the field home.

On the day after the race the Erie *Dispatch* printed the following article: "Major Taylor, the colored bike star, who attracted so much attention here at the race meet yesterday, is a rare exception to his class generally. He is fairly modest, rather conservative, and not overly proud nor stuck up. He is very white for a colored man and has other qualities that should recommend him to the public generally. He does not drink or use tobacco in any form, never uses profane language, does not race on Sunday and attends church regularly. He is a married man and has saved $25,000 from his winnings and investments covering the past four years.

"Taylor rode in excellent form in the four-cornered special match race yesterday always holding himself back until just before the tape was reached, just to encourage the boys, then he darted ahead with ease and grace that was alone worth going to the track to witness. Later in the season he will ride a special match race with Willie Fenn, the amateur champion, to decide the National Championship for the year of 1900. Major Taylor won about $300 in the races here.

"Major Taylor is not as light in complexion as George Dixon, but he is a dandy in dress and he has a muscular development that is the envy of every slim-jim that sees him."

# CHAPTER XXXVIII



Returning to my home in Worcester, Massachusetts following my success on the Montreal track I set to work training in earnest for my championship match with Willie Fenn, the amateur champion of the country. I had but one week in which to prepare for this all-important event as the winner was to be designated as the champion match rider of the country. Two prizes were hung up for the event, a gold medal and a purse of $500.

I was reluctant about this match. It seemed to me that I was giving away considerable odds when I signed up to face Fenn. It had required an entire season of strenuous training and bitterly contested races to gain for me the professional championship title that year. In my race with Fenn I stood to lose my laurels at one fell swoop.

On the other hand Fenn won his national amateur championship title in a single event which was held at Buffalo. I figured that in case I defeated Fenn his reputation would not suffer, for a professional is assumed to be superior to an amateur with a somewhat similar rating. However, if Fenn defeated me that was something else again. Much was printed concerning my attitude toward the race, which was exactly the same as the one taken by me in Montreal a year previous under almost similar circumstances. The nub of my feelings in the undertaking was that if Fenn led me over the tape it would mean the end of my racing career.

However, I signed the agreement to face Fenn on the Hartford track, which was considered his home oval. Incidentally I considered Fenn one of the most remarkable riders in the world. He had his own particular style of racing and I realized that the one who won our match race would turn the trick in one of the most fiercely contested events ever held on an American track. The fact that I was in excellent physical condition and my knowledge of the fine points of the game, such as generalship and track tactics, gave me confidence that I could lead Fenn to the tape. Offsetting my knowledge of track strategy was the fact that Fenn was a powerful and very fast rider and I knew that I would have to be at my best to defeat him.

Hartford bicycle fans always claimed Fenn as one of their own. He was extremely popular in that city. I also had a number of very good friends in that city and there was much speculation on the eve of the much discussed race as to who would win, the amateur champion of the country or the professional champion of the country.

It was stipulated that the first heat would be paced, the second unpaced and the third, if necessary, would be determined by the toss of a coin.  I won the first heat and volunteered to ride it over again when Fenn claimed a foul.  I won the run-off of the heat and also won the next heat thereby clinching the championship of the country for amateurs and professionals.

WILLIE "BILL" FENN

On the day after the race one of the Hartford dailies printed the following article:

"Major Taylor Wins Championship Title Again.  A large crowd of bicycle enthusiasts saw Major Taylor, the professional champion of America, defeat Willie Fenn, the boy wonder, who is the amateur champion of the country, in a specially sanctioned match race at the Hartford Veledrome last evening.  Major Taylor won the event quite handily.

"Fenn has been doing some phenomenal riding all season and his many friends in Hartford thought he would easily be able to defeat the invincible Major Taylor.  The match was finally arranged for the mile distance, best two in three heats, one heat to be single paced, one to be unpaced and the third, if necessary, to be decided by the toss of a coin.  Fenn wore a confident look when he came out on the track but was a trifle nervous. His appearance was a signal for applause.

"Shortly afterwards Major Taylor came out. He looked very unconcerned and as though he had some business to attend to and was in a hurry to finish it. Thayer of New Britain was put in as pacemaker. In the first heat Taylor laid back and allowed Fenn to take the pace but followed closely until the last turn on the home stretch, then jumped, and took the lead finishing several lengths ahead. Fenn protested, claiming a foul which was allowed, and about twenty minutes later the heat was re-run. Major Taylor looked angry this time, and at the crack of the pistol he jumped and caught the pacemaker which position he held until the last of the fifth lap, when Fenn made a sprint past both Major and the pacemaker and tried to shake the Major off. However, Taylor paid no attention to Fenn but at the finish made a jump and beat him out three lengths, time 2:25.

"In the next heat judges were placed on each turn and in this heat Fenn warmed matters up some, but started his sprint too soon, although Major was obliged to take the last turn wide as Fenn had the pole, and many thought surely Fenn would win the heat, but when about twenty yards from the tape, Taylor made one of his famous jumps and won by several feet."

This was the first time in my career that I had been obliged to re-ride a race on account of a protest. In fact Fenn did not enter a formal protest but complained that I had ridden him too close on the turn. I was more confident than ever that I could again take Fenn's measure when he began to complain so I quickly volunteered to ride the race over as I wanted the decision clean-cut.

The second heat of our race proved to be the final, and as in the preceding race Fenn put up another great battle. His last three-eighths was a magnificent exhibition of brute strength against experience and skill. Fenn was an exceptionally powerful rider and could ride the last lap of a race just as fast as the first one—at top speed. In our race he was evidently riding under the direction of his manager who had instructed him to take the lead in the last three laps, and with one lap to get wound up in, he thought he could sprint the last two so fast that I would be unable to kick past, so I did not interfere in any way, but simply allowed Fenn to ride his own race.

At three laps to go the pace was all one could ask for, at two to go I was sitting pretty but the pace was torrid. As the bell announced the last lap I was still in second place and as we passed the spot where I generally made my jump I was pedalling for all I was worth to hang on. Fenn was now sure he had me beaten. However, just as we entered the home stretch I threw all I had into my jump and nipped him at the tape.

It was a good job, newspaper men agreed, but a most risky one as I put great confidence in my jumping him in the last twenty-five yards. I had intended to pass him in the middle of the turn but he swung so wide it was impossible for me to carry out my plan, so I had to disappoint him in the last few yards of the race. The result of this race gave me the undisputed claim to the title of Champion Match Rider of America.

Although Fenn was a Connecticut boy and naturally a big favorite in Hartford my victory over him was a very popular one. I considered this match by all means my outstanding success of the season.

# CHAPTER XXXIX



Under the old order promulgated by the League of American Wheelmen, the winner of each championship event on the National Circuit Tracks was declared the champion of the season for the distance ridden, but in the season of 1900 it was decided that a series of championship races would be held at the various distances on the several tracks of the country in the National Circuit, the winner of each event being allowed a certain number of points. At the close of the season the rider having the most points for the one mile championship races was declared the one-mile champion and so on through the list of other distances. The rider having won the greatest aggregate number of points was declared unreservedly the National Champion of his class, either amateur or professional.

I quote as follows from the "Cycle Age" of October 4, 1900:

"American Championship Decided by Points. Now that the championship races of 1900 are over and Major Taylor has been officially declared National Champion, the thought arises that the method of deciding champions under the new regime is much more satisfactory than under the old.

"When a championship depends upon one race it may be won by a rider who is not in reality the champion by merit. For instance, in the International Championship Race at Paris this summer, the French rider, Jacquelin, gained the title of International Champion. Immediately following this International meet came the Paris Exposition of even greater importance from standpoints of competitors, prizes, crowds, etc., and Jacquelin failed to defend his crown, being beaten by Meyers and Cooper. Jacquelin has also been beaten well in several almost successive races since the International meet.

"When a championship is won, as Major has won the 1900 National Championship, by a series of races, it shows conclusively that the winner is the true champion. The champion point table shows forty points for Taylor as against twenty for Frank Kramer his nearest competitor. He is without doubt the best sprint race rider of the aggregation with which he raced."

A New York daily printed the following article relative to the 1900 bicycle championship:

"Major Taylor Is Champion. Worcester Whirlwind Proves Himself the Fastest Man of the Year. The championship among sprinters for the season has been won by Major Taylor, the colored boy, who also was champion last year under the L. A. W. He has now achieved his fondest hope after a number of years of steady riding in championship form. He scored the highest number of points in the N. C. A. series by an immense lead with Frank Kramer second, and Owen S. Kimble third.

"Major Taylor scored more points than any of the N. C. A.

MAJOR TAYLOR—American Champion, 1900

sprinters and double his nearest competitor, Frank Kramer. Five increased point championships have been run during the season in which the winner scored eight points instead of four which is the allowance for the winner of a circuit championship. Major Taylor won four firsts which gave him thirty-two points, one second gave him four points, and he won a circuit championship which gave him four points, making a total for the season of forty points with Frank Kramer having but twenty. Major Taylor won every championship but the mile at Montreal in which he ran second. Taylor won the quarter, third, half and the two-mile, also the one-mile circuit championship events.  The five-mile was not contested.

"Major Taylor's supremacy during the season has been unquestioned.  His victories being easily accomplished in most cases.  It was Owen Kimble, the Kentuckian, who gave the "Major" the bitterest battles of any of the contestants, and he managed to beat Major out occasionally.  Whenever they came together in a final it was always sure to be a battle royal.  On Monday at Hartford Major Taylor rode a special match against Willie Fenn, the amateur champion, for the National Championship title and defeated the amateur in straight heats.  It was a great race.

"The following is an official record of the professional series for the season of 1900.  Rank of the riders, championship contestants were rated as follows for the first ten fastest riders in America:

TEN FASTEST RIDERS, PROFESSIONAL SERIES, SEASON OF 1900

| Rider | First | Second | Third | Points |
|---|---|---|---|---|
| Major Taylor . . . . . . . | 5 | 1 | 0 | 40 |
| Frank Kramer . . . . . . | 1 | 3 | 4 | 20 |
| Owen S. Kimble . . . . . | 2 | 1 | 1 | 18 |
| Howard B. Freeman . . . . | 2 | 0 | 0 | 8 |
| Earl Kiser . . . . . . . | 0 | 3 | 0 | 8 |
| Johnnie Fisher . . . . . . | 0 | 0 | 2 | 3 |
| Jimmie Bowler . . . . . . | 0 | 1 | 0 | 2 |
| George Collette . . . . . | 0 | 0 | 1 | 2 |
| Bobby Walthour . . . . . | 0 | 1 | 0 | 2 |
| Al Newhouse . . . . . . | 0 | 0 | 0 | 0 |

# CHAPTER XL



So popular was the bicycle racing game, and bicycle riding on the part of the general public, that by 1900 all of the bicycle builders of the country had the crack riders riding their wheels. They used this method as an advertising medium and it paid liberal rewards as it was a rare person, indeed, either man or woman, who did not own a bicycle or even a tandem. In that era a bicycle occupied much the same position as the automobile today.

While Tom Cooper and Floyd MacFarland, two of the greatest sprinters in this country, were riding in Europe during the season of 1900, the American Bicycle Company whose wheels they were riding, carried on an advertising campaign in the Parisian daily and weekly papers. It was a costly campaign but the company felt amply repaid for spending a large amount of money to inform the Continent that Cooper and MacFarland were riding all of their races on two of their best known models of bicycles.

Before the season opened that year I was secured by the Iver Johnson Arms and Cycle Company of Fitchburg to ride their make of bicycle that season. This firm was very conservative, and I was the first rider that was ever engaged to participate under its colors. Although other bicycle manufacturers had been engaging the stars to ride their wheels in races throughout the country for years I was passed up, because of my color, until this company engaged my services.

Mr. Johnson went a step farther than any bicycle manufacturer had ever gone before in his quest for championship honors for his bicycles. He also selected the late Harry Elkes, one of the greatest middle-distance riders that ever pedalled a bicycle, as my team-mate. And true to Mr. Johnson's predictions, to say nothing of his good judgment, I won the sprint title in 1900, and my good friend Harry Elkes won the laurels in the long distances.

This is the only instance in the history of bicycle racing in which a firm of bicycle manufacturers engaged two champions to ride their wheels simultaneously in the same season. Not only did Harry Elkes and myself win the championship laurels for both the sprints and distances that season we appeared under this company's colors, but we continued our victorious march until Elkes, my team-mate, was killed while riding in the 1901 season at Boston.

Manager Purtell of the New York branch of the Iver Johnson Company made the following statement to the New York newspaper men concerning my selection to ride for his company: "The Iver Johnson Company have pinned their faith in Major Taylor, the phenomenal colored rider, who won the championship in 1899. His almost unbroken string of victories, culminating in his winning of the American championship title, swayed us as we pondered on a selection to ride our models this year. We debated the value of Major Taylor and his victories from an advertising standpoint with some of the leading advertising agencies of the country.

"At first my company was rather skeptical because this was a very radical departure in advertising. However, we decided to give it a fair trial, and not only did we make Major Taylor's victories prominent in our display advertisement, but we kept all our agents constantly informed of his successes on our wheels. I am frank to say that the money we paid Major Taylor was the best investment we ever made. Not only was this made certain to me by the reports of our agents, but through the frequent orders that came direct to us specifying the type of wheel Major Taylor was riding."

Here is an extract from one of the Iver Johnson catalogues: "Major's career since riding the 'Iver Johnson' has been particularly successful. No one has been able to demonstrate superiority over him. In the spring of 1901 he defeated every rider who competed with him, in Europe, his tour being regarded as the most remarkable in the history of cycling.  This fact is all the more astonishing, when it is known that he has had to earn his title of 'champion' in the face of obstacles which do not beset the path of the average rider.

"Taylor has to his credit several world's records; briefly enumerated, they are:

1     Mile, standing start, 1:41 2/5; made in 1898.
1/4 Mile, paced, 20 sec.; made in 1899.
1/2 Mile, paced, 41 sec.; made in 1899.
1/2 Mile, unpaced, against time—55 2/5 sec.; made in 1900.
1     Mile, Special, paced, 1:19.
1/2 Mile, Special, paced, 40 1/5 sec.
1/3 Mile, Special, paced, 27 1/5 sec."

Harry D. Elkes began riding the Iver Johnson in November, 1900, and his successes dating from that time, have partaken of a national character; for in Europe, as well as in America, he has clearly demonstrated his right to the title of "Champion of pace followers."

Elkes has not only excelled in competition as a pace follower, but has made many World Records, briefly enumerated, the most important of these are:

Competition Paced Records:

8 to 14 miles, 16 to 17 miles, 21 to 24 miles, 26 to 39 miles, inclusive.
One Hour Competition, distance ridden, 39 miles, 1045 yards.
Against time, paced, 2 to 25 miles, inclusive.
Three Hour Competition, distance ridden, 97 miles, 1932 yards.

# CHAPTER XLI



Shortly after I had been crowned sprint champion of America at the close of the 1900 season I expressed an oft repeated desire for a match race with Tom Cooper before I closed my season's log. He was riding in Europe at the time and was very successful.

There were several reasons why I was especially anxious to meet Cooper. In the first place he was one of the prime movers in the effort that would have eliminated me from the bicycle tracks of the country in 1899, if it was successful. Secondly, he had drawn the color line against me in answer to my repeated challenges to him. Thirdly, the only match race that had ever been arranged between Cooper and myself fell through in the fall of 1899 because track officials decided the Milwaukee track on which we were to have ridden was not properly constructed.

So intent was I on getting a match race with Cooper that I decided to remain in training for the indoor season at Madison Square Garden and for the races on the old Park Square bicycle track, Boston. Meantime I took advantage of the opportunity to participate in a tour on one of the biggest vaudeville circuits in the country riding a series of "home-trainer" races against Charlie Murphy. My riding on the "home-trainer" tended to keep me in first-class physical condition. Through my work on this machine every day I felt that I would be able to step out against Cooper on a very short notice and give him the race of his life.

It was arranged that I would start my series of races on the "home-trainer" in my home town, Worcester, Massachusetts. I quote the following article from a metropolitan newspaper of the era:

"Vaudeville Attraction. Major Taylor and Charlie Murphy in 'Home-Trainer' Races. Major Taylor, national cycle champion of 1900, is to enter the field of vaudeville as have so many others who have gained fame and fortune in the athletic world. He will shortly make his début on the stage and with the assistance of his partner hopes to make a big hit.

"He will not attempt to star in his own company as did Eddie Bald when the Buffalo rider had his 'Twig of Laurel' on the road for a few short weeks. Major Taylor's vaudeville stunt will consist of riding 'home-trainer' races against Charlie Murphy whose mile-a-minute ride behind a locomotive in 1899 gave him world-wide prominence."

(157)

Charles R. Culver, manager of the Worcester, Mass., Colosseum, managed Murphy and myself on our vaudeville tour. Mr. Culver who was widely known in bicycle racing circles of the country readily agreed to one stipulation that I made—that I would not be asked to ride on Sunday. We had a very successful season on the "home-trainers," big crowds attending our performances in the theaters. Murphy was advertised as having ridden the fastest mile on record, while the billboards proclaimed I held the one-mile motor paced record, and all the records up to two miles on a circular track. By a strange coincidence I made my theatrical début in Worcester, and I shall never forget the rousing reception I got in my first appearance on the old Park Theater stage.

Thanks to the practice I obtained on the "home-trainer" I was in the best condition of my life on the eve of the races in Madison Square Garden.

That fall Floyd MacFarland wanted me to team up with him at the six-day races at the Garden. He told me that if I would agree to team up with him in the grind he would do most of the plugging, thus making it as light for me as possible, so that I would be fresh for the finishing sprint on the final night. I rejected this proposition, however, and insisted that MacFarland and I alternate mile after mile in the race. I did this despite the fact that I knew my going through with the program would undoubtedly injure my chances in the final sprint.

As MacFarland and I came to an agreement in this matter Mr. Fred Johnson of the Iver Johnson Company with which firm I was still under contract asked me not to participate in the six-day race. He said he was prepared to offer me a contract for the following season provided I would not start in the long grind, and in deference to his wishes I did not enter the event.

It was significant that MacFarland sought me out when he was choosing a partner for the six-day race. By no stretch of the imagination could he have been termed friendly to me, and my friends were elated when they found he had made overtures to me to pair up with him in the classic. However, the armistice between us was short lived as subsequent developments will indicate.

Nevertheless, on the eve of the long race at the Garden the lanky Californian not only wanted me to team up with him, but he submitted a proposition for me to join forces with him the following season in the course of which he planned a trip across the water that we might compete against all comers in the bicycle centers of Europe. When I turned down these race suggestions, MacFarland became peeved and then signed up the late Harry Elkes and the pair of them won the six-day grind. In fact, he was so worked up over my decision not to ride with him that he became more anxious than ever to have me dethroned as the sprint champion of the country. His campaign to this end covered the entire 1901 season, and brought about my failure to repeat my 1900 championship performances.

MacFarland figured that he and I could win the six-day race and that on the strength of victory we could dictate our terms to the officials of the European tracks in 1901. He told the newspaper men of New York that if I rode under his management I could defeat all of the champions of Europe, including the great Jacquelin, famous French champion, who was unquestionably the best sprinter in Europe. He stated further that he believed the champion of America also meant the champion of the world.

MacFarland was so sure that I would sign up with him for a tour of Europe in 1901 that he struck off an itinerary for my consideration. Being a hard-headed business man he was also satisfied that our invasion of the Continent would be a good paying investment. In the summer of 1900 he managed Tom Cooper on his trip through Europe and their efforts netted a tidy sum.

I was informed by MacFarland that the first prize in the Grand Prix at Paris was $2000, and that an equal sum was given to practically all of their big races over there. On top of that the rider gets more of the prize money across the water than he does in this country. While in Europe the training expenses of a rider are paid by the manufacturer under whose color he rides. In this country the rider has to meet them himself. On top of that European track-owners engaged regular trainers and rubbers for the riders whereas, in this country the rider had to carry a trainer with him at his own expense, which item included railroad and hotel outlays.

*A fair field and no favor to go out and try,*
*A square deal and the spirit to do or die.*
*A fair field and no favor—don't be a big bluff—*
*A square deal and fair play, now show your stuff.*

## CHAPTER XLII

### HOW I DEFEATED MY OLD RIVAL TOM COOPER—MADISON SQUARE GARDEN

At last the stage was set for one of my most desired races. I was pitted against the famous Tom Cooper of Detroit in a special championship match race over the mile route, best two in three heats for a purse of $500, winner take all. The event was featured on the opening night of the six-day bicycle race in Madison Square Garden in 1900. So anxious was I to race Cooper that I readily agreed to all of the conditions suggested by him with but one exception—that was that a loser's end of the purse be provided for. I insisted on a winner-take-all basis maintaining that the loser did not deserve a share of the purse, and eventually I carried the point.

Since Cooper had but recently returned from a very successful season throughout Europe I realized he would be in excellent fettle for his match race with me. To make doubly sure that I would be in top form for this classic I discontinued my vaudeville engagements on the "home-trainers" and put in two weeks of special training on the Ambrose Park track in Brooklyn.

If ever there were two riders on earth that I wanted to meet in match races above all others they were Eddie Bald and Tom Cooper. Since a match with the former was out of the question, because he drew the color line, my next best choice was Cooper. Now after three or four years of dickering and yearning my opportunity to meet him was at hand. When I signed the contract to race Cooper I was in perfect physical condition and was confident I could take Cooper into camp.

Earlier in the season Cooper and I had been signed to race a special championship match on the Milwaukee track. However, that event was called off when municipal inspectors declared the track unfit. In all my years of waiting to oppose Cooper in a match race that Milwaukee engagement was the first in which we were actually signed to an agreement. Our Madison Square race was, therefore, the first in which we had ever been pitted against each other in a special match.

I quote the following article from one of the New York papers relative to this special championship match race:

"Major Taylor, the Marvelous Colored Sprinter, Upholds His Supremacy. Defeats his old rival, Tom Cooper, in Straight Heats. Major Taylor by a clever jump on the eighth lap of the first heat gained a lead of ten yards on Tom Cooper, and beat him out badly at the tape in the first heat of their championship match race.

"The first heat was unpaced and both men held back at the pistol, shortly Cooper reluctantly took the lead, Taylor trailing until they entered the back stretch on the eighth lap. Then he suddenly dashed down the banking and took the pole and a lead of ten yards with it. The ex-champion pedalled pluckily and pulled up a few yards, but he could not catch and pass Taylor who won easily, time 3.06. There was tremendous shouting and cheering.

Tom Cooper—and trainer "Mother Webb"

"Taylor also won the second heat of his match with Cooper, but only after a great finish, which brought the large audience to its feet with excitement. By agreement a pacemaker was put in, Louis Grimm. Taylor caught his rear wheel and followed closely until the pacer dropped out at the end of the seventh lap, and then the real fight began. Struggle as he could Cooper was unable to pass Taylor. The white champion made his final effort at the bell. He drew up along side Taylor on the back stretch and they swung on to the stretch and over the tape with Cooper lapping Taylor's back wheel, Taylor having won the heat and the match in the time of 2.08 4-5. The colored champion was cheered wildly.

"Tom Cooper used very poor judgment in both heats. In the first he opened up a gap on the pole allowing Taylor to jump through and take the lead. In the second heat he permitted Taylor to have the lead on the last three laps and all Major Taylor had to do was to hold the position of advantage on the pole to the finish.  But it was a great race and a most popular victory."

As I tore over the finish line in the final heat of my race with Cooper my thoughts flashed to the night a comparatively short time previous when as a New York paper put it, "he electrified the immense throng in the same old garden by outsprinting the great Eddie (Cannon) Bald in a hot finish in his first professional race."

This race stands out in my memory as one of the greatest victories I ever won. . It is as fresh in my memory today as it was on the night of the championship match race with Tom Cooper in the old Madison Square Garden.

I clearly recall an incident that occurred as I was leaving my training quarters for the first heat of that great match race.  It centers about Tom Eck, the white-haired veteran and mentor, who was acknowledged trainer and manager of numerous bicycle champions in that era.  On this occasion he was handling Cooper.  I can see him now carrying Cooper's wheel on his shoulder toward the starting line.

As Eck passed my trainer and myself he called out to the former, Bob Ellingham, "Well, Bawb, Tawm will now proceed to hand your little darkey the most artistic trimming of his young life.  In this first heat Tawm is going to give the Major his first real lesson on the fine points of the French style of match racing.  Tawm has a fine assortment of brand new tactics, fresh from Paris, and if the Major will practice the strategy in this heat until he has it down fine, coupled with what he already knows about the game, he may in time be able to give Tawm a pretty smart race.  However, Bawb, I have cautioned Tawm that in the best interest of the sport and for the good of all concerned, not to beat the little darkey badly."

Of course this comment by Eck was designed solely to get me nerved up.  He felt that it would so upset me that I might possibly lose my head and make a false move or slip-up in the race thereby bringing about my downfall.  Eck's comments served an entirely different purpose, however, as it made me all the more determined and confident.  I smiled as I heard my trainer inform Eck as follows: "It is true, Mr. Eck, that Major Taylor has never raced in Paris and will, therefore, be obliged to ride this race on what he has been able to pick up on this side of the pond.  What he may lack in track strategy he will have to make up in gameness and speed.  However, he is always willing to learn and never lets an opportunity slip by to teach the other fellow a point or two if possible."  Cooper smiled confidently as he overheard the repartee between our two trainers and I reflected Cooper's broad grin.

The six-day riders were called off the track proper but continued riding on the flat surface inside the track. There was an understanding among them that there would be no attempt at lap stealing until the heat of the match race was over when they would be given the pistol signal to renew their six-day argument in earnest.

At the start of the first heat Cooper attempted to force me into the lead. After trying every trick he knew, including an assortment of French numbers, he gave it up for a bad job and took the lead and settled down to business.

I can recall every move he made in this heat as vividly as though it were run only yesterday. I actually measured the revolutions of his pedals in comparison with my own to determine what gear he had up. When I was satisfied that it was an 108-inch gear I could tell from experience just what tactics he would employ. My forecast was strengthened when I discovered he was using a seven-inch crank. I figured he was relying more upon the difference between his 108-inch gear and my 92-inch gear and his seven-inch crank as compared to my six-and-three-quarter-inch crank, to quote a jibe given by Cooper's trainer a few moments before "to teach me the fine points in the art of the French style of racing," rather than through a burst of speed. It was apparent to me that Cooper figured he had an edge on me through the size of gear he was riding as compared with mine together with the advantage he thought his crank held over mine rather than a display of speed and good judgment.

Cooper evidently figured that if he could get the jump on me down the steepest part of the banking, he should get his big gear wound up in fine style and I would never be able to get around him in the last lap and beat him to the tape. I knew that once he got that big gear rolling it would be a very difficult task for me to beat him out at the finish line. Therefore, as we rode I was very busy figuring out his plan of action and planning my campaign to meet it.

Sure enough with three laps to go Cooper gradually edged away from the pole toward the outside of the track. At the same time he began to pick up his sprint as he mounted the banking at a lively clip just after crossing the tape at two laps to go. This strategy Cooper planned would aid him materially in making his great plunge *à la Française* on entering the back stretch. However, I had him timed perfectly and beat him to it by jumping from low right into high speed so that by the time I reached the pole I was going at top speed. I gave him everything I had. The spectators cheering frantically.

I gained about ten or twelve lengths with only one and a half laps to go. When I saw I had Cooper hopelessly beaten and that it was unnecessary to extend myself further I was about to ease up, and then I suddenly recalled Tom Eck's sneering remarks about his warning

Cooper not to beat me too badly for the good of the sport. Riled by that taunt I kept right on tearing to the tape. Meantime Cooper sat up down the back stretch—he had been badly outgeneraled, outsprinted and outdistanced. It was not my usual custom to do business in this way. This was the first time I ever really tried to distance an opponent.

Shrewd old Tom Eck hadn't a word to say as he and Cooper walked to the latter's dressing room, neither did my trainer nor I.

As Cooper and I were called out to resume hostilities in the second heat, he looked nervous and pale. Eck looked worried but this time failed to utter a sound. Louis Grimm was put in as pacemaker and a very fine job he made of it. As the pistol barked I made a bid for his rear wheel and I held it for seven laps after which I went to the front and taking it easy watched Cooper closely from under my arm.

I saw every move he made and when he noted that I was not going to mount the banking he started to do so. As a matter of tactics and in order to keep him on the pole I started to sprint the moment he started up the banking. My move forced him to come along with me on the pole and as soon as he was back there I eased up again. Twice this trick was repeated and as Cooper sensed my strategy he made a desperate effort to jump past me. That was physically impossible as he could not pick up speed as quickly down on the pole with his big gear as I could with my smaller one.

So I kept him fighting furiously around on the outside of the track for a lap and a half. When he began to weaken I jumped for the tape which was then a lap away. My jump gave me about two lengths lead which advantage I maintained to the finishing line. In the excitement incident to that mad dash for the tape, the old Garden fairly ringing with thunderous cheers, I made a very serious error that came very nearly causing me the heat after all.

I made a mistake in the number of laps to go and sat up as I crossed the tape. As the bell clanged to designate the last lap, however, I realized my error and quickly regained my stride. Cooper meantime had not miscalculated on the number of the laps and he tore after me with a terrific burst of speed. We had a desperate neck-and-neck struggle for the honors throughout the entire lap. His big gear was now wound up in fine style but I managed to hold my advantage and led him across the tape by half a wheel's length. That margin settled the race and squared for all time my score against Tom Cooper. My principle grievance against Cooper centered about his strenuous efforts to have me debarred from the race tracks of the country in 1899. The drive being camouflaged cleverly to cover up its real cause, color prejudice, on the part of my rivals who realized I was their peer on a bicycle.

Had the purse been $5,000 instead of $500 it would have been a mere bagatelle compared with the supreme satisfaction that I felt over my defeat of Tom Cooper. If ever a race was run for blood this one was. Incidentally, world-wide prestige went hand in hand with the victory. Neither Cooper nor Eck offered to shake hands with me at the close of the race nor did they utter a word of congratulation. I have never seen a more humiliated pair of "Toms" in my life than were Cooper and Eck as they marched silently to their dressing room.

As a matter of fact, I was equally silent as Ellingham and I repaired to our dressing room. I had never indulged in boasting over my conquests either within the hearing of my opponents or elsewhere. I felt that real sportsmanship demanded that an athlete wear his laurels modestly. I know very well that some of the greatest riders of my day had a different idea about that, and I am also aware, that many of the present-day stars do not share my theory in this respect. It is still my belief, however, that no real champion in any line of sport could or would resort to such ungentlemanly conduct. But many times I have had all I could possibly do to refrain from handing out a bit of the old sarcasm.

Cooper was keenly disappointed at the outcome of our championship match race. Naturally he was anxious to win the $500 purse, but he was far more desirous of defeating me on this occasion as he had planned to retire after the race—provided he had administered a crushing defeat to me to mark the end of his brilliant racing career.

In response to a general demand on the part of the six-day bicycle enthusiasts in New York, the management of the Madison Square Garden signed me to race two exhibitions on the track while the grind was on. Apparently I had got the public fancy in my spectacular victory over the great Tom Cooper. So high was the enthusiasm of the moment that the management of the track practically permitted me to name my terms for the exhibitions. I rode the quarter of a mile in 2/5 of a second under the world's record and later covered the half mile in 4/5 of a second lower than record. One of the New York dailies commented as follows on my victory over Cooper:

"Major Taylor's Great Victory over Tom Cooper makes him Equal to the Great Jacquelin. Major Taylor's victory over Cooper places him on a par with the celebrated French rider, Jacquelin. The merits of the two have been compared as far as could be without an actual race. Jacqueln defeated Tom Cooper in a match race this summer in Europe, and had Cooper been able to defeat Taylor in the Garden the French champion would be considered faster than the 'Worcester Whirlwind.' "

My thrilling victory over Tom Cooper paved the way for my first invasion of Europe in 1901. Tom Cooper had made a very fine impression in Europe through his great riding in 1900. Therefore, the bicycle enthusiasts of the Continent were deeply interested in my welfare and whereabouts following my sensational victory over him in Madison Square Garden that winter. Hardly a day passed thereafter that I did not receive a cablegram asking my terms for a series of championship match races with the stars of Europe in 1901.

European riders who participated in the 1900 six-day race at Madison Square Garden were eagerly sought out by newspaper men upon their arrival home. It was apparent that they were anxious to get first-hand information on my riding ability. Very favorable comment caused track promoters all over Europe to seek my services for match races forthwith.

The following article was printed in a Paris sporting newspaper shortly after the 1900 six-day bicycle race in New York had become a matter of history:

"Jean Gougoltz and Other Foreign Stars Have Arrived in Paris. Contrary to the general rule of returned cyclists they declare that they were treated beyond expectation by the American riders. Robert Coquelle, the French newspaper man, who was with the invaders said upon his return to Paris that America is a great country and the riders are very fast. Major Taylor, he said, is built like a bronze statue. He simply played with Tom Cooper in their match race, and he will defeat every champion in Europe. He has signed a contract and is coming to Paris next spring."

It was arranged that I would race Jacquelin, the sprint champion of Europe, in a series of special matches. The first two to be held in Paris, May 16 and May 27. I was also signed to meet Willie Arend, champion of Germany, Thorwald Elleggarde, champion of Denmark, Momo, the champion of Italy, Grognia, champion of Belgium, Gougoltz, champion of Switzerland, and all of the leading sprinters of Europe. Other American invaders in Europe that season were Billy Stinson, Johnnie Nelson, and Harry Elkes, all of whom were motor pace followers.

# CHAPTER XLIII



Now that I had defeated all the topnotchers among the sprinters I drew some attention from the middle distance riders. But a few weeks elapsed between the time I defeated Tom Cooper in our special championship match and my signing to oppose Harry Elkes the peer of middle distance riders behind pace for a series of match races. He and Floyd MacFarland a fortnight previously won the six-day race in New York.

In this match I agreed to race Elkes for a purse of $500, winner take all, the first heat to be a five-mile pursuit race, the second a one-mile paced heat and the third, if necessary, to be decided between those events by the tossing of a coin.

Coming in the wake of our races in connection with the six-day grind at Madison Square Garden, Elkes and I were in top racing form. Country-wide interest was aroused in our special match race in view of the widely different types of riders entered. Elkes was easily the best middle distance rider in the country while I was rated as champion among the sprinters.

A Boston daily printed the following item relative to my match race with Harry Elkes in that city: "There is no end of talk concerning the match race between Major Taylor and Harry Elkes at the Park Square track tomorrow night. It is one that is sure to give great satisfaction to the public. It will be run off in two heats, possibly three. The first will be a one-mile sprint, single paced, which ought to be won by Taylor. The second will be a five-mile pursuit race in which Elkes should have a little the best of the argument. If each should win a heat, the toss of a coin will decide whether the third will be a one-mile sprint or a five-mile pursuit race. If Taylor should win the toss he will prefer the one-mile sprint; provided Elkes wins the toss he will choose the five-mile pursuit race. The match will be for blood as neither man can afford to have his reputation suffer by a defeat."

Again I quote from a Boston paper which printed the following article on the day following my match race with Harry Elkes:

"Major Taylor Defeats Harry Elkes. Worcester Whirlwind Passes Fast Bunch in Final of the Handicap from Scratch. Major Taylor won his match against Harry Elkes at Park Square Garden last night, but had no easy time doing it. In the one-mile heat, paced by Oscar Babcock, Taylor won through a sprint on the last lap and down the home stretch which enabled him to cross the tape a length ahead of Elkes.

"The second heat a five-mile pursuit race was won by Elkes. Taylor stopped riding in the third lap his rear tire having been wound too thickly with tape causing it to bounce and skid so badly that the 'Major' was obliged to give up the race. The last heat was a mile unpaced in which both men started from the tape. In this race Taylor again demonstrated his superiority, but Elkes was at his rear wheel when the tape was crossed. Major Taylor was cheered to the echo.

"The other big race of the event was the one-mile handicap professional in which Major Taylor, Bobby Walthour, Alex McLean, Harry Caldwell, Arthur Ross and Archie McEchren qualified. In the first heat Major was on the inside and at the turn into the back stretch rode on the flat floor and then shot ahead of McEchren and Ross crossing the tape first. McEchren lodged a protest with the referee, Bemis, claiming that Taylor had no right to go to the inside and that he should have stayed on the track. Major Taylor claimed that he could do nothing else as he was crowded off the track. The decision was reserved until the matter could be looked into more thoroughly."

A few days later another of the Boston dailies carried the following self-explanatory item:

"Referee's Decision Against Major Taylor. Major Taylor who finished first in the one-mile handicap from scratch at the Park Square Garden Tuesday night will get no part of the purse. The race was run off in heats, and immediately after the final, Taylor's riding was protested by the other contestants on the grounds that he violated the racing rules by passing on the inside instead of swinging around on the outside when passing the other contestants on the banking.

"Pending the decision the management of the races withheld payment· of the prize money. F. M. Bemis, a Boston newspaper man, was referee of the races and last night he announced his decision on the protest in which he declared that Major Taylor was guilty of a rule violation which disqualified him from the race. By the decision A. W. Ross will receive first money, McEchren second and Walthour third.

"The text of the decision is that Major Taylor was disqualified for violating one of the most important rules of track racing which forbids any rider from passing inside another rider, excepting in the home stretch. In the back stretch of the last lap, with McEchren racing on the black line marking the pole, Taylor passed him on the inside instead of on the right and took his place at the head of the line in such a manner as to endanger not only his own neck, but the safety of every man left in the race. If the champion is allowed to do this the same privilege must be given every other rider. It is this helter-skelter method of riding that this rule is intended to prevent. Taylor's defense was that he was in a pocket and that the only way out was to pass on the inside. But it is a dangerous precedent to establish that a rider may break one rule if others break another rule.

"When Major learned of the referee's decision he said that he was not surprised, because in his six years of racing he had only once been given the benefit of a close decision."

I regretted, however, that this rule had been rendered against me for it was the first time I had ever been disqualified for unfair riding. The riders did not want me in the handicap race in the first place. They felt that I had just won my match race with Harry Elkes which netted me $500 and that that should be enough for me. However, I didn't think that was sufficient reason to keep me out of it, so I started from scratch in the final and ran away from the back-mark men who were out to flag me, meaning to slow me up, and let the front markers get away. I sprinted like mad until I had caught the leaders with three laps to go, when the back bunch rushed up and quickly pocketed me.

The pace was so fast they realized that they could not retain their positions and hold me there. One rider on my right tried to bring me down with a bump that sent me flying off the track on to the flat floor entering the back stretch. It was only through skillful riding and a good break of luck that I managed to stay up. There was only one way out of my predicament. It called for quick thinking and action. Taking a long chance I dashed for the next turn and reached it a length ahead of McEchren and mounted the track taking the lead which I held until the tape was crossed.

It was the most frantic effort I ever made and had I failed in the attempt every rider would have come down with me and perhaps some one might have been badly hurt. Yet I would have been taking an equally desperate chance on the flat surface had I attempted to slow down before reaching the corner. At any rate I got away with it successfully and shall always remember the stunt as the most amazing feat I ever accomplished on a bicycle. Although I did not get credit for it from the officials the crowd appreciated it and I was given thunderous applause.

The referee's decision was another of those rank ones that I had handed me on numerous occasions. I soon got over it, however, as I was fast learning to accept them as part and parcel of the day's work.

On this occasion I again won two first places on the same program.

# CHAPTER XLIV

MY FIRST TRIUMPHANT INVASION OF EUROPE

In the short space of two months I participated in fifty-seven races in various European cities. In view of the fact that I refused to ride on Sunday one will readily see that my schedule called for almost one race a day while I was on the Continent. There wasn't one race in which I participated that could be called easy by the widest stretch of the imagination. It was one of the most strenuous campaigns that I ever took part in and this despite the fact that I had planned to compete in the championship circuit races in this country as soon as I arrived home from Europe.

Among the cities in which I rode against the champions of Europe were: Roubaix, Bordeaux, Nantes, Orléans, Paris, Toulouse, Agen, Lyons, France; Verviers, Antwerp, Belgium; Berlin, Hanover, Leipzig, Germany; Turin, Milan, Italy; Copenhagen, Denmark; and Geneva, Switzerland.

Among the riders whom I opposed in my sweep through Europe, which compares in a measure with the recent trip through this country by Paavo Nurmi, the great Finnish runner, were: Edmond Jacquelin, champion of France; Quivy, one of the best French riders; Dutrieu and Fouaneau also of France; Thorwald Elleggarde, champion of Denmark; Willie Arend, champion of Germany; Louis Grognia, champion of Belgium; Charles Gascoyne, champion of England; Palo Momo, champion of Italy; Muringer, one of the topnotchers of Germany; Ferrari and Bixio two of the greatest sprinters in Italy; Van den Born who was recently defeated by Grognia for the championship of Belgium which Van den Born had formerly held.

Other well-known riders of the day were: Poulain, who became champion of France in 1902; Marteles, former champion of France, Bonnevie, Coutenete, Dangla, Chodeau, LeVeler, Marsollies, all great French riders, and the famous French tandem team, Lambrecht-Legarde; Protin, former champion of Belgium; Huber, former champion of Germany; Crause, a great German sprinter; Sidel, former champion of Germany; Cornelli, former champion of Italy; Anzani, former champion of Italy and now world famous as a builder of airplanes; Dei, former champion of Italy, now a bicycle manufacturer; Tommosillo, former champion of Italy; Gougoltz, champion of Switzerland; Sid Jenkins, the British champion.

I shall never forget my first race in Europe. It took place in Berlin on April 8, 1901, and the distance was one kilometer, and all hands started from scratch. The German champion Arend won

( 170 ) "

this race, Elleggarde champion of Denmark was second and I finished third.

My greatest handicap on this occasion was the cold weather as I was always at my best when it was extremely hot. On top of that drawback I arrived in Berlin the day preceding the race and was unable to take a practice sprint on the track until the day of the race. I also found myself at a disadvantage in not being able to speak the

WILLY AREND, the German Champion

language of the country—this being a novel experience for me since the race was run according to French tactics. This meant loafing until the last two hundred or three hundred yards when a furious sprint for the tape was the order. It allowed considerable loafing until it was time for the jump. This enabled my opponents to confer as they rode the race and make their plans out in the open because they knew I could not understand them.

No sooner had Arend crossed the finish line to win the race than the greatest demonstration I had ever seen on a bicycle track took place. He was presented a monster horseshoe of roses after which the officials, the band, and the public filed out on to the track in perfect order. One section of the crowd carried Arend's wheel while others bore the champion on their shoulders. The band played the "Watch on the Rhine" while the entire gathering sang the words of the German national anthem as they made a complete circuit of the track. I added my bit to the festive occasion by shaking hands with Arend as I congratulated him warmly on his splendid victory. Down in my heart, however, I felt that it would not be long before the tables were reversed with Arend seeking me out to shake my hand as he congratulated me over leading him across the finishing line.

My chance to even up the score with Arend came a few days later

Start of the Final of the International Championship Race

on the same track and I trained as I never had trained before for my come-back stunt. Besides Arend and myself the promoters secured Sidel another great German rider and Elleggarde, the Danish champion, to ride in this four-cornered International Championship race. My three opponents on this occasion were all great sprinters and were in excellent physical condition.

On the day of the race the weather was all that one could wish for and my form was vastly improved in the intervening week. It was agreed that the race would be decided on points. I won the first heat scoring one point on Arend who finished second, one point above Elleggarde who was third while Sidel was last. Elleggarde, Arend and myself lined up for the final. In the deciding heat I julled a neat little trick on the field that worked out perfectly. I had my trainer pace off about one hundred yards from the tape down the home stretch and make a mark in the sand along side the edge of the track with his foot to mark the spot. True to my calculations my three opponents started to sprint for the tape with almost two laps to go.

That was just what I wanted them to do. They thought I was going to make my jump from the spot that my trainer had made in the sand and they planned to speed me by it so fast that I would be unable to start my jump therefrom. When I pulled frantically for the last lap they had already sprinted a full lap and as we reached the last turn I made my jump. After a most furious effort I had won by about two lengths.

The applause that greeted me was as great as that accorded Arend a few days previously when he defeated me. The "Star Spangled Banner" never sounded sweeter than it did on this occasion, the band playing it as I rode my lap of honor around the track. Arend, Elleggarde and Sidel congratulated me as did thousands of American admirers who appeared at the track to cheer for me.

One week later I made my début in Verviers, Belgium, the home of Louis Grognia, the champion of that country. It was a championship match race between Grognia and myself. I won the first heat after a desperate fight in the last two hundred fifty yards. Grognia won the second heat and I took the final and the race.

In the second heat an incident occurred that had never before fallen my lot in my racing career. I had forced Grognia into the lead and was watching him closely. I allowed him to mount the banking on leaving the tape in the final lap and even permitted him to start his jump down the banking first, feeling certain that I could beat him to the tape even after giving him those advantages. When we reached the pole he had a length's lead on me which he increased to another before he reached the tape beating me by about two good lengths.

Grognia's defeating me in this heat gave me the surprise of my life and incidentally threw a scare into me that I shall never forget. I was dumbfounded as I realized all too well that Grognia had gained on me in the home stretch, a feat that no opponent of mine in my years of racing had ever been able to do. The thought kept running through my mind that if Grognia defeated me in the third and final heat of this race in the same manner my invasion of Europe might just as well end then and there. My chief objective on my trip to the Continent was a race with the great Edmond Jacquelin, who had acquired his title as champion of Europe by setting back all of the champions I was to do battle against, and should one of them lead me home in the interrim, the zest would naturally be out of our big match race. With these facts in mind one may well realize I was completely upset by Grognia's terrific sprint which enabled him to win the second heat.

As we were called out for the final heat I had my mind all made up as to the style of race I was going to ride. In the breathing spell between the second and third heats I delved into my bag of cleverest tricks and tactics and extracted therefrom my outstanding favorites.

I finally decided that I would ride practically the same style of race in the final heat that I followed in the second with one exception— I made up my mind to jump off the banking first. This strategy enabled me to reach the tape first, a little more than a length ahead of Grognia. I breathed a sigh of relief as I rode my lap of honor. It was one of the most trying races that I had ever contested in Europe. However, I felt amply repaid as the Belgians gave me a splendid ovation despite the fact that I had dethroned their idol, Grognia, who was the last stumbling block between Jacquelin and myself.

Louis Grognia—The Belgium Champion

# CHAPTER XLV



After having competed in ten races in the various sections of Europe I was called upon for the feature event of the tour—the match race with the French champion Edmond Jacquelin. This race of races was held at the "Parc du Princess" in Paris on May 16, 1901.

At the time of this match I felt I was in excellent physical condition for the big fuss and desired only a warm day for the race. I was doomed for a disappointment, however, because the day was cold and raw and despite the fact that I wore an extra heavy sweater I shivered as I took my warming-up trips over the track. The fates had also decreed that I was to be beaten on this occasion by the great Jacquelin and I took my reverse gracefully. I offered no excuses.

EDMOND JACQUELIN—Champion of France

Although Jacquelin defeated me in our first meeting I learned a very valuable lesson while he was turning the trick. That was that Jacquelin's well-known mental hazard (that deadly jump) through which he gained his margin of victory in most of his races availed him naught when he pulled it on me. From experience I learned that try

as he might Jacquelin couldn't jump away from me and in each of
our heats I was right at his rear wheel as we crossed the finishing line.
Incidently, I realized that Jacquelin was as good a rider as I had heard
him proclaimed and that with a warmer sun and balmier air I could
have given a far better account of myself.

At the conclusion of the second and deciding heat of our match
race Jacquelin astonished me by his childish antics.  He was so carried

MAJOR TAYLOR—Champion of America

away with his victory over me that he lost his head completely and
thumbed his nose at me immediately after crossing the tape all the
way around the track.  As I stood bewildered by Jacquelin's actions
his thousands of friends and admirers poured out of the grandstands
and carried him about the track on their shoulders.  In all my ex-
perience on the tracks of this country and Europe I had never before
suffered such humiliation as Jacquelin's insult caused me.

However, Jacquelin's conduct was to react as a boomerang.  I was
hurt to the quick by his unsportsmanlike conduct and resolved then
and there that I would not return home until I had wiped out his
insult.  My opportunity to square the balances came in a fortnight
and I did little else but plan for that race in the interim.  I made up
my mind that I would lead Jacquelin home in this championship match

race by such a margin that there would be no doubt, even in his mind, as to who was the better rider.

So on May 27 I had planned my campaign in a way that I figured would bring the best results. I was in prime condition for this race and was still further favored with a hot day. So pleased was I at the weather conditions that I felt this was going to be my day.

Upwards of thirty thousand eager, impatient bicycle race enthusiasts

Start of First Heat of Second Grand Challenge Match

greeted Jacquelin and I with a storm of applause as we came out to face the starter. The Frenchman had his same arrogant smile as he mounted his wheel. As we rode slowly from the tape in the first heat there was great cheering. After some maneuvering Jacquelin and I tried to force each other into the lead. In so doing both of us came to a dead stop. We were practically side by side, Jacquelin being slightly ahead. Balancing a few moments, I backed slowly half a revolution of my crank until I brought myself directly behind Jacquelin. That's just where I wanted to be. The grandstands were now in a frenzy. Realizing I had out-maneuvered him on this score Jacquelin laughed out-right and moved off in the lead prepared for business.

I was so satisfied that I could bring him into camp on this occasion that I again allowed him to ride his own race. I played right into his hands and actually permitted him to start his famous jump from his favorite distance, about two hundred fifty yards from the tape. However, I was very careful to jump at the same instant and the sprint down that long straight stretch must have been magnificent. Jacquelin was four lengths behind when I dashed across the tape. The applause was deafening.

Twenty minutes later we were called out for our second heat. It proved to be the final heat, as per my plans. I worked in a bit of psychology after both of us had mounted and were strapped in. I reached over and extended my hand to Jacquelin and he took it with a great show of surprise. Under the circumstances he could not have refused to shake hands with me.

I knew from the expression on his face that he was well aware

That Bewildering Hand Shake—Start of Second and Last Match

of the fact that my hand-shake was a demonstration of sarcasm pure and simple. My motive was to impress on Jacquelin that I was so positive that I could defeat him again that this was going to be the last heat. Followers of boxing will recognize my action as a parallel to what happens at the boxers' meet at the start of the final round.

As the French idol gathered the full significance of my gesture he mumbled something, shrugged his shoulders, and set his jaw. His sneering smile disappeared and a frown encompassed his face.

No sooner had the starter's gun sent us away than Jacquelin seriously accepted the lead without the usual jockeying. However, as we came to the last quarter I took the lead and with two hundred fifty yards left to go we tore off the steep banking together, and as we entered the home stretch and dashed for the tape, I kicked away from him—the resentment I bore towards Jacquelin for the insult he offered me

Finish of Revenge Match

serving to pace me as I never had been paced before.  When I crossed
the finish line Jacquelin was again four lengths behind.

As I crossed the tape I quickly pulled a small, silk American flag
from my belt and waved it vigorously in front of the vulgar Jacquelin
while we circled the track.  Meantime the people were howling their
approval and tossing their hats into the air as I deftly turned the tables

My  "Military"  Salute

on the French hero. It appeared that the vast audience, although
stunned for the moment by my victory over their idol, were delighted
to have me take some of the conceit out of him. They were also
elated at the method I pursued to even up the insult he had offered
me at the close of our first match. Jacquelin was severely censored by
the press and public for his ungentlemanly conduct. He made a
gesture that was merely a military salute, so I thought it only fair and
quite proper to return my salute in this manner as ample revenge for
his insult.

Meantime the band struck up the "Star Spangled Banner" as I
rode my lap of honor with a big bouquet of roses on my shoulder
which were symbolic of my victory. Hundreds of Americans poured
onto the track and gave me a splendid ovation as did thousands of
natives, men and women. This was my greatest triumph in Paris.

## CHAPTER XLVI

THE HARDEST FOUGHT MATCH RACE OF MY CAREER—AGEN, FRANCE

From Paris I journeyed to Copenhagen where I met Thorwald Elleggarde, the sensational Danish champion, in his home town in a championship match race. He was the peer of the stars of Europe in open competition while Jacquelin was the king of the field in match races. Elleggarde won the world's sprint championship on several successive occasions prior to my match race with him. Arend the German crack was possibly more brilliant than Elleggarde but the latter was the most consistent performer among the European stars. Although I arrived in Copenhagen only a day before my race with the great Dane and so had little time to get accustomed to the track, which was a third of a mile and built of cement, I had no fear of the outcome. Nevertheless, I was in my best form as usual. Elleggarde won the first heat, I took the second while the big Dane captured the third and the match.

There was a tremendous attendance at this race the weather being well-nigh perfect. Notwithstanding the fact that the first heat was called for nine o'clock P. M. the use of artificial lighting about the track was superfluous. I recall that the track, thanks to the midnight sun, was lighted almost as clearly at midnight as it would be at midday.

In the first heat, being unaccustomed to the track, I forced matters with Elleggarde a bit too soon and was beaten by inches to the tape. There was a wild demonstration on the part of the Danes present, so overjoyed were they at his victory over me. However, I reversed the tables by winning the next heat by a length after a terrific sprint right over the tape. The big crowd awaited breathlessly for the final heat anticipating another hectic duel on that last lap.

However, these Danish people got a thrill as Elleggarde and I rode on to the last lap that they had not looked forward to. As we swung onto the back stretch I started my jump and was just kicking past him when my rear tire blew out with a bang and I went down with a crash. Elleggarde hesitated for a moment as though making sure that I was down for the count and then dashed for the tape for all he was worth, evidently fearing that I might remount and tear after him. Since my feet were strapped to the pedals I could not free myself and had to be content with raising myself on one elbow and watching the big Dane sprint like mad for the tape.

The thought went through my mind at the moment that Elleggarde had displayed a very poor brand of sportsmanship under the circumstances.

Right then and there a feeling sprang up between us and it continued to grow more and more bitter as time went on.   Our sentiments as a result of this fluke race brought about a revenge match on the famous Agen (France) track in which I was the victor.

It was the consensus of opinion among sports writers of Europe that as a matter of sportsmanship Elleggarde should have volunteered to ride the final heat over in our Copenhagen match race.   Their

THORWALD ELLEGGARDE—Danish Champion

criticism of his refusal to do so hurt the big Dane and brought about our being signed up for a return match which would, the newspaper men claimed, determine the real victor of the Copenhagen race and the Agen match at one and the same time.

Just three weeks to a day from the date of the Copenhagen fiasco Elleggarde and I hooked up in our revenge match race at Agen.   It proved to be the hardest match race that I ever competed in.   Elleggarde was determined to wipe out the stain of his fluke victory over me in Copenhagen, while I was out to prove that I would have led him home in that race only for the accident to my tire, had he been sportsman enough to ride it over again after I had been painfully hurt in the last lap.

The Agen track was a beautiful course, built of concrete and measured three laps to the mile.   Ideal racing weather greeted Elleggarde and I as we went to the starting line, while the immense throng gathered about the track gave us a rousing reception.   It was apparent that all hands wanted the better man to win this momentous race and I knew that the French bicycle enthusiasts would acclaim the winner regardless of whom he proved to be, provided he won the race on merit alone.

The first heat was paced by single riders—which was just to my liking. However, I was greatly surprised when Elleggarde led me home in this dash by six or eight inches in a manner that left no

Start of the Deciding Heat of the most bitterly fought Match Race I ever contested

doubt in the minds of all who saw the race as to who was who. After a brief rest we came out for the second heat which was unpaced. This time Elleggarde appeared to be more confident and determined than I had ever seen him before. I decided to ride a different style of race this time and we fought it out for a full lap, neck and neck, with a heart-breaking finish down the home stretch and right over the tape. I had just about the same advantage over Elleggarde in this heat that he had on me in our first heat, not more than half a foot. There was great excitement.

Then came the most trying test of all, the one that would tell the story, and settle for all time the question of supremacy between Elleggarde and myself. Incidentally, I felt positive that this heat would decide two matches simultaneously—my race with Elleggarde in Copenhagen as well as the current one and judging from the way he rode this race in Agen he must have felt the same way. It was a grudge fight and there was no friendly hand-shaking either before or after our heats on this track. The enormous throng was cheering frantically as we came out.

In this third heat I allowed Elleggarde to take the lead for the first two laps. Then I suddenly jumped past him just coming up to the bell on the last lap. After taking command of the situation I eased up a trifle until he challenged me, then I made my final jump for the tape. He had me timed just about right. It was anybody's race down the back stretch, around the turn, down the home stretch and right over the finish line. It was a savage fight but I had the advantage again by about six or eight inches. The cheering was deafening. I can never forget it.

We were nearly exhausted at the close of this heat despite the fact that we were both in perfect physical condition. Judging from the physical expression on Elleggarde's face, and from subsequent events this race must have settled for all time any hope he might have had of ever defeating me in a single man-to-man race. As a matter of fact we met a number of times after that gruelling race but I never again experienced a great deal of difficulty in defeating him. It is apparent to me now that my victory over Elleggarde on the Agen track on that eventful day broke his morale as far as I personally was concerned. The outcome of this great match proved that it was the hardest match race that I ever won.

Soon after my races with Elleggarde I jumped to Berlin where I defeated the champions of four countries in a five-cornered international match race at 1000 meters. It was arranged that we would ride three heats, winner to be determined on a point basis.

The field included Momo, the Italian champion, Elleggarde, champion of Denmark, Protin, Champion of Austria, Arend and Huber, the premier sprinters of Germany, and myself.

From Berlin I next went to Leipzig where I won a three-cornered match race over Willie Arend, champion of Germany, and Huber, the former champion of Germany. At Antwerp I defeated Grognia, the champion of Belgium, Momo, the Italian champion and Protin, the champion of Austria, in a four-cornered international match race. At Toulouse I scored another victory over Van den Born, the former champion of Belgium, and Cornelli, the former champion of Italy.

In a match against the tandem team composed of Grognia and Prevost at Bordeaux I was defeated, but won out against Lambrecht and Legarde, another tandem team in Lyons. On this same occasion I won the 1000-meter handicap event from a field of stars which included Lambrecht, Legarde, Grognia, Prevost, Marteles, Van den Born, Cornelli and others. At Geneva I rode my final engagement of that season and defeated Gougoltz and Henneburn another famous tandem team.

My first European tour had proven even more successful than the trip made by Arthur Augustus Zimmerman, my famous predecessor, when he was champion of America. All told I competed in 16 cities, most of them being the capitals of European countries, and was successful against the champions and leading riders of six countries. I was defeated in only two single man-to-man match races, Jacquelin and Elleggarde turning the tricks as has been explained. Incidentally, my first invasion of Europe, in 1901, netted me 42 firsts, 11 seconds, 3 thirds, and 1 fourth prize.

# CHAPTER XLVII



Despite the fact that I took the first available boat home I was unable to take part in the opening of the National Circuit on July 4, 1901, at the Manhattan Beach track. As a matter of fact I did not start riding until the latter part of July, by which time the fight for the championship honors for that season was well under way, and my rival Frank Kramer had rolled up a lead which I found it impossible to overcome in the balance of the season. In my races that year it appeared to me that rival riders were more jealous and hostile toward me than ever, possibly due to my successes in Europe. I ascertained that the riders headed by Floyd MacFarland had made a pact which was aimed to block me from becoming champion of America again. As subsequent developments will show they lived up to the letter of their agreement, and I was unable to win the laurels again.

I was eliminated from the 1901 campaign for the championship of the country only after a series of the most bitterly fought contests in the history of the sport in this country. One of these was the half-mile championship race which I rode on the Manhattan Beach track on the very day I landed from Europe. It almost resulted in a near riot among several of the riders, their trainers and managers. The trouble centered about the foul tactics employed by the field to bring about my defeat, the tremendous gathering in the grandstand showing their disapproval of the tactics used against me in no uncertain manner. Only a few moments before the big assembly had given me a remarkable ovation as a testimonial of the good work I had done in Europe the preceding weeks.

Floyd MacFarland of San Jose, California, was the ringleader of the gang of riders who had sworn among themselves to bring about my dethronement as champion of America at all costs. I have always been taught that one should "speak naught but good of the dead." I have also heard it said that there are ofttimes circumstances that justify comment and criticism even at the expense of the dead. I shall always remember the late Floyd MacFarland as the instigator and leading perpetrator of practically all the underhanded scheming that brought about my failure to win the championship laurels that year or thereafter.

At every race in which MacFarland's name and mine appeared on the program, he made it a point to stir up a conspiracy against me. Even when he was not scheduled to compete in a heat with me he would get busy amongst the other riders in my heat and organize combinations which aimed to prevent me from winning. If I were fortunate enough to qualify in the heats, MacFarland would line up those who were opposed to me in the final and instruct them, many times with a threat to win, even if it were necessary to throw me in order to bring about that result. Many times the toss of a coin would decide which one would bring me down.

Knowing of this diabolical scheme on the part of my opponents I took great delight in outgeneralling and outcycling them and breezing across the tape ahead of such combinations. To me this was the sweetest revenge a man could enjoy. I recall clearly a championship race at Manhattan Beach track in which I defeated Frank Kramer despite the foul methods pursued by the field against me.

I quote from a New York paper concerning that race as follows:

"Major Taylor Defeats Frank Kramer in Championship Race. Yesterday was a red letter day for the track at Manhattan Beach. Never in the history of cycling has there been an afternoon more filled with finer sport. It was replete with record breaking and hot finishes, surprises and exciting incidents.

"The program began with the Grand Circuit championship of the half-mile race in which Frank Kramer, Major Taylor, Willie Fenn, and Owen Kimble, Taylor's bitterest rival, were entered. Kimble led Taylor in the trial heat of the first semi-final heat, the colored boy being apparently content to take second place so long as he got into the final.

"In the second semi-finals, two riders each, and only one to qualify, Kramer beat out Hausman, and Major Taylor ran right away from Kimble leaving the final a duel between the two closest rivals Frank Kramer and Major Taylor.

"They made a real French-style race of it, the first part being ridden very slowly and jockeying, and at times almost standing still, but eventually Taylor forced Kramer into the lead but he pulled up abreast of him as they entered the last turn down the back stretch, and in the sprint for home the colored boy reached the line two feet in front of Kramer. He was loudly cheered for his splendid victory which was clean and decisive.

"As a result of Major Taylor's victory over his rival a storm of indignation swept through the camp of a clique of white riders with whom Taylor is, of course, unpopular. A relative of Kramer's went to Taylor and offered to bet him $500 that Kramer could beat him, but Taylor said that he never bet, that he was in the game to ride for someone else's money and not against his own.

"William A. Brady accepted the challenge in behalf of Major Taylor and Floyd MacFarland came to the front as the man who would back Frank Kramer, and for a half hour there was a futile argument with huge rolls of money being used in the gestures in front of the grandstand. Kramer wanted to ride in mile heats unpaced but Taylor, as challenged party, wanted a paced mile (single paced) and an unpaced mile, the toss of a coin to decide the style of the third heat if deemed necessary. Taylor finally gave in and the forfeit was posted.

"Brady then offered a purse of $1000 for the race aside from his bet and named Wednesday night, August 7, as the date. Kramer refused to ride at night and the money was drawn down. The bitter feeling between the two riders is so unmistakable, however, that the pair will undoubtedly clash before very long. Owen Kimble said afterwards that he is perfectly willing to meet Taylor in a match race at any time."

Another fiercely-fought contest took place shortly after that Manhattan Beach affair at Madison Square Garden. It was a half-mile championship race with only two men in the final which was in keeping with the new ruling of the bicycle governing body of the country that season. This edict practically assured all such races ending in two-men matches between the two fastest men on the track.

The scheming MacFarland as usual supposed that he had everything arranged for Kramer to win the final of this race without effort on his part. But unfortunately for Kramer, MacFarland, et al, Willie Fenn mussed things up by winning, so that Kramer failed to qualify in his semi-final heat. Then MacFarland got busy among the riders starting in my heat of the semi-final, arguing that the only chance "to trim the nigger" was to pocket him and hold him there. MacFarland argued that it was very simple to do this on a small ten-lap track such as the old Madison Square Garden contained. The riders did as they were ordered to do up to the seventh lap, but at three laps to go I upset MacFarland's well-laid plans and slipped through the pocket and won by several lengths, defeating Wilson, Kimble and Gascoyne amid tremendous applause.

The pace was hot from the start and at five laps to go I intentionally slipped into a pocket remaining there until we came up to the seventh lap. Then, crouching as low as possible, I dropped back about a half length and at the psychological moment I kicked through like a flash. Once out in front I sprinted for all there was in me, winning by a good five or six lengths. I could hear the audience roar with delight when I jumped out of that pocket and I was given a mighty ovation at the conclusion of the race. It was unusual under the circumstances but there were no complaints filed by the other riders against me or on the racing tactics I employed in this race.

Tom Cooper, who was also shut out of his heat, together with MacFarland, who did not ride that night because of injuries received a short time before, got their heads together in a determined effort to bring about my defeat in this race. No sooner was the race over than MacFarland started to berate the riders in the final for allowing me to get out of the pocket after once having me boxed in so perfectly.

"And you call yourselves bicycle riders," he said sneeringly. "Call that bicycle racing, do you, huh?"

"Well, perhaps not," said one of them, "but you call yourself a bicycle rider, don't you Mac?"

When this last question was asked MacFarland interposed with a statement that he had forgotten more about bicycle racing than his audience would ever know.

"If you know so much about racing tactics—," continued the rider. "Well, we all saw him get out of a pocket on you the same way last week. Why did you let him get out? Why the h—— didn't you hold him in?"

The enlongated Californian seemed suddenly to lose his speech.

Relative to this race in the old Madison Square Garden I print the following article from a New York newspaper:

"Major Taylor Gains More Points. Wins the Half-Mile Championship in Madison Square Garden. The real interest of last evening's bicycle racing program in Madison Square Garden centered in the half-mile championship race. The starters included Major Taylor, Kramer, Cooper, Fenn and Wilson. The new plan of starting four men in the trial heats so as to bring the final down to a duel, or practically a match race of two, proved very successful. The second semi-finals of the final are just the same as match races. Each of the heats of this event aroused great enthusiasm among the spectators, they brought the great crowd to their feet.

"In the trials Cooper and Hausman were shut out by Kimble and Gascoyne, while Newhouse and Caldwell were shut out by Taylor and Wilson, while Fenn and Kramer shut out Tom Butler. Jenkins was left in the lurch by Fisher and Freeman. In the first semi-final, Major Taylor, Wilson, Kimble and Gascoyne started. An attempt was made to pocket the Negro, but he was too wary, getting out in front three laps from home he made a burst of speed that opened a gap of several lengths between him and the others, and won by about six lengths.

"Tom Cooper, in his racing togs, and the invalided MacFarland, in his street clothes, were standing on chairs watching the race. It was a rare spectacle to watch them. How they shouted with satisfaction when they saw Major Taylor pocketed in his heat, but the manner in which their jaws dropped when they saw the 'Major' shoot out of the pocket to the front was more interesting to watch than the race itself, that is, to those who know the feeling that exists in the camp of the other circuit riders.

"In the second semi-final heat Fenn, Kramer and Fisher started and to the surprise and disappointment of everybody who hoped to see Frank Kramer and Major Taylor fight it out in the final, Kramer was shut out with Fisher. Kramer sprinted on the outside trying to pass Fenn but failed and was beaten for second place by a foot.

"In the third semi-final heat Taylor and Wilson met first and Taylor did just as he had done in every other heat. He remained behind until three laps were left to go, then he dashed to the front and won by a clean length. Fisher and Freeman made a grand duel of it. They started with loafing tactics, but Freeman caught Fenn napping at about three laps from home and jumped him for a lead of five yards or more. Fenn did show his sprinting ability, however, going after him, he nailed him at about fifty yards from the tape and beat him out by about six inches. This brought the final down to a match race between Willie Fenn and Major Taylor.

"The latter started out to make a slow race of it and Fenn began by running up and down the banking forcing Taylor into the lead. But when he did get ready the colored boy jumped to the front with a rush. Fenn was wide awake, however, and he made as good a race of it as Frank Kramer did at Manhattan Beach, but he could not catch and pass the colored rider before the tape was reached, and Major Taylor won by a length. It was an exciting finish that brought the crowd to its feet again cheering wildly. MacFarland was a worse licked man than Fenn, so keen was his disappointment at being unable to place Kramer in the final against Taylor."

# CHAPTER XLVIII



Soon after I had won that great race in Madison Square Garden I was pitted against practically the same field at Providence. In the final of the one-third-mile circuit championship race the starters were Frank Kramer, Iver Lawson, Jimmie Bowler and myself. In this event the same old bitterness evidenced itself as it did in every race I competed in following my return from Europe in the summer of 1901. I made all of my races a continuous battle, not so much of speed as of wits—the odds being against me as I had to work single-handed against all of the others who combined to bring about my defeat.

As was his custom MacFarland had conspired with my opponents in the race and given them their instructions as to how to trim me. It was apparent to me, however, that the stars tossed Mac's instructions into the discard and used their own judgment in the race.

They made no attempt to pocket me this time, but instead, Lawson, who was supposed to be assisting Kramer to win, became confused at my tactics. He got his wires crossed with Kramer and both became upset as Bowler suddenly came up with a mad rush on the inside and could have gone right through, but he hesitated. When he made up his mind it was too late as I had jumped around the outside. Lawson and Kramer ran me high up in the banking as we were entering the last turn down the back stretch. I raced for dear life around the turn, into the home stretch and over the tape with a good foot to spare, with Kramer second. I finished up quite near the grandstand while Kramer was far down on the pole.

The crowd was on its feet screaming, "Taylor, Taylor!" Simultaneously MacFarland with his group of schemers who were standing near the finish line, jumped up and began shouting wildly for "Kramer, Kramer!" The judges had decided I won but MacFarland and his henchmen were giving such a demonstration that confusion reigned about the officials.

When Kramer rode up all of the riders headed by MacFarland rushed up to him and carried him over to the officials, some of whom were still deliberating on a decision. I stood off to one side to note what influence MacFarland's underhanded tactics would have on the officials. They hesitated for some time, the crowd meantime continued screaming for me while MacFarland and his gang made the air ring for Kramer.

Finally the judges weakened and called it a dead heat.  I suppose they thought that was the easiest way out of the predicament for them. The spectators, however, who sat nearest to the tape and most of the people in the grandstand believed I had won and the dead heat decision was met with a storm of hisses.

Not content with having been awarded a dead heat, some of Mac-Farland's gang protested against me claiming I had teamed with Bowler in the race.  I smiled at this proceeding as it was an old trick of Big Mac's.  Whenever a rider in my heat refused to work with him or his associates against me he always claimed they were working with me, provided I won.  So Kramer protested and the referee ordered the race run over between Kramer and I, but MacFarland refused to allow Kramer to ride it.  As soon as the tumult had died down I stepped over to the referee and demanded that the race be run over immediately between Kramer and myself.  I stipulated that the winner take first and second money and the points in the champion-ship table.  I also offered to make a side bet of a sum equivalent to the sum of the first and second prize money and suggested it be ridden over right there and .then.

However, the race did not take place.  The officials did not take very long to decide that question, they had no objection to seeing an-other good race thus giving the public an extra run for their monev, but the scheming MacFarland turned the proposition down pronto. He insisted Kramer's protest stand, meantime the prize money was tied up for several weeks.  The protest went up to A. G. Batchelder, chairman of the racing board of the N. C. A., who threw it out and ordered the money equally divided.

Concerning this "dead heat" one of the Providence papers printed the following article:

"Major Taylor and Frank Kramer Ride Dead Heat at the Vele-drome Track.  Major Taylor and Frank Kramer rode a dead heat on the Veledrome track last night in the final of the one-third-mile circuit championship race before a large audience.  This event was not only the best race on the program but it was the most exciting race ever witnessed on the local track.

"When the referee's decision was announced Frank Kramer entered a protest which is to go to the N. C. A. officials on the grounds that there was team work between Major Taylor and Jimmie Bowler which did not give him a chance.  Lawson finished third and Bowler fourth.  The time for the final was :38.

"The one-mile professional handicap race was won by Jimmie Moran, the famous Chelsea milkman, who made a runaway of it in the final with Jacobson second, Lawson third and George Collette fourth.  Neither Major Taylor or Frank Kramer started in this race.

Patsy Keegan won the mile consolation race in which Kimble and Stevens went down but were not injured."

Such a remarkable demonstration following the dead heat decision was another attest of the Providence sporting public's desire to see me get fair play.

A few nights later I again defeated Frank Kramer in the one-third of a mile championship event on the Hampden Park Colosseum at Springfield, Massachusetts.

One of the Springfield papers carried the following article relative to that race:

"Major Taylor, Colored Sprinter, Again Wins Championship Race. Major Taylor, the Worcester Whirlwind, who is a great favorite in Springfield, defeated Frank Kramer in the one-third of a mile championship event on the local Colosseum track last night in a magnificent finish. It marked the first time that Kramer and Iver Lawson have ever ridden in this city and they made a very favorable impression, Lawson taking a leading part in the one-third of a mile championship race.

"The greatest interest naturally centered in the championship race. In the first heat Willie Fenn, who was expected to cut a big figure in the final, was shut out by Tom Cooper and Owen Kimble. Major Taylor appeared in the second heat and as usual was given a warm welcome. He has been laid up the past few days and he limped when he came out on the track. He had no difficulty in pushing the pedals of his machine, however, and he won his heat in a pretty sprint in the last lap.

"In the third heat Frank Kramer gave a fine exhibition of fast sprinting and won easily, while Iver Lawson, another stranger to Springfield enthusiasts, but one who stands near the top in the percentage table, just managed to finish second to Fisher, and thus qualified for the semi-final, both of which were very interesting. In the first one Major Taylor, Owen Kimble, Tom Cooper and Floyd Mac-Farland were the stars that faced the starter. Cooper and Mac-Farland did some great teamwork, but on the bell lap the 'Worcester Whirlwind' breezed past the two of them, and when he went over the tape Kimble was tacked on to him and thus finished second.

"Frank Kramer, Lawson, Gascoyne and Fisher came out for the second final and another great race was promised. Fisher who was waiting for Kramer to sprint tacked on behind and was pulled into the home stretch and almost to the tape in second position on Kramer's rear wheel. Lawson came up with a great rush on the outside and captured third place by a few inches.

"The semi-final brought together Major Taylor and Owen Kimble —the colored boy and the big southerner—and as can well be imagined the southerner fought his hardest to defeat his dusky rival, but to no avail. That wonderful sprint of Major Taylor's stood him in good stead and he flew past the big southerner as though the latter were standing still. Major Taylor received a great ovation from his Springfield friends and admirers. Kimble, although defeated, was also given a generous hand for the fine race he put up against Major Taylor.

"The finest sprint of all the heats was in the second semi-final between Frank Kramer and Iver Lawson. These two men were well matched. The first lap was a loaf but both riders sprinted the entire distance of the second lap and finished less than a wheel apart at the tape with Kramer in the lead. This meant Frank Kramer and Major Taylor would battle it out in the final which was certainly a treat to witness.

"The 'Worcester Whirlwind' was easily the favorite with the crowd. The start was slow as Major Taylor evidently tried to force Kramer into taking the lead. On the second lap Kramer started his great sprint but Taylor was right there with him and certainly rode to win. As they swung into the home stretch Major seemed to give a final dig to the pedals, and the boy from Jersey suddenly saw the back tire of Taylor's wheel in front of him crossing the tape. Major won by a good open length and climbed up a few more points in the championship table of points. It was a splendid race and pleased the spectators immensely judging from the applause Major Taylor received."

The outcome of this event did not increase my popularity among the other riders. MacFarland used every trick in his bag to eliminate me from the final. He told every man in that race with the possible exception of Owen Kimble just how to ride it in order to shut me out. Kimble, who beat me occasionally, turned a deaf ear to MacFarland while he made his appeal to the other riders for that reason.

Incidentally, I knew that Kimble was one of the most formidable of my opponents. The least slip on my part in any of the races between Kimble and I meant victory for Kimble; that's how closely we were matched. I was always forced to use my very best tactics when I found myself pitted against Kimble in a heat or final. On the occasions that Kimble defeated me I felt his victory was not accomplished on his natural speed but through an abnormal burst of speed that seemed to generate within him through his inborn hatred of my color. Of all the races Kimble ever rode I am satisfied he was at his very best whenever he opposed me.

At this Springfield meet the entire field was especially bent on "getting me." MacFarland was especially anxious to have Kramer defeat me in that final. Big Mac and Kimble tried their hardest to freeze me out of the semi-final. I spoiled their plans, however, by refusing to ride into the pocket which they had perfected. Instead I followed in third position until I decided it was time to cut loose, then I rushed past the two of them with a vengeance and headed for the tape. I was so confident that I could trounce the whole bunch of them that I again allowed MacFarland to go the last two laps with Cooper hanging on him, a very dangerous proceeding on my part. However, I came from third position on the back stretch in the last lap beating them out by three lengths. It wasn't very difficult for those who witnessed the race to surmise what tactics MacFarland instructed Kramer to use but it was to no avail. MacFarland did not belabor the other riders, however, for failing to stop me on this occasion.

There was a bit of sentiment tied up in this famous Hampden bicycle track as far as I am concerned. In my boyhood days I grew to know Springfield, Massachusetts, through frequent references to it in the celebrated bicycle weekly "The Bearings." In those days this beautiful half-mile dirt track promoted the greatest races in this country at that time, and I always longed to ride in Springfield. Since the last championship meets were held there annually the residents of the city came to know the greatest riders in the world, as it was not difficult to attract them to this track, which was one of the fastest in the country.

Besides this, George Hendee, one of the greatest riders in this country in the heyday of the old high wheel, was a native of this city. As a boy I knew that after having defeated everybody on this side of the Atlantic, Mr. Hendee was challenged by the celebrated English champion, Saunders Sellers. Sellers came to America to meet Hendee and succeeded in defeating the Springfield idol on his home track.

The famous Arthur Augustus Zimmerman, known throughout the cycling world as the "Jersey Skeeter," succeeded Hendee as champion of this country on the high bicycle. Zimmerman was widely known for his skill as a performer on the old "ordinary" in and about Springfield where he had ridden many of his championship races. After making a great name for himself on the old "Star" Zimmerman took to the modern bicycle, becoming one of the greatest racers of all time on it. Zimmerman through having ridden a number of his championship races on the Hampden track was immensely popular in this city.

On this same historic track the famous W. W. (Willie) Windle of Millbury, Massachusetts, established a world's "ordinary" record, 2:25 3/5 for one-mile. Windle and Zimmerman had many a hard fought race on this selfsame Springfield track, the most notable one being the race which was won by Zimmerman with a special prize of $1000 team of horses and a trap fully equipped.

# CHAPTER XLIX

## THE MOST DRAMATIC EPISODE OF MY CAREER—WORCESTER

Through the strange turn of affairs the most outstanding incident of my career was staged in my home city, Worcester, Massachusetts, in the summer of 1901. It followed the National Circuit meet races at Springfield, Massachusetts, and brought to Worcester the pick of the bicycle riders of the country, as the program included the one-mile championship event.

This one-mile national championship event with its increased points was the feature event of that program. Great as was this incentive the real motive that sent all of my rivals to participate in this big race at Worcester was their desire to humiliate me before my fellow townsmen. As a matter of fact the winner of a national championship race secured eight points whereas in a circuit championship event he would only gain four. That fact had no little bearing on my desire to win before my thousands of friends in Worcester, and it also served to spur on my rivals.

As usual there was the customary combination trumped up to bring about my defeat regardless of cost in this race. MacFarland, of course, was at the bottom of it and he had such able assistants as Owen Kimble, Frank Kramer and Tom Cooper to aid him in putting across his underhanded tactics. In addition to that MacFarland entered the races himself to make sure that his instructions were carried out to the letter. It would have been a great feather in his cap to have caused me to trail the field in my home town. The feeling had become so strained that the riders in MacFarland's clique felt that to defeat me would bring admiration that would dwarf the prize money and even the victory in the race itself.

Knowing that the final heat of this national one-mile championship classic would virtually result in a match race of the two best men in the country, I had no fear of the outcome provided I got into the final. The immense gathering at the old Colosseum track was right on edge with excitement. Likewise the crowd knew that there would be some excellent racing in the trial heats and semi-finals in which none but the best riders could survive. Since the final was scheduled to be ridden without pace of any kind the throng also knew it would be a test of brains as well as brawn. The people anticipated a scorching race in case Owen Kimble, Frank Kramer, Tom Cooper or even Floyd MacFarland opposed me in the final, and they were not disappointed. They all conceded that I would be in the final but they could not decide whom my opponent would be, so evenly matched were the other riders in the big race.  They knew that MacFarland and Kramer bore ill will towards me and that Kimble being a southerner had no use for anybody of color.  I was, therefore, on my best behavior.  Physically I was well nigh perfect.

In the course of this meet in Worcester one of the most unpleasant incidents of my life took place, but for fear of hurting the sport the fracas did not reach the public print and I am making it known

Floyd MacFarland—Handicap Champion and "Mentor"

now for the first time.  In the heats of the mile championship, MacFarland, my most formidable adversary, resorted to every unfair means he had at his command to have me eliminated.  He carefully instructed the riders in my heats as to how to trim me, but I managed to win each time despite their scheming and after some very furious riding I got into the final.  MacFarland's underhanded strategy came to naught and all bets were off when his *protégé*, Kramer, gummed things up completely by failing to get into the final.  He was so anxious to oppose me in the final that he actually fouled Owen Kimble in his semi-final heat and was promptly disqualified.  That meant that Kimble and I would battle it out for the laurels.

In the dressing rooms immediately after Kramer had been disqualified a rumpus started. It centered about the efforts of MacFarland and Kramer to attack Kimble. Only the timely arrival of a squad of policemen prevented bloodshed.

As Kimble and I were leaving our dressing rooms going out for the final tussle, MacFarland yelled to Kimble as a parting shot, "The nigger will trim you, the nigger will trim you." Kimble boiled and wheeled about as if to rush at MacFarland but policemen prevented that step.

I felt badly for Kimble despite the fact that I knew he disliked me very much because of my color. In order to relieve the pressure somewhat I made the finish as close as possible and I know that Kimble appreciated the stunt. I knew what Kimble or any of the other riders would have done to me under similar circumstances even in my home town, but I sympathized with Kimble and made it a close finish although in the perfect physical condition I was in that night I could have easily distanced him. I was given a royal ovation.

MacFarland and his crowd gave me a cheer as I made my way to the training quarters at the end of the race. I knew they were only acting and paid little attention to them. But I plainly heard them aim cutting remarks at Kimble to further humiliate him. The worst one of them was voiced by MacFarland himself, it was, "So you'd rather be trimmed by a nigger than to be defeated by a white man, would you? Well, how do you like it, how do you like it, you ———!!!!——— southerner?" Three times MacFarland yelled this at Kimble.

It was a tense moment, the rest of the riders, their trainers and their managers stood breathlessly awaiting developments. They knew such taunts would rouse Kimble, the southerner, to action and they were not disappointed. Kimble suddenly sprung from his cot and pleaded with me to come with him. I refused saying it was not my fight, but he insisted saying that he did not want to fight but only wanted to show "Mac" and his yellow bunch up.

Once in the presence of MacFarland and his gang Kimble placed his hand on my shoulder, and addressing particularly MacFarland and Kramer, said, "Yes, Major Taylor did defeat me and he didn't have to run me off the track or foul me to do it either. He did it like the real champion that he is and although his face is black he is not only the whitest man in the whole d— crowd, but the fastest man on the track. I do not consider it a disgrace to be beaten by him because he always does it fairly and that is more than any of you can do." Then he turned and shook my hand saying, "Major Taylor, I congratulate you on winning this championship race. You're the fastest and squarest man among us."

In this dramatic manner Kimble silenced the whole crooked outfit. They dropped their heads in shame and slunk away. Even Mac-Farland was unable to utter a word of a comeback. Kimble's speech closed the altercation although I heard several of the MacFarland gang threaten under their breath to get even with Kimble. No doubt Kimble was serious at the time and probably meant all the complimentary things he said about me but down in my heart I felt that he simply used that means to bring MacFarland and his crowd to their knees when they cut him to the quick by their insulting language.

One of the Worcester dailies carried the following story relative to that race:

"Major Taylor Rode Like a Whirlwind Last Night. Was Out to Win and Succeeded. Was Cheered by Thousands of Admirers. Major Taylor made good his promises to his Worcester friends by winning the one-mile championship event at the Colosseum last night. People yelled themselves hoarse with satisfaction and jubilation as the dusky champion heat after heat trimmed his opponents. The 'Major' was out to win and did it to a queen's taste.

"His victory over the field was little better received than was the decision by the referee in which Frank Kramer was disqualified from entering the final, and which also caused the big lanky MacFarland to take a quick seat on the bench where he belonged.

"Frank Kramer rode the crooked race in the semi-final with Owen Kimble who started in that heat with the leader. Kimble got the jump and Kramer rode foul in order to secure the pole, crowding Kimble down on the running boards and throwing him off his stride. The crowd saw it and demanded that the referee disqualify Kramer, which he did at once. This gave complete satisfaction although everybody had wished to see Taylor and Kramer come together in the final.

"Owen Kimble took his heat with Iver Lawson second, there being only two men in the heat. Kramer defeated Lester Wilson in his heat, these being the only two in the heat. Willie Fenn, Howard Freeman and Floyd MacFarland were the starters in the third heat. Freeman, who started the jump and got too far ahead of Fenn to be bested, landed first with Fenn second and MacFarland third. Major Taylor won his heat against George Collette and Johnnie Fisher. Major rode a great race. He watched his man who was Fisher, of course, and at the right moment shot out from them and trimmed them nicely.

"Major Taylor took his heat in the semi-final from Fenn, Fisher, and Freeman doing a nice job on them, his wonderful sprint being all to the good. In the grand semi-final Taylor laid in behind

Fisher, trailing him all over the track, and at the proper moment whizzed past him and reached the tape first by all kinds of lengths.

"In the final heat with Major Taylor was Owen Kimble, the Major's old rival. Kimble wanted to win this race very badly for he is a southerner imbued with all of the prejudices of that section. He worked hard to win, resorting to several foxy tactics to induce Taylor to take the lead. He was fair, however, and did not attempt anything foul, but when Major got him in the back stretch in the fifth lap Taylor jumped him, and sprinting furiously around the disk won by several lengths. Major received a great ovation from his many Worcester friends and was obliged to ride a lap of honor while the audience cheered lustily. It was a great race.

" 'Nellie' Bly and Charles Porter set up a record for a motor tandem on the disk, negotiating the distance in the fastest time that has yet been made for the saucer track, 1:26 2/5."

# CHAPTER L

MY SENSATIONAL VICTORY OVER FRANK KRAMER—MADISON<br>SQUARE GARDEN

Shortly after the National Circuit Championship Meet in Worcester the long looked for, and eagerly awaited match race between Frank Kramer and myself was arranged. Kramer had but recently been proclaimed the champion of America having won eighty points in the Circuit Championship races to sixty for myself as runner up for the honors and thirty for Iver Lawson who was third.

No sooner had the laurels been awarded than many sports writers and a host of friends of mine declared that the fact that I was unable to compete in the circuit races that year until the season was well advanced, because of my strenuous tour of Europe, alone prevented my repeating my championship victories of the three preceding years. Regardless of their claims, however, I conceded him the honor without an'mosity.

Nevertheless, these arguments in my behalf brought about the match race between Kramer and myself in which they claimed the real championship of the country was at stake. It was settled that we would ride three heats unpaced, the victor to be determined by the rider finishing first in two of them. A purse of $500 was offered for the race with the stipulation that the winner take all. Despite the fact that my good friend, William A. Brady, the present theatrical producer in New York, stood ready to make good his offer of several weeks previous to bid $1000 on my chances, it had no takers. Floyd MacFarland on a previous occasion declared his willingness to back Kramer, whose manager he was, for a like sum, but just prior to the match with Kramer, MacFarland's money had not been posted.

Realizing that his reputation as sprint champion of the country was more or less at stake in this match race with me Kramer had trained diligently for the event. Nor had I allowed any grass to grow under my feet and when we were called to face the starter on that memorable night Kramer and I were in excellent physical condition—ready and anxious for what I believed would be one of my most important matches. As has been previously mentioned there was ill will between Kramer and myself, the same being due in a large measure to the fact that Floyd MacFarland, who had no use for me, was arranging Kramer's races for him. His instructions to Kramer were to beat me at all costs.

I might mention here that the real cause of MacFarland's grievance against me centered in the fact that I did not team up with him

( 201 )

in the recent six-day bicycle races at Madison Square Garden, and that later I refused to go to Europe under his management. Then and there MacFarland declared that I would never again be champion of America. He conspired with the entire field of American riders to this end, and I must admit they were obviously successful in their unsportsmanlike combination against me.

So anxious was MacFarland to have his *protégé*, Kramer, defeat me in this special match race that he even went so far as to order Kramer to throw me in case he felt he could not defeat me fairly and squarely. MacFarland was undoubtedly spurred to this heroic measure by the fact that Kramer was champion of America and that he (Kramer) would have a hard time explaining to the public why I, the runner-up to him in my abbreviated season, should be able to defeat him. Of course, that was a trying predicament for Kramer and big "Mac" as they could ill afford to have me defeat Kramer whose laurel wreath was still fresh on his brow.

I instinctively knew that MacFarland and Kramer would leave no stone unturned to bring about my defeat in this match race so I hauled forth my best bag of tricks for use in it.

For nine laps of our first heat Kramer rode according to Hoyle. However, as I started to jump him on the turn just entering the back stretch on the last lap, he bumped me purposely, and bumped me hard. I was prepared for this move though, and instead of my being knocked off my wheel Kramer was the one to hit the boards as a result of the collision while I managed to stay up.

MacFarland lost no time entering a vigorous protest for Kramer, claiming that I had fouled him. He loudly demanded the race be rerun and I made my way to the referee's stand and volunteered to ride it over again. But the referee informed me that he had seen the collision from his vantage point and added that since I was put on the defensive by Kramer's deliberate foul tactics the heat would not be run over again under any circumstances. The referee further informed me that Kramer had left the black line on the pole and swung up the banking purposely to knock me out of my stride.

No sooner had I crossed the tape in the first heat than a pop bottle thrown by an excited Kramer sympathizer in the gallery narrowly missed hitting me on the head. The missile struck the track a short distance in front of me and scattered the spectators who were gathered inside of the railing. Between Kramer's bumping me and the pop bottle incident I began to think that this was scheduled to be one of my most hectic nights—but luck was with me on both occasions and I felt that was a lucky omen for the next heat of the match race which proved to be the final when I brought Kramer into camp a second time.

As we came out for the second heat it was apparent that he and MacFarland were in anything but a congenial mood. It was clear to me that the pair of them were grimly determined to take me into camp in the remaining heats by hook or crook. Meantime I was wondering what underhanded tricks they had up their sleeves for the occasion and also if there were any more pop bottle throwers who were waiting to assault me in case I turned Kramer back in the pending heat.

However, I held firmly to my plan of action in this heat and played right into Kramer's hands by allowing him to ride his own race right up to four laps to go. Then dropping back a couple of lengths I jumped past him. This time he remained on the pole and I had no difficulty in getting around him winning by over a length, thus ending this fiercely fought match race. I shall never forget the splendid ovation that greeted me as I rode my lap of honor about the historic old Garden. The New York bicycle enthusiasts knew full well of the conspiracy and feeling fostered by MacFarland and put into effect by Kramer to bring about my defeat as champion that year and they were not slow cheering me loud and long when I forced Kramer the champion to trail me in this special match race, despite the foul tactics employed by him against me.

Among the bicycle riders and sports writers of the country it was agreed that while Kramer won the championship of America for 1901, MacFarland got most of his prize winnings. MacFarland was a good manager—for MacFarland. As a matter of fact I must admit that MacFarland accomplished his two-fold purpose that season in masterly fashion. Not only did he dislodge me as champion which was his outstanding goal but he also made more money through handling Kramer than he did on his own actual winnings on the track that season.

# CHAPTER LI



Following a short conference with Victor Breyer and Robert Coquelle I signed a contract with them under the terms of which I was to tour Europe for them a second time in 1902. These same two residents of Paris managed my tour of the Continent in 1901. Under the terms of the contract I was to get a bonus of $5000 for two months riding in addition to whatever prize money I would be able to win. May and June were mentioned as the months I would ride overseas and both match and sprint races were stipulated together with the circuit I was to cover.

In a statement to sports writers on the New York dailies Mr. Breyer made the following statement shortly after I had agreed to ride under his management in Europe:—"I consider Major Taylor as the savior of cycling in Europe. Until he made his appearance in France last spring there was every indication that the great outdoor sport was dying. However, with Major Taylor's appearance on the European tracks the pastime took on a new lease of life and quickly jumped back into public favor. Taylor's great racing on the Continental tracks also drew thousands of new patrons to the sport.

"He was looked upon as an idol, and when he took his departure for his native shores it was with the universal regret of all the cycling enthusiasts of Europe. They demanded the presence of Major Taylor and as a result I made this trip to America to get his signature to a contract for another tour of Europe. I consider Major Taylor the greatest racer and drawing card of them all. I am delighted to get him signed up again and I will sail for Europe in a few days one of the happiest men in the world."

Mr. Breyer declared that among others I would meet the world's champion, Thorwald Elleggarde, the great Danish rider whom I defeated in a special match race in France the season before. Shortly after I had won from Elleggarde, the latter won the world's championship in Berlin. My European managers had mapped out a very strenuous campaign for me in the course of which I was to oppose the champions of every country in Europe once more.

Upon my arrival in Paris in the latter part of March 1902, I found conditions even more conducive to a successful season than I had in the previous year. I knew that next to being in excellent physical condition the most important feature in a rider's success was the climatic conditions. It also helped me considerably to know that I had made thousands of friends in my previous invasion of Europe and this thought reacted favorably upon me as I trained for my strenuous season against all the foreign champions. A decided edge that I had on my 1902 tour as compared with my trip in the preceding year was the fact that my first race in the former year was scheduled for May 9, which was just a month later than my opening race in 1901—that was decidedly in my favor.

In my first appearance on the 1902 tour of Europe I defeated Walter Rutt, the champion of Germany, Sydney Jenkins, the English champion, Bourotte, the French champion, Muringer, a German champion and Lorrain a French champion in Paris.

My next engagement was in Maestricht, Holland, where I figured in a match race against Harri Meyers, the brilliant champion sprinter of that country. It marked my first visit to the Netherlands and gave me an excellent opportunity to ascertain the Dutch brand of sportsmanship. Meyers was extremely anxious to down me and he battled me around that famous track with grim determination. But after defeating him by a very close margin in the first heat the judges declared our second brush a dead heat and in the run-off of it I again lead Meyers home by six or eight inches.

The race took place before a tremendous crowd. The weather was perfect and our three heats were mighty struggles throughout the final laps. The first heat was a real test of speed and we had landed in to the home stretch on even terms. It was a furiously fought fight inch by inch right up to the finishing line where I crossed only about six inches ahead of Meyers.

I had heard that Meyers was a wonderful rider and although this was the first time I had ever met him in a race I agreed that he was all that. In our first heat he demonstrated to me that he had not been overrated by my managers. He had a great jump, all kinds of speed, excellent judgment—in fact he seemed to possess all of the necessary requisites, including plenty fight, that go to make a real world-beater. On top of these attributes, Meyers had the further advantage of riding against me in the presence of his own people and on his own home track, every inch of which he knew by heart through his many victories there.

I am frank to admit that things did not look any too rosy for me when Meyers and I came out for the second heat of our race. However, I tried to appear indifferent but I was really deeply concerned, realizing full well that I had one of my most trying races ahead of me. I was still cogitating in my mind what my tactics would be in this heat as I knew only too well that I had a rival on this occasion who was well worthy of my steel. Since I had used my very best judgment in the first heat against Meyers I was still debating in my mind whether to use the same tactics or to try something different.

At the last moment the second step seemed inadvisable since he had ridden me such a tight race in the first heat. I felt he was too dangerous a man to experiment with.

Heat No. 2 was practically a repetition of the first. I tried to work my jump, but to no avail as Meyers was too quick. After our first brush in this heat I knew that he could jump practically as quickly as I. However, I was satisfied that I could undoubtedly hold my sprint longer than he, so I tried it and forced Meyers into a sprint a trifle sooner than in the other heat. Then we settled down to a killing sprint to the tape. Since I. had beaten him in the first heat I had confidence that I could lead him home again and I did by a very close margin. The judges, however, decided it was a dead heat, and backed by thousands in the grandstand, they ordered another heat ridden.

Meyers knew I had won the heat and practically admitted it to me in the dressing room. In answer to my direct question as to who in his estimation won the race, Meyers shrugged his shoulders and said reluctantly, "Well, they gave it to me." He refused to amplify that statement further.

Then I said to him, "Harri, I always heard that your reputation for honesty and fairness as a gentleman and rider were irreproachable. I also know full well how much you would like to win this match as it is to be your last race. I appreciate you would like nothing better than to retire with a victory over me as a fitting climax to your brilliant career. Well, in the next heat I am going to try something that I have never attempted before. I am going out there on the track before your home folks and intentionally see just how far I can distance you."

I was deeply grieved by the rank decision against me in the second heat and plainly showed my feelings to Meyers as I made the above boast to him.

To carry out my threat to him I changed my tactics for this third heat as I felt this move would serve to confuse him. But he was not to be rattled. I never met a cooler rider. At the crack of the pistol I went to the front with a determination and once in the lead I watched him closely. We jumped together and after the third ferocious struggle down that home stretch I repeated my performances of the first two heats, winning again by only a scant foot.

Meyers, although defeated, was far from being disgraced, for I had but little to boast over in my victory over him. This race with him strangely paralleled my victory over Elleggarde at Agen, France, the previous year. Incidentally these two matches were the most desperately fought of all my European match races.

I was successful in all my single, or man-to-man match races in Europe that season. Among others whom I defeated that year were notably: Grognia, champion of Belgium; Thorwald Elleggarde, world's champion and champion of Denmark (twice); Walter Rutt, champion of Germany; Lambrecht, a champion of France and Tom Linton, world's champion behind pace.

My first match with my great rival Elleggarde in 1902 took place in his home town Copenhagen, Denmark, on the same track where

Harri Meyers—Champion of Holland
Major Taylor—Champion of America

he defeated me—in a fluke match race in 1901. An immense throng was on hand for this event.

I was confident that I could defeat Elleggarde again but at the same time I decided to take no chances. I considered Elleggarde every inch a champion and remembering the unsatisfactory ending to our match race on the same track a year previous, I decided to take his measure before his own people and thus avenge my defeat at his hands on the same track. I also wanted to drive home to that tremendous audience, through action and not through words, that I still considered his victory over me as very hollow. One may well imagine my pleasure on this occasion when I defeated Elleggarde in straight heats. Despite the fact that he rode a great race against me on this

Taylor and Elleggarde in a "Friendly" Warming Up Spin on the Buffalo Track, Paris

Start of the Second and Final Heat of the International Championship Match,
Taylor Won by Two Lengths

occasion it was by no means on a par with his brilliant performance against me at Agen.

A fortnight later I again took Elleggarde into camp, this time in Paris, again demonstrating my superiority over the world's champion in straight heats. He fought hard in an effort to redeem some of his lost prestige, but try as he might I ascertained that he was not the Elleggarde that I had to defeat in such a thrilling struggle in Agen.

In the course of this invasion I was pitted against the greatest tandem team on the Continent, Bourotte and Gougoltz, in a special match race at Calais. It was arranged that we would ride three heats of 1,000 meters each, the winner of two heats, being declared the victor. I won this match after a great fight.

After defeating Walter Rutt, champion of Germany, in a special match race in Paris I prepared for my final race of the tour. In view of the fact that a fortnight before I was matched to meet Rutt in Paris, he defeated me in a three-cornered race, Arend being the third man on the Hanover, Germany track. Rutt's friends were confident he could defeat me in our special match race at Paris. However, I won in two straight ·heats but only after having been pushed to the limit by the robust and youthful Rutt.

Then came my final match race of the tour against the famous Welshman, Tom Linton, who had beaten everyone behind motor that season. Linton and I were matched to ride behind pace in this race, best two heats in three to determine the winner. The first heat was a distance of two kilometers, the second at five kilometers and the third distance to be determined by the toss of a coin.

Since Mr. Fred Johnson of the Iver Johnson Company, under whose colors I was riding that season, happened to be in Paris on this occasion, I had an added incentive to try to defeat the speedy Linton. However, I was handicapped, inasmuch as I had only my sprinting wheels with me on the trip since I did not anticipate doing any paced work. Nevertheless, I decided to go through with the match and figured that I might be able to jump away from the tape and open up a gap that Linton would be unable to close. My plan worked out successfully but in leading Linton over the tape by half a lap in the first heat, I had to break the world's record by six seconds. I also won the five kilometer heat from Linton after a short rest, breaking another world's record in turning the trick by a margin of 2 3/5 seconds, automatically winning the match.

In the course of my second successful invasion of Europe (1902) I won forty first places, fifteen second places, and two third places. I won every single man-to-man match race in which I figured, but in the three-cornered events and four-cornered I was not so fortunate as every rider combined against me making it impossible for me to take my percentage of victories.

*A fair field and no favor for one and for all.*
*A square deal is promised both great and small.*
*A fair field and no favor and, if you are game,*
*A square deal is sure to bring glory and fame.*

## CHAPTER LII

### HOW I LOST THE 1902 CHAMPIONSHIP TITLE THROUGH VICIOUS UNFAIRNESS

Returning to this country I found the circuit championship season well under way with Frank Kramer leading for the honors with a margin of thirty points. I was satisfied that he could not be overtaken, so well advanced was the season, but I determined to give him a good fight for the laurels. He won the championship, however, but not before the bicycle enthusiasts of this country had witnessed some of the greatest races in the history of the sport in America. Because of conditions and circumstances already explained in a previous chapter there can be no repetition of those hectic battles between Kramer, the Mac-Farland faction, and myself.

While I was racing in Europe in the early months of 1902 the officials of the Nation Cyclists' Association had seen fit to change the system relative to the number of men eligible to start in the final of each championship race. Hitherto the rules called for only two starters whereas now it was stipulated that there would be four starters in the final heat of championship events. It seemed to me that this change in the rules was aimed directly at me. Evidently the powers that were believed the old system had proven advantageous to me in the 1901 campaign, but they could not afford to change the system until the season was over for obvious reasons. No doubt Floyd MacFarland was a prime mover for this shift in the regulations as he felt that with two men only in the finals I would undoubtedly have a decided edge on the field. The season of 1901 had convinced MacFarland, Kramer and the rest of the outfit that the man to man arrangement in the final was made to order for me.

In the very first circuit races that I took part in after my return from Europe it was clearly demonstrated to me that the four-man final heat system further militated against my success. I realized that Kramer's advantage of thirty points over the field in the scramble for the championship was in itself a mighty hurdle for me to clear.

I quote from a New York newspaper article relative to the first race I competed in under the new ruling. It refers to a pocket that the riders forced me into in the final of the Half Mile Championship event and was typical of the tactics employed against me throughout the remainder of the season:

"Major Taylor defeated in the half-mile national championship race. Major Taylor finished second to Frank Kramer in his first race for the national championship on the Manhattan Beach track last night before a large audience. The final of the half-mile championship event brought together Frank Kramer, Major Taylor, Iver Lawson, and George Collette, probably the four fastest sprinters in the country.

"Kramer and Lawson set the pace and Taylor was pocketed on the second turn, but jumped through on the turn into the home stretch and beat Collette and Lawson out in a magnificent sprint, and he forced Kramer to the utmost. Kramer won by barely a foot. The time was 1:04 4/5.

"In the one-mile handicap Taylor starting from scratch rode himself out setting the pace in an effort to catch the limit men, and did not finish. Taylor was forced to do this as none of the other riders would share the brunt of the battle with him."

My next race was with Willie Fenn who was the Amateur Champion of the country in 1900 on his home track at Hartford, Connecticut. It was a special match race, best two in three heats, consisting of a one-mile unpaced race, one-mile single paced race and a two-mile pursuit race for a purse of $300, winner take all. The one-mile unpaced race, which was a French innovation, was looked upon generally by newspaper men as being my favorite style. The pursuit race was the style of riding at which Fenn was considered unbeatable. The result, therefore, virtually hinging on the one-mile paced event.

Fenn was a very powerful rider and one of the best in the country. He had a wonderful sprint on the end of a very fast mile but he did not pack the punch which would give him the winning margin at the end of a race. I won this match in two straight heats.

In commenting on my race with Fenn one of the Hartford dailies printed the following article: "Because of having refused to compete for the N. C. A. championship title this year Major Taylor seems to have been the victim of a press censor of that organization, as a result he has received very little credit for his wonderful performances, one of which he gave at the local track last night when he took Willie Fenn into camp in two straight heats in a hotly contested match race.

"Nor did Major Taylor receive due credit from certain quarters for his remarkable work while abroad this season. In other words Major Taylor cannot now be featured on the circuit since he prefers to ride independent races, and recent newspaper articles have a tendency to knock him. However, his winning forty first places in fifty-seven races on foreign tracks stamps Major Taylor as one of the greatest match racers of all time. In his European starts the Colored Flyer was up against combinations, especially in three and four-cornered match events, that made it practically impossible for him to win all of his starts. However, he won every man-to-man match race in which he competed. The jockeying resorted to in his European races was about the worst Taylor has ever had to contend with as the foreign riders are past masters of this game.

"In the three-cornered matches first one rider would shoot to the front, then if Taylor went for him and caught him he would suddenly stop and the man in the rear would jump past and win the race. If Major didn't go after him, of course, he would win. No man living could win against this kind of team work, but Major Taylor was obliged to enter these matches as the track owners and promoters claimed that in a match race between two men only it was a contest with the foregone conclusion that the American would be victorious every time, and the crowd would not attend."

A few days later at the Vailsburg track I was the victim of a pocketing combination in the half-mile championship race which was won by Kramer. I quote the following article from a Newark, New Jersey, daily:

"Half-mile championship to Kramer. At the Vailsburg track yesterday Frank Kramer won the half-mile championship event, with Owen Kimble second, Iver Lawson third, and Major Taylor fourth, after a hard struggle. Kramer dodged the two-mile handicap but Taylor who started from scratch finished third. The race was won by Johnnie Fisher of Chicago (60 yds.), Pat Logan of Boston (210 yds.) second, "Plugger" Bill Martin of Australia (120 yds.) fourth, time 4:07 3/5."

In the final of the half-mile championship on this occasion the riders opposed to me combined so successfully to bring about my defeat that I was forced to finish fourth in a championship race for the first time in my career. However, I gave my opponents the ride of their lives before their foul tactics brought about my defeat. The crowd realized the unsportsmanlike tactics adopted by my three opponents in this race to prevent my winning, and they were greeted with round after round of hisses and cat-calls from the grandstand, the racing enthusiasts being quick to show their disgust at the methods adopted against me. Meantime, I was forced to ride an extra lap, throughout which I was given one of the greatest ovations of my life.

The following letter was printed in the New York *Sun* the day following the race on the Vailsburg track mentioned above:

"To the Editor of the New York *Sun:* Sir: On the Vailsburg track last Saturday the spectators had it plainly demonstrated that all hands were out to kill the chances of Major Taylor to score a win over Frank Kramer. Major Taylor won both of his heats in the half-mile national championship with ridiculous ease, and there were thousands who expected to see him land the final, but what was the result? The line-up was Kramer on the pole, then Taylor, Lawson and Kimble. At the gun Taylor dropped in back of Kramer, and Lawson forced Taylor off the track into the dirt.

"Entering the bell lap Kimble had the pole with Kramer second, on the banking Kimble swings up and drops down beside Taylor, leaving Kramer a free pole, while Lawson comes and closes up on the other side of Taylor so that when they entered the home stretch he was jostled and held fast until he had to sit up. Of course Kramer won, but there were hundreds, yes thousands, who would have given the price of admission to see Major Taylor have a good square chance at him. The Hartford *Times* said: The riders have pocketed Major Taylor in the same way on the track in this city. If it were not for the fact that he is really the *fastest* sprinter in the world he would not hold the championship one week against the combination of white riders.

"Is there no way to prevent such contemptible tricks as are repeatedly put up by some riders who would secretly rejoice if they could upset Taylor and cripple him for life? Such riding is unworthy of decent, self-respecting and sport-loving people, and makes a white man blush with shame to know that a colored rider is today, with the exception of Fenn, the banner man for clean sport and gentlemanly conduct. Come now, what we want is to determine the ability of these two men, Taylor and Kramer, alone on the track, so I ask the *Sun* to use its efforts to bring about a series of match races with Willie Fenn as pacemaker to the bell lap. The N. C. A. and all its angels could not rob the colored man then of a chance to do his best. Yours truly, A Lover of Clean Sport."

A day or two after the Vailsburg affair I opposed Willie Fenn in a special match race at Hartford. Fenn won the first heat, a two-mile pursuit race in 2:07 2/5, but I won the next two heats, the first being a half-mile unpaced race in 2:21 and the other a one-mile paced race in 2:07 2/5. Although Fenn won the first heat and I outclassed him in the next two races, he failed to put up the same battle that he did in our first desperate match, his morale was broken.

# CHAPTER LIII



I shall never forget my first appearance in Ottawa, Ontario, August 3 and 4, 1902. At the railroad station I was met by a large delegation of cycling officials, newspaper men, sporting celebrites and cyclists who gave me a rousing welcome to their beautiful city.

I was doomed to disappointment in a short time, however, when my trainer informed me that our racing machines had been lost *en-route*. We later learned that they could not possibly arrive inside of twenty-four hours. Inasmuch as I was scheduled to ride on the afternoon of the day on which I arrived in Ottawa I was keenly disappointed at this turn of affairs. The public in turn shared my sentiments in the matter when I was introduced to them before the grandstand with the announcement that I would be unable to compete in that day's program.

Hardly had I taken a seat near the track before I noticed a rider having a warm-up sprint around on the back stretch. This lad proved to be Willie Morton, a prominent Canadian amateur. My attention was first called to Morton by his position on his wheel. It was very similar to my own. As he dismounted and stood near me I inquired for the name of the bicycle he was riding, the gear, the length of the cranks, the pedal reach, the weight and the like. He answered all my questions including the name of the wheel which was a Massey-Harris and manufactured in Toronto.

At this point I asked him if he would allow me to use his wheel in the championship race if I promised not to alter his bicycle. Morton's face fairly beamed at my suggestion. "Why certainly, Mr. Taylor, you may use my wheel, and you may alter it to suit your position," said Morton. "If you can win this championship," he continued, "on my bicycle it will be a wonderful souvenir for me of your visit to Ottawa."

I promised him I would do my best in the race. Then I borrowed a racing outfit from several of the amateurs gathered about the track and made a wierd appearance when we were called out for the first heat of the Quarter-mile Championship in those odds and ends of faded, loose, ill-fitting garments. This was very much against my pride as I admit that I was extremely vain about my racing colors.

Without making a single adjustment on Morton's wheel I took a few trial laps on it to get accustomed to it, after which I told the officials that I was prepared to enter the race. Shortly after, Morton, using the same bicycle, qualified for the Five-Mile Ontario Amateur

Championship. No sooner had he dismounted than I mounted his wheel and finished third in the first heat which qualified me for the semi-final. Then Morton went out on the same wheel and qualified in the semi-final heat of his event. Once more I replaced Morton on the saddle and this time finished second in the semi-final heat of my race in which only two men qualified. Then Morton won the final heat of his race and I did likewise a few minutes later, as I had become accustomed to his wheel in the preceding heats and gave a splendid account of myself in the final.

I was a trifle nervous when we lined up for the final heat realizing that I was pitted against two of the best riders on the track, Frank Kramer and George Collette, and was mounted on a wheel that I had never ridden before the first heat of this event. Topnotchers in championship racing circles would never have dreamed of riding a big race on a borrowed bicycle. So all the crack riders at the track that day, both amateurs and professionals, were laughing up their sleeves when the announcer made it known I was going to ride in the championship race on a strange bicycle. However, I felt that my perfect physical condition plus my confidence in myself would offset this disadvantage. I received a most flattering ovation for my well earned victory.

This final heat of the Quarter-Mile Championship was virtually a match race—in which two riders were contesting against one. I was the one. Owing to the short distance the race covered, both Collette and Kramer made a bid for the lead at the crack of the pistol. In order to keep out of a pocket I dropped back on the pole and took a long chance of being able to fight around them in the home stretch. Collette undertook to hold me at one time, but Kramer took him around the turn too fast and by a supreme effort I managed to jump through just entering the stretch. I was then able to outsprint Kramer in a desperate battle down the home stretch, winning by a length. Realizing the handicap I rode the race under the large crowd of enthusiasts in the grandstand were shouting themselves hoarse for me to win, and they gave me a mighty ovation as I broke the tape ahead of Kramer.

I quote the following paragraphs from an Ottawa newspaper of the following day:

"Major Taylor in fine form defeats Frank Kramer in Championship race in Ottawa. At the bicycle races of the N. C. A. at the local track yesterday there was a record-breaking attendance. The feature of the program was the Quarter-Mile Championship Race, the final of which was won by Major Taylor, with Frank Kramer second and George Collette third.

"The Ten-Mile Championship, flying start, was captured by George Scribner, Jimmy Bowler second and 'Plugger' Bill Martin third, the time being 22:30 which establishes the world's record from three to ten miles. In the Consolation Two-Mile Lap Race, Willie Fenn finished first, Johnnie Fisher second, and the time was 4:15. The Five-Mile Ontario Championship Race was won by Willie Morton, 'Toronto' Jones second."

Early next day my bicycle trunk arrived and I was extremely anxious to show the bicycle fans of Ottawa my real speed on my own outfit and under my own colors. In fact I was impatient for the starter's pistol to send us away on that Half-Mile Championship Race. I won my first heat in fine style and the semi-final without much difficulty and toed the mark in the final with such stars as Johnnie Fisher of Chicago, Frank Kramer the champion, and Willie Fenn one of the outstanding stars of the day. This also proved to be a match race. There were no pacemakers employed to pace the final of this event which gave my opponents a fine chance to pull off some funny business at my expense.

They made the most of their opportunity by forcing me into a pocket halfway down the back stretch. I made two or three desperate efforts to break through but Fisher and Fenn held me in tight. Later I did manage to jump through but not quite soon enough and I was beaten by a few inches by Kramer.

I chuckled that evening as I recalled my having won my race on the first day of the meet on a borrowed bicycle and losing out on my own racing machine. Many times since I have wondered whatever became of Willie Morton's bicycle that saw double service and two championship victories on successive days on that Ottawa track.

A local newspaper printed the following self-explanatory paragraph the day after the race:

"Major Taylor beaten by inches only in Half-Mile Championship Race. Almost a Dead Heat between Kramer and the Worcester Whirlwind. The final days cycling races at the Varsity Oval were in every way a great success, both in record attendance and exciting contests. It was a civic holiday and business generally was suspended.

"The Half-Mile Circuit Championship Race was particularly exciting. It was almost a dead heat between Major Taylor and Frank Kramer, the latter winning by only a few inches. The results were as follows: Half-Mile Circuit Championship won by Kramer, Taylor second, Fisher third, Fenn fourth—time 1:07.

"Civic Handicap, Five-Mile Professional Race, won by Keegan (250 yds.), Menus Bedell second (250 yds.), F. B. Beachamp, Australia, third (300 yds.) and Saxon Williams fourth (250 yds.). Keegan's time was 10:46. The Half-Mile Consolation Professional

Event was won by George Collette, Eddie Bald second, and Menus Bedell third, time :59."

It is a coincidence that at the close of the 1902 season in this country I rode a Massey-Harris bicycle on my triumphant tour of Australia. Due to a freak of fate I borrowed a Massey-Harris wheel for the above mentioned race in Ottawa that year and was so successful on it that the manufacturers of the machine engaged me to ride it on my proposed tour of Australia.

# CHAPTER LIV



For the first time in my racing career I selected a teammate for the One-Third-Mile National Championship Race at the Manhattan Beach track in the summer of 1902. In keeping with the rules of the N. C. A. I announced just before the race started that I would team up with Willie Fenn in the final heat. Kramer announced he would team up with Kimble. My selection proved to be a good one and I won the final heat with Kimble second and Kramer third. The time being :45 1/5.

In this race I was particularly impressed with the ridiculous ease with which I won over such a fast field and proved to me the advantage of a worthy team-mate. Incidentally this showed me the tremendous disadvantage under which I had been laboring when I fought two or even three of my rivals unassisted.

But let a New York daily newspaper tell the story of the race:

"Major Taylor wins Championship at Manhattan Beach. Major Taylor aided by the teamwork of W. S. Fenn won the final of the One-Third-Mile National Championship Race at Manhattan Beach today, defeating Frank L. Kramer and Owen S. Kimble. Taylor would not have qualified for the semi-final but for the disqualification of Jimmie Bowler, who had unintentionally run into Taylor, but without harming the latter's chances. Marcus Hurley won the big Ten-Mile Amateur Handicap from scratch after a hard race. The consolation for the professionals was captured by Floyd MacFarland from John Bedell by inches. Collette who led all the way down the stretch, finished third. One-Third-Mile Championship won by Major Taylor, Owen Kimble, second, Frank L. Kramer third. Time :45 1/5. Five-Mile Handicap Professional won by W. S. Fenn, scratch, Owen S. Kimble, 150 yds., second, G. C. Scribner, 100 yds., third, W. A. Robe, 200 yds., fourth, E. C. 'Cannon' Bald, Buffalo, 200 yds., fifth. Time 11:07 4/5. Two-Thirds-Mile Consolation Race won by Floyd Krebs, John Bedell second, George Collette third. Time 1:21 3/5."

Still another New York newspaper commented on that race in this fashion:

"How Major Taylor and Willie Fenn turned a clever trick. Two heads can usually figure better than one, and the trick turned by Major Taylor and Willie Fenn last Saturday at Manhattan Beach track whereby the Worcester Whirlwind won the Circuit Championship event could hardly have been improved upon. "Old Kentuck"

Kimble, always hot on the trail of Major Taylor, has taken a new lease of life this season, having participated in nearly every championship final and scoring, is not to pair with champion Kramer, under the revised rule. The veteran decided that he was capable alone and unaided to attend to the case of his ancient opponent. Kramer, too, with a string of eleven championships to his credit possessed a goodly supply of confidence.

"But the 'Nutmeg boy,' Fenn, and Major Taylor planned wisely and well, and not only did they plan, but they executed. Once around the one-third-mile belt of cement called for quick action, and it came quick. Kramer at the lead at the outset ran up the bank, Taylor following, then Kimble with Fenn bringing up the rear. Turning into the back stretch Fenn jumped down to the pole. Taylor deserted Kramer's rear wheel in a jiffy, and was prepared for the forthcoming sprint, Kramer went for the 'Major,' and down the back stretch flew the trio, with Frank Kramer fighting desperately to get up on the outside.

"Swinging around the last turn into the stretch the 'Major' concluded he had enough pulling, and emerged from cover. Owen Kimble fought hard to pass his rival, but the best he could do was to finish lapped on the winner's rear wheel. Kramer ran a disconsolate third, with Fenn a happy and contented last, but he completed a good day's work by appropriating the five-mile handicap, in which he rode from scratch, and again Kimble was the rider to fight the leader, and again the representative from Kentucky had to be satisfied with second place money. Scribner's effort was praiseworthy, with Rutz just beating out Eddie Bald, the former king, who is laboring to regain his once invincible form."

A short time later I again defeated Kramer in a sensational two-mile circuit championship race on the Baltimore track.

I quote the following article from a Baltimore newspaper:

"Frank Kramer beaten. Major Taylor wins two-mile championship. Collette and Fenn are also beaten. The National Circuit Championship Bicycle Races at the Coliseum track last night attracted a big crowd. The program was made up entirely of sprint races, the riders being the crack sprinters of the country.

"Major Taylor, the diminutive Negro rider, won the big event of the evening defeating his strongest rival for the National Championship honors, Frank Kramer. Major Taylor qualified by winning first place in his trial heat, and first in the semi-final heat, and won the final. Kramer was first in his trial heat, second in his semi-final and second in the final. The heats as well as the final were ridden slowly excepting the spurts which were not more than two or three laps of fast sprinting. The winner, Major Taylor, received great applause from the enthusiasts."

I was now in excellent physical condition and riding better in each successful meet. Willie Fenn was quite anxious to team up with me in this event but I declined telling him that I felt so well-trained that I was certain I could win the two-mile sprint single-handed.

## CHAPTER LV



This famous track was the scene of many hectic races but I doubt
if it ever staged one where the feeling was so intense as it was on this
occasion.   The event that brought Kramer, Bedell, Lawson and my-
self together for this bitterly contested race was the One-Third-Mile
Circuit Championship and the five-Mile Handicap.   Inasmuch as this
was the closing meet of the season on that track every rider was deter-
mined to win at all hazards.

At the last minute I was informed that there was a plot afoot to
throw me off my wheel in the events in which I figured.   Several of
my friends advised me to keep out of the competition fearing that I
would be injured by the rival riders.   However, I figured this was a
ruse to keep me out of the competition and decided to go in and ride
to win no matter what happened.   Subsequent developments showed
that my informants knew whereof they spoke and twice I came within
an inch of being deliberately thrown in the course of the program.

A New York newspaper carried the following paragraphs concern-
ing that memorable occasion:

"Major Taylor was pocketed in the championship at Manhattan
Beach.   MacFarland and Mate could not beat Major.   The cycling
season on the Manhattan Beach track wound up yesterday and there
was plenty of excitement owing to the deliberate pocketing of the
colored rider, Major Taylor, by Bedell and Lawson in the final of
the One-Third-Mile Championship Event.

"Major Taylor was so badly pocketed in the event that he was
forced to sit up in the home stretch while Frank Kramer who was just
behind jumped around the trio and won out.   The team work was so
palpable that the thousands of spectators yelled their disapproval of
the unsportsmanlike action of Lawson and Bedell who were promptly
disqualified by referee Merrihew, giving Taylor second place, which
was a most popular decision.

"A short time afterwards Major Taylor was enthusiastically ap-
plauded when he defeated a big field in the Five-Mile Handicap
Event which he won from scratch and in which MacFarland who
had announced his intentions of teaming up with Frank Kramer fin-
ished second, but Frank Kramer was not in the first five.   By a quick
jump at the start in the five-mile race Major Taylor left MacFarland
struggling alone for two laps before he could get to Kramer, his
teammate, and the well laid plans of the pair went for naught in the
finishing sprint, Taylor winning easily, amid tremendous applause."

MacFarland, the master mind, framed the obviously unfair tactics that beat me in the final of the One-Third-Mile Championship Race. Notwithstanding the fact that Bedell and Lawson were disqualified for their foul tactics in this race, they received for the part they played and the unsportsmanlike proceedings as much of the purse as the actual winner. MacFarland was only too willing to sacrifice the entire purse if necessary in order to get the points that went with winning this championship race for Kramer, regardless of how he got them. I believe that no injustice would have been done Kramer had he been disqualified also.

I took sweet revenge in the next race, however, much to the satisfaction of the spectators who vociferously hooted and hissed the winner of the championship race and his conspirators. Stung to the quick by the cowardly actions of the trio against me in the championship event I started out to win the five-mile race with a determination that I had seldom evinced before. I was confident I could take the field in this handicap event in which I started from scratch with MacFarland. Incidentally he figured that he had it all "fixed" to hand me another setback in this race.

At the crack of the pistol I jumped away from MacFarland and went after the seventy-five-yard man, never easing up until I caught him. Then I remained behind him enjoying a little breathing spell until MacFarland swung by with Kramer and Lawson tacked on his rear wheel, the latter being planted there to keep me away from Kramer. The pace had been terrific throughout and with three laps left to go big "Mac" took a good look around to see that the combinations were placed as per orders. Satisfied, he started tearing at his pedals for the tape just as we entered the home stretch with three laps to go. It was his intention to cover two laps at top speed and then let Kramer and Lawson fight it out with me in the last lap.

The crowd was roaring as we swept across the tape with MacFarland setting a withering pace. Kramer was in second position, Lawson was in third place and I brought up the rear as I was tacked on Lawson's rear wheel. Around the turn we flew, each one doing his utmost to stick to MacFarland's relentless pace. Still in fourth place from which position I could see every move my opponents made, I noticed MacFarland gradually drawing away from Kramer at a lap and a half to go. Kramer was struggling for dear life to hang on but to no avail.

Whenever his knees began to wobble I knew Kramer was in trouble, and since Lawson made no attempt to close up the gap made by MacFarland, I knew that he too had been indulging in more speed than was good for him. Summoning all the strength I had left in me I went after MacFarland and as I passed Lawson and Kramer neither of them offered the slightest resistance, they were all burned out. So I quickly slid up behind MacFarland and watched the other two from under my arm as they continued to fade away in the rear. MacFarland was still in command and "going great guns." On entering the last turn he suddenly swung up the banking and yelled, "All right, Frank, go, go!" Imagine MacFarland's astonishment when he

Iver Lawson—The "Speedy Swede"

saw me slip past him instead of Kramer. He almost fell off his wheel with surprise. As I flew past him he muttered a terrible oath that was tinged with blue, but I had visions of the first prize money that was awaiting me at the tape so I did not wait to hear the rest of his sulphuric outburst.

As I rounded into the home stretch I could hear the frantic cheering of the crowd which seemed to increase until I breezed over the tape fully ten lengths ahead of big Mac, who had beaten out the very one whom he was assisting in an effort to trim me—Kramer. Lawson finished third while Kramer was out of the picture altogether.

The pace was torrid right from the start of the race and of the more than thirty starters all but about six dropped out of the race, completely burned off, before the halfway mark was reached. It surely was a leg tester, and the last lap was a genuine test of gameness, as we were all physically "shot." If ever there was a speed test in bicycle racing it was that one. It demonstrated clearly to me the value of stamina and topnotch physical condition. While MacFarland and Kramer sustained another telling setback in this event it was a wonderful personal triumph for me. The crowd was not so slow to sense it and I got a mighty ovation as I rode my lap of honor. I only wish it was possible to describe the wonderful thrill and satisfaction of winning that particular race, the crowd seemingly went mad for the time being. I chuckled meantime as the band played a "Hot Time in the Old Town Tonight."

MacFarland was so angered at the outcome of the race that he belabored Kramer and Lawson in the presence of all of the other riders, trainers and managers for "permitting me to win." Later he threatened to clean out the training quarters but did not get that far in his efforts to vent his rage on anything or anybody that crossed his path.

The spontaneous applause that the spectators gave me on this occasion again demonstrated to me that the honest fair-minded, sport-loving public always demanded fair play in athletic sports regardless of color. If ever there was any doubt about that fact in my mind it was thoroughly wiped out on this occasion.

It was some time later that I learned that MacFarland had arranged with all of the other riders in that five-mile race to run me off my feet in it. Had I only known this at the time I would have given the bunch a real trimming as per my father's suggestion—at Indianapolis.

Still another New York newspaper printed the following account of the Manhattan Beach track program:

"It was unsportsmanlike. The worst charge that can be made against a man who enters a contest where a fair test of endurance and skill is supposed to be guaranteed, is that of unsportsmanlike conduct. Any contest that is not on the level is worse than none at all, for it degrades a certain class of athletes who try to make an honorable living by superior training and giving the public the benefit of their prowess, and it places them in the same category with the card sharp and the whole Bunco fraternity.

"Whether the skin of the contestant be white or black he is entitled to what he is worth, and to defeat him the winner should be able to prove himself the better man. which should hold true in cycling, prize fighting, wrestling, baseball or any other sport. The conduct of John Bedell and Iver Lawson at the Manhattan Beach track yesterday afternoon was reprehensible in the extreme.

"In the final of the One-Third-Mile National Championship Event they deliberately 'pocketed' Major Taylor, the colored rider, thus dealing a victory to Frank Kramer, the champion. It is pleasing to note that the referee knowing that a reputation of such foul tactics would soon destroy the game for lack of true sportsmanship promptly disqualified Bedell and Lawson.

"To illustrate Major Taylor's superiority, a little while afterwards he defeated a fast field of riders in the Five-Mile Handicap Event from scratch, while his erstwhile competitor, Kramer, could not finish better than fifth. Throughout this season Major Taylor has been harassed to a point of desperation by these cheap fellows who seemed determined that he shall not win the championship of America again. In every race a combination seems always in order to defeat Taylor by unfair tricks, even if they themselves fail to score.

"Wherever there is an attempt to pocket a rider or foul him in any way the event should be called off and the guilty ones barred from racing for the remainder of the season, if not forever. When people who support the races pay their way to see a contest they want it decided on its merits no matter who carries off the prize. With anything like a fair show, or an equal chance and the honest observations of the rules of bicycling racing Major Taylor would be Champion of America again."

Shortly after the above mentioned races Kramer and I were signed for a special match race on the Newark, New Jersey, track. It was stipulated that the winner of the best two heats in three would take the entire purse of $500. The first heat was to be over a half-mile route, the second a full mile, while the third, if necessary, was to be determined by the toss of a coin.

While I had defeated Kramer in the first two special match races we figured in, fate decreed that he was to defeat me on this occasion in two straight heats. If ever a man had a good alibi for being beaten I had, had I elected to use it. But instead I took my setback as a good sport should, shook hands with Kramer congratulating him and acknowledging him to be the better man on that occasion.

I now for the first time will make public the facts leading up to my defeat at the hand of Kramer. I wish to state at this time that Mr. Fred Voigt, manager of the Newark track, was aware of my troubles of the moment which brought about my defeat. But at my suggestion he did not divulge the facts to anybody.

Leaving Worcester with my wife at six o'clock on the morning of the race I planned to have breakfast on the train. *En route*, however, we learned that there would be no dining car on the trip so we had a cup of coffee in the short stop that we made at Springfield. Continuing our trip we arrived in Newark about noon with our minds all made up to have a substantial lunch. Our plans were somewhat upset when we were refused service in three restaurants because of our color. Now I had a hard race before me, I was discouraged and disgusted by this turn of affairs and I decided to forsake the race and return home. In the depot I ran across Manager Voigt and told him of the difficulties that we had experienced.

He sympathized sincerely with me and offered to take me to lunch with him. This was impractical as it was then but a short time before the scheduled hour for the race to start and I refused his kind offer with thanks. After an urgent plea by Manager Voigt centering about the amount of money he had tied up in this event, and knowing that the public would be keenly disappointed, together with the possibilities of difficulties with the N. C. A. officials, I reluctantly decided to go through with the race.

With heavy steps I made my way to the track knowing full well that I could not do myself justice in such an important race as confronted me on an empty stomach. Nevertheless, I rode for all I was worth against Kramer but he defeated me by a wheel's length in the first heat and by about eighteen inches in the second and deciding heat. So impressed was Mr. Voigt with my gameness that he made me a present of $400 at the conclusion of the race as a loser's end.

I quote as follows from a Newark newspaper:

"Major Taylor defeated in Special Match Race. Major Taylor was badly defeated by Frank Kramer in a special match race on the Vailsburg track yesterday for a purse of $500, winner take all. The first heat was a loafing race for half the distance until Kramer sprinted for home, winning by a wheel's length. The first heat was a half-mile.

"In the second heat Kramer again took the lead and the pair of riders galloped around the track for three-quarters of a mile. When the sprint started Kramer was leading on the pole. Taylor tried hard to pass him on the home stretch but could not, Kramer again winning, this time by about eighteen inches, the last heat was one mile."

# CHAPTER LVI



Shortly after Frank Kramer had defeated me in our special match race at Newark I took ample revenge on him for that setback at the Revere Beach track. To make my victory doubly sweet on this occasion I again scrambled the plans of the master schemer, MacFarland, and his colleagues, Kramer and Lawson, who sought by underhanded methods to insure my defeat.

Kramer, MacFarland, Lawson and I won our way into the final heat of the Half-Mile Championship Event on this occasion. MacFarland's job was to do the pulling in the final with Kramer hugging his rear wheel. Lawson in turn was to hold Kramer's wheel as a matter of protection in order to keep me away from Kramer as far as possible, Kramer being scheduled to win.

With four laps left to go MacFarland started to sprint at a terrific pace. I was in fourth position when we crossed the tape with three laps to go with Lawson switching continually. Big "Mac" was now pacing at his maximum speed. Carefully timing Lawson just entering the turn with two laps left to go I gave his back wheel a side slap with my front wheel at the same time uttering a yell which caused him to swing out sharply from the pole. Almost simultaneously I replaced Lawson on Kramer's back wheel.

Entering the back stretch I repeated the same trick on Kramer with similar success giving me MacFarland's rear wheel, the winning position. This I held until MacFarland swung out just enough to allow Kramer (as he thought) to slip through on the pole. I jumped through so quickly that MacFarland had no chance to close down on me as he saw me flash past him instead of Kramer, and I kicked to the front, winning by two lengths amid thunderous applause.

MacFarland's cursing and swearing were plainly audible to me despite the thunderous applause I received at the conclusion of this most sensational race. MacFarland was fit to be tied as were the other two when they realized what had happened. After crossing the tape MacFarland rode along side of me waving his arms and shaking his fists at me in a threatening manner. He even promised to beat me up as soon as he got me in the dressing room.

However, he found time to cool off a bit while he lodged a protest with the judges as I was riding my lap of honor. The judges saw through big "Mac's" flimsy attempt at a protest of the race since it had been ridden according to the letter of the rules and they waved him away.

Hurt by MacFarland's voluble abuse and put on the defensive by
his threats to do me bodily harm I quickly made up my mind to defend
myself against him and the rest of his gang if they bothered me in
my dressing room.   This is the first time in my racing career that
I ever lost my head to the extent of planning to fight for my rights
at all costs.   As they came into my room I was waiting for them
with a length of two-by-four which I had picked up from a lumber
pile near the grandstand.   Before they had a chance to lay a hand on
me I made one vicious, healthy swing at MacFarland but he dodged
the blow.   Then the entire outfit tried to close in on me but I was too
fast for them even on foot.   I dropped my club and made for the
dressing room where my trainer and I were obliged to take refuge
until the police interfered.   Fortunately there was no bloodshed.

At the following circuit meet at Baltimore I coached Willie Fenn
to a victory over Kramer in a heat of a championship race.   This
stunt by Fenn was particularly pleasing to me in view of the fact
that he had decided not to ride in the race because he was not feeling
fit.   He was threatened with suspension by Chairman Batchelder, and
I talked him into riding even promising to instruct him as to how he
could defeat Kramer in his heat.

Fenn was impressed with my advice.   I told him further that if
he would watch me ride in my heat and keep close tabs on every move
I made he could adopt my measures and take Kramer into camp in
his heat.   That bid of advice seemed to encourage Fenn and he prom-
ised that he would follow my instructions to the letter—and he did,
actually shaking Kramer off up the home stretch and winning a place
for himself in the final.

Taking my tip Fenn rode in last position in his heat until there was
but a lap and a half to go.   Then he went to the front with Kramer
on his rear wheel where he remained until Fenn drew away from him
coming up to the tape.   The bunch of riders were delighted to see
the popular Fenn pulling away from Kramer, the champion, and the
crowded grandstand also cheered their sentiments.

Just before we were called out for the deciding heat Fenn, highly
elated, came into my dressing room to thank me for my instructions
which served him in good stead when he defeated Kramer in their
heat.   He was all smiles as he told me it was the easiest race he had
ever won, then a puzzled look came over his face as he said, "But,
Major, you're in the final heat and so am I, now what do you advise
me to do?"   Patting Fenn on the shoulder I advised him to go out
and employ the same tactics and ride his head off in an effort to beat
the field.   Thanking me, Fenn said he realized he probably could not
beat me, but added he would like to land inside the money.   "That
being the case," I told him, "if you can tack on to my rear wheel in

that last lap, Bill, you can count on landing second money. Meantime if you see a chance to beat me to the tape hop to it and welcome."

At the start of the final heat I dropped into last position with Fenn riding in third place which gave me his rear wheel, forcing the other two competitors into the lead. These positions remained unchanged until within a lap and a half to go then I made a bid for the tape with Fenn on my rear wheel. I crossed the line first and Fenn, true to my prediction, walked off with second money.

As I rode my lap of honor on the Baltimore track I received one of the greatest ovations of my entire career. It made me think back to the time when track officials in that city rejected my entry fearing, as they said, that my riding would not be pleasing to the bicycle enthusiasts. The demonstration of the moment again proved to me that the sport loving public always wants to see the best man win in every branch of athletic sports regardless of race, color or creed.

From Baltimore the circuit riders moved on to Hartford, Connecticut where we participated in the One-Third-Mile Championship Race. On this occasion Kramer, the champion of the country, was again shut out of his preliminary heat and was, therefore, unable to participate in the final heat.

A Hartford paper carried the following paragraphs concerning that race:

"Major Taylor wins easily. Major Taylor had little difficulty in winning the One-Third-Mile Championship Race at the Hartford Veledrome last night. In the first heat R. M. Alexander got a good start on the second lap and Jackobson got the jump on Kramer in the last lap, beating the champion out at the tape. Major Taylor won his heat and his semi-final with ease. He had little trouble in defeating Iver Lawson in the first heat and in the semi-final he won out by ten lengths from 'Plugger' Bill Martin. Lawson won the second semi-final by defeating Jed Newkirk. Owen Kimble won the fourth semi-final by defeating Johnnie Fisher.

"The final of the championship was won by Major Taylor from Iver Lawson, while Johnnie Fisher finished third and Jackobson was fourth. Time :41. Frank Kramer failed to qualify in his preliminary heat and, therefore, did not start in the final. Major Taylor's victory was well received by the Hartford bike fans."

At the closing meet of the season at the new six-lap Coliseum track at Philadelphia, a few nights after the Hartford meet I received one of the rawest deals that has ever been my lot. I had become more or less used to the underhanded methods adopted by my competitors and had laid my plans accordingly. However, on this occasion I also had to contend with a conniving promoter, who is still prominent in the sport, who with MacFarland took the prize money which was hung up for this race and ran away with it.  While I won the race and Bowler finished second we received no prize money whatever while Kramer and Lawson who finished in third and fourth position got it all.

After MacFarland had tried every trick imaginable to bring about my elimination in my heat of the semi-final, as was his custom, he sought out Timmie Bowler in an effort to get him to team up with Kramer and Lawson to further insure my losing in that heat.  Bowler had no use for Kramer, Lawson or MacFarland and so MacFarlands' plan to incur Bowler struck a snag.  No sooner had Bowler qualified for the final than he proposed teaming up with me, as teaming up was permissible that season in a ruling by the N. C. A. moguls, providing participants announced their intentions to the referees, who in turn made it public.  I rejected Bowler's offer, however, telling him that I felt I could beat both Kramer and Lawson and himself in the final single-handed because of the excellent physical condition I was in, and needed no assistance.

I recall that this race was held on a beautiful summer's night, it was warm and ideal in every way for racing.  Besides that I was never better trained in my life and I had all the confidence in the world in my ability to beat the field, combinations or no combinations. Then, too, I loved to ride before a Philadelphia audience as I knew they were well-versed in the sport and were very liberal in their applause regardless of who won, provided good sportsmanship prevailed in the conduct of the event.

My last word to Bowler as we started out to face the starter's gun in the final heat was that I was going to win the race and that if he wanted to finish in second place all he had to do was to tack on to my rear wheel and stick there.  There was no teaming up between us because as I had previously informed Bowler I felt confident I could whip my three opponents in the final heat if need be, in case they all teamed against me.  Bowler followed my instructions to the letter and sure enough he rode into second money, Kramer being third, and Lawson fourth.  The applause was thunderous as I rode my lap of honor.

Bowler was naturally elated over the turn of events and thanked me sincerely as he quit the training quarters saying he was due in Chicago on a business matter the next day. A few moments later he rushed into my dressing room yelling like a madman.  It developed that the manager of the track and MacFarland had run away with the prize money that Bowler and I had won.

I wish to make it plain that the judges and the referee awarded me the race which I had fairly won without question or comment in regard to collusion from neither Kramer nor Lawson and the public, after cheering wildly, left the arena satisfied that I would receive the winner's end. But when we called at the box office for our share of the prize money we were informed that the manager and MacFarland had absconded with it, leaving word that they had given Kramer and Lawson first and second prizes and that Bowler and I had been disqualified for teaming.

Incidentally neither Bowler nor I ever received a penny for winning that race and as far as I know nothing ever happened to the pair. I later appealed to the chairman of the racing board, although I knew I had no redress and was licked from the start, but I thought he would at least give them each a slap on the wrist. He promised to investigate, but like most such "investigations" this gesture on the part of officials was merely a stall which allowed the thieves to get away to a good start. The only difference between these bandits and Jessie James' gang was that these robbers used bicycles instead of horses.

# CHAPTER LVII



Following in the footsteps of my illustrious predecessor, the first American Sprint Champion, Arthur Augustus Zimmerman of Freeport, New Jersey, I invaded Australia for the season of 1903. Since Zimmerman, who was my boyhood hero, had made a very successful invasion of the land of the kangaroo five years previous to my jaunt there, I bent every effort to duplicate or even exceed his wonderful performances there. Also since I was contemplating retiring from the sport I felt that my career would hardly be completed unless I measured my speed against Australia's best, feeling that this was really the only other world, in a bicycle sense, that I had not conquered.

Frankly, if it were not for the fact that I had previously given my word that I would participate in the 1903 season in Australia I would have permanently retired from the sport with the close of the 1902 season in America. Several factors prompted me to take this step. In the first place I was satisfied that I could never regain my American championship title, which I had won in three consecutive seasons, 1898, 1899, 1900, with the entire field of riders combined against me. On top of that I felt that my seven world's records including the fastest mile ever ridden behind motor pace and also the world's sprint title, to say nothing of my three very successful invasions of Europe, warranted my retirement while I was still at the top of the heap. I also felt that since I had fulfilled and even exceeded the wonderful prophecy of my discoverer, Mr. Louis D. (Birdie) Munger, that I was entitled to the rest that I had so rightly earned, especially since I had won enough honors for any one man on the bicycle track.

However, I had given my word to the bicycle meet promoters in Australia that I would compete for them in the 1903 season and I stood ready, if they gave the word, to go through with that plan. They insisted and within a month of the close of the American season I was *en route* to Australia, via San Francisco. I was accompanied on this long trip by my wife, the voyage being something in the nature of a honeymoon trip.

When I called for my steamship tickets in San Francisco the agent informed me that there was a rigid color line in effect in Australia. This was the first intimation I had had that any such condition prevailed there and I was very much disturbed. It seems that the color line was drawn in Australia to keep out the Japanese and Chinese as it was feared that they might cause labor disturbances there if allowed to enter in large numbers as has since happened in California.

My first thought upon getting this information was to cancel my Australian tour but my dauntless fighting spirit and courage served me in good stead and I decided to go through with the agreement. It was particularly discouraging to me to realize that I would be up against such a proposition in Australia, as I somehow figured that race prejudice flourished only in this country. It certainly was a distressing outlook. Before I had left San Francisco, however, my wife and I were subjected to indignities through the sharp drawing of the color line in that metropolis. Because of it we were unable to get hotel accommodations or food. We breathed a sigh of relief when we got aboard ship the following day but were shortly in throes of severe attacks of seasickness which added to our misery. For the first time in my life I was thoroughly discouraged at the turn affairs had taken. It seemed to me that even nature had taken up the cudgels against us. However, I had faith and eventually the sun burst forth again for us.

Meantime I told my wife I felt the color line tip that I had received relative to Australia could hardly be founded on fact. I did not believe that the promoters would have gone to the expense of taking me away out there unless they knew for a certainty that I would be permitted to land. Furthermore, in order to protect their own interests, I assured her, they would be obliged to see to it that we were treated courteously as we entered the country. I also reasoned that if we could exist in America where race hatred and color prejudice are so rampant we could undoubtedly get by in Australia or in any other country. So pondering on this line of reasoning we took new courage.

I shall never forget the courtesies extended my wife and myself by the purser on the ship. It developed he hailed from Westboro, Massachusetts, which is close to my adopted city, Worcester, Massachusetts. Although he had never seen me ride he was well acquainted with Willie Windle of Millbury, Massachusetts, another of my boyhood heroes, whom he had seen ride a number of times. The purser had followed my racing career carefully and he quoted a number of my records and outstanding achievements without hesitation. Daily he presented a group of fellow passengers to me and we talked for hours about bicycle racing and other sports, thus helping pass the time pleasantly. Gaining his confidence I asked the purser if it was true that there was a color line in Australia. He assured me that it was a fact adding, however, that the step was in the nature of a labor measure rather than as against members of my race as a whole. "You need have no fear, Mr. Taylor," he said, "because anybody with your personality and gentlemanly conduct will command respect over there, or wherever he may go."

With my experiences in San Francisco still fresh in mind I had my doubts about my personality getting me any advantages but I thanked the purser for his kind words, nevertheless. I was satisfied that my personality had secured very little for me in my native land, America, especially as regards fair play, equal rights, political rights and any other number and variety of rights. I vowed to the purser that if they drew the color line against me in Australia I would certainly be a passenger on his return voyage.

Reaching Auckland (New Zealand) I was cordially greeted and interviewed by a group of newspaper men, sport promoters, and prominent cyclists. Naturally I was anxious to ascertain whether or not I should be permitted to land in Australia because of the color line. They assured me that I would have no difficulty passing the immigration regulations and declared my manager had already looked after that detail of my trip. They informed us, however, that Australia did draw the color line, but not as far as I was concerned.

I shall never forget the wonderful sight that greeted us as the steamer rounded the Sydney Heads, the most beautiful natural harbor in the world. To me it was worth the price of the voyage just to sail from the entrance of the harbor to the pier, a distance of seven miles. As I stood drinking in the wonderful scenery the purser came running up to me all excited. Pointing over the rail of the steamer he exclaimed, "Look, look, do you see all those American flags. Do you hear those whistles and horns, now do you think you will be allowed to land in Australia?"

It was a most delightful experience and a very impressive one too, and I shall remember it as long as I live. I could not restrain my tears as I looked over the side of the liner and saw hundreds of boats and all kinds and sorts, both steam and naptha launches, decked out with American flags with their whistles tooting and men and women aboard them with megaphones greeting me with this salutation, "Taylor, Taylor! Welcome Major Taylor!" My friend the purser was as pleased with this royal welcome accorded me as my wife and I were. I told him I felt sure I was going to love Australia and that I would undoubtedly be obliged to delay my trip back to America until the last minute.

Presently the pilot came aboard and with him a number of newspaper men including Messrs. Percy Hunter and Tom Scott under whose management I was to ride. Mr. Hugh MacIntosh, secretary of the League of New South Wales Wheelmen, who later promoted the Johnson-Burns fight in Australia, was also on the welcoming committee. After being cordially welcomed to Australia by that trio I was interviewed by a squad of newspaper men.

As we stepped ashore my wife and I were greeted by thousands of cheering people. We were taken to the Hotel Metripole where a beautiful suite had been reserved for us. At the hotel I was introduced to a number of prominent people and was later escorted to the City Hall where I was formally welcomed by the Lord Mayor of Sydney, city officials, prominent citizens and sporting celebrities. It was a rousing welcome and I shall never forget the flattering compliments the several speakers tendered me in the course of the banquet which followed.

A Sydney newspaper read as follows:

"The cycling champion of the world, Major Taylor, who arrived from America by the R.M.S. *Ventura* on Sunday, was received by the Lord Mayor (Alderman T. Hughes) at the Townhall yesterday. Amongst those present were Messrs. David Walker (general sec. Y.M.C.A.), C. W. Bennett, H. S. Cusack, T. F. Byrne, and a number of prominent officials of the League of New South Wales Wheelmen."

The Lord Mayor's speech was in part as follows: "The Lord Mayor cordially welcomed the visitor as the Champion Cyclist of the World, one who had met and defeated the foremost men in Europe and America, and who now comes to Australia to gain, if possible, fresh victories, and while wishing Major Taylor every success, he sincerely hoped that the Australians would hold their own against him, (applause), although he realized that they had a very difficult task before them.

"They were all pleased to see a man of Major Taylor's standing in the world of sport visit Australia even though he should sweep over the land like a whirlwind, for those who entered into competitions with him were bound to profit by the experience, whether they were successful or not. (Applause.)"

A Sydney newspaper carried the following excerpt of the banquet: "The Lord Mayor proposed the visitor's good health. Mr. Percy Hunter, who supported the toast explained the negotiations which had taken place to secure the visit of Major Taylor, and detailed the difficulties that were encountered before the engagement of the champion was finally settled. He thought that the presence of Major Taylor in Australia would give the sport a new impetus. Major Taylor responded to the toast in a neat speech and expressed the hope that he would be able to come up to the expectations, and that the public would not be disappointed with his performances. Dr. A. M. Gledden proposed prosperity to the League of Wheelmen to which Mr. O'Brien responded, assuring Major Taylor that he would receive a fair field but no favors.

"Mr. J. J. Virgo, General Secretary-elect of the Y.M.C.A. proposed the health of the Lord Mayor. He considered that it was a gracious act on the part of his lordship to receive Major Taylor, who, he was assured, fully appreciated the honor accorded him."

The first place in Sydney that I wanted to visit was, of course, the great battle field—the bicycle track. It was located in Moore Park, being built of concrete, measuring three laps to the mile, about forty feet wide and banked to about thirty or thirty-five degrees. It had a peculiar shape being almost round. The famous Sydney cricket field was located inside the bicycle track which was almost completely surrounded by grandstands.

The Famous Sydney Cricket Ground and Track at Night. At the Start of each Race all Lights are turned off, except those directly over the Track

After spending a few days sight-seeing and shaking off my sea legs I announced I was ready and eager to start my training.

I was much impressed with the hospitality of the Australians from the outset, everyone I met seemed anxious to be of service to my wife and I and we were deluged with invitations to visit or be the dinner guests of hundreds of people whom we met in the course of our stay. However, I knew that I would have to curtail my social activities if I desired to be at my best at my profession, bicycle racing. So I devoted all my spare time to training as I knew my program had been previously arranged for me, since the time allotted for my practice stunts was very limited.

Had I been less serious in my training preparations I could never have gotten in shape for my first race which came only a fortnight after I landed in Sydney. It took me but a few days to lose my sea legs, then I went to work in earnest preparing for my initial race in which Don Walker and Joe Megson, the two best sprinters in Australia, together with the cream of the sprinters in that country, took part. This was scheduled to be held on January 3, 1903. Thousands of people came to the track daily to watch my training preparations and most of them were impressed at the seriousness with which I went about my work.  The riders expressed astonishment at my training stunts and the great amount of work I did, all of which was new to them.  Likewise they were surprised when I went out on the track to work with them as they had an idea that I preferred to do my training in secret.

My Australian rivals seemed pleased at the frankness that I showed as they plied me with questions relative to my bicycle, such as the gear,

Major Taylor and Trainer Sid Melville at the Sydney Cricket Grounds and Bicycle Track

length of cranks, height of frame, the pedal reach, etc., and were again astonished when I gave them the privilege of examining it for themselves.  Most riders regarded these points as vital secrets but I did not hesitate to give this information to any who desired it.  I even answered questions concerning my tactics in races, and as far as I know this showing of my hand never reacted against me.

I gradually rounded into shape and things began to look rosy for a very successful visit in Australia, the greatest sporting country on earth.  I can not emphasize too strongly the pressure off of my mind upon learning that I would have no worry from the color line while I was here.  This was a tremendous load lifted off my shoulders and it permitted me to go about my training unhampered.  In addition to this the climate was just to my liking for racing, as it was delightfully balmy.  My manager selected for me as a trainer, Sid Melville, one of the most faithful and loyal trainers a man could have.

While working out on the Sydney track daily I made a close study of all my new opponents who included the pick of Australasia. In this way I ascertained their strong and weak points and incidentally I discovered that my opponents were not high class sprinters with the possible exception of Don Walker, who was the champion at that time. However, my rivals comprised the greatest aggregation of fast riders as a group of any country I had visited, including even America.

I found also that some of the riders who had the best head for tactics were woefully lacking in heart and courage, while those who had the greatest courage and gameness lacked speed and strength. One of the star riders whom I watched in practice had the head and the gameness but possessed only stamina enough for one heat. After winning one heat this rider could not repeat and for this reason he seldom got into the final, but in that one heat he was a very dangerous contender.

I also found that my superior knowledge and experience in match racing also stood me in good stead. In all of my important races in America and in Europe the big purses were for scratch events and match races, but I found the opposite plan prevailed in Australia where the handicap races take the big purses. Hence the riders of that country were exceptionally strong handicap men and equally as fast and strong in open events, but they were not especially "up" on the fine points of the game, such as tactics and track generalship in match racing. But they were as game a set as I ever competed against and quickly adopted some of my best tactics, forcing me to invent some new and strategic moves.

Just before my first race I was informed that the Quarter-mile Championship of Australia would be the feature attraction on . the opening night's program. Mr. Percy Hunter, one of my managers, after watching me work out one day asked me how I felt. I told him I was pleased with my condition and would be sorely disappointed if I failed to win my first start. I also told him I was anxious to be at my very best form to repay the good people of Sydney in my own way for the many courtesies they had extended me. Although I did not tell Mr. Hunter I was still unaccustomed to sprinting for the tape on an almost round track. Naturally this caused me considerable annoyance until I became familiar with it. As a matter of policy, however, I never complained about the track as I felt that would have been giving the other riders an advantage over me in addition to the worry it was causing me.

From long experience I knew that if I could win my first race or even hold my own against the best riders in Australia, after the period of training that I had had, I would have little to fear in my tour of the country. I felt also that I would improve my condition through riding this first race and each time I competed throughout the season. The Australian riders were already at top form, having been racing for two months before I arrived.

Their style of riding handicap races was new to me. A rider never started in a handicap race over there with the idea that he would win on his own, they always worked in combinations of two or three, and sometimes even more, to help pace the contestant whom they had figured stood the best chance of winning. In the event of his winning the race he would split his winnings equally among those who had assisted him.

Another thing that interested me very much was the method adopted by the riders to defeat the scratch man. According to the Australian rules a rider was not obliged to start in a race even after qualifying. The intent of this rule was undoubtedly to spare the riders from being compelled to race with an injury, or after being taken suddenly ill. But in time the riders took advantage of this rule and used it for shady purposes. By taking advantage of it they could remain out of the final intentionally in order to create a gap too great for the scratch man to close up to his nearest competitor unassisted.

For example, if there were ten or twelve men in the final and they were placed out ahead of the scratch man on marks ranging from 10 to 150 yards, the first four or five men nearest the tape would scratch. This would leave as many more riders on the longer marks nearest the limit man, making a gap of 75 or 80 yards for the scratch man to bridge before he really could give them a race. Meantime the long handicap men were alternating the pace, burning the track with speed, while the scratch man was straining every nerve and muscle to overtake them, which in most cases would be physically impossible.

In a combination of this kind, of course, it was understood in advance which rider was to win. Thus the entrants who scratched not only came in for their split of the purse, but could safely bet their last dollar on the result. That's where they made their clean-up. So far as I have been able to learn Zimmerman and I were the only riders who never entered in any such combinations.

# CHAPTER LVIII



"The sole topic of conversation yesterday in cycling circles was the forthcoming visit of the world's champion, Major Taylor, to race here in January and February next. The enterprise of the promoters of the big cycling carnivals being held this summer, in securing the presence of the famous negro, met with praise on all sides. The fee which is being paid for Taylor's presence—£1500—is the largest ever given to a racing cyclist in any part of the world, and although this seems an enormous sum to pay any man to come out here and race, the promoters should reap a good reward by securing very large attendances at their meetings to see this wonderful sprinter opposed to the Australian cracks. As Taylor is to appear in sixteen races in all, he will have ample scope to display that lightning sprint which has earned him so much fame and placed him head and shoulders over the rest of the world's crack sprinters.

"When the great A. A. Zimmerman visited Sydney some five years ago he only appeared twice in Sydney, and over 30,000 people attended to see him race each day. Major Taylor is a faster sprinter than Zimmerman ever was, and League authorities here naturally expect that just as many people will attend their next meetings to see the wonderful negro race as attended to see Zimmerman opposed to our best men.

"Major Taylor is recognized all the world over as the world's premier sprinter, as he ought to be, for, after conquering all the champions of his own country, he visited Europe on two occasions—this season and last—and easily defeated the premier riders there. On his return to America this year, after a successful European tour, he had to put up with a great deal from the Americans, who will stop at nothing in order to defeat him. They do not seem to care who wins so long as it is not Taylor, and in nearly every race he was deliberately blocked and 'pocketed' in order that he should not get home first. Whenever he did get a clear run it was Taylor first and the rest anywhere. The American officials must have been prejudiced against the negro wonder too, or else they would not allow such a state of affairs to exist. Taylor can depend on getting a fair deal from the Australian riders during his forthcoming visit. Even should our riders have any intention of resorting to unfair means to defeat the world's champion, the officials would soon put a stop to it. Every athlete that has yet visited Australia, whether black or white, has always received a fair deal from his opponents. This cannot be said of the European and American riders, who have never given Major Taylor a straight deal if they could help it.

"The world's champion sprinter was on the Sydney Cricket Ground track yesterday for the first time since his arrival in Sydney. He only did a little slow work. He will be on the track twice daily now until the opening day of the carnival, on January 3, when he hopes to be in something like proper shape to do himself justice. Taylor has a nice position on a machine, and is a nattily put together athlete. As he rides around the track it can be seen at a glance that he is a great rider, and no doubt he will prove a favorite with the public here. Tremendous interest is being taken in his performances, and it is safe to say that when he makes his first appearance on the Cricket Ground on Saturday week there will be a crowd to welcome him quite as large as that which saw Zimmerman race here on two occasions. Major Taylor puts in some of his time at the gymnasium of the Y.M.C.A. every day. Towards the end of the week the champion intends to begin fast work behind the powerful Massey-Harris motor. He realizes that in Walker he has a sprinter of the very best class to beat, and consequently will leave 'no stone unturned to achieve his true form.

"The largest crowd that had attended any bicycle racing program in Australia since the great Zimmerman was there in 1895 attended my first appearance in Sydney on January 3, 1903. There were over twenty thousand paid admissions to this program, Zimmerman's two races in Sydney attracting sixty thousand people. Included in the gathering were practically all of the city's official family, numerous former cycling stars and enthusiasts and not a few tourists from all quarters of the globe."

I quote the following article from one of the Sydney dailies:

"The feature race of the program at the Sydney Cricket Grounds Track yesterday was, of course, the début of Major Taylor, and his meeting with the Australian Champion, Don Walker. There were three first-class events on the program in which all of the cracks appeared. They were the Wyalon Half-Mile Handicap, the Quarter-Mile International Championship Race and the Walker Plate, a five-mile scratch event.

"All of the racing proved interesting and two or three of the events aroused a greater pitch of enthusiasm than has ever been witnessed here before. One of these was the victory of the World's Champion in the International Championship race in which Major Taylor showed a flash of one of the sprints for which he became so justly famous. And again the crowd became wildly excited when Don Walker, the Australian, defeated Taylor and the big field of first-class men in the Five-Mile Scratch race which wound up the program.

"The sport provided was entirely to the taste of the huge audience, everyone went away in the best of humor having enjoyed a sporting treat, and fully determined to see more of the meetings between the two champions, the next of which takes place tonight when Taylor and Walker will fight their battle over again.

"When the riders went out to indulge in their preliminary practice Major Taylor was accorded a most flattering reception by the specta-

Don Walker—Australian Champion

tors. He must have been pleased with the welcoming cheer that went up all around the grounds as he pedalled around the track. This welcome was an earnest demonstration of the fair play and consideration that he would receive on the Australian track in his struggles with Australian rivals. The Australian champion, Don Walker, on appearing a few minutes later was as cordially received and it was apparent that if the Australian could prove his superiority over the distinguished visitor the victory would be a most popular one.

"The racing started shortly afterwards with the heats of the Half-Mile Handicap, the first heat being won by Dick Mutton from virtual scratch with a fine burst of speed. The second heat was won by Dan Sheehan from S. Simon, who rode a good race. The third heat brought out Don Walker, who thrice demonstrated that he was in magnificent form. In it he met several other good men in the persons of R. Lewis, J. Chalmers and E. Payne. Walker showed his form by running onto Lewis' wheel at one bound and paced in turn by Payne, Chalmers, and Lewis, this bunch cut out a very hot lap until just leaving the back stretch for the second time, Walker was seen moving around on the outside, getting clear he set sail for the leaders with a great rush amid intense excitement. He cut the front men down in the home stretch and won by a length from Payne, Lewis being a close third. The time from scratch was :57, which was remarkably good.

"The next heat saw Major Taylor on his mark placed five yards behind scratch. This was the first occasion in which a man has ever started behind scratch on a track. The champion was loudly cheered as he took up his position and at the gun fire he jumped like lightning onto Gudgeon, who set sail for the field with Taylor trailing his wheel in fine shape. Some fast men were out front and Gudgeon carried the champion along very fast. When the home turn was reached the riders had a long break and when Taylor settled down for his home run he flew over the last thirty yards at an incredible rate of speed but he was just too late to win, though he was travelling five yards to the winner's one at the finish. He placed third. McLean was first and Drinkwater was second.

"Walker won the final heat, Ben Goodson, the fast and plucky Queenslander, was second, and Boidi, the Italian star, was third, the time being :57 3/5.

"The race next discussed was the Quarter-Mile International Championship. In this event Major Taylor proved victorious, his lightning jump and speedy sprint being too much for Don Walker, who, however, finished with a remarkable burst of speed, making up a lot of ground in the last fifty yards and finishing a good second.

"This event caused the wildest excitement of all and while everyone on the grounds would no doubt have been glad to see the Australian win, no one begrudged the visitor the victory and gold medal, especially in view of the acknowledged fact that he has not yet reached his best form. No discredit attaches to Walker's defeat for he was beaten by the foremost tactician in the world, and it is probably due more to Taylor's better knowledge of tactics than to any superiority in speed over Walker that he will take the Australian medal away with him.

"The pace was slow at the Northern Pavilion, where Lewis on the inside suddenly went with a rush and made a clear break, but Taylor with his marvelous jump got going immediately, and Walker was dropped a couple of lengths. He picked up his sprint quickly and the three made a terrific dash for the tape with Taylor winning by half a length from Walker, who barely beat out Lewis for second. Major

Taylor was accorded a tremendous ovation for his great victory as he rode around the track with the Stars and Stripes fluttering from his hand.

"The final of the Quarter-Mile Championship summary is as follows:—Major Taylor, U. S. A., first; Don Walker, Victoria, second; R. W. Lewis, New South Wales, third, time :32.

"The program wound up with the Walker Plate, a five-mile scratch race.  Like a true sportsman, Major Taylor came out for this event

Start of Final Heat of Quarter-mile International Championship Race

although he might well have claimed exemption on the ground that his condition was not good enough to stand the strain.  It is all the more to his credit that he rode, though he hardly expected to get through the race, but the fine performance he subsequently put up surprised him considerably.

"The race was fast throughout, but the last three laps were run at a terrific pace, the last quarter being turned in :26, an Australian record.  This tearing pace naturally told on Taylor, whose condition is not yet up to the mark, for a race of this distance, but it had absolutely no effect on Walker's strength.  After a fine run on the back stretch where he had the good fortune to trail the wheel of Lewis, who is a magnificent judge of position, he swept around Taylor

who was trailing Gudgeon and Mutton, who were finishing a terrible
lap, and clipped over the tape a clear length to the good.

"The enthusiasm as Walker rode around after his splendid win
was wonderful.  The people stood on their seats and cheered wildly
again and again as the riders re-circled the track.  Major Taylor
rode along side of the Australian Champion and congratulated him
by shaking hands.  The crowd burst out cheering anew and the day
ended with the honors even and with the good feeling between the two
champions unimpaired."

Taylor Winning Final Heat of Quarter-mile International Championship,
Sydney, Australia

# CHAPTER LIX



Following our first clash at the opening program Walker and I were interviewed concerning each other's ability under fire.

I was quoted as follows:

"Major Taylor Regards Don Walker, the Australian Champion, As One of the World's Best. I consider, he said, that I have made

Two Great Rivals, TAYLOR and WALKER

wonderful strides while in Sydney in view of the fact that I have only been about ten days on my wheel since I landed. I really did not expect to get in to sprinting form so quickly. The training record I have made while here is far better than any I have previously accomplished in any country. In fact I never before attempted to ride on such a short preparation.

"What do you think of Walker now? Well, my previous high opinion of Walker has not changed by his showing yesterday. It is difficult to compare him with the continental riders as they go in for an entirely different style of training and racing. All of their races are of the short sprint order. Neither Jacquelin or Elleggarde could have stood three minutes of the pace changing, ripping, five miles which Walker defeated me in yesterday.

"The last three laps' pace of that race were corkers and made me absolutely tired, and I finished very slow. But I did not complain at that because I really did not expect to be able to finish at all. I am quite certain there is not an American today that can defeat Don Walker.

"What about the Quarter-Mile Championship? Well, that was a distance that suited my present form better. In that race I had nothing but sprinting to do. I could hold a short sprint like that at my top speed, still it was not easy, as Lewis is another fine sprinter, and gained another good break when he jumped. I touched his rear wheel just as I was about to pass him. It was a narrow escape. This was due, however, to my rear wheel's skidding slightly when I jumped suddenly. I do not think I ever travelled faster than I did over the last sixty yards. Walker came very fast at the finish.

"I received very fair treatment from all the riders and I admire the way they ride, and the pace they can set. They are a much better lot of men than is generally known in other countries, and taking them all around I think they are far better in handicap races than American riders.

"Speaking of his effort in the Half-Mile Handicap, he said, I had a good position throughout the race, but Gudgeon was a bit slow off the mark. I might have won by going out on my own sprint a little earlier, but I thought by so doing I might spoil my chances for the other races. I can plainly see that a scratch man needs a bit of a motor to win in the handicap money in this country."

The following is quoted from Don Walker:

"I think that Major Taylor has nothing more to learn about the racing game, and even after he achieves his form I don't think he will sprint any faster than he did in the Quarter-Mile Championship Race yesterday. The quickness with which he made his famous jump was absolutely a revelation to me.

"I was watching him closely and was all ready for him, and expecting him to jump every moment, but when Bob Lewis got going on the inside, Taylor was gone like a flash of gunpowder. Before I could attempt to hold him he had two lengths on me. We then had less than two hundred yards to go to the tape, and of course, you know what that meant. I buckled and hustled but to get around a man like Taylor in a fresh sprint in 200 yards is a task verging on the impossible.

"A sensational incident occurred just after the three of us started at top speed. Taylor touched Lewis' back wheel just opposite the members' pavilion, I thought Taylor would come down, and eased off speed for a fraction of a second and swerved somewhat up the banking. But the champion made the most remarkable recovery I have ever seen, and seemingly without detracting from any of his speed, and from that point on he travelled faster than I have ever seen anyone sprint. He pulled right clear of Lewis, who is one of the best sprinters in Australia when fresh. I was full of sprint and coming fast. I think I sprinted faster than I ever did before but it was not fast enough to catch Taylor, who seemed to ride the last dozen yards at an increased pace.

"I can see that to have a chance of beating Taylor in that style of race I shall have to get going actually with him, and race every yard of the way. It must not be forgotten, however, that in this kind of racing Taylor has proved absolutely invincible, having beaten every sprinter in the world time and time again. I have hopes of turning the tables on him though before the carnival is over, but I have honestly to acknowledge that in the jump which we had in the final yesterday he was my superior.

"Did his touching Lewis' wheel interfere with your prospects at all? In one way it did, but I cannot blame Taylor for that. It was more for what I fully expected to happen, after he hit Lewis' wheel, than what actually did happen that caused me to run a yard or two up the banking, but Taylor made such an extraordinary recovery that he not only kept up, but he scarcely swerved from his track, so he could not have interfered with me. Of course, on the track one must always be prepared for emergencies. You can't wait. If nothing happens so much the better.

"Do you think you have met your Waterloo in Major Taylor? I won't say that. I don't like to say anything that sounds like a boast. I really believe that I can make the short sprint closer than it was in the Quarter-Mile Race yesterday before the champion leaves us.

"You can beat him in the Walker Plate, how about that? Yes, but I don't count that against him. His ride in that race only increases my admiration for him, for his ability and the pluck with which he goes through his races. Which of us Australian riders could have put up such a sprint in the Quarter-mile Race, and then have gone through a five-mile race in which the last quarter was run in Australian record time, and finish right on the line with the winners after being off the boat only a fortnight after a long sea voyage? No, I take no credit for beating Taylor in the five-mile race. I think his performances yesterday, considering his form, as wonderful, and something that none of us Australians could ever accomplish. I won't consider that we Australian sprinters have defeated him until one of us has beaten him in the short sprints, such as the quarter, third, half and one-mile distances, the recognized championship distances. These are the true tests of speed pure and simple, for all the riders start their sprints absolutely fresh, and the fastest man reaches the tape first."

R. W. Lewis who finished third in the Championship race, and also interviewed said:

"I thought that I was actually winning the quarter-mile championship race, and the pace we were travelling at convinced me that in the short distance that intervened between us and the tape I had a very good chance of remaining in front. Near the members' stand I felt a sensation, as if I had a puncture. It did not, however, interfere with my speed. I realized afterwards that Taylor had hit my rear wheel. Then suddenly something flashed past me. Then I gave up thinking I could win.

"Major Taylor's jump past me was most extraordinary, because I was sprinting at my top speed, and the pace was proven by the manner in which I was able to race Walker. I think Taylor has a wonderful jump, and although I think he will be defeated by some of the Australians when they learn to jump away a bit faster, he will make our racing very interesting. He has wonderful control over his machine, and seems to be a true sportsman. For a great sprinter he has fine endurance. His coming out in the five-miles riding, considering he is not in form, should make him popular with the public. He put up a great race in the five-miles, and that he stuck to the finish proclaims him a great rider, for I don't think I was ever in a faster three laps than those that wound up that race yesterday."

Lewis was one of the fastest sprinters in Australia. He was the first Australian rider to do a mile inside of 2:25, and several years previous to my tour he had reduced the record to 2:08. That he was riding extremely well at the moment was amply proven by his defeating Gudgeon and Mutton, two other Australian stars in the third semi-final heat of the championship race.

A few days later one of the Sydney dailies carried the following self-explanatory article:

"Major Taylor's opinion of Gudgeon, one of the best New South Wales riders, is very high. Gudgeon has come rapidly to the front recently, and made a name for himself by beating all the cracks in Melbourne at the Australian meeting in the International Scratch Race. He hails originally from Cobar and is a big strong rider with quite considerable sprint, and uses a big gear. Taylor first made his acquaintance in the heat of the half-mile handicap in which the world's champion started from five yards behind scratch.

"He was giving Gudgeon twenty yards start, but caught him before the New South Wales rider had got going. When he did begin to move, however, he carried the world's champion in great style. Taylor afterwards expressing the opinion that 'riding behind him is like riding a motor.' Taylor again saw something of Gudgeon in the Walker Plate, in which Gudgeon was very prominent in the final three laps, in which Taylor trailed Gudgeon's wheel throughout the last lap, but Gudgeon dead-heated with Mutton, and beat the champion home.

"It is a pleasing trait in Major Taylor's character that he denies acknowledgment of the capabilities of no rider, and though Mutton and Gudgeon both beat him home, there was no trace of discontent in his reference to them. 'New South Wales,' he said, 'should be proud of having two such fine riders.' They are in his opinion fit to take their place with the best handicap men in the world.

"Some one asked Taylor if he thought Gudgeon was in MacFarland's class. MacFarland is known as the handicap king in America, and he has a wonderful record of wins in this class of racing. Taylor replied, 'MacFarland is not in the same class, but Gudgeon is the best handicap rider I have ever seen, and I believe he will make a champion in time.' "

The newspaper went on further to say, "We have vanquished the world's schulling, held our own in boxing, swimming and other lines of sport, but so far we have failed to produce a world's champion at bicycle racing.

"When Zimmerman was here he had a world's reputation, but he was not so much a world's champion as Major Taylor. We did beat Zimmerman several times, but it is only fair to admit that he was unlucky in the matter of health and scarcely showed at his best. In the same way as Megson, Lewis Payne, Martin, Palmer, Kerr, Beachamp, Goodson and many others who went to England and America, met with varying successes, but owing to climatic conditions and other reasons they never won a championship abroad.

"The recent championship I put by as worthless in comparing the merits of Taylor and Walker, that is, beyond the fact that Major Taylor can use his head, which we knew before, and which he must necessarily do to beat the Jacquelins and Elleggardes at their own game. If it simply becomes a matter of tactics, Major Taylor will always win when well.

"Could it be guaranteed that Taylor will go on improving in form (and it must be remembered that all the conditions were strange to him on his first appearance) in the next fortnight in proportion to what he picked up in a little over a week then there would only be one in it, but I very much doubt if he can. Form is a very elusive thing. You can't hurry over an athlete's preparation. The condition Taylor has may be of the 'mushroom' order, not lasting.

"Taylor certainly made a wonderful recovery after bumping Lewis. As we have said before, Taylor is a master of his machine, and he proved it in this instance. Without detracting from Major

Taylor's victory in the championship we consider that the supremacy between the two men has yet to be settled. Walker said before the final of the championship that he was afraid Taylor, who was an expert in that kind of race, might jump him. Taylor is undoubtedly a great rider, but Walker has few superiors. The American came with a great reputation, and it was not tarnished, but rather brightened by the result.

"Like Zimmerman, almost his first race gave him a championship victory. As a matter of fact if Taylor improves for the next few weeks in the same ratio as he has picked up form in his ten days he would be able to beat all our best men pointless. I am taking his measure by his efforts in the five-mile race. It bordered on the marvelous for a rider, who after three other races, to finish as he did in the long race. Would any of our riders shape up as well under the same circumstances if they went to America?"

# CHAPTER LX



Two days after my début on an Australian track, the same being located at Sydney, I appeared for my second program on the same course. Don Walker, the champion, and the cream of the fastest riders in that country were also entered in the various events. The handicap event was a half-mile race and there was a scratch event for the same distance in which Walker and myself were entered.

Winning Half-mile Handicap from 5 Yards behind Scratch and
establishing World's Record

The O'Brien Plate, a popular five-mile scratch race, wound up the evening's program.

Concerning my second appearance on the Sydney track one of the local dailies had this to say:

"The Major Taylor Carnival was continued last night and it proved to be a strong attraction. The racing was of the highest order. Major Taylor's heat in the Half-Mile Handicap was a revelation. Starting five yards behind the tape, he flashed along at a terrific pace to victory. He was unpaced throughout the race and finished in :56 1/5, a competitive record.

"In the semi-final heat Major Taylor started from the same mark as Don Walker. They were seen going at top speed and caught the field at the North Pavilion. At this point interest was momentarily taken from Taylor through an accident. There was a crash and a rider flew into the air minus a bicycle, while two others were spread-eagled on the track. Drinkwater had fallen, and Hardy shooting over the prostrate man's machine was hurled against an overhead electric light support breaking the glass. Drinkwater was injured, but Hardy without having any bones broken suffered much pain around his loins and back. Meanwhile, Major Taylor on hearing the crash swerved in and Larry Corbett finished first, equaling the world's record of :56 1/5 which Major Taylor had made in his first heat.

"Taylor's showing in the final heat was wonderfully good. He and Walker caught the field together. Walker got hopelessly blocked and Taylor also looked inextricably so, but Taylor streaked through and won by inches amid thunderous applause. The time, :55 3/5, still further clipping the world's record which was set in the first heat and tied in the semi-final by 3/5 of a second."

# CHAPTER LXI

### ANOTHER VICTORY AND ANOTHER POCKET

A large crowd was present at the third meet in which I participated in Sydney. The program was designated the "Major Taylor Carnival" and included the Summer Wheel Race, which carried with it a purse of $500 and attracted a large entry list of prominent handicap riders, heats of the $750 One-Mile Handicap, and Invitation Race of one lap, a Half-Mile Scratch race, a Half-Mile Handicap and the Ten-Mile Scratch Race.

I won the Half-Mile Scratch Race, and the Lap Dash Event, but was shut out of my heat in the Half-Mile Handicap when I was caught in a pocket.

I quote as follows from a Sydney newspaper clipping printed the day following this race meet:

"Major Taylor's Wonderful Sprint. Leaves Walker Standing. The excitement displayed last night at the Sydney Cricket Grounds when the Major Taylor Carnival was conducted was at times intense. The huge crowd of 15,000 people journeyed to the track primarily to see the colored cycling wonder, Major Taylor, ride. In the course of the program they became fully satisfied that his world-wide reputation as the fastest sprint rider in the world is not one bit exaggerated.

"The heats of the Summer Wheel Race were well contested. It was in the third heat that most of the interest centered, for in this Major Taylor made his first appearance of the night. He was greeted with applause. The champion started ten yards behind scratch, with Gudgeon on the ten-yard mark and Chalmers on the thirty-five yard mark.

"It was a one-mile race, but the big crowd was much disappointed when Taylor failed to get up with the long markers, and consequently did not make the finishing effort. There was an uproar though in the next heat when Don Walker, the Australian champion, was paced up to the front mark men at half the distance by Wilksch and Mutton, and finished a length ahead of Rolfe in one of his famous sprints. He received a great ovation.

"In the first heat of the Invitation Scratch Race of one lap, Megson, Gudgeon, and Burton started, but the former succumbed to the other two at the tape in a very close finish. Major Taylor, Bob Lewis, and Chalmers met in the second heat. Chalmers made a dash for the tape at the half lap mark and Taylor went after him. When the tape was crossed it was difficult to determine which of the two had really won, the judges deciding it was. a dead heat, the excitement became intense in the meantime.

"Don Walker succeeded in winning his heat and a little while afterwards the competitors lined up for the final. Walker was on the inside on the pole, Chalmers next, then Gudgeon, then Major Taylor. The pace was cut out by Gudgeon, with Walker, Taylor, and Chalmers in that order. Walker went out at the east pavilion but Taylor kept close up, and they settled down for the finish. At the members' stand Taylor made a quick dash and shot towards Walker like a flash, passing him in a brilliant sprint for the tape which he reached fully three clear lengths ahead and the enthusiasm that followed was tremendous.

"Don Walker was regarded by the great majority of those present as a certain winner of the final. At the pistol he remained on the pole and kept watching for Taylor, who, however, let him remain in the lead right up to and past the clock, when amid tremendous and excited shouts 'Walker wins, Walker wins, the darkey's beaten, the darkey's beaten,' Taylor, crouching very low, flashed past Walker as if he were anchored, winning by three lengths.

"The spectators were dumbfounded and Major Taylor had ridden almost around the track before his marvelous performance was fully realized. He beat Walker by four lengths in about seventy yards, and that while the Australian was right in the middle of one of his famous sprints."

Another Sydney newspaper carried the following comment the next day:

"It seems to us that while Don Walker is, perhaps, fast enough to pace with Taylor, the latter will out-general the Australian, as he has had far more experience in riding against the world's best, both in America and on the Continent.

"That is what we wrote last week and it seems to have anticipated the situation, except that Taylor has that tricky little kick which gets up a sprint so quickly, but we doubt if he is actually much faster than Walker.

"Everyone was prepared for the Special Invitation Lap Race in which Taylor and Walker were to settle their relative claims as to whom is the fastest sprinter in Australia at the present time.

"So far, however, Taylor has the best of it and we must admit his superiority, but it is mostly in head work that he surpasses the Australian. Walker is a phenominal rider in some respects but he lacks one or two essentials for a world's champion. He has not the good head of a Walne or Megson, nor the lion heart of the latter, which is not his fault but his misfortune.

"A great deal of excitement was caused in the second heat of the Lap Dash by Chalmers of New Zealand who nearly out-sprinted the star of the evening, Major Taylor, at the finish, when the American nearly left it too late to make his jump. Although he did leave Lewis very easily, Chalmers flashed across the tape with him and the decision of the judges was a dead heat.

"It so appears, however, that Major Taylor's great reputation has overpowered Walker, and he has not yet recovered from the spell. What, for instance, could have been more in Taylor's favor than for Walker to go to the front in the final of the Lap Dash last night? No doubt he thought he was doing the best thing, because of having made a mess of it in the opposite direction on Saturday by remaining too far behind in the hunt of the Quarter-Mile championship.

"Walker's only chance of defeating Taylor is to keep with him and sprint when he sprints, and in doing that a comparatively low gear will be found to be of advantage in those short sprints where the struggle is only for a few yards, and it is essential to sprint quickly.

"But giving Taylor all the credit, it must be recollected that these short loafing races are just made for him, while our own riders have been more used to genuine hard riding all the way. It may be 'fine art' as they term it on the Continent, but we confess that we do not care about it, and no doubt the public here will become enamored of it. At present Walker is the only one fit to pace with Taylor, but by and by, we may see Walne or Megson equal to challenging him in a special match race.

"The world's champion Major Taylor's form has improved, judging by his finish in the Half-Mile final on Monday night, he is improving with every appearance. His famous sprint, which won him the half mile, was a revelation.

"For ten yards it was any odds on Boidi, the Italian crack, who was a good sprinter, but Taylor fairly flew, and with a terrific jump near the tape he defeated Boidi at the finish. Australian riders had never seen such a stunt before, especially in view of the fact that Boidi had a lead of three lengths in the home stretch. It was a wonderful sprint and the large crowd present recognized its merits by giving the champion a fitting reception.

"This was the first half-mile handicap race in which Walker has been defeated this season, however, he was not disgraced in having his colors lowered by the world's champion. Walker was blocked and Taylor was too, for a while, but gamely pushed his way through the field. It was a very risky thing for a champion to do. Walker recognized this and would not follow through.

"After his race in the half-mile handicap Major Taylor was looked upon as a certainty in the half-mile scratch race later on, but he did not have a chance to get up for in his heat he was badly pocketed and had no earthlv chance of getting out of it and winning. It must have been an unpleasant experience for the World's champion to find riders whom he could easily defeat finishing in front of him while others held him safely in the 'pocket.' Every person present saw plainly that Taylor was blocked. He might have protested, but this he never does. He is used to being deliberately pocketed by the other riders, and has had this experience all over the world, however, he will no doubt profit by this experience and not allow himself to be shut in again.

"It is all in the game, however, and Taylor recognizes the fact, still it is an unpleasant experience for any crack rider to have to sit in and watch others sprinting for the tape when he knows he could have won."

# CHAPTER LXII


### A DOUBLE VICTORY DESPITE A POCKET

Commenting on the fact that my first two race meets had tended to create a revival of the sport in that country, one of the Sydney dailies pointed out that upwards of 35,000 people paid to attend these events. It pays tribute to the enterprise of the promoters who paid me a large sum of money to go to that country to race, and declares there is no question but what their efforts will meet with great financial reward. Further it pointed out the great public interest that centered about the races in which Don Walker, the Australian champion and myself have participated in.

Further this Sydney newspaper also stated:

"The majority of the Australian public now thinks that Major Taylor is too good for the Australian champion, but there is plenty of time yet for Don Walker, and he will continue his big efforts to retrieve his laurels in his pending races with Taylor.

"Perhaps we may yet have a chance of beating Major Taylor in a mile race run hot from start to finish, but when one recalls his great sprint in the recent half-mile handicap race which he won, and his remarkable ride in the five-mile race on his first appearance in Australia, there is little to hope for even in a mile race run hot all the way.

"Were he at his best, Billy MacDonald, who has just arrived from Westralia, would have a hope of beating Taylor in a fast race run from end to end. "Mac" has the strongest and longest sprint of any of our riders and a full lap at his full top speed is enough to satisfy any glutton."

This same Billy MacDonald was entered in the races that were held a few day's later at Sydney, as were also the champions Walne and Morgan who arrived from Melbourne on the eve of the race. Others entered were Don Walker, Gudgeon, Lewis, Wilksch, Mutton, and Megson. Commenting further on MacDonald this same newspaper carried these lines:

"MacDonald is in good form and will no doubt be troubling the judges in some of the finishes, however, the remainder of the first class men will have some difficulty in finishing ahead of the two champions, Major Taylor and Don Walker, who have been going along training steadily on the track every day and will face the starter in their very best form.

"The easy manner in which Major Taylor has defeated Walker, the Australian champion on two occasions has led to a great deal of argument. A great many, amongst whom are several experts, contend that it is not Don Walker's true form to be defeated so easily even by a world's champion. They attribute the Australian champion's defeat to the difficulties he has had in timing his sprint in his races against Major Taylor, and are anxiously looking forward to the meeting of the two cracks tomorrow night in the One-Mile Scratch Race, and a First Class Handicap, in which Walker is expected to run the world's champion much closer at the finish, if he does not turn the tables on him.

"The League Cup race (one-mile scratch) will suit Walker much better than the shorter races and if it is a fast run race he will have a good chance of downing his great opponent. The fast mile will actually test the stamina of the world's champion, and if Walker takes the lead and goes the last lap in front he will not defeat Taylor. The Australian should use his head in addition to his legs just as Taylor does. The Australian beat Zimmerman in a straight out sprint and his many admirers think he will yet finish in front of Major Taylor. It is expected Walker will adopt some of Major Taylor's tactics when they meet tomorrow night."

The principal event for this next meeting in which I participated was the one-mile scratch race, (open to first-class riders only), the prize being $300. Another event on the program was a first-class handicap at a distance of one mile, a two-mile handicap race, a heat of the Summer Wheel Race (one-mile) and the Megson Plate event (five-mile).

A Sydney daily carried the following article relative to that program:

"Marvelous Ride by Major Taylor. 15,000 People Present. A crowd of over 15,000 attended the Cycling Carnival at the Sydney Cricket Grounds last evening. The fact that Major Taylor, the world's champion, and various Australian cracks would meet in the several events was responsible for the large attendance. His riding last night was indeed a revelation and his marvelous jump when hard pressed shows that the Australians, expert as they are in cycle racing, have still something to learn from the old world.

"The marvelous riding by Major Taylor, the world's champion, roused the spectators to a great pitch of enthusiasm.

"In the League Cup, a one-mile scratch event, Walne won the first heat by thirty yards from Rolfe, Megson won the second heat from Sheehan, and Chalmers defeated Walker and Crowell in the third heat.

"Major Taylor led Payne and Middleton over the tape in their spirited heat which was the fourth of the race. When Payne bolted in the last lap it looked like he was going to win, but Major Taylor with a phenominal jump cut him down in the last 30 yards and secured

the verdict by a length.  Excitement was now at fever heat.  Morgan
won the fifth heat from Ernest Pye and MacDonald the sixth heat
from Gudgeon and Lewis.  The final of this race will be run
Saturday.

"Major Taylor rode again in the First Class Handicap, one mile,
and starting from scratch accompanied by Walker made a quick sprint
to the nearest man of the cracks who were out on the marks.  Lewis
and Wilksch were the men out on the limit marks (80 yards) and the
pace was hot from the outset.  At a lap and a half to go Major
Taylor moved up on the outside in order to get a position, and rode
the rest of the distance up on the bank, but the world's champion
moved steadily around close to the railing, passing one after another
of the dozen best Australians who constituted the field, until he shoved
abreast of the leaders.  Then in a magnificent sprint for the tape he
cut down Walne who was leading and fought out a hard finish with
Burton, Taylor winning by a clean length amidst thunderous applause
from the big crowd.

"Taylor's beating of Payne in their heat in the League Cup event,
in which Taylor was pocketed, through his own fault, and his victory
in the mile handicap were most meritorious.  In the last event the
victor had a very severe ride against a splendid handicap field.  Still,
though the best man won no doubt, the result of the race was not a
true indication of the merits of those engaged in it.  Burton is a solid
rider, but he would not have been second in a true run race, but it was
a rushing, grueling contest, and some always have more lurch than
others.  Yet Major Taylor uses his head so well in conjunction with
his heels that he almost commands lurch if the term may be used.

"But we suppose that Taylor will admit that he has had a fair share
of luck in his racing here, and particularly in getting into shape so
quickly.  All through last night's Carnival Don Walker was really
our only first fight-man to oppose Taylor, but now we have Walne,
only recovering from two falls, 'Newhaven' Jackson, who will ride
better at every appearance and ditto Billy MacDonald, who has just
landed from Westralia, all likely to give the Major trouble if he
makes the slightest mistake.  There is also George Morgan, who is
one of the best, but who has to shake off the effects of a tumble-down
game of pace following against the Continental paced cracks at
Melbourne.

"It is well worth recording that one or two of those mentioned did
not think Major Taylor quite so good as the general run of followers
of the sport, and who will do their utmost to finish ahead of him.
The confidence in themselves is a very good thing, half the victory in
fact, and it is quite likely that one of them may win the big scratch
race.  As the race was run, we believe Walne would have beaten

Taylor on Wednesday night when he tried to steal that march, but the grueling falls the Queenslander had a few days ago did not enable him to finish in his usual figure.  How far this theory is right or wrong will be shown later.  The best judges in Melbourne say Walne was riding in his old form prior to his fall, and the Austrial Wheel Race was a moral certainty for him to win—bar the accident."

# CHAPTER LXIII



There were more than 15,000 people present at the continuation of the Major Taylor Carnival.

I quote as follows from one of the local daily papers relative to that program:

"League Cup won by Walker. Major Taylor defeated by Mac-Donald. Last night's race meet on the Cricket Grounds bicycle track was rendered notable by the defeat of Major Taylor on even terms in the first heat of the semi-finals for the League Cup. MacDonald, Chalmers and Sheehan were the riders opposed to Taylor in this heat, which was paced by Harris. At the bell Chalmers shot out with Mac-Donald on his wheel and the champion on the outside. MacDonald led up to the members' stand when Taylor came at him and caught him. To the spectators the race seemed over, but MacDonald still had something in hand, for with a magnificent sprint he drew away from the champion in the last twenty yards and won by half a length.

"Major Taylor when seen subsequently, said he had no excuse to offer for his defeat. He said he had been fairly beaten. He said he was in good form and he had gotten a fair run. MacDonald has but recently come over from Westralia and was hardly expected to strike form so soon. He had previously expressed the belief that he could beat Taylor, and though his ride was undeniably a fine performance, it must be admitted that he had all the best of the conditions. Mac-Donald, riding in behind Chalmers, was sheltered to some extent from the north easterly breeze which caught the riders in full force. Taylor riding on the outside was necessarily more exposed to it than any of the others. In the final heat Walker won with MacDonald half a length behind for second place.

"The second appearance of Major Taylor was in the first heat of the Half-mile First-class Handicap. The champion, Taylor, starting from scratch caught Wilksch from the 15-yard mark in less than half a lap, but could not make up the gap which separated him from Pye on the 40 yard mark. Paced by Orr, Pye won very easily. Walker won his heat in this event. In the final heat Pye, Morgan, Walne, Middleton and Walker were the starters. Although Walker made a great effort to overtake Pye he was beaten by him for first honors by several lengths."

By this time the Australians were pretty well worked up as they debated the relative merits of the best Australian sprinters and myself. Relative to this controversy I quote the following article which was printed in a Sydney newspaper the day after I was defeated by Mac-Donald:

("Major Taylor Versus the Best Australian.) The question whether Major Taylor can defeat the best Australian sprinters is still rather undecided. The League officials have decided to conduct a contest Scratch Mile Tournament on the closing night of the Major Taylor Carnival, January 21, for a purse of $625, $500 to go outright to the winner. It is felt this should definitely decide the question. Under the conditions of the event this race will eventually develop into a match between Major Taylor and the best Australian.

"The riders will be asked to compete in three preliminary heats. They are Walker, Chalmers, MacDonald, Megson, Morgan, Walne, Gudgeon, Jackson, Mutton and Wilksche. Should any of these not desire to start, the referee has the right to substitute R. W. Lewis, Pye or Rolfe. To decide who will represent Australia, the three winners of these heats will meet in a final. The successful competitor in this final will race Walker over a mile course on Wednesday night, and the winner of that race will on the same evening meet Major Taylor in a one-mile race, best two in three heats for the $500 purse.

"Walne or Morgan should win tonight's tournament judging from their present form. The race between Walker and either of these two on Wednesday night should result in a victory for the former who will thus secure the well-earned right to defend Australia against the great American rider who has come out here with the reputation of being the world's fastest sprinter. The final of the test will be an international contest in every sense of the word, and should fill the Sydney Cricket Grounds with enthusiastic spectators.

"That Don Walker should meet the man called upon to uphold the credit of Australian cycling against Major Taylor in this tournament may be taken for granted by any one who watched him in his recent races. However, the chances of Walne and Morgan can not by any means be lightly considered. After MacDonald's recent win over Taylor, no doubt, many people will fancy his chances, but Taylor's defeat can hardly be considered conclusive, as far as the merits of the two men are concerned. In the heat of the League Cup Race Major Taylor was really riding against three men in combination. MacDonald had the assistance of Chalmers as a pacer, and also received warning from a rider on the track when Taylor was about to jump. Then, too, possibly Taylor made a mistake by coming out while MacDonald was still sheltered from the wind by Chalmers, and attempting to sprint before the turn into the finishing stretch. Mac-Donald was paced right through the wind and got his big gear thoroughly wound up. Then with the stiff wind at his back he came around the turn with a magnificent pace, leaving Taylor no time to make the second jump before the line was reached.

"In the final, MacDonald had to ride without this pacing assistance and with the result that he was beaten by Don Walker, who finished with his usual easy style. Although the finish appeared to be fairly close it was easy to see that Walker might have won by a greater distance had he desired.

"Taylor's defeat on Saturday by MacDonald in the semi-final of the League Cup is of no importance, in so far as determining the relative speed of the two sprinters is concerned, for on the track by himself with the champion, MacDonald would have no chance to win. Taylor was handicapped somewhat by MacDonald's inadvertently running him up the bank almost to the railing in front of the ladies' pavilion.

"When MacDonald had to ride without the assistance in the final, Walker defeated him with ease, so on this form it does not seem likely that he will stand a chance of winning a place to race with Major Taylor Wednesday night.

"After the race Major Taylor had no complaint to make but merely said that he would like to race MacDonald for a match for as much money as he wished to ride for."

These editorial comments on MacDonald's victory over me stirred up a hornet's nest in Sydney. Some of the dailies berated their contemporaries for belittling MacDonald's win over me. Likewise the reporters on the rival papers were in disagreement relative to Walker's substantial victory over MacDonald, especially as to reports of its having been so easy to win.

The upshot of this newspaper controversy on the merits of MacDonald and myself as sprinters, was that MacDonald challenged me to a match race for a purse of $500, winner take all, best two heats in three. However, this event was never held for reasons which are outlined in a subsequent chapter.

# CHAPTER LXIV



In the final meet of the Major Taylor Carnival I won the Centennial Mile (handicap) in 1:57 4/5 thereby establishing a new record for Australia. That this race was hotly contested is indicated by the fact that it attracted seventy-one of the best riders in Australasia and 18,000 spectators.

Concerning this final heat I quote as follows from one of the Sydney newspapers:

"Remarkable Performance by Major Taylor. Sets New Record for Australia. Gudgeon Beats the Cracks. Major Taylor's exhibitions in the heat and final of the Centennial Mile race which was held at the local track last night, were up to his reputation. He made a competitive record for Australia in the final of the mile handicap event, riding from scratch, 1:57 4/5. Taylor's riding was very fine to look at, but we used to see Martin do something like it. Had he not made up his mind to start in this race his share of entertaining the public would have been very small, for his only other appearance was in the heat of the Major Taylor Plate (one-quarter-mile) in which there was no real competition and it was a cake walk for him. Throughout the night he did not meet one of Australia's best.

"I never saw such extraordinary riding among first-class men since the League has been in existence. How badly they are shaping up for want of form or other causes, can be reckoned by Megson's riding. He never rode worse in his life than at this carnival, and yet he beat Gudgeon in the quarter-mile and was only just beaten in turn by Gudgeon in the one-mile. The latter in the night's racing showed himself next to Walker. He will in fact have to race Walker tonight for the honor of meeting Taylor. Fancy Pye beating Jackson in a race of this kind, and Middleton, a tough old battler, who was never in the first fight, downing Morgan, who afterwards won the five-mile scratch race. If this is not a Chinese puzzle to explain, I do not know what is.

"If those who wanted to see Australia's best man chosen at his best, and not the glorification of Major Taylor, nothing could have been worse than the way the Test Mile heats were arranged and the way they resulted. There was, first, disappointment in that Walker should be chosen instead of being made to race in heats like the rest. It was most injudicious that the question of who should meet Taylor was not decided on Monday night. Now Walker and Gudgeon will have to ride a mile race to find out, and they have to then meet Taylor 'fresh' in mile heats, besides that, if it be Walker who wins his way to meet Taylor he has also in the same night to compete in the semi-final and the final of the quarter-mile event. The Major Taylor Plate (quarter-mile) should have been disposed of on Monday night and the rider definitely chosen to meet Taylor. As it is now, what hope has anyone that Major Taylor will be beaten? Most likely Walker will beat Gudgeon and have to meet Taylor, and past experience shows

Winning the Centennial One-mile Handicap, establishing Australian Record

what a poor prospect Walker has of beating Taylor at his own game in mile heats, but should it happen that Gudgeon be the rival, then the only hope would be that his condition would enable him to saddle up well."

Another Sydney daily under the caption of "More Magnificent Racing" commented as follows on the same heat:

"The magnificent finishes witnessed by 18,000 spectators at the Major Taylor Cycling Carnival on the local track last night will undoubtedly sustain the great interest manifested in cycling hereabouts. The racing throughout was excellent and at times became so fast that the crowd could scarcely restrain themselves.

"Another illustration was given the spectators of the marvelous capabilities of the world's champion, Major Taylor. His defeat on Saturday by MacDonald disappointed some, but his performances last night must amply justify his great reputation. In the Centennial Mile (handicap—250 yard limit) he put up a new record for the Australian tracks and he showed such remarkable sprinting in the other events that the spectators yelled themselves hoarse.

"The racing in the heats of the Centennial Mile was fast and brilliant.  The fifth heat in which Major Taylor showed proved one of the features of the evening.  In it he showed some of his splendid skill by sweeping up his field at terrific speed, then lying in the center of the bunch until the bell went.  He then had the appearance of being pocketed, but neatly cut himself out, and started to sprint 250 yards from home, leaving the other five riders who had been in front of him standing still.  With a marvelous jump he got to the front passing the line six or seven lengths ahead of Orr, amidst tremendous enthusiasm.  His victory, which was accomplished in the very fast time of 2:00 1/5, was exceedingly popular and the air rang with stirring cheers.

"The final offered Major Taylor another splendid opportunity for showing off his marvelous powers.  Starting off scratch, he caught Lewis, who started from the 35-yard mark, in half a lap.  He hung on for about a lap, then set out by himself to bridge the big gap.  Unpaced, he fairly flew up to the riders and caught them amidst thunderous cheers and applause.  At the grandstand he was lying seventh.  Near the score board, he jumped away, taking the lead 250 yards from home.  From this point he cut out a terrific rate of speed, winning by a length from Orr in 1:57 4/5, a new record for Australia.  His performances earned for him a magnificent reception.

"The Major Taylor Plate, a quarter-mile dash from scratch, brought forth some exceedingly fine racing.  Major Taylor, in whose honor the event was named, won his heat from Dan Sheehan and Ben Goodson by a length and a half, the champion making his famous jump when a length behind Goodson on entering the home stretch.

"The preliminary heats to select the rider most qualified to meet Major Taylor and Don Walker on Wednesday night in the International Test Mile were also run off.  Bob Walne defeated Bill MacDonald by half a length in the first heat in 2:07.  Arthur Gudgeon defeated Joe Megson in the second heat by a wheel.  Dick Mutton and Eddie Wilksch rode a dead heat in the third heat.  In the first semi-final Gudgeon defeated Walne by two lengths, Wilksch being third.  Three pace makers assisted the riders and the race was very fast, time being 2:01 4/5.  Gudgeon will meet Don Walker Wednesday night and the winner of this heat will meet Major Taylor on the same evening in three one-mile heats for a purse of $500, winner take all.

"With each appearance Major Taylor emphasizes his claim to the title, World's Champion Cyclist."

# CHAPTER LXV



A crowd of 30,000 attended the final meet of the Major Taylor Carnival equalling the best attendance mark created in the course of Zimmerman's championship tour in 1897. That evening I won the International Championship Match in two straight mile heats and the

Final of One-mile International Match, with Gudgeon leading on the Bell-lap

Major Taylor Plate, quarter-mile scratch race in two heats from the cream of Australia's star riders.

A Sydney daily told the story of those two races, the only ones on the program, in the following paragraphs:

"Major Taylor Shows Superb Form by Winning International Mile Championship Match Race and Quarter Mile Scratch Event. Despite a light rainstorm upwards of 30,000 people were at the Sydney Cricket Grounds bicycle track last night to witness the International Championship Match Race between Major Taylor champion of the world, and Arthur Gudgeon of New South Wales. Never before has the enthusiasm been so prolonged as it was on this occasion, and it is doubtful if the program could have been improved upon. Unfortunately the weather was not of the best, rain falling throughout the evening. In spite of this fact the spectators remained at the track although a very large number could have obtained shelter.

"The first event, in which most interest centered, was the contest between Don Walker and Arthur Gudgeon to decide which of them should meet Major Taylor in the International Championship Match Mile Race. Almost everybody expected Walker to win. But Gudgeon rode around the track after vanquishing the rider who has all along been regarded as the best in Australia. The pace throughout the race was exceedingly fast and although Walker came with a terrific sprint he could not overtake his rival. Thus the question as to who was going to oppose Major Taylor was settled and the spectators were sure that the New South Wales rider was to be the American's opponent.

"Half an hour afterward Taylor and Gudgeon appeared in the first heat of the International Match Race. Two good men, Scheps, and Payne were the pacemakers. Taylor hung onto them while Gudgeon followed, but his ride for the first two laps was not pleasant owing to the way Taylor's machine wobbled. At the score board on the last lap Gudgeon moved up alongside his opponent and remained until the members' stand was reached. Then like a flash of lightning Taylor left Gudgeon, who was, however, bothered by Taylor's wheel swerving. Gudgeon put up a fine finish but suffered defeat by two good lengths. The last 150 yards was covered in the exceptionally fast time of :08 2/5. The American was accorded great ovation.

"The second heat was decided half an hour later. This heat was run on the Continental style of racing, no pace being used. It may be confessed that the method is not a good one, from a spectator's point of view, although the men are called upon to use a good deal of strategy.

"For the first lap Gudgeon led, but the pace was exceedingly slow. When the bell went, however, there was a quickening of pace, and Taylor jumped to the front of Gudgeon unexpectedly. Near the scoring board Gudgeon made an effort to pass the famed rider, but did not succeed, the pair racing in line until the members' stand was approached. Then Taylor left his opponent and won, this time by three lengths. His victory was greeted with the loudest applause, as it was recognized that Taylor had settled all pretensions that any Australian could defeat him in a straight-out, single man, match race. Gudgeon dismounted and shook hands with Taylor at the conclusion of the race and Taylor congratulated Gudgeon for his fine effort. 'You have the strength and speed,' said Taylor to him, 'all you need to know is how to use them.'

"Taylor made two more appearances, the first in the semi-final of the Major Taylor Plate, quarter-mile scratch event, which he won easily. The second and last appearance of Major Taylor in this race came in the final heat in which he opposed Walker and Walne. Taylor led both of them home, although Walker made a good finish with him. An incident happened on this event which showed clearly Major Taylor's good sportsmanship. Owing to the slippery track Bobby Walne, soon after the starting of the semi-final, unfortunately fell. Immediately Major Taylor eased up and returned to the starting place. This action was especially recognized by the spectators.

"Major Taylor is all that he was represented to be. He has put up a phenominal record for the time he was here—beaten only once, in the semi-final of a scratch race, by MacDonald. The feat will stand to MacDonald's credit, as the defeat of Zimmerman stood to that of Walker, Parsons and Pither.

"But I still contend, allowing that Major Taylor is the champion, that our best men rode a good deal below their form, and though they may be unable to beat Taylor, the difference between the American and the Australians is not so great as it appears on the surface."

I was deeply impressed with the treatment accorded me by the sport loving public of Sydney in my first month's racing there. Likewise I was grateful for the fair treatment accorded me twice by the race track officials, the riders and the newspaper men of that metropolis. Incidentally I was pleased with my record on the track in that city, the weather being ideally suited to my training stunts, thereby enabling me to round into top form in an incredibly short space of time. I shall always recall most pleasantly my first stay in Sydney.

# CHAPTER LXVI



After my six weeks' stay in Sydney my schedule called for a series of races in that other great Australian city, Melbourne. I was especially anxious to be at my best when I showed there, but the fates had decreed otherwise. I contracted a bad cold on the last night of the Carnival in Sydney when I rode in the rain, and it was aggravated by the trip on the sleeper *en route*. The result was that I was confined to my bed for two weeks with an attack of influenza. However, I quickly recovered my form once I started training anew and eventually made good before the people of Melbourne.

Although the public was keenly disappointed at my inability to ride because of my illness they were most considerate of my welfare. The newspapers treated me with the utmost respect, and kept the public informed from day to day relative to my condition. Naturally I was anxious to show my appreciation of these kindnesses and longed for the day when I could resume my training and thus regain my wanted form. I had still another reason for wishing to get back in my saddle—to defeat a number of Australian riders who were boasting of their having defeated me, while I was still under the doctors' care.

But to get back to my first entry to that beautiful city of Melbourne. One of the dailies in that city printed the following article relative to my arrival there:

"World Champion Cyclist, Major Taylor Arrives. Given Enthusiastic Reception. Cyclists of the past, and cyclists of the present, to say nothing of the general public, gathered in full force at the Spencer Street Station to-day to welcome Major Taylor, the world's champion bicyclist. Mr. Mountain, Chairman, and Mr. Heide, secretary of the League of Victorian Wheelmen, after much struggling managed to reach the reserved carriage in which the champion and his wife travelled. It was with difficulty that the vehicle was able to move out of the surging crowd to the hotel where Mr. and Mrs. Taylor are quartered. Major Taylor was shortly taken to the Port Phillip Club Hotel where a monster public reception awaited him.

"Here there was a better chance of inspecting the world-famed cyclist. His appearance disappointed a great many who expected to see a big brawny individual. Instead they saw what might be described as a pocket edition of what they expected. Major Taylor is barely average height, but he is very muscular and sinewy. He has the prominent jaw so characteristic of the prize fighter and the cyclist. He is modest and unassuming and very gentlemanly in deportment.

"Major Taylor was formally welcomed to Melbourne by representatives of the leading organizations.  Besides the leading lights in the sporting world Lord Mayor Alderman Jefferies, Mr. Fitzgibbons, chairman of the Metropolitan Board of Works and many others shook hands with Major Taylor and bid him welcome to Melbourne.  Mr. Mountain, chairman of the League of Wheelmen proposed the guest's health in very eugolistic terms.  He laid special emphasis on his sportsmanship and manly reputation and also on the honorable way he had won the distinction of champion and afterwards maintained it. (Cheers.)

"Mr. McCullagh, secretary of the Melbourne Bicycle Club, who supported the toast said he knew Mr. Taylor was a gentleman as well as a sportsman, and hoped that his visit would have a good effect on the sport in Australia.  He continued with much enthusiasm saying, 'In behalf of the Melbourne Bicycle Club I wish to welcome Major Taylor.  The Australians are singularly fortunate in having at the same time as visitors the champion sprinter of the world, and the champion middle distance rider of the world, Robel, the German pace follower.'  Mr. Scott on behalf of the Australian Natives' Association expressed the hope that Major Taylor's visit to Melbourne would be both enjoyable and profitable.

"In response Major Taylor spoke briefly and modestly.  He said that he could not quite express his feelings.  'Mr. Mountain.' he continued, 'had been kind enough to say that all had heard of his many wonderful performances on the track, but no one present, he felt sure, had heard anything of his ability as a speaker.'  (Laughter.)  The champion said that he had no idea until he arrived that Australia had so many splendid riders.  His judgment had been affected by the poor display of the Australians in America.

"I never underrate an opponent," he said, "but look upon every rider as being, perhaps, just as fast as I until I have defeated him." (Cheers.)  (This sentence describes the man as he is.)

"He said he hoped to be able to ride so as to merit all the flattering compliments that have been heaped upon him.  In closing he said he will do everything in his power to further promote the sport of cycling in Australia, adding that doing so would be a source of pleasure to him."  (Cheers.)

After I had regained my health and was hard at my training stunts, a reporter for one of the Melbourne newspapers watched me perform and wrote the following paragraph relative to my style, etc.:

"Taylor tests his seat till he finds his position right, then sees to it that his feet are strapped properly to the pedals, and that the pedals are working freely.  When satisfied he surveys the field ahead of him and getting a firm grip on his handle bars, he waits for the pistol.  The smoke has hardly left the muzzle before the champion is in full swing and driving like mad in pursuit of the leaders.

"Like all sprinters he is wonderfully quick off a mark, but his capacity during the race to pick up his wheel and sprint within a sprint is a revelation. A. A. Zimmerman gave us several exhibitions of the art, Bert Harris showed us one example of it, which none who saw it will ever forget, and the ungainly Bill Martin has on many occasions let the people see something of the knack, but Major Taylor bears the palm from all others in this particular. The pity of it is that he cannot be kept here long enough to teach Victorians some of the secrets of the accomplishment.

"Major Taylor, the celebrated American Negro sprinter has made his bow to the Victorian audience, and his name has been added to the list of champions from the 'other side,' who it has been our pleasure to see. We have had Zimmerman, Barden, Lesna, Jack Green, Platt Betts, Bert Harris, Bill Martin, Robel, Dicketman and others, but excepting the great Zimmerman, whom we saw but once or twice at his best, the greatest of them all is Major Taylor.

"Major Taylor was applauded for his fine ride under such disadvantageous circumstances, when he was introduced at the Australian Natives' Association meet recently. This was a novel method of introducing the world's champion to the people of Melbourne since Mr. Taylor is still ill and therefore unable to participate in the meet. He simply rode an exhibition lap, but showed in it that he is rightly a world's champion. Later he was also introduced to the Governor, Lieutenant-Governor, and many others, all of whom expressed their sympathy with the champion, whose illness they very much regretted. Sir John Madden endeavored to brighten the 'Major' up by telling him that if cycling went back on him, he would make a first-class lightweight boxer or even a jockey.

"The style of Major Taylor on his machine appears peculiar because of his abnormally short pedal reach. It seems as if he could do with about an inch of his seat post drawn out, but for all that he can get over the ground quickly.

"Major Taylor is a very cleanly built, neatly packed parcel of humanity. He is short in stature, with good body and hip development, and slender legs with ankles which a fashionable ballet dancer might envy. No comparison of his build would be better, perhaps, than that of a thorough-bred race horse. He has blood and his every movement is instinct with it, being highly strung, alert, nimble, quick to take advantage of an opportunity, and with an indomitable determination to pursue to the very end.

"Stripped for action, and wearing only his snug fitting light blue jersey with black collar and cuff bands, he looks exactly what he is, a great sprinter. From the eye which sees, and the head which directs, down to the hip which drives and the ankles which work with poetic ease, Major Taylor is the personification of grace and lightning-like rapidity. His skin shines like satin, and his face smiles pleasantly under his center-parted, closely cropped, curly hair as he walks to the starting point. He is a typical Negro.

Major Taylor—Champion of America, 1900

"Then the smile gives place to an expression of thoughtfulness, the lips become compressed and the brow puckers with wrinkles as he sees that everything is in order. He neglects nothing. Champions never become champions without learning the lesson that we all must learn, there is no such thing as trifles. But issues often depend upon what many in slap-dash fashion unthinkingly call trifles unworthy of consideration. Not so, however, with Major Taylor.

"In the make-up of a champion it is also essential that he have what is known to the sports' world as gameness or courage. Major

Taylor proved he has much of that quality in his make-up by riding on the Melbourne track a few days after his arrival here, despite the fact that he was ill and far from his best condition. He was defeated in the Federation Handicap (one-mile) running fourth to Pye, Forbes and MacDonald. In the second heat of the Australian Cup Handicap (one and one-half miles) he finished third to Murphy and Woods, their handicaps being too great for him to overtake in his weakened condition.

"It is not generally known that 'Major' is Taylor's christian name, and not an American pseudonym. Of all the cycling champions who have visited these states, Taylor is without doubt the most unassuming. That he can ride a bicycle there is no question, and it is to be sincerely hoped that the Victorian public will yet have an opportunity of seeing this great sprinter at his best."

# CHAPTER LXVII

No sooner had I left my sick bed than the officials of the Melbourne race track, known as the St. Kilda Cricket Grounds, pressed me to sign up for a match with Don Walker, the Australian champion. The bicycle race followers of that city were keenly disappointed because my illness had prevented my racing there for two weeks. After a few practice sprints, however, I decided that I was in pretty good shape, and agreed to take on Don Walker.

We agreed to ride three heats—a half-mile, one-mile, and the third heat of one-mile, if necessary to determine the winner, for a purse of $500, the winner take all.

The following from a Melbourne daily had this to say concerning this match:

"Before the Grand Challenge Match started the book-makers wavered considerably in their choice of a favorite. First, they elected Walker and loudly proclaimed that they would not take less than three to one against him. Presently the odds ranged from three to one downwards. Taylor became the favorite when the sun came out, and as Walker and Taylor toed the scratch, the book-makers would take nothing less than three to one against him.

"Walker had the running at the outset of the first heat, but as there was no pace this was of no advantage to him. Taylor, knowing that everything depended on the final jump, forced Walker into the lead, and the first part of the race was a crawl, with Taylor a length behind. Walker craned his neck all the way around the track looking for Taylor's famous jump.

"At the bell, Walker, who had commenced to pedal rapidly but was still watching, was a length and a half in the lead. Half way round the positions were unchanged, but both men were sending their machines along merrily. At the scoring board Taylor suddenly lifted his wheel and there was a great howl from the crowd who had at last seen Taylor's famous jump. He shot past Walker who seemed to stand still in comparison.

"A quarter way up the stretch the race seemed to be all over, but in the last 20 yards Walker showed speed which quite rivalled the champion's kick. A magnificent finish resulted in Major Taylor's favor by a wheel. Had Walker not been surprised by Taylor at the score board it is by no means certain that the American would have won. Both riders were warmly cheered.

"Chalmers and Farley paced the second heat. Taylor was favored from the outset. Taylor took no heed of the pistol at the start, but sat quietly, being confident that the pacers would not get very far away from him. Thus he forced Walker into the lead again. Several laps passed at a very moderate pace. Taylor never moved his nose from the handle bars, but his eyes were very sharp and he never missed a point. On the back stretch in the last lap Taylor began to tighten up his grip on the handle bars and the crowd yelled frantically to Walker, 'Look out, look out!' Near the score board, bunching himself up in an extraordinary fashion, and with a spring, he landed a couple of lengths ahead within a few yards. There was a general exclamation of amazement at the electrical jump of the champion. Walker was only momentarily nonplussed. Bending to his work he rode magnificently and within a few yards of the finish he had drawn level with Taylor to the unbounded delight of the people, but Major Taylor still had a kick left, and won by a foot which gave him the match. He was once more applauded generously.

"Major Taylor tied Don Walker for first place in the final of the Half-mile Scratch Race. Among the entrants in this event were included a number of the very best sprinters in Australia. Taylor's racing was excellent, for not only was his sprinting and general riding of the best, but his tactics and judgment were thoroughly sound.

"By winning three events out of four and riding a dead heat in the fourth, Major Taylor retrieved his diminished laurels and asserted his claims to the reputation which had preceded him to Australia. He had at last recovered his form and raced under conditions which allowed him to display his real riding powers."

My next and last race in Melbourne found me pitted against George Morgan in a challenge match, best two in three heats of one-mile for a purse of $500. It fell Morgan's lot to ride me in this event through his having won previously a number of trial heats in what was known as the Test Mile Tournament, the prize for which totaled $600.

Others entered in this tournament besides Morgan were Walne, Beachamp, Pye, Jackson, Barton, Chalmers, Wilksch and Dan Sheehan, the best riders in Australia with the exception of Don Walker. It was arranged that should I win in straight heats, Morgan and myself would afterwards compete in the one-mile scratch race against all the other star riders.

The following article is quoted from one of the Melbourne dailies:

"Major Taylor Wins Again. Defeats Morgan in Special Match Race. Any shadow of suspicion that may have lurked in the public mind that Major Taylor, the American racing champion, was not the man his reputation made him appear to be, was dispelled effectively by his great riding on the Exhibition track last night. On this occasion he was opposed to George Morgan, who had won the coveted honor of meeting Taylor in a special challenge match race on one-mile, best two in three heats for a purse of $500, winner take all, in a series of test mile heats.

"The first heat was unpaced. At the sound of the pistol Taylor sat back on his saddle and checked the spin of his pedals. Morgan tried to do the same, but could not ride slowly enough for the 'Major' who forced Morgan to the front. Then he settled himself in a position to hang onto Morgan's rear wheel. Four times around the track the men crawled, with Major Taylor cautiously watching every movement of Morgan's pedals. When the bell went for the last lap, Morgan pulled to the top of the bank, but even then the American did not rush matters. The riders did not begin to really race until they were half way around the track, when suddenly Morgan set out for the tape, and led around the turn until half way down the straight had been covered. Here Taylor made his essay and there was a ding-dong tussle a few yards from the tape, when the 'Major' gave his wonderful finishing kick that seemed to lift his machine to victory by half a length amid thunderous applause.

"The second heat found Morgan manifestly outmatched by his opponent's sprinting powers. They proved too much for Morgan, although he pressed Taylor more closely than in the first heat. The American won by more than half a wheel giving him the match.

"The two men met again in the final of the International Scratch Race, which proved to be the most exciting thing on the program. The contestants were Walker, Wilksch, Filsell, Morgan, and Taylor. The last named won his heat in an almost marvelous manner. In the last lap he appeared to be hopelessly pocketed. Nearing the upper end, however, he succeeded in extricating himself by riding around on the outside thus beating his opponents at their own game. Then he shook them off one after another and got home a winner by a few inches only. In the final heat he was not successful, Morgan having achieved the victory."

Another Melbourne newspaper printed the following article on the day after the race:

"Wonderful Riding by Major Taylor. Fine as was Major Taylor's riding in his match race with George Morgan yesterday, it was second class when compared with what followed in Taylor's heat of the one-mile scratch race. In this event there were Pye, Walne, Chalmers, and Major Taylor. Middleton paced for about two and one-half laps when Chalmers went to the front with Taylor lying fourth. At the bell Taylor dashed through on the inside for Chalmer's wheel. At the same moment Pye rushed up on the outside and got his front wheel overlapping Chalmer's driving wheel, thus hemming Taylor in. The pace was now terrific and the thousands of spectators yelled with excitement when they saw Taylor's predicament.

"Half a lap from home a roar went up as Walne came with one of his old sprints on the outside. In an instant he was a couple of lengths in front of Chalmers and Pye, the American still being in the 'pocket'. 'Taylor's beat, Taylor's done,' the crowd roared. But now they saw the world's champion at his best. One hundred twenty yards from home a change came over the scene. Taylor eased up, let Pye go on and in an instant had jumped his machine on the outside of Pye. It looked a hundred to one against his chances of overhauling Walne, but in ten yards he had his machine moving as Victorians had never seen a bicycle travel before.

"The champion fairly flew. He passed Chalmers and Pye in a flash, and then set down to take away Walne's two length's lead in 30 yards. It looked impossible but Major Taylor made it possible by one of the most marvelous sprints ever seen, for he came like a meteor, and beat Walne over the line by inches.

"Such a finish fairly staggered everyone present. It will be many long years before the American's phenominal ride is forgotten. The spectators went home amazed at Taylor's marvelous 'jump.' Major Taylor speaking of his ride afterwards said it was the best thing he had done in Australia. 'That's the way I usually do business back home,' he said."

Still a third Melbourne newspaper made the following comment on that same race meet:

"Combinations Against Major Taylor. The final of the International Scratch Race in Melbourne yesterday in which Major Taylor won his qualifying heat in such a sensational manner, was by no means a true indication of Taylor's best form. In it Taylor was a victim of a combination amongst the other starters. The combination was well organized to bring about his defeat.

"In the last lap the field got around the Negro and so securely hemmed him in that he had no possible chance of getting out. He realized this and sat up half way down the home stretch. These tactics were certainly unfair because the champion did not have a fair chance. Many of the spectators believed that the riders, Walker, Wilksch, Morgan, Filsell, and Farley, felt that Major Taylor could defeat any one of them in a fair and open race. So they combined to prevent him from snatching another victory from them. Owing to the way that the men crowded around him Taylor was actually obliged to back-pedal just before he crossed the tape.

"It is almost impossible to figure how Taylor shunted his attack of influenza so speedily. A few days after he left his bed, his temperature reading 104, he was back in good form and proved it by riding a mile in 1:50 2/5, the world's fastest behind single pace, four men taking him half a lap each. Taylor 'jumped' the last 180 yards in :11 1/5 and finished wonderfully strong. How Don Walker ever figured that he had a hope with Major Taylor surpasses the writer's understanding. Major Taylor is a superman on a bicycle."

Although I was a sick man when I reached Melbourne, I left that city in a blaze of glory in the wake of the remarkable races referred to above. I shall never forget the utmost courtesy with which I was treated while I was very sick in that city by the newspapers, track officials, and the general public. Although they were keenly disappointed because I was unable to ride for two weeks after my arrival there owing to my illness, the residents in general treated me with the utmost consideration and fairness.

# CHAPTER LXVIII



Returning to Sydney from Melbourne I was especially anxious to
prevent a recurrence of my attack of influenza.  I knew that within
a week I would be called upon to compete in the Sydney Thousand, a
one-mile handicap race, the purse for which, $5,000, was the largest
ever offered for a bicycle race.  Naturally I was anxious to win that
race, and was very enthusiastic as I pointed for it through my last few
races at Melbourne which indicated I had returned to top form follow-
ing my illness of a fortnight.

However, it was decreed by the fates that I was not to participate in
the division of that record breaking purse.  I qualified handily enough
in the first heat, but found some of the riders combined against me in
the semi-final heat in such a glaring manner that the officials ordered
the heat re-run.  When the heat was run over again the group that
was working to defeat me was still in power and I failed to win my
way into the finals.  The conduct of the field, especially that part of
it which was organized to prevent my winning, stirred up a hornet's
nest throughout Australia, and for weeks thereafter the newspapers
attacked the "sportsmanship" of the riders who were apparently bent
upon anyone's winning the race but myself.

Thanks to the combination referred to above Norman Hopper, an
American rider, who had a handicap of seventy-five yards, won the
Sydney Thousand, but in the division of the spoils he had to split his
winnings so many ways that, it is said, he received about $600 for his
share, instead of $3,750 which was the first prize.

A Sydney paper commented as follows on that semi-final heat:

"The League people did a barefaced thing over the semi-final of
the Sydney Thousand, last night.  When half the race was over it
was painfully evident that the back-markers including Major Taylor
were quite out of it.  The back division owing to some misunder-
standing or something else allowed the limit men to get a long un-
catchable lead.  The horrified officials realizing that the American
champion could not start in the final of the big event promptly called
it 'no race.'

"The official reason given for annulling the heat was that the back-
division did not do their share of pacing.

"A beautiful theory truly.  Why on earth should the winning di-
vision be penalized because of the want of judgment of their op-
ponents?  Briefly the handicap men were in this position; if the back

markers don't catch up to them the race is declared off, if they do catch up the limit men haven't much chance to win. Naturally they can't keep ahead when racing level, or they would not be allowed hundreds of yards start in the first place. New South Wales professional cycling has witnessed some funny catch-penny methods, but surely the public's collective leg was never so merrily pulled as on this occasion."

A second daily commented on the semi-final heat in the following paragraph:

"Last night's cycling capped the record of bungles and other things. The back-markers in the semi-final of the big money event would not pace worth a cent, with the result that Major Taylor was beaten, and the public hooted as only those 'taken in' can hoot. It was the most disgraceful bit of sport ever seen in Sydney. Taylor's re-run heat was obviously thrown away by trying to make his own pace, he burst himself and could not sprint at the finish. If the officials wanted to impart fairness the whole of the back-markers except Major Taylor in the semi-final should have been wiped out for life. At any rate the riders have shown their cronk hand, and the public should grip the pro-offered paw with a will."

Still another Sydney newspaper commented on this "no race" incident as follows:

"The real facts of the 'no race' incident in the Sydney Thousand seemed that the referee had good reason to believe, that the way the back-markers resolutely refrained from making pace, that there was a sort of conspiracy to keep the money in the country. Major Taylor had overtaken the back-markers, therefore, they considered they had no more chance, and they were not going to burst their aggregate boilers to help him bridge the gap between him and the front man. Without their assistance it was practically impossible for him to overtake the long starters and the referee decided it was no race.

"The race was ordered to be run off on Monday night, and when Monday night came the back-markers still refused to make any arrangement with Major Taylor as to pacing and the League does not seem to have taken any steps to put in pacers. At the start Taylor overtook the back men and then went on in a desperate effort to overtake the front starters without any pacing at all. He succeeded in getting in to the front bunch, but in an exhausted state. Immediately he dashed on, the back-markers paced one another so well that Morgan (10 yards), was able to dash to the front and win from Simon and Thorne, 120 and 80 yard men respectively. It was good tactics, but it was certainly not good sport, and merely a low-down trick to keep the best man from winning. An ugly complexion was put on the matter by Major Taylor's statement that he could have bought the chance to win, but refused."

In the Sydney Thousand there were entered one hundred fifteen of the best riders from New South Wales, Victoria, New Zealand, this country, South Australia, Westralia, England, Italy, Ireland, British Columbia, Tasmania and Denmark. It was arranged that but eleven of that picked number would be eligible to start in the final heat. Among those who were entered in this classic were such stars as George Morgan, Joe Megson, Arthur Gudgeon, Ernest Pye, Dick Mutton, Don Walker, Bill MacDonald, Frank Beachamp, Charlie Burong, Richard Cameron, James Filsell, Ernest Payne, Bobby Walne, M. Campbell, Arthur Middleton, Larry Corbett, A. O'Brien, Dan Plunkett, George Sutherland, F. Scheps, C. Boidi, and N. C. Hopper.

The handicaps ranged from 5 yards to 240 yards, while I alone started from scratch. In order that all of the entrants might be at their best when they clashed in the several preliminary heats of this big race the officials had the various heats held on separate nights.

Concerning the first heat of the Sydney Thousand in which I qualified, one of the Sydney dailies carried the following paragraphs:

"World's Greatest Cycle Race. Opening Heats Run. Major Taylor Qualifies. The Sydney Thousand Carnival was begun at the Sydney Cricket Grounds yesterday afternoon. The greatest interest centered in the fifth heat of the big race in which Major Taylor champion of the world, started from scratch. Owing to the want of an agreement regarding pace amongst the back-markers, Walker and Walne, Major Taylor had to ride the hardest portion of the race alone. Three men were placed for the semi-final, but the front men paced so well that the champion had considerable difficulty getting into that third position. That, however, qualified him for the first semi-final. Walker finished fourth and will in consequence ride in the special semi-final, but Walne failed to qualify.

"In the semi-final heat the officials declared it 'no race' and ordered it run over again."

In the semi-final it was apparent that some of the riders had gotten their heads together and decided that I should not win under any circumstances unless I entered into an agreement with them. In the first heat of the semi-final the workings of the combination were so flagrant that the officials ordered all the riders from the track before the event was finished, and called it "no race." Then the officials ordered it re-run immediately, despite the fact that I pleaded with them for a half hour interval in which to recuperate following the terrific race I had ridden against the entire field unassisted prior to having the heat termed "no race." While the officials were impressed with the fairness of my request they heard MacDonald object to the step and ordered the race run over at once.

I quote as follows from a Sydney daily concerning this turn of affairs:

"Taylor collapsed after his great effort in the first heat of the semi-final which was called 'no race' by the officials.  As Taylor had had such a straining ride the committee decided to interpose a five-mile motor race to give him time to recover.  To this MacDonald objected and it was then decided that as a set-off a second motor race should be interposed between the fifth semi-final and the handicap third heat, which by interposition of the motor race would come in right on top of the others.  MacDonald also being in that heat.

"Taylor was on scratch, MacDonald and Beachamp on the ten yard mark, Pye had fifteen and Wilksch thirty, with Morgan, Gudgeon and Middleton nearest to Taylor.  In the front bunch were Murray, Payne, Whitson, Thorne and Foster, Taylor dashed past the back-markers, as in the other heat and took them along at some distance.  Then Wilksch took a turn for half a lap.  The front division was going strong, but the back division appeared to have lost interest in the prize at stake.  Taylor looked for some of them to pace, and the crowd howled and yelled saying it was not sport.  While the back men were being hooted, the front men were going for all they were worth, and of course, they won and Taylor was out of the final.

"There were cheers, hoots and groans, so much interspersed that it was like a pandemonium.  Payne was first, Thorne second, Foster third, and Whitson fourth.  Taylor was cheered wildly, and Mac-Donald was hooted not only then, but all through the remainder of the night.  Whatever dissension or difference of opinion exists in the internal arrangements of these sports, Taylor has proven himself a clean sportsman, and the adoption of the tactics of the cricket hoodlums, instead of impressing the American visitor, must oppress him."

Another Sydney newspaper commented on the re-run heat of the semi-final in this manner:

"In the re-run of Taylor's heat of the semi-final of the Sydney Thousand certain riders in the back division again refused to pace, but this time the race was allowed to stand, though as a matter of fact there was more cause for ruling it 'no race' than there was on Saturday.  The rear men knew that they could not live in a sprint with Taylor, and they could not see the force in pacing him to victory.  Since Major Taylor won fourth place in this heat he qualified to ride in the special heat for fourth place winners, the first two in this heat to go into the finals.

"There was considerable doubt in the minds of the public as to whether Major Taylor would be fit to ride in the fifth heat of the semi-final for which he had qualified by getting fourth in the second heat after his great unpaced ride in that heat. It was scarcely expected that he would be able to go out so soon. His appearance was a signal for another popular outburst of applause.

"There were ten men in the race which was robbed of interest through the back-markers refusing to take their share of pacing to overtake the front bunch. Major Taylor caught MacDonald in a few yards, and paced the back division for half a lap. To the disgust of the crowd no one else would take up the pacing, and the five limit men continued to increase the gap between them and the back division until all prospect of them being caught vanished. Payne was first, Thorne second, and Jameson third.

"Major Taylor was loudly cheered by the spectators, who showed their disapproval of the conduct of the other riders of the back division."

The final of the Sydney Thousand was won by Norman Hopper, ex-amateur champion of America, who was aided by good pacing. Don Walker was second, Thorne third, and Forbes fourth.

# CHAPTER LXIX



As I have mentioned in the foregoing chapter the heats of the
Sydney Thousand ranged over a number of weeks. This plan was
adopted to insure the several entrants being in excellent condition for
those heats, especially since some of them competed in other events on
the cards referred to.

On the day that the opening heats of the Sydney Thousand were run
I participated in the Kent Plate, a one-mile scratch race, for a purse of
$250, in addition to winning my heat of the Sydney Thousand. The
field in the Kent Plate race included the stars who were gathered from
all parts of Australia, the Continent and the United States. In fact
so many were entered in this crack event that the officials deemed it
necessary to run nine heats, three men in each heat, to determine the
three fastest who were to participate in the final. It worked out that
the Kent Plate was a three-cornered battle between Don Walker,
George Morgan and myself. It was conceded that Walker, who was
champion of Australia, and Morgan, his closest rival, had proved
beyond any question of doubt that they were the two fastest men in
Australia that season, and they were counted upon to give me a great
tussle for the laurels.

One of the Sydney newspapers carried the following item relative
to this three-cornered race just before the battle started:

"Before the start of the Sydney Thousand Don Walker was ex-
tremely anxious for another match race with Major Taylor. He is
sure that with the experience he gained in his previous contest with the
world's champion that he can defeat the American marvel. He will
have his chance this afternoon, and the three riders will thus have a
clear run throughout. On his showing at the races already held
Major Taylor will defeat the two Australian cracks, but they may,
however, be depended upon to put up a good battle right up to the
tape. There is also great rivalry between Morgan and Walker, and if
Taylor beats them out, their sprint for second place will be something
out of common.

"Notwithstanding the many defeats that Major Taylor has inflicted
upon them this season both Morgan and Walker have followers, who
expect to see them yet turn the tables. It is asserted in behalf of Mor-
gan that Taylor only defeated him by a foot or so in each of the heats
of the match in Melbourne, and there is not a very great difference
between the two. However, Major Taylor wins the majority of his

races by only a foot or so, and seems content to win by only a small margin, which is just as good as twenty lengths to him. Taylor's form is even better now than it was at the January meeting when he was practically undefeated, and he keeps right on improving at every appearance. Experts here are now satisfied that he is really the marvel that the Continental and the American press proclaimed him to be."

I won by a wheel in my preliminary heat with Mutton second, and Lewis third, the time being 2:05 1/5. In the first semi-final of the Kent Plate I was opposed by Beachamp and Filsell. Concerning this race I quote the following paragraph from a Sydney daily:

"This was a slow race in which Filsell made a good showing, but Major Taylor always had the race well in hand and eventually won by over three lengths, Filsell being second and Beachamp bringing up the rear. Don Walker won the second semi-final heat and Morgan was victor in the third. Taylor's time was 2:14 2/5, Walker's was 2:08, while Morgan won in 2:05."

Another Sydney newspaper carried the following item on the day following the final of the Kent Plate event:

"Taylor Riding Brilliantly. Makes Show of Walker and Morgan in the Final of the Kent Plate. In the final of the Kent Plate race Taylor was opposed by Morgan and Walker. The American took the lead half a lap from home, and simply playing with the pair, won with ridiculous ease, which was a slap in the eye for those who were booming Morgan as a likely winner, for the best he could do was finish third, with Walker second. The time was 2:01 1/5.

"I have previously commended Morgan for holding the opinion that Taylor is not invincible. Other riders seem to have made up their minds that it is no use trying to beat him. But if yesterday's riding is the best Morgan can give us, he can join the other brigade at once. As to Walker, his chance against Taylor is hopeless, for he has had many tries, and is doing worse now than at the start."

My next big race was in the Castlereigh Plate, a first-class scratch event, limited to only 18 starters at a distance of five miles.

A Sydney paper read:

"Later on Major Taylor rode in the Castlereigh Plate, a five-mile scratch race. He kept in a handy position all through the race, and was led by Pye with only a half lap to go. The final sprint was a good one. Taylor soon had Pye in difficulties, but Joe Megson came at him. Taylor, however, stuck to his task and won out with something to spare."

On the second night of the Sydney Thousand Carnival I started in the York Handicap, a half-mile race. Concerning this event I quote a Sydney daily:

There were eight starters in the fourth heat of the York Handicap, a half-mile race, in which Major Taylor rode from scratch. He got away very fast and rode at a wonderful rate of speed for a full lap. When the time came for the finish he sprinted leaving his field, and won easily by three lengths. The final was also appropriated by Major Taylor, but only after a very plucky ride.

"The American was up to the field at the bell, but it was not until the last 200 yards from the tape was reached that he began to move to the lead of the field, then he was obliged to fight his way through the thick of the bunch, but once out of the rut he dashed for the tape, winning easily.

"It was certainly a daring piece of work, and one which no other rider would have attempted. Major Taylor was given a great reception as he rode around the track after winning. Hopper, who started from the 35 yard mark, finished second, while Filsell from the 25-yard mark was third. The time was :56 2/5.

"Major Taylor was fined ten shillings for careless riding in the final of the York Handicap. From the position he was placed in no other rider could have won that race. On passing the members' stand he was badly pocketed, but saw an opening through which it seemed almost impossible to get through. However, Major Taylor made a quick dash through it, and spread-eagled the field around him and won easily. This was a most daring thing to do, and one of the racing men remarked he never saw anything like it for daring in his life. There was nearly a spill, and the officials saw fit to impose a fine on the victor.

"Plugger Bill Martin was a most daring rider when getting through a field of riders, but he never did anything like what Major Taylor showed us in this race. It only goes to show that it must be a very bad pocket that Major Taylor cannot extricate himself from."

Another daily had the following paragraphs relative to that fine:

"Much Ado About Nothing. The fining of Major Taylor for an alleged taking of a very dangerous risk in going through where there was not sufficient room in the York Handicap has created no end of discussion in Sydney. One journal made it out to be the most desperate thing ever seen on a track. Now this offense is a very serious one indeed, and riders have been dealt with seriously for doing it. If Major Taylor had done half what was alleged by that daily, he certainly would have deserved a twelve months' disqualification.

"However, I don't think he took any risk at all, and he says he did not, as the riders in front of him swerved out at the psychological moment which allowed him a clear passage. But it goes to show the peculiarities of official penalties."

After successfully eluding the hoodoo of all bicycle races, a spill, up to this time, he caught up to me in the final event of the closing program of the Sydney Thousand Carnival. It came in the final of the Oxford Plate, a special first-class half-mile handicap. The crash happened just as I had taken the position which would have surely landed me in first money. Wilksch and Sutherland were the riders who figured in the mixup, as I crouched for my jump, and in a twinkling the entire field was scrambled all over the track, but fortunately no one was seriously injured.

In commenting on my tumble one of the daily papers had this to say:

"Major Taylor's fall at the cycling sports last evening points to the fact that the same gang was determined to bump him out regardless of all costs. It would be well to bear in mind that this was Major Taylor's first spill in his racing for the past two years."

# CHAPTER LXX



Following the race meet on the Sydney Track I went to Adelaide,
South Australia, to participate in a three-day meet in that city, under
the auspices of the League of South Australian Wheelmen.  I was
tendered a wonderful reception upon my arrival in Adelaide in which
officials of the city, promoters of the bicycle racing, and racers of the
country took part.

On the opening day I participated in five events and was beaten
only once.  That was in the seventh heat of the Walne Stakes (half-
mile handicap event) in which I made my début before the Adelaide
audience, Thorne, who started from the forty yard mark nipping me
at the tape.  I won the final of the Walne Stakes and the Sir Edwin
T. Smith Stakes, and was first in my heat in the Adelaide Wheel
Race, besides winning the fourth heat of the Sir Edwin T. Smith
Stakes (one-mile scratch event).

I quote the following account of the first day's racing from an
Adelaide daily:

"A hearty round of applause indicated that Major Taylor was on
the track to take his place in the last heat of the Walne Stakes, which
served to introduce him to the Adelaide public.  Taylor quickly picked
up Gudgeon's rear wheel and in turn with Hopper they took the
champion along in pursuit of the leaders.  A hot pace was set by the
front men who evidently wished to have something to say at the finish.
Major Taylor left his colleagues at the score board and put in a
splendid effort.  He flashed past King within a few lengths of the
tape, but Thorne was not to be overtaken and won by three-quarters
of a length in :58 2/5.  This was the fastest of the heats and allowed
Taylor to start in the final.

"In the final heat Taylor and Walker were on scratch, Walne had
ten yards handicap, Shean fifteen, Farley thirty, Mathais thirty-five,
Thorne and Payne forty, and Scheps forty-five.  Walker was off the
mark before Taylor, but the latter soon caught him and took his wheel.
Payne led by two lengths at the bell, and Walker was pacing the back
men.  He gradually overhauled the handicap men and then cut down
Scheps and Thorne who had been leading. Walker was in the straight
and had not commenced to sprint when Taylor set off at a great rate,
and Walker, seeing the futility of chasing him, did not finish as he
usually does.  Taylor won by several lengths.  Thorne was third.

The time was :57 1/5. Major Taylor was loudly applauded as he pedalled around the track afterwards.

"Twenty-seven riders answered the call for the four heats of the Sir Edwin T. Smith Stakes, a Blue Ribbon (half-mile scratch) race. The last heat brought out a representative field. Major Taylor was quickly off his mark, but was content to draw back and allow Forbes and Farley to set the pace, when the bell went Farley was leading

MAJOR TAYLOR, winner of the Sir Edwin Smith Stakes and Blue Ribbon

with Taylor on his wheel. Then came Forbes, Walne and Wilksch, Marshall having retired. Wilksch made his sprint near the score board, but Taylor was quickly in pursuit, making a magnificent sprint and crossing the line half a wheel in front of Wilksch, with Forbes in third place, and Walne trailing.

"The final of this event was by far the most exciting race of the evening. The contestants were Major Taylor, MacDonald, Wilksch, Sheehan, Mutton, Walker, Hopper, and Forbes. This race was notable for the splendid pacing. The field was close together at the bell when Taylor, Walker and MacDonald shot to the front. MacDonald went away with a magnificent sprint with Major Taylor pressing him hard, but he was not easily captured. The pair were on even terms, however, as they raced for the tape, but MacDonald was not able to match the American's final jump and lost the race by over a wheel's length. Meantime Walker had run himself into a pocket and

Wilksch and Morgan finished in front of him. The winner and MacDonald received an ovation. Lady Smith invested Major Taylor with the blue ribbon and salvos of cheers rent the air as the distinguished visitor circled the Oval with the coveted ribbon fluttering in the breeze.

"There were fifty-four starters in the six heats of the Adelaide Wheel Race, a two-mile handicap. There were eleven men in the fourth heat, including Major Taylor, Morgan and Mutton, who were on the back marks. The front markers were overhauled at the end of the fourth lap with Taylor lying fourth. The American sprinted at the stand and ran home lengths in front of Mutton, Nalty finishing third. Major Taylor won his heat in the brilliant manner which characterizes all of his riding. He declined an invitation to ride into a pocket, and getting a clear run by the time the straight was reached, he made hacks of his competitors, and won amid loud cheers.

"The final of the Adelaide Wheel Race was run on the third day of the meet. The fourteen stars in the final were Major Taylor, scratch, Forbes, twenty yards, Gudgeon and Mutton, forty, Chalmers, seventy, Aunger, eighty, Filsell, ninety, Mathais, one hundred thirty, Hunt, one hundred forty, Thorne, one hundred fifty, Schneider, two hundred ten, McAuliffe, three hundred, King, three hundred fifty, Madden, three hundred sixty. A handicap of three hundred yards in a two-mile race is considerable of an advantage, but as Major Taylor is in splendid form it is thought he will be able to lead the field home."

In the American Whirl (one-half-mile handicap) I won the third heat in which I started ten yards behind scratch. I also won the third heat of the Morgan Stakes (one-mile handicap) starting fifteen yards behind scratch. I won the final of the Morgan Stakes, but finished second to Scheps (forty-five yards) in the final of the American Whirl. In the lap dash (one-third mile handicap) I started five yards behind scratch and was defeated by Schnider (fifty yards) in the first heat. The final of the lap dash was scheduled to be held the closing day of the meet.

An account of the day's racing appeared in one of the Adelaide newspapers:

"Hearty applause greeted the competitors as they appeared on the track for their preliminary sprint. The brilliant American champion, Major Taylor, received a cordial demonstration while he pedalled around the track. What a master he is on the bicycle! A forceable illustration of his wonderful sprinting powers was provided in the fact that for the first time in the history of South Australian cycling, an Adelaide gathering saw a rider start from behind scratch. Taylor was heartily cheered as he took up that high position of professional honor, the penalties inflicted by the handicapper called for magnificent work by the champion.

"In the American Whirl, a half-mile handicap event, Taylor was placed ten yards behind the scratch mark, but with a fine burst of speed he got home from Farley in the third heat. Scheps, the plucky South Australian rider, defeated the crack in the final, and was applauded for his splendid efforts.

"Fifteen yards behind the tape was Major Taylor's position in the Morgan Stakes, a first-class one-mile handicap, which he won by

MAJOR TAYLOR (with white waistband) in a Pocket

magnificent skill. The American was five yards behind scratch in his heat of the lap dash. But notwithstanding the wonderful sprint he made, Schneider, fifty-yard man, was not overtaken by him.

"In the third heat of the Morgan Stakes a splendid field was seen. Taylor riding from fifteen yards behind scratch had to bridge the gap of twenty yards to get on even terms with Don Walker, and one hundred five yards to make up on the limit man. From the start the champion with wonderful judgment and dash plowed his way skillfully through the fast field, and quickly picked up Walker. Gudgeon took the back-mark men up to the leading division, at the end of the first lap, with Taylor on his wheel. An easy pace set by Marshall brought them into the bell, when Champness took charge from Gudgeon, Morgan, Taylor, Mathais, Walker, Corbett, and Wilksch.

"The field opened out at the river end and Taylor promptly jumped into fourth place. At the northeastern turn the pace quickened. Taylor began his sprint rather earlier than usual and ducked his head at the score board. Coming up the stretch with a wonderful sprint he got across the tape comfortably from Morgan and Mathais.

"In that heat there was an attempt to pocket Major Taylor, but the American was on the 'qui vive.' A formidable field was left to battle for first place in the final. Taylor got away from mark smartly and dashed past Morgan and Forbes, and set off in hot pursuit for the leading bunch whom he captured at the southern turn, after a splendid effort. Farley and Aunger were out in front by themselves, while the second division consisting of Chalmers, Rolfe, Filsell, Mathais, and Taylor, now slowed down. Forbes pulled off the track and at the bell Farley and Aunger were well in the lead with

MAJOR TAYLOR winning the Morgan Stakes

Taylor, Rolfe, Mathais, Morgan, and Filsell in the order named. Morgan was unable to stick to the hot pace and retired from the race.

"Quickly Taylor shot out at the turn just entering the back stretch with Rolfe sticking to his rear wheel. The American flew past Chalmers and with a magnificent sprint crossed the tape six lengths ahead of Farley. Rolfe was third, Mathais and Aunger next. Major Taylor, the winner, rode a splendid race showing both superior speed and tactics, and was loudly cheered by the vast throng. The time was 2:04 4/5.

"Lap dashes always spell excitement and yesterday's events were no exception to the rule. In the first heat Major Taylor was placed five yards behind scratch, and he failed to catch Schneider, who started from the fifty yard mark. Taylor caught MacDonald and Burton and took them along at a merry clip, but he could not overtake Schneider. The American got a bad start, being a length behind with Burton, MacDonald, and Nalty in his wake. The final in this event will be decided on Saturday, Major Taylor's second place allowing him to enter that heat."

On the third and final day of the Carnival at Adelaide I won the lap dash final, starting five yards back of scratch, by two lengths from Hopper (twenty yards) with Walker (scratch) third, and King (80) fourth. I won my heat in the one-mile International Championship event and won the final with Don Walker and Chalmers finishing in that order, the time being 2:02 2/5. Then I won the final of the Adelaide Wheel Race in 4:09, the fastest time ever made in this race from scratch, and the final of the Walker Stakes, a mile and a half handicap.

Record breaking crowds attended the first two day's meeting at the Adelaide Track and the third and final day saw a gathering far in excess of the opening day's, there being twenty-two thousand present on this occasion. The Adelaide Wheel Race was the feature of the program. In this event, a two-mile handicap race, I had to concede the limit man three hundred sixty yards. There were fourteen riders in the event including the cream of Australia. There were forty starters in the Walker Stakes in which I started twenty yards behind scratch, the limit man having a handicap of two hundred fifty-five yards. In the International One-mile Championship event there were forty-four starters including Hopper, and all the Australian stars.

One of the Adelaide newspapers carried the following article relative to the final day's racing of the Carnival in that city:

"In addition to the two International victors, Major Taylor, the world's champion cyclist, and N. C. Hopper, the other American representative, who was formerly amateur champion of that country, were all the first class riders from every state in the Commonwealth and New Zealand.

"The final of the Lap Dash gave the spectators a treat, Major Taylor giving his most magnificent exhibition of sprinting to win the laurels. Only a rider of Taylor's caliber could have conceded eighty yards to such a strong handicap man as King, the race covering only one-third of a mile.

"Don Walker got away to a good start, and set a pace that took Taylor along for half the distance. Then the American ran high up on the bank and with a wonderful burst of speed jumped into the leading position and crossed the tape two lengths in front of Hopper with Walker and King following in that order.

"There was some excellent racing in the One-Mile International Championship Event. Major Taylor's success in the second heat was a foregone conclusion, and at no period of the race was he pressed for victory. In the final of this event Farley and Marshall furnished the pace right up to the bell. Major Taylor then took charge from Walker, Chalmers, Hopper, Burton, MacDonald, Payne and Morgan. Burton went out and Taylor trailed him. Gudgeon took Mac-

Donald up on the outside, but in the race for positions, these two faded away. Taylor settled down for his terrible sprint for the tape in the meantime, and won handily from Don Walker and Chalmers in the fast time of 2:02 2/5 amid tremendous cheering.

"The great Adelaide Wheel Race proved to be a magnificent test. Major Taylor had twenty yards to make up before catching Forbes, Gudgeon and Mutton, but he was up with them on the first lap. The

Final of the One-mile International Championship
Taylor         Walker          Chalmers
American     Australian     New Zealand

leaders, McAuliffe, King and Mutton assisted each other with clock-like regularity.

"Passing the judges for the first time around Taylor put in a magnificent sprint and caught the middle division at the first turn. This splendid effort practically decided the race, for the three leaders were within reach with three laps to go. On entering the home stretch preparatory to the final lap Madden had command, leading McAuliffe, King, Hunt and Aunger until Chalmers shot forward with Taylor lying on the outside. The success of the American was now assured, which was further demonstrated when he leaped to the lead followed by Gudgeon, Chalmers and Aunger. He jumped for the tape in front of Aunger, who was too smart for Chalmers, Schneider finishing fourth.

"Taylor was greeted with rounds of applause as he pedalled around the track. In the history of the Adelaide Wheel Race which was introduced as the premier event of the South Australian League in 1895, being contested annually ever since, only once previous to yesterday has it been won from scratch, Walne turning the trick in 1898. Incidentally up to yesterday's win by Major Taylor the Adelaide Wheel Race has always been won by an Australian rider, although contest-

Start of the Adelaide Wheel Race

ants have included international champions. Major Taylor's time, 4:09, is the fastest time ever made in this race from scratch, clipping :07 1/5 off the previous record which was made by Walne, when he won in 1898.

"Major Taylor stands head and shoulders above all the other competitors at the meeting just closed on the Adelaide track. He started in fourteen races, scoring eleven first's and three second's. The next best scorer was Don Walker with four first's, three second's, and two third's. Major Taylor's riding was a revelation in these three programs and nobody begrudges the brilliant sprinter the $1,250 in prize money he is taking away from this state. His superior judgment and faultless tactics were delightful to witness, and his sprints for the tape which he accomplished with a phenomenal burst of speed were far and away the finest efforts ever seen on an Adelaide track.

"The enterprise of the promoters in securing this hero of the world's cycle tracks was substantially rewarded, a credit balance of $2,350 resulting.  Excluding the appearance money of $750, Major Taylor has won nearly $500 in prizes.  His chief victories were the Walne Stakes, Morgan Stakes, Sir Edwin T. Smith Stakes, the Adelaide Wheel Race, the Lap Dash (1/3 mile), and the One-mile International Championship Event.

# CHAPTER LXXI



Flush with my successes on the Adelaide track I made my way to Melbourne for a return engagement. I was entered in the feature event of the Australian Natives' Association program, the International Five-mile Championship race on April 13, 1903. This meeting was probably the biggest bicycling event in Australia, judged from the viewpoint of the races and the throngs that attended the programs.

Since I was going to leave Australia for my European tour following this race at Melbourne I was especially desirous of winning this international race. In addition to that incentive for doing my best on the Melbourne track I was desirous of adding another international trophy to my collection. I had won the Quarter-mile International Championship race at Sydney, and the One-mile International Championship event at Adelaide and this Five-mile International Championship race was the third one on my Australian schedule. Incidentally since I had won the Quarter-mile International Championship race for my first victory on the Australian tour, I was very desirous of winding up my tour of that country with a victory of the International Five-mile event.

The starters in this race were Don Walker, Jack Chalmers, Joe Megson, Arthur Gudgeon, Richard Cameron, A. C. Forbes, George Morgan, Ernest Pye, Bill MacDonald, E. F. Wilksch, Norman Hopper, C. E. Burton, J. Filsell, R. (Dick) Mutton and myself. I won this race with Walker second, and Chalmers third.

One of the Melbourne newspapers carried the following story relative to that race:

"Honors in the International Five-mile Championship race were carried off by the American champion, Major Taylor, from a field of fifteen starters, after a brilliant set-to up the home stretch with MacDonald, Walker and Chalmers.

"Morgan and Cameron retired from the race early, the former through a tire blowing out. Megson, Mutton and Filsell were the early pacemakers, and with four laps to go Filsell made a break from the field. He did not last long, however, then Wilksch resumed the lead but the American champion soon dashed to the front, but was instantly replaced by MacDonald. For a brief space it looked as if Major Taylor would be blocked, but he cleverly worked his way clear on rounding into the home stretch and with a magnificent sprint he defeated Don Walker by a length and a half, while Chalmers was two lengths in back of him.  The time was 12:01 2/5.  The American received a tremendous ovation.

"In the handicap events, however, Major Taylor was not successful owing to the fine form of the handicap men on the big marks.  It seems that the crowd that has been racing against Major Taylor since his advent in Australia has evidently got hold of the right tactics at last.  Major Taylor's riding yesterday is said to have been very disappointing, outside of his fine riding in the International Five-Mile Championship Event, and certain back-markers, who recently put their heads together in Adelaide can doubtless explain the failure."

That International Five-mile Race marked the end of my Australian tour and a few days later I sailed for Paris where I was under contract to ride.  In my four months' stay in Australia I participated in twenty-seven races, winning twenty-three first places, and four second places.  Included in that grist were the only three international events in that country and I won first place in each of them.

My conquests on the tracks of Australia netted me a total of $10,735.  I received a bonus of $7,500, and won $2,235 in prize money and received $2,500 additional for establishing new records.  In addition to my prize winnings my Australian trip taught me several new wrinkles in the art of handicap racing.  The Australian riders are skilled in this style of race, and they certainly taught me more about it than I ever dreamed was in the book.

My stay in Australia is one of my most pleasant recollections, especially in view of the fact that I entered the country with dire misgivings because of my color.  While I experienced team-work and combinations in my racing tour of Australia, I am satisfied that the field was interested in bringing about my defeat simply because I was champion, and not because of my color.  With that color bugaboo dispensed with I got more pleasure out of my highly successful Australian tour than had hitherto been my lot in my entire racing career.  This psychological feature enabled me not only to follow in the footsteps of my boyhood hero, A. A. Zimmerman, the world's champion, but also to exceed his performances in Australia.

# CHAPTER LXXII



Owing to a mishap the ship on which I sailed from Australia to France was delayed one week, causing the trip to take a full month. As a result of that accident I had to ride in Paris the day after I arrived there, and of course, I was defeated as I was on several subsequent occasions pending my return to top form. On top of my lack of condition the season in France was well under way, giving my opponents a decided edge over me in the matter of condition. Another drawback I experienced in France was that my schedule called for my spending much of my time on trains, so that the only training that I got came in actual competition on the tracks.

All told I won thirty-one first places, twenty-two second places, nine third places, and two fourth places in this invasion of Europe. In the course of this tour I made my first appearance in England, and was given a hearty ovation upon making my début in London.

In the course of this tour of Europe my great successes were scored in my match races with Elleggarde, the champion of Denmark, whom I defeated twice in single match races. I also scored victories over Jacquelin, the former French champion, and over my old friend Owen Kimble, the Kentuckian, who was one of my bitterest rivals on the tracks of this country. On my appearance in England I figured in a three-cornered match race with Charles Piard, the French champion and Sidney Jenkins, champion of England. I was successful in three straight heats.

Relative to my first appearance in England one of the London daily papers carried this item:

"A crowd of ten thousand persons gathered around the track at the Memorial Grounds, Cannington, yesterday to witness what proved to be a most admirable program of bicycle racing. The fact that Major Taylor, the 'flying Negro' champion, would make his appearance here largely helped to augment the normal gate. A most enticing program had been prepared, consisting of a three-cornered match race between Major Taylor, America, Piard, France, and Sid Jenkins, England. Taking first the international races which consisted of three one-mile heats, it may be sufficient to say that Major Taylor won all three of them.

. "He has little to learn in the art of finessing, and possesses a wonderful sprint which landed him a winner at the tape every time. The time taken in riding the second mile heat was 5:22 4/5, and will serve to show the extreme difficulty the men had in keeping on their machines as they maneuvered up and down the banking for positions.

"Major Taylor watched his men as a cat does a mouse, and although he was nearly pocketed on the last turn into the stretch of the second heat, he managed to get through and hold his men easily.  The third heat was set at a more regulation speed, and the 'Major', giving us a glimpse of his true sprinting powers, went after Jenkins and Piard

SID JENKINS—British Champion

and divided the pace for the greater part of the mile.  The Negro champion easily beat them across the tape the third time, and was given a splendid ovation.

"After the race Sid Jenkins of Cardiff, a prolific prize fighter and winner of nearly all the championships, said 'I have been beaten by the fastest rider in the world today.  That's the only excuse I have to offer.'  Sid Jenkins holds all the National Cyclists' Union's professional championships and is our best representative in the professional ranks.  He has been racing for twelve seasons, and during that time has won many important races both at home and abroad.

"Charles Piard, the French crack, won the world's amateur sprint championship at Rome last year.  He was seldom beaten while an amateur.  After joining the professional ranks he soon made a good name for himself and is regarded as the fastest professional in the French ranks."

On this my third tour of Europe my most notable victories were my two single man-to-man contests with Elleggarde; the great Danish champion. The first of these races was held in Antwerp where I was successful in two straight heats. The second match was in Paris before a tremendous crowd. I won the first heat, lost the second, and led Elleggarde home in the third and deciding rush. This was one of the hardest races I ever rode, bearing in mind that Elleggarde was always a hard man to beat. My defeat of him on this occasion was second only to the defeat I administered to him at Argen, France, on my first trip to Europe in 1901.

Another hard battle in which I engaged in my 1903 European tour was with Harri Meyers, the star Hollander, whom I had also defeated in my second visit to Europe in his home town Maestricht. On the latter occasion Meyers defeated me in the second heat, but I turned the tables on him in the third and deciding heat. However, I had to extend myself as Meyers' victory in that heat gave him a world of confidence, and he tore around the turn into the home stretch on the last lap of the third heat with a terrific burst of speed. I made my jump on him half way to the tape and nipped him at the line by a half length.

BY PAUL HAMELLE AND ROBERT COQUELLE

## PREFACE

Had this book been published two or three years ago, I would
have understood the need of it, or else a preface—the word is some-
what ambiguous to my view of introducing or presenting this book.

At that time the sport, not so much known as it is now, was far
from the popularity that it now enjoys, for that reason a few explana-
tory lines for a book so well named, Major Taylor could have deemed
a necessity.  But since the idea has had a rapid stride, and he has
conquered every one in the field, a few of our contemporaries can
say in truth, that they did not know, at least by reputation, the Negro
champion cyclist, hero of the book of which the authors, my good
friends Paul Hamelle and Robert Coquelle, gave me the undeserved
honor of writing a few introductory lines.

These gentlemen, who having perceived the blazing name of Major
Taylor on billboards, lamented the slackening of the discipline, and
the loss of the old army traditions, resulting in the exhibition of one of
our officers in the bicycle races, is rather in a class of its own, if he
isn't in an insane state of mind as a result of such a thought.

Today there is no longer any one among the young and the old
people, both men and women, who do not know the names of the celeb-
rities in the sporting history in general, and that in particular, of the
famous "Flying Negro" whose achievements are equal to those of
Coquelin Regane.

Certainly, not the least known psychologists of our day do not
believe that such glorious achievements exaggerated to their point of
view, of muscle against brain of which they are still disputing, is worth
commendation.  Far be it from me to take issue with them.  For one
reason space will not permit me to do so, and this being the principal
reason, at any rate it will not be discussed, as my pen is too unskilled
to uphold an argument of such critics.  I am confined to my own
opinion.  And this opinion is for the work of Hamelle and Coquelle,
the best of all presentations since it justifies their ambitions of having
written a book destined to interest everybody, without exception.  Who
among our foreign contemporaries that hasn't applauded Major Taylor
in one of the numerous countries where he victoriously carried the
Stars and Stripes, has not heard from someone of his records in the
sport?  Very few evidently.

(304)

If that constituted the most agreeable part to fill in my short testimonial it would be superfluous to add that none were better qualified to entertain the public with his big doings and to bring back reminiscences than our two friends, who at the same time introduce him in this interesting story; as exciting in some of its chapters as is the life and the appearances of the Negro champion himself, who before winning the European track races was able to triumph over the prejudiced competitors among his countrymen, despite the fact that he was not of their race.

Scrupulous and refined writer as well as a journalist, whose work augments in scope and in importance every day, he can lay claim to distinction without boastfulness, for he isn't in a "combination" class, or in a set class in his profession. He is only among those who say and write very truthfully just what they think, and in what they believe to be just. As for his partner, my old comrade Robert Coquelle, he is one whom we may call a chip of the block, in every meaning of the word. Liking, he himself, his profession, less for what it brings him in financial return than for himself and especially knowing his subject so much more than he has lived so to speak, he gained glory in succeeding where many failed. In getting Major Taylor to attempt the venture, big for the Negro at that epoch, and in getting him to come across the ocean to popularize in Europe the bicycle sport (which was then dormant as a result of circumstances) he also succeeded. He was first also to accompany the Negro champion on his tour of the country, and knew the honest sentiments and glowing thoughts (even for those who do not share them) of the frizzled haired negro, in whose brilliant eyes lurked instinctive suspicions. It is to him we are indebted for knowing, in the proper sense of the word, the honor of this little book. He was in a manner the inventor of "Major Taylor", as Paul Hamelle had been the signer. Of this contribution, there could be only success. I leave it to all the readers the care of judging it. VICTOR BREYER.

### GIANTS OF THE TRACK

In the domain of the cycle, is Major Taylor the King of Cyclists? This question which would readily be answered in the affirmative by sportsmen, leaves a certain doubt in the minds of the critics.

The world of the wheel is one of the polytheism, each person adoring his own god whom he places above all others; and the number of these gods has been growing constantly larger, ever since men have propelled bicycles.

In England, men still have a real devotion for Cortis. Ask any Englishman between the ages of thirty-five and forty, who was, in his opinion, the greatest cyclist of the world. His answer will most certainly be "the first one who, on a sixty inch bicycle and on a flat dirt track, made 20 miles in an hour the 'lone wanderer,' who died at the antipodes, and whose statue may be seen at the entrance of his native village, or on one of the tracks where he became famous." And do not argue with this firm believer; he would soon convince you (with irrefutable arguments) that all our modern celebrities are as nothing when compared to this giant of prehistoric ages.

Nevertheless, the cyclic admirers of young England pay tribute to other gods, each of which has his particular High-Priest. Harry Leeming, the trainer, thought Saunders Sellers, the conqueror of George Hendee, the greatest natural cyclist "who had ever sat astride of a bicycle." Our old friend, Tom Eck, who brought out John S. Johnson, who in turn espoused the case of so many champions, had the same opinion of Herbert Snyder; Wilson, manager of the Crystal Palace, asserted that Zimmerman, even at his best, would not have been worthy of loosening the shoe-strings of Frederick Osmond, his pupil at the height of his fame. In this, his opinion differed from that of McCredy, himself champion, who had to do with both, and who with a multitude of Americans, numerous Frenchmen, among whom the great Mousset, many Germans, Belgians and Australians swear only by the flying Yankee, the great Zim, the Grinder, with whom no one may be compared.

Notwithstanding this general opinion, the great Choppy Warberton, he who knew a rider when he saw one, proclaimed loudly that the Belgian Houben had completely overwhelmed the great American. While Culver, the "scientific trainer" declared Walter Sanger superior to Zim, whom he defeated four times in the six races they had, a fact which certainly could be taken as an argument. A few of our Frenchmen, among whom Mousset, named Cassignard only with that expression of regret for him who could have been . . . an expression which means "Tu Marcellus eris," you shall be king, if your brains are not shattered on one of the milestones. And we know of others who esteem that Bourrillon is the greatest rider the old world has ever produced for them even; he would be equal to Zimmerman. The tall MacFarland has written that Jacquelin was the greatest tactician and the greatest sprinter of the world, without excepting even the great Zim. Dick Howell, Fred Wood, Percy Furniwall have their devoted adherents; Cannon Bald and Kramer also, but more so, Major Taylor who has visited so many countries and made in all of them Taylorites who now see everything through colored lens.

Is the opinion of the Taylorists more exact than that of others, the Jacquelinists, the Baldists, the Furniwallists, and the other "ists"? That is the question.

To tell the truth, there is no greater racer. At a certain height, there is no longer superior nor inferior, for the plausible reason that no margin can be set among men who, by definition, may not be classified. Moreover, what would be the means, when it is already so difficult to assign a rank to two men who competed every day during many seasons, such as Elleggarde and Meyers; what would be the means to establish a lawful hierarchy, one that will not be the result of sentimental preferences, among men who have never met, who lived at different times, raced with different machines, trained on tracks by different methods, between a Cortis and a Major Taylor?

That the Taylorites have a reason to want their colored idol to have first place in the temple of the cycle gods, that Taylor is the "primus inter pares" among the members of the big family, is doubtful; which by way of compensation he is not, even though the Major is of that family, and if not the greatest, he is, at least the most extraordinary, the most different, the most picturesque, and the most popular, on whose self the greatest legends have accumulated and history of whom isn't complete in a story.

This story, unfinished, we wish to revive in these pages even without all marvelous elements, reduced to exactitude of facts, it is startling!

BEFORE THE OUTSET

We are not writing about the ancestry of our hero. From what negro tribe, in either quarter, does he descend—and on what date and what merchant ship did his negro foreparents come into port? On all these points his biographers are mute because they are ignorant of these facts. But this incertitude does not diminish our opinion if it is true that mystery makes greater those whom it drapes. The fact is that the history of his family starts with himself, Marshall Walter Taylor, born on November 26th, 1878, at Indianapolis, who owed all to nature and nothing to his ancestors, unless it was good health and strong constitution, being himself among those we name poetically of the "ancestors", or, to speak as his country men "a self made man", that is to say " a son of his making."

Where did the title of "Major" originate? Or is "Major" a synonym for Marshall, which was his baptismal name? First name or surname, it doesn't matter, the story knows of only the Major.

We pass over his childhood years, which do not bring out any of the anecdotes of which we would like to have known something, as they might have some bearing on his destiny. Without doubt his time was occupied, as that of all his little fellowmen of the black and white races, between school with teachers, and at home with parents. With the natural instinct, characteristic of his race, to learn readily, he received a solid primary instruction, and a good education, which was later to make him an exception— a negro gentleman and champion on the bicycle race-track, and to whom reporters on both sides of the water paid homage.

In the great race of life much depends upon the start, and his was a good one. At thirteen years of age he first took to the wheel and the pedal that was to carry him so far and to such a lofty position. Major was a well built negro boy and only asked an opportunity to make good. Over there (in America) everything is made by machinery and the machinery is very complicated. Mechanism appealed to him strongly. At his duty Major did his work twice as quickly as the other men, thus attracting the attention of his employer and in this way he gained the nickname "Speed Boy."

The meeting of Major with Mr. Munger in 1895, at Indianapolis, where the negro had established himself, was itself on the limit of two periods, the legendary and the historical. Munger was a genius and prophet. In this sixteen-year-old boy, he saw one that would be champion. He predicted to Major that if he followed his instructions to the letter, by abstaining from intoxicating liquors, the use of tobacco in any form, and retire early, rise early, and train regularly, or in other words if he took excellent care of himself, he would become the fastest bicycle rider of the world. Just how the negro followed the instructions in the hope of realizing the predictions made by Mr. Munger remains to be seen.

### HIS DEBUTS

Uncertainties characterize beginners; the best of them feel their way; the majority test their strength on the road before taking a chance on the circuit or the boards. Among those who did this is Major Taylor. He was still a resident of Middletown when he enrolled in the road event in New Jersey. All that we know is that he met and defeated the hero of the Irvington-Milburn Road Race, the famous R. M. Alexander. Who among us remembers this illustrious personage? The début was encouraging and Major persevered. It is said that he defeated "several local amateur performers."

His professional débuts were held in the six-day race at Madison Square. One day, a little before the six-day race, (which was won by the Englishman, Hale) M. M. Powers and Kennedy received a call at their office from a little negro lad. He gave his name as Taylor and wanted to engage himself in the big event. The managers hesitated at first to accept his entry, and the boy came near to being sent away, that is, sent to shine the Fifth Avenue gentlemen's shoes. They contended that the presence of this little negro would not be right at a race; it would stir the whole of New York. Finally, after some time, Taylor was admitted on his honor to race for six days and nights on the wooden track of Madison Square Garden in the company of Hale, Rice, Schock, Ashinger, Waller and other celebrated riders. Taylor started without an extra machine, without help and without food. He raced day and night. He was looked upon with indifference and hatred by those who felt the negro a dangerous being. He went round and round buffeted and pushed by his competitors.

And the scorer? He must have been square at times for in the evening of the sixth day it was announced that Hale was first with 3073 kilometers to his credit. Taylor was eighth with 2789 kilometers. It was not bad, but it did not begin to show the endurance and speed of which Taylor was master. But others had given him example. Fred Wood, who had taken part in the 100-mile race had tried the one and ten mile, also the 25 and 50; and how about Fred Osmond, Bob English, and Webber and how many others? Taylor, the negro "Proteus" who by turns or simultaneously, as we shall see, pedalled the tracks, amateur and professional, recordman and champion, acrobat and athlete.

He added to his débuts as sprinter in the spring of 1897 and quickly he placed himself in the lead. It wasn't that the American allotment was weak, far from that; the Pleiade (meaning seventh star) of Zimmerman, Sanger, Butler, Windle, Bliss, Zeigler has preceded the less brilliant battle of Bald, Cooper, Gardiner, and Kimble. To gain admittance to such company, this newcomer, who was handicapped by color prejudice, must have better qualities than the others; but that did not prevent him from taking part.

It is not our intention to take exact inventory of his successes and failures. It would more than fill a book. We only want to trace this travelled career with its "ups and downs" considering the minutes that are most significant and picturesque.

Let us note at this period of '98, who was the equal, if not the superior of the "bests," who on the 8th of July won the Championship of 1000 meters in Philadelphia, beating Cooper, Gardiner, "Cannon" Bald, Kimble and Company. Who beat, at this time, Michaels at his own game? It was the Major. The papers were short of titles to qualify "the Colored King, the Black Cyclone, Black Cloud's wondrous sprint, Taylor outshines the stars, Black Whirlwind," etc.

However, on the 27th of September he fell behind the "Blond Adonis of Chicago," Arthur Gardiner. He will remember this defeat for a long time, as this date is important in the history of "sports." This was the last ordeal under the rules of L. A. W. in which all the great cracks took part.

All of the year of '99 and the beginning of 1900 is a grey and empty page of the sport romance of the negro. It was at the time of the birth of the N. C. A. and the finishing of the L., A. W. Yet, Kimble can worry over him; Cooper has returned to Europe. It is true that at Madison Square, Munger's prophesy had been realized. The hero of the European season, Jacquelin himself, is at his height. It will always be a big regret in the sport-world that these two great athletes could not have met a year sooner to decide which of the two was the champion of the world.

On the American tracks, Major reigns without a doubt. It was on the 30th of October in order that he might prove what had been said of him, he beat "Murphy of the mile-a-minute fame," before a Worcester audience who had come to applaud their negro idol.

### THE TRIBULATIONS OF A NEGRO AT HOME

Jules Verne wrote a novel on the misfortune of a chinaman in China. It would be easy to write a volume about the incredible misfortune of our hero, Major Taylor, and it would not be a novel. His misfortunes have just one cause, his color, and his marvelous speed.

The Americans of the North made war with those of the South to break the negro chains and there are no longer slaves in bondage from the Atlantic to the Pacific. But there always seems to be an inferior race, doomed to receive all of the insults, disgraced by their liberators, parked in special hotels, and lynched for the slightest offense. They are free by right, but outcast indeed. "Isn't that so, Major Taylor?"

That our hero did not give up his profession, which his fellow cyclists made so perilous and bitter, our poor descendant of Ham, with all the athletic qualities we know of, must have had great endurance, which is characteristic of his race, to be able to suffer without revolting. From the day he appeared on the track, or at least, from the time he began to shine, everything went against him. There was much jealousy and he feared his treacherous rivals. If he could only have joined in with his fellow riders, entered into their contrivances, participated in their fraudulent schemes, then perhaps they would not be so pitiless about his color. This negro boy was timidly honest; he did not want to cut up the purse. "Did they not play mean tricks on him?" One of the tricks, the most classic, is the "pocket." Two riders take positions before the dangerous rival, one beside him, and a third one behind him—then let him try to free himself! They need not be timid with him, they swing him and encircle him, they jostle him, for he is black. If need be, they throw him, or maybe, the pin does its work in the tires. One day Taylor had to declare forfeit on account of the mishaps. At the time of the final his three spare tires were punctured; some of the doings of a revenger. Finally the public, although white, revolted. A spectator wrote to the *Sun* of New York. "We have today proof that every rider is combined against Major Taylor to destroy his chances of beating Kramer. Isn't it enough to make a white man blush from shame, that a negro is the only carrier of a banner of honesty and is gentlemanly on the track?" "But the judges?" "Aren't there any honest judges in America, or are they blind?" "No, but he is an American, that is the reason."

In reading over again this pitiful story, one of the authors recalled a little verse which reminded him of his childhood. A little negro lad was being beaten by three white lads. The scene discloses a green umbrella shading a young negro boy in red underwear.

> "A negro blacker than a crow
> Was out walking one beautiful day,
> He opened up his umbrella
> For the heat was excessive.

But Louis, Caspard and Wilhem saw him,

> And burst out laughing at the Negro

When a fifth person

> The great simpleton approached,
> With his large ink-well
> "Children, don't be so naughty,"
> Said he, "Leave this negro alone,
> Can he help it, if he is black
> Instead of rose?"

> But would you believe, these lads
> Laughed right into the face of the simpleton,
> And mocking all the more,
> The poor negro boy with the black face.

But you can't laugh all the time.

> "The simpleton got mad
> He grabbed the little brats,
> By the arms, the hair, and waists,
> And plunged them into the ink.
> The three begged for mercy,
> Deeper he plunged them into the ink."

In our history, the negro is here, and so are the urchins. But the simpleton is missing, or rather he is there also. He is the president of N. C. A. He is against his accomplices. But he closes his eyes. They are white, he is black. The judge like others is convinced that Major cannot be beaten in a race between two, but he thinks that it would be improper that a colored man should be champion of America. And such is the opinion of Major's fellow riders.

It is true that Major Taylor attracts a large crowd, his presence doubles the receipts. The American Association makes a rule that one must attend each and every one of the race meets, whether he be well or sick. There is no excuse for him. If one fails to be present he must pay the fine of one hundred dollars, whether he has a doctor's certificate or not. In 1900 Major Taylor and Nat Butler had a fine imposed of five hundred dollars for non-appearance at a meeting. Butler's fine was not paid, but Taylor must pay his in full. There is a limit to everything, even to a negro's patience. One day, when Taylor was suffering from wounds received in an accident caused by malice, his head bandaged and his side all raw, the referee ordered him to mount. This time, he had gone the limit. Major refused to mount and when they threatened to fine him, he declared that rather than pay it, he would leave the track forever. It is useless to say that from that time on, his purse was left intact, because they could not do without him.

Certain hardships are sometimes good for one. This harsh school made of Taylor an excellent pupil. He was forced to fight against the doings of his good friends! Major acquired the qualities of watchfulness and skill. He knew all the tricks and ropes of the trade. Nobody knew any better the zig-zags, the turns and the speeding up. He is as sure of his machine and uses it as skillfully as Paganin used his violin.

What attracted Major Taylor to ride on this side? Was it the sickening thoughts of ill-treatment or the desire to see something new, or to become rich in the racing-world? He decided his course in the beginning of 1901 and left his native land and came to visit us.

We are at the turning point of this history. Until now he ran his career in America. Major was a great star, but an American star. He was a roving star, if not a shooting star. His life was the most shifting that a champion has ever led, never stopping, sometimes he could be found in Australia, sometimes in America, never knowing whether the season was summer or winter. He was usually in the trains or on a boat excepting when in the saddle of his bicycle. If we should try to follow him in his tournaments, we would soon become dizzy and as we are now in America let us stay here.

## TAYLOR—KRAMER

Taylor, Kramer—Kramer, Taylor. From 1900 to 1902 the American sport holds everything between these two names. Very rarely, someone takes the lead between these two kings, but occasionally appear amongst them Iver Lawson and Owen Kimble.

It looks as if it were a law or perhaps a habit of this sport that the champions are always in pairs: Howel–Wood, Temple–Rowe, Osmond–Snyder, Zimmerman–Sanger, McCready–Medinger, Cassignard–Fournier, Jacquelin–Morin, Bald–Cooper, Elleggarde–Meyers, Taylor–Kramer. In looking over this list, how few are the singles! They are Cortis, Furniwall and Bourrillon. Law or coincidence, the duel is a fact, and a happy fact.

The interested of the season are attentive if they can concentrate on two individuals, instead of on a crowd. Instead of one man taking lead and his competitors fighting for the second place, two first-class athletes come forth to dispute the lead. In all cases, the duel-race is the most pathetic. The riders, the public, and the press are more attracted than the performers to the Zimmermans against the Sangerites, Baldites against Cooperites, Morinites against Jacquelinites, (remember Taylorites against Kramerites).

One day, a short while before Taylor's reinstatement by the N. C. A. he applied for a position on one of the racing teams of a prominent American Cycle Manufacturer and the first words in reply to his request were "to offer his services to someone else." Taylor knew that they had already engaged Kramer, the Phenix (King Pin) of all the Americans. The refused Taylor returned as he had come, but swore that "the day, when by chance Kramer should be put in his way, there would be a quarrel and someone would regret his answer."

The negro's word held good, his meeting with the director dates back from the early part of 1900, at which time we saw that the superiority of Major was not a doubt after the result of their match at Manhattan Beach.

Frank Kramer was the ex-king of the amateurs, and the prophets were not far out of the way when they said, "You shall be king." In fact, at the end of 1901 his friends admitted that he was the champion of America by twelve points ahead of Major. But figures don't mean everything. They don't say that Major just landed from Europe after a three months' campaign, and began his circuit with thirty points behind the leader, without mentioning the fatigues of the previous campaign, and of the crossing; but the tables turned, to the advantage of the traveler, who again became very strong and Kramer felt the enemy at his heels, and tried to bar the way of the championship to the negro.

I think it was in Hartford that MacFarland and Kramer had tried in every way to hold back the negro. While directing the tactics, the big Mac had fallen, bringing down with him his associates and had even endangered himself. Major did not pass. Back in the training quarters of the riders the big Californian swore at everybody, and when Taylor followed by Kramer entered, "Permit me, Mr. Taylor," said MacFarland, with a sneer and becoming suddenly a teaser, "to present to you, our white Champion of 1901—Mr. Frank Kramer." Without showing any confusion, Major thanked one, and felicitated the other and remaining serious he said, "Kramer, you were a gentleman and a fair rider before your association with this MacFarland, but I am sorry to say that since you are in his company, you are also just as crooked as he. You have the championship title, but Mac-Farland has your money." History does not tell us the answer of the one challenged. But, nevertheless, Taylor was no longer the champion of America. As a small compensation he took three national championships out of six, the one-fourth mile, one-third mile and the mile, and left Fenn with the two miles and Kramer with the five miles and twenty-five miles.

It is at this time that several good sportsmen offered a purse of $500 to the winner of a match, which would give an equal chance to the two heroes of the season for the championship of America in Madison Square, the place chosen for this meeting.. When the night came the grandstand was filled. At the sound of the pistol, the two men started; Taylor had what the Yankees called "Blood in his eyes." At the eighth lap Kramer held the pole, when Taylor started on one of those sprints which made him so famous, and Kramer seeing him coming left the pole to cut off his opponent, but Major had gone for good—seeing for his goal the purse and revenge. In the collision, Kramer fell and Major who had avoided the fall (nobody knows how) won by one lap.

When the gong sounded for the second time, Kramer leaped from his training quarters furious as a bull, but the little Major did not heed him; the track was 10 laps to the mile. To begin with Taylor forced his competitor to work at the sixth lap instead of the eighth as before, he jumped Kramer before he could blockade him. It was up to Kramer to let loose. He caught up to Major at the turn, but the former looked under his arms saw him coming and in a second the whirlwind left him standing and won easily.

This victory was both sensational and significant. Spectators were obliged to admit that the real champion was not the one to hold the title.

## KRAMER—TAYLOR

1902. It is Kramer's year. He is in full possession of his means which are great. At the end of each event the headlines were: "Kramer wins as usual," "Kramer wins in a whirlwind" or "Kramer always in the lead."

Kramer once told a reporter who asked him the secret of his success, "I have worked and worked hard. I did nothing else but try and try again. Each defeat that I got made me more determined to conquer until finally my determination became a part of me."

To become champion one must want to be one. Kramer and Major are two hot-headed men with the same idea. Therefore, it results in a wonderful duel.

And again the white champion has thirty points ahead and at the end of July the black champion, who, returned from Europe, rejoins the circuit. In the first race on the 26th of July, Major allowed himself to be pocketed. The *Cycle Age* wrote that "Major ought to learn to get nearer the outside; he wants to hug the pole. At the rate of speed that he was going, it would have been impossible to pass him, but it is his own fault. He ought to know by this time that you can't ride the same with four men in the line as with two men." Kramer is always ahead at the critical moment, but he (Taylor) doesn't even bother to take the lead.

The *Racing Board*, we should have mentioned, thought the same as the Hartford *Times*, that there did not exist a man capable of riding in front of the negro. And then others claimed that the champion of America should be a white man. He got such a good lesson from the 26th of July that in the following race of the quarter of a mile, he forgot his way of waiting, and jumped at the right moment and Kramer did not see him again. The campaign progressed; the successes and defeats of the two great rivals alternated.

With more experience and time Major was advised that he could easily fight his opponent. The rules permitted team-work provided that they be declared. Taylor joined in with the honest Fenn, already named "the very light Yankee." This combination together with the "very dark brunette" was not long in bearing good fruit.

It was at Manhattan Beach on the 9th of August in the one-third mile race, "the old Bald" at least twenty-five years, in a bold awakening of energy had beaten the negro by a few inches. But the arrangement Fenn—Taylor will wipe away this incident in a brilliant way in the final of the one-third mile. There were four of them, Kramer-Kimble, Fenn—Taylor. Kramer takes the lead followed by the pair, and in reaching the turn, Kramer hesitated, when like lightning Fenn who had been following jumped past the tape. In a flying plunge

Taylor took possession of the rear of the friendly wheel and the two sped to the goal.

Kramer awakened from a dream, tried to overtake them, and joined them at the turn—but it was too late for Kramer; he had missed the trick.

Kimble in the scuffle hastened to the tape and with such speed that he finished within a short distance of the negro.

No difference of opinion existed between the papers as to the outcome between the whites and the black.  This is where the black glorifies, the masterpiece of skill, one of the prettiest endings that has ever been seen in a race.  The white spurned what he qualifies as "an act of high brigandage, accomplished under cover of the laws permitting team-work."

Kramer soon took his revenge in Buffalo by winning over his conquerer of the previous night, in the five-mile race which counts double.  And at the end of the season he still kept the same gain on Major which he had when he had rejoined the circuit.

The wishes of the *Racing-Board* are fulfilled, a white man is the champion of America and for the second time.  The *Sportsmen* are less happy.  There is a doubt as to the value of the two men.

The big match is held September 6th in Vailsburg (on a track of 400 meters).  They will race in two heats, the first race is on the half-mile.  Kramer held the pole and took the lead, but he slowed up pace until the bell.  Major, on the outside suddenly started, Kramer joined him on the turn; Taylor slowed up perceptibly, looked behind him.  Did he want to keep his strength for the final plunge?  Then Kramer who had been stuck between Major's rear wheel and the pole let loose, took the open and now attacked.  He entered on the right side by a half length, forcing the other ones from side to side.  No exhaustion from either one and Kramer, like a hurricane, reached the line first—a length and a half before Major.  Time 1 m. 23 1/5 seconds.  The conquered one complained of having been inconvenienced.

And now for the second heat; Kramer was confident as the two men placed themselves at the post for the mile race; he takes the lead at an easy pace.  Both of them ride side by side as far as the bell.  Then Kramer suddenly jumps enough to kill Major's start.  Kramer was riding hard and it was a big fight near the last turn.  The Jersey man was quite a distance ahead, but Taylor with a great effort got back his lost ground except two feet which separated him from the conqueror and the red line.  Time 4 m. 18 2/5 seconds.  This was the last match race between the two great rivals.  The Major triumphed twice out of three, single man-to-man match races.

But we have been delayed in America, that is to say the American history was practically unknown to us. The fact that there was some parts unknown, we had to imagine the rest.

We shall make more progress in Europe, where we have nothing else to do but revive our memories, and the visions or sensations, which are still fresh in our minds. The surprise, and then of course a doubt when news from one of the authors of this book, when in America, broke the news to the sporting element in Europe, that Major Taylor was to cross the ocean. The mysterious man of whom we have heard so much about in the last three years. The doubt of his coming and we will also say, the doubt as to his merits. We were being paid for having been a little skeptical in regard to these American Aces, who from a distance seemed to devour everything, and when near vanished like smoke. The man who was coming—who would he be like? The great Zimmerman, Banker, Johnson, or the mid-distance man between the two, Tom Cooper.

He was not the usual type of negro, who aroused curiosity and sympathy. Everything apparently came the negro's way, and by the proper adjustment of affairs, his color which had always been a serious drawback for him in America, was already a benefit to him in this country. Upon Taylor's arrival at Cherbourg, and in Paris, there was a rushing of reporters and photographers. For one solid week, Taylor was the man of the hour. There were races staged both on and off the track and bazars were held.

Superstitions and moral laws forbade racing on Sunday. This was the cause of great comment. There was much discussion as to the habits of the Major, regarding the clothes he wore, what he ate, and how he trained.

At last the sky seemed to be against our shivering son of the sun, who is never really himself only when it is very hot. In the rain and cold he works only with a grouch, thus his début in Berlin was a defeat, as was the case with Zimmerman who was defeated by the Italian, Dani, in his first race in Europe. The following week Major took his revenge against his conquerors, who were not dubs, Elleggarde and Arend. The series of his victorious voyages through the foreign continent was not interrupted until the 16th of May.

The 16th of May, we were impatient for this date, when a race on the very narrow incline at Auteuil was to take place, between the champions of two worlds, of two schools, of two colors, and who excited the cycling world, Major Taylor and Edmond Jacquelin. The tri-color and the blue, more blue than the sky, which on this day was cold and gray, lined up at the tape. They started slowly, amidst the delightful cheers which rendered us motionless, then the bell sounded, they rode straight ahead, Jacquelin jumped for the tape, and Major caught him instantly, and was after him pedalling desperately and about passed, but his opponent successfully resisted the attack, and with another terrible lunge won by three-quarters of a length. The first heat was over.

Then the second heat was on, Jacquelin was waiting for his opponent to give chase and in the last two hundred meters, he breaks away for a decisive victory, using his famous maddening jump. Jacquelin's victory amazed the speechless crowd, they were overjoyed and broke the lines and carried their hero triumphantly to his dressing-room, while in the neighboring division the Major mumbled in his lingo "finis." He was no more champion, but he was brave and offered no excuses. He acknowledged that he had been fairly beaten, because he was not fast enough. He soon recovered from the disappointment and came out with a challenge to his conqueror for a match race, which challenge Jacqelin accepts.

Here we are now on the 27th day of May. Things have changed. There is a blue sky and a warm atmosphere and by chance there is some of the warmth of atmosphere in the minds of the performers. This time Major won a spectacular victory which did not astonish the spectators. Twice he literally left behind his disabled adversary by two tactics. The first time by taking the lead and repulsing, with perfect ease, a wicked attack. The second time in waiting for the last two hundred meters in order to jump, and he won out by many lengths. This was the final heat.

The Belgian correspondent of the American Newspaper *Cycle Age* wrote to his paper the next day, "You were perfectly right when you told us that you did not have a rider in America capable of defeating our greatest men. And this without Champagne or Bordeau wine, but with good, clear, sanitary drinking water."

Without losing a day Major Taylor commences his glorious campaign of triumph making apparently nothing of it, yet giving to all the impression that he was of a superior class, or in a class by himself. Alone, Elleggarde opposed him with a resistance which already assigned the blond as the future rival of the black champion, his Kramer on this side of the "Herring Pond." Major defeated Elleggarde on the day previous to the "Grand Prize of the Republic" and it is very likely he, Major, would have been the victor, but living in accordance with his teachings, Major would not race on Sunday.

The spring of 1902 brings him back to France, but we do not wish to narrate this campaign in detail, as his victories all look alike. The most astonishing was his match of the 30th of June with Tom Linton, Champion pace-rider. They rode over two and five kilometers behind motorcycles, as pacemakers. Major Taylor defeated the specialist in fine style and also broke the world's record. These performances were accomplished with a sprint wheel geared only at seven meters.

With many other victories he had some reverses. Would that mean that he was slipping? Not at all, not by the sportive law, which reminds us of the old horror of nature for the empty. The distance between Elleggarde, the sprint champion, and Major Taylor was diminishing rapidly. The other riders having gained likewise. Walter Rutt, German Champion sprint rider surprised Taylor once or twice, and Taylor in turn crushed Elleggarde immediately upon his return from Rome where he had just won the World's Championship for the second time.

Major found a worthy adversary in the person of the Hollander, Harri Meyers, who returned to the track after a year's absence, to win the three-cornered match, between Major, Elleggarde, and Meyers. This fantastic match-race will never be forgotten. It took place at the Veledrome, Buffalo, on that eventful night of June 1902.

It is now Major Taylor's third European season, and he has gone steadily forward. He hurries steadily on, first to meet one rival, the flying Dutchman, so powerful, so quick and so bold, also the second rival, the flying Dane, Elleggarde, now in full possession of his rare condition, and who, at times impressed us as the sensation of being the negro's equal. We are mentioning that Jacquelin had been the man of the 16th of May, as he took the victory at Auteuil. The courageous Willie Arend, the German Champion, the dazzling Grognia, the Belgian, who many times checked and imperilled our visitor, are among the numerous foreign champions out-classed by Major Taylor.

Since Major Taylor left America he has had little rest excepting while he was on his way to America or to Europe for the racing seasons. He is here and there and everywhere; yesterday in Antwerp, today in Paris or Turin, and tomorrow in Berlin, and the next day in Copenhagen. Here he competed in handicaps, scratch races, and with pacemakers, and won practically all the races.

It is not for the pleasure of it that Major Taylor pedals, we don't believe that he cares any more for it than our old friend Fred Wood did when he said, "He would have given the damned wheel to the devils." But there is one thing sure, Major does not allow his legs to get rusty. This man of sport is above all else a man of business. The old Anglo-Saxon saying that "time is money," is applied more to the cyclist who races for money, and he makes the best of his time as his legs are not everlasting. For this reason the negro travels the world over, without respite, and he will continue to race without enthusiasm, as a business while he feels "in the pace." For this reason we bring him back each spring at the same time the swallows return.

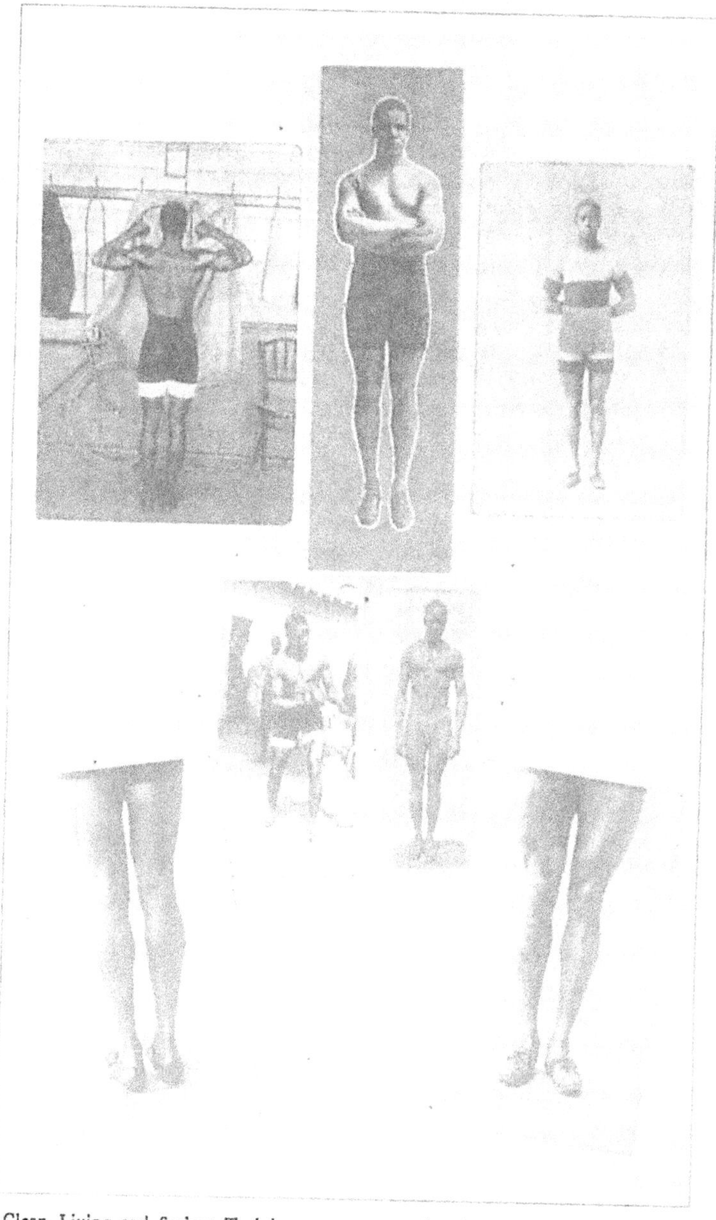

Clean Living and Serious Training are necessary for the Perfect Condition shown Above. It has often been said by Leading Sports Writers that Major Taylor's Legs were the best ever developed for Bicycle Riding

### MAJOR'S SECRET

Do not look into the mysterious "crystal ball" for Major's secret of success, that is of his sport fortune. Major was able to overcome fatigue by his good habits. And we will recall the advice of Mr. Munger when he instructed Taylor "not to drink, smoke,—to go to bed early and arise early," and more than that he said in a few words,

Perfect Condition and Correct Position

"live a clean life, and train systematically and one day you will be the fastest bicycle rider in the world."

Major Taylor followed these instructions to the letter and even more strictly when we see what fatigues were imposed upon him. His drink consisted of milk and water, very plain food, but plenty of that. He trained systematically, yet moderately as we saw by his work. He walks or runs with the step of an athlete.

In training for the races there are two periods, the first consists of using the punching bag for a time, then the massage plays an important part, also the use of the bicycle; the second part is sometimes worked out alone on the bicycle, then again behind motor, but more often working together with the other riders. Taylor's training actions are much more active than those of the great Zimmerman, but they are more capricious. In conclusion there is nothing very mysterious about the rules and methods—in fact, nothing could be more simple than his training.

There is a lot in explaining the requisites which produced this phenominal negro sprinter. The Major, as we have already explained, possessed the gift of a strong will. He was born to pedal, and built to be a champion. You can all see the silhouette of light and the harmonious strength in his body of bronze living in the supple body. It has been said that he had the form of a Marquise, and when in action the feline gait of a black panther, watching the moving jungles of bicycles; at times he creeps and is ready to spring, then he jumps, the final dazzling sprint where the rider goes as straight as lightning with no visible effort, and without the slightest twist of his blue jersey, motionless on the whirlwind of black feet which turn faster and faster until he has won. "Taylor has won"—nobody understands just how. "By what witchcraft," they ask each other. With a Jacquelin we can puzzle it out, we can see this great athlete propped on his handlebars, while each ·formidable thrust of his strong body sends him forward. We admire the strength of his action, and we understand his victories, but we must confess that we do not know how it is done by Major Taylor. His tactics like his style, escape our definition and we are not sure that he has any.

Major Taylor, properly speaking, is not a general of the track. He ignores the daring attacks, the confused improvisation of our own Jacquelin; he is not the genius, and his game is more on the negative. It is more like that of Merin, with a few happy alterations. He watches his prey then bounds. Major Taylor is a very primitive man whose thought conveys in a savage manner to distinguish the work of the legs from that of the head. The agreement is so perfect between the brain which commands the other functions that we must renounce in doing the part of one, and the others; as volition and execution blends in a victorious movement.


### THE MAN IN THE BLUE JERSEY

We have without doubt agitated too long a time before our colored gesticulator. It now remains to show a few of the means that make his movements so quick in racing. The outline of the man next to the picture of the athlete, they are both inseparable.

We have stated that Major Taylor's color was the cause of the ill-feeling against him back home, in his own country, and we hasten to add first and not alone, and perhaps by principles that we become accustomed to everything, and Major's "friends" would have without a doubt finally forgiven his color, but there is one thing that they will never forgive, and that is his honesty. Major Taylor brought into his profession, a conscience more delicate than was required on the race tracks. Possibly, he was agreeable to race for a bit of the "hard cash" but as precise as positive,

Ah! if this negro had consented to follow the prevailing customs, all would have been well—they might have understood each other, but he positively refused to enter into their shady schemes, and split purses, but such gross impertinence has no name. "What money I win, I keep," he stated. "I only split with the hotel keeper who lodges me, and the railroad man who transports me," and thus he remained the good sportsman to the end. He was always modest when victorious, and game in defeat, but never refusing a hand or a compliment even though the winner was a MacFarland, as it once happened in Indianapolis, Major's hometown. It was the finish of the National one-mile championship, when even before dismounting his wheel, he rode alongside of the big Mac, and said, "Well, for once you did it fair, how does it feel?"

With that conservative and thorough respect for the athletic law, as well as the moral law, Major Taylor stands in a class of his own. He does not drink, smoke, blaspheme or gamble, and he avoids, as much as possible, the company of those who do. He keeps pretty much to himself and many times rents a room in the neighborhood of the track. His conduct is a living blame to some of his comrades, simply because he puts into practise the lessons taught him in his catechism, which he always carries in his grip. He never mounts his wheel for the races without saying a silent prayer. He positively refuses to race on the Sabbath. This rider is unlike those who surround him. If he exasperated his comrades, he certainly has surprised and astonished us; we have never been able to understand how one man, especially a colored man, could refuse to make a fortune because the opportunity to make it, came on Sunday. The boulevard sports smiled at the superstition of the negro, but thousands of Parisians did find the time to applaud him during the week. Laugh as you wish, we lift our hats to the one who in these times of stupid egotism, sacrificed his interest for a principle. The family influence seems, however, to have been one of the chief motives of our hero's life.

With his first prize earnings he acquired a home in Worcester, Massachusetts, which helped to soften the last days of his devoted sister Gertrude, who was ill. And not one of those who knew him was surprised to learn that two years ago this good son and brother, prepared himself to become the model husband of Miss Daisy Victoria Morris. She was a very lovable colored lady, light in color, and a fervent lover of sports. She was also a graduate of Hartford

University.  These are some of the facts about the girl who won the heart of a man who never succumbed in a match of two until Cupid promoted this heart race, where Major lost his first match-race.  In so doing the Major won the best and highest prize in all his career, Miss Daisy Victoria Morris.

Perhaps the popular magazine, the "Colored American" exaggerates the past success of the husband in order that the wife may enjoy some of his popularity.  But it is quite permissible to forget two or three poor matches lost and remember only the numerous ones in which he was the victor, when it be considered that the greatest match of all was run with Cupid.  Things bring us back to our starting point.  Major Taylor, the rider, whose dazzling career we have just retraced, was he not the superior of Kramer?  Also Elleggarde, thus mentioning only two of his rivals.  To those who dare to answer and who have not heard of a panegyric made a little book of good faith, we refuse to express ourselves.  We remark in this competition that the question is rarely put forth.  The question is rarely asked whether Kramer or Elleggarde are superior to Major Taylor, or even his equal.  This puts between them a little to his advantage.

However, it is too soon to judge.  The three men are still there and have not given their last words.  Frank Kramer is still the American Champion, and Thorwald Elleggarde is still champion of the world, according to the latter.  This same opinion is popular in Europe.

Major Taylor returns from Australia with the grand passe which we know, and before him are vast projects.  The world is not so large but what they may meet again.  Who can say after all, if between the three veterans of the track some unknown youth may make his appearance, and settle the difference by defeating them all.  Luck is very changeable, and Walter Rutt whose name causes a great deal of noise is likely to give some trouble.  He is a very speedy rider.

# CHAPTER LXXIII


### MY DEFEAT IN NEW ZEALAND

Shortly after I arrived at my home in Worcester, Massachusetts, from my third invasion of Europe, I accepted another invitation to tour Australia. I made quick connections for San Francisco and sailed for Sydney the day I arrived on the coast. When the ship touched at Christchurch, New Zealand, I received a cablegram instructing me to participate in a number of races in that country.

Despite the fact that I suffered from sea sickness for most of the trip, I took part in a race meet the day after I landed in New Zealand. Naturally I was unable to do myself justice and was defeated in the New Zealand Wheel Race, a one-mile scratch event, by a native rider named George Sutherland, the champion of New Zealand. In this scratch race all of the best riders of that country were entered including Sutherland, Forbes and Chalmers.

A local newspaper printed the following item relative to that race:

"Major Taylor gave a fine exhibition of speed, but not being thoroughly trained, having just left the boat which took him across the Pacific, was unable to defeat the strong opposition that he was called upon to face. The race being won by the local champion, George Sutherland, who showed remarkably fine form.

"The victory generally speaking was popular, though a section of the public hooted Sutherland, apparently being under the impression that he was responsible for Taylor's being blocked in the last lap, causing Taylor to be forced on the grass.

"Considerable discussion has been caused by the attitude adopted by a combination of riders toward Major Taylor in this the New Zealand Wheel Race. To the uninitiated it is necessary to explain that the element of 'pacing' places cycle-racing on a different footing from any other sport. The term 'pacing' is generally understood to describe the state of things well recognized in cycle-racing circles, by which a rider following closely behind another competitor receives such a substantial advantage, an advantage that increases with the speed adopted by both, that a third-rate rider may have little difficulty in outsprinting at the finish a champion, who has been leading, or pacing him for a full lap or upwards. It is as though the man behind were being actually towed by a rope. This accounts for the disinclination, except where prior arrangements are made, of riders to go to the front, and brings about the 'loafing' which disgusts the public.

"The exigencies of pacing causes riders to combine and agree to share the task of leading, and thus increasing their aggregate speed.

Thus the combination which undoubtedly existed yesterday for the purpose of defeating Major Taylor was but a most successful development of the combined efforts of team-work on the part of the rival riders. Each of the three riders concerned recognized that if riding singly without sharing the pacing, the redoubtable negro would catch them· in a lap, at the end of which they would be nearly as tired, through their unpaced 600 yards, as he. Taylor would then have simply ridden behind them until, through the benefit of their kindly shelter, he had recuperated quickly, and then would have shot by. As it was, the trio worked their cards so well that when Taylor, by a remarkable effort, overtook them, one of the three was able to shoot from behind his mate's wheel and get away before their opponent had recovered quickly enough to respond.

"Where team-work seemed to be legitimate, the governing body will probably be called upon to decide. But it necessarily exists to a greater or lesser extent in every handicap race, amateur or professional. . Upon the amount of the stakes depends the thoroughness with which the riders complete their arrangements. A remarkable instance of the manner in which team-work is occasionally developed occurred in the Sydney Thousand last March.

"The first prize amounted to $3,750. Of the eleven riders in the final heat six on the middle and limit marks agreed to pace one of their number, Hopper, while the five back-markers pinned their faith to Walker. A desperate race ensued in which the front-markers got their man home first by fifteen yards in record time, thus securing the prize, which was subsequently divided, as previously agreed upon. Had Major Taylor not been in the New Zealand Wheel Race, the three riders specially referred to would still have been compelled to come to some arrangement to share the pacing. Otherwise they would have had no prospect of overtaking the limit riders. Theoretically, every competitor should ride to win unaided. In actual practice this is impossible.

"The effect of team-work legitimately carried out, is to produce faster racing, and to those who understand it, more exciting contests. In Major Taylor's case, the handicapper set him a task which, probably owing to the fact that he was unexpectedly called upon to race immediately after a long voyage proved too severe. A section of the public, and also of the officials, considered that Taylor had been ill-treated, but it seems hardly fair to blame the three riders immediately in front of him for having made their wits assist their legs in keeping away from the renowned cyclist.

"Major Taylor after declaring he was disappointed at having been defeated said it was not altogether unexpected on his part, owing to the fact that he had had no time to train, and so could not do himself full justice.  When asked about the blocking which took place in the last four hundred yards, he would say nothing, his only answer being, 'I wish to say nothing to detract from Mr. Sutherland's victory, I take off my hat to him, and congratulate him on winning a fair, hard-run race.  It was his day, and he deserves all the credit.' "

In the other races in which I participated in various sections of New Zealand, I was unable to get going and the results were generally the same as those that marked my début at Christchurch.

Before I left Christchurch I took occasion to thank the people of that city and New Zealand in general for the many courtesies extended to Mrs. Taylor and myself during our stay there.  I was especially grateful to the press of the country for their fairness to me and as a parting request I asked the reporters to express my regret at not having been able to do myself justice in my races in New Zealand.  I told them I would welcome an opportunity to return to the country trained to the minute and prepared to show them my best racing condition.  I have always regretted my experience in New Zealand especially since it was the only country I have ever appeared in where I failed to win a majority of my races.

# CHAPTER LXXIV

WINNING INTERNATIONAL TEST SERIES, DEFEATING LAWSON

Upon my arrival in Sydney from New Zealand I learned that I was to participate in a series of Four International Test Races extending over a period of four weeks. The stipulated distances were the half-mile, four-mile, five-mile and the crux of the entire program—the one-mile.

This competition was limited to twenty selected riders, the winners of the half, four and five-mile distances received fifty dollars for first place, ten for second and five for third for each event. Points were to be awarded in the half, four and five-mile distances in the order of finish—one for first, two for second, and so on. The twelve men with the lowest number of points would be entitled to start in the one-mile event, and the winners of places in this distance will be the winners of the prizes for the competition, independent of the points secured in the half, four and five-mile events.

It so happened that only a few days elapsed from the time I arrived at Sydney on this 1904 tour before I participated in the first heat of the International Test Mile on the final day of the meet, when I hoped to be at my peak form for what proved to be the outstanding race of my career up to this time.

I won the first heat of the half-mile distance of the test series, defeating Mutton, the New South Wales champion. Lawson won the second heat having no trouble defeating Gudgeon, the local rider, by several yards. MacFarland won the third, and Don Walker the fourth. The final was won by MacFarland, Lawson was second, I was third and Don Walker was fourth. At the conclusion of the race the referee ordered it to be re-run on the following evening, asserting that there had been bumping between Lawson and myself to my particular disadvantage. The time was :56 1/5.

On the night of the re-run of this race MacFarland and Lawson refused to ride so the field narrowed down to Don Walker and myself. The result of this heat was a dead heat, the points being equally divided between Walker and myself, the time being 1:00 1/5.

The second distance in the International Test series was four miles and was called shortly after Don Walker and myself had ridden a dead heat in the final of the half-mile distance of this same test. The four-mile race was won by Iver Lawson, I was second, Hardy Downing third, and Floyd MacFarland fourth. Time: 8:26 1/5.

In the five-mile event of the International Test Series Iver Lawson finished in first place, I was second and Floyd MacFarland was third, the time was 10:35 1/5, world's competition record.

In the one-mile event of the International Test Races, comprising four all told, which really decided the international title, I finished first, Iver Lawson second, Bill MacDonald third, and Hardy Downing, fourth. The time was 2:03 3/5.

Concerning the running of the final of the half-mile International Test Race I quote as follows from one of the Sydney newspapers:

"Major Taylor, Iver Lawson, Floyd MacFarland and Don Walker, a remarkably brilliant quartette, and undoubtedly the four fastest riders in Australia today, were the starters in the final. There was terrific excitement as the four champions pushed off. Boidi paced and Taylor took his wheel, the pace being on from the jump. Walker riding behind Taylor, then came MacFarland with Lawson next. As the bell rang MacFarland as usual rushed to the front with Lawson on his wheel. Taylor having the pole took MacFarland's wheel as he was going past, which put Lawson on the outside of Taylor. This blocked him from taking his sprint, there being no room for him to go between MacFarland and Lawson.

"As they sprinted into the stretch Taylor, recognizing the hopelessness of trying to get to the front against his two countrymen, who formed a combination that was wellnigh impossible for any rider to beat single-handed, had to drop right behind and come around on the outside. There appeared to be some bumping in the back stretch, and Lawson crowded Taylor down on the grass, which prevented either Taylor or Lawson from finishing properly, and MacFarland won by a length from Lawson, with Taylor third, and Walker fourth.

"The crowd treated Lawson and MacFarland to a vigorous hooting for their combination, as they thought, against the champion of the world. The bumping between Lawson and Taylor during the last lap interfered with the only Australian in the race. It was, therefore, not a fair test, and for fully 30 yards Taylor was on the grass. The referee, Mr. Wilkie, and the Stewards, J. Arnold and W. Watts, after a consultation decided that the event should be declared 'no race,' and it was to be run off on Saturday night.

"It appears after the running of this event that Taylor's only chance against MacFarland and Lawson is to take Lawson's rear wheel and race the latter on the outside. He will never win trying to get between the two, as he endeavored to do last night. The brilliant riding of Lawson and Taylor throughout the evening brought forth great applause. Taylor rode in four events, while Lawson appeared in only two.

"When the four men, Lawson, Taylor, MacFarland, and Walker, were called to re-ride the final of this half-mile International Test Race, Lawson and MacFarland refused to start which was their privilege, leaving the issue to Taylor and Walker. There was a surprise in store, however, and a much better race from a spectacular point of view was seen than if Lawson and MacFarland had ridden. Walker rode the race of his life, tackling the world's champion in resolute style. After the pacer had retired, the pair raced as if locked together, and the cheers as the two men dashed dead level for the tape were deafening. Both riders strained every nerve, and fairly threw themselves at the tape.

"While a great many thought Taylor had just won, others gave the verdict to Walker, while the three judges were unable to separate them, and called it a dead heat. They both received a tremendous ovation. It was decided to divide the points for the race between Taylor and Walker."

Concerning the four-mile race of the International Test series one of the Sydney newspapers carried the following account:.

"The positions in front were continually changing, the lap prizes ensuring a fast pace throughout. For the first two miles and a half Taylor rode in the middle of the field on the outside, with Mac-Farland and Lawson just behind. Taylor was trailing Gudgeon. Filsell bolted away from the field two miles from the finish, and Palmer also tried to get a break, but Gudgeon took the field up. Megson and Mutton were riding last.

"At three laps to go MacFarland, Lawson, and Stevens moved up behind the leading bunch, consisting of Gudgeon, Taylor, Farley, and MacDonald. The pace was now terrific, for the competitors were moving at their top. Gudgeon and MacDonald went out a lap and a half from the finish closely followed by Taylor, MacFarland, and Lawson, but at the bell MacFarland shot to the lead with Lawson, who had followed him throughout the race on his wheel, and Downing and Stevens behind the latter.

"As the quartette of Americans, who form about the best 'combination' in the world, flew past him, Taylor set after them and got Downing's wheel. MacFarland put in a terrific last· lap, and as he rounded the bend for home at the ladies' pavilion Taylor was over three lengths behind him, and looked to have no chance, for here Lawson left MacFarland's wheel and set sail for the finishing post.

"Taylor, however, put in a marvelous run, and finished at such a rate that he was barely half a length behind Lawson at the finish, with Downing the same distance off, third, and MacFarland in fourth place. The four Americans thus filled the places. Don Walker retired from the contest two laps from the finish. Time, 8:26 1/5."

I quote the following account relative to the five-mile International Test Race from still another Sydney daily:

"Twenty started. The pace was rather slow at the beginning of the race, but livened up after, MacDonald, Gudgeon, Taylor, and

Farley rode up near the front throughout, while MacFarland, with Lawson on his wheel, and followed by Downing, were watching Taylor closely and riding just behind the world's champion. Much the same positions were occupied by the crackriders throughout, and nothing of any moment occurred until a hundred yards past the bell, where MacFarland flew past the field, with Lawson on his wheel. Taylor had the pole, and raced with MacFarland as he was going past him, but he did not get enough room. Lawson had to go on the outside of Taylor, and as they were rounding the bend for home Taylor and Lawson bumped. The former was thrown out of his stride, he set sail after Lawson, but suffered defeat by a length. Time, 10:35 1/5, world's competition record."

Then came the grand finale of the International Test Series, the one-mile event. Iver Lawson won the first heat, over Sheps and Filsell. I won the second heat from Stevens and Mutton in 2:08. Hardy Downing won the third heat from Walker and Palmer in 2:12. Bill MacDonald won the fourth heat in 2:14. I won the final in 2:03 3/5 with Lawson second, MacDonald third and Downing fourth.

Concerning my heat in this race one of the Sydney newspapers printed the following paragraph:

"Plunkett paced, and Stevens took his wheel, from Taylor and Mutton. The pacer made the pace very solid, and the position remained unaltered until Taylor shot past Stevens at the members' stand, a 100 yards from the post. Stevens started the sprint a half lap from home, but Taylor was watching him closely, and beat him home in a fast sprint by a clear length, with Mutton a similar distance off. Time, 2:08."

Relative to the final of this race the same newspaper published the following paragraph:

"Farley and Goodson were put in as pacers, and MacDonald followed them from Taylor, Downing, and Lawson. The two pacers changed every half lap, but the positions of the contestants did not alter until MacDonald started the sprint three-quarters of a lap from home, with Taylor on his wheel. Downing got moving at the same time, with Lawson, and he almost got level with MacDonald at the end of the shilling stand. As they got to the far end of the members' pavilion the issue was seen to lay between Taylor and Lawson, for the latter sprinted up to his rival.

"They swung into the straight almost abreast, but with Taylor slightly in the lead, and one of the most brilliant and desperate races ever witnessed between any two men ensued. The spectators arose in one mass, as the two men strained every nerve, and the shouts could be heard for miles. Lawson could never get up to Taylor, who beat

him by a clear length.  The victory was immensely popular.  Mac-
Donald was five lengths off third, and Downing last.   Time,
2:03 3/5."

And so ended the hardest contest of my second invasion of Australia.
In this series of four races in the International Test Carnival I rode a
dead heat for first place with Don Walker in the half-mile, was second
to Lawson in both the four and five-mile events, and won the feature
number of the entire series, the one-mile event, the last race determin-
ing the international laurels.   In these hectic tests I was obliged to use
everything I had in me, but the final results were highly pleasing.

# CHAPTER LXXV

Mv first appearance in Sydney on my second tour of Australia occurred on January 1, 1904, in the State Cycling Carnival. Subsequently I participated in a number of racing programs at Melbourne and Sydney between the events in the International Test Events, with the following results. I rode in the Christmas Handicap, one-half-mile, in which I failed to qualify, and the New South Wales, one mile handicap in which I won my heat, but failed to place in the final.

In the Commonwealth Stakes (five-miles) scratch event I finished second to Mutton with Gudgeon third. I finished third in the Brisbane Handicap, one-half mile, McLean (75 yards) won and Iver Lawson, who started from scratch with me, finished second. In the final of the First Class Handicap race, riding from scratch, I finished second to Carter (110 yards), Glencross (130 yards) third and King (90 yards) fourth. Time, 1:59 2/5.

I failed to qualify in my heat of the Commonwealth Stakes, one-mile, one of the numbers on the Melbourne Bicycle Club program in Melbourne. Nor did I place in my heat in the two-mile event. I was put down in the three-mile event and naturally failed to qualify.

Returning to Sydney I rode from scratch in the Furracabad Handicap (one mile) finishing fourth. Farley (sixty yards) won, Don Walker (ten yards) second, and Downing (ten yards) third. Time, 1:57 3/5. Iver Lawson won the McCullagh Plate (five-mile scratch event) in which eighteen started. I finished second and Mutton third, time, 10:37 2/5. The last lap was ridden in :31 2/5. "This is the fastest five-miles ever ridden in the world," read part of the article concerning the event.

In the final of the Summer Wheel Race (one-mile handicap) I rode from scratch finishing fourth to Carter (ninety-five yards) first, Kett (100 yards) second, McLean (140 yards) third, with Iver Lawson (scratch) fifth. The time was 1:54 4/5.

Four heats were required to determine who was who in the Melbourne Handicap (one-mile). Twelve men qualified for the final. Floyd MacFarland (scratch) won. Riding from scratch I finished second, and Goodson (80 yards) was third. The time was 1:55.

In addition to the International Test events which are dealt with in the preceding chapter, I participated in a number of races, all but two of which were handicap events, finishing first once, second on four occasions, third once, and fourth twice. While taking part in these races I encountered some particularly rough riding, besides a number of pockets in which I was thrust, the climax coming when I was maliciously thrown by another rider in the course of a race at Melbourne.

The following paragraphs will deal with the trials and tribulations I encountered on the occasions mentioned.

Referring to my riding in the Commonwealth Stakes, which was a feature of the State Cycling Carnival in Sydney, January 3, 1904, I quote the following paragraph from a Sydney paper:—"After a few laps two of the field tried to steal a march on the others, but Taylor put in a lap's pacing and soon took the others up. Webster got a break on the field and the others slowing it looked as though they would run away with the race. Five others, including Taylor, bolted at three laps to go, and they forced the pace, evidently to give Taylor as little rest as possible. At the bell Gudgeon went out with Taylor on his wheel. Two others rushed on the outside and Taylor was blocked. Mutton got in the lead a quarter of a lap from home, and it was not until Mutton had a three-lengths' lead that Taylor got out of the pocket. He, however, reduced Mutton's lead considerably once he got a clear run, and putting in a magnificent run he only suffered defeat by a wheel. Time, 11:15."

A Sydney daily commented as follows on the Brisbane event which was held in connection with the International Test Cycling Carnival in that city:

"Major Taylor and Lawson, on the scratch mark, had a big gap of 55 yards to bridge, and on the form shown by the front and middle rankers in the heats, their chance of winning did not appear too bright. Lawson rushed to the front, with Taylor on his wheel, and after a half-lap Taylor changed pace. They put in terrific sprints each, and caught the field as they approached the members' stand. The two champions, however, were here blocked, and could not get through. Lawson had the better of a bad job, for he went round on the top of the banking, while Taylor tried to get through the middle of the field, and was hopelessly blocked. When he got out at the ladies' pavilion he finished at a terrific pace, and was going a lot faster than Lawson. G. McLean got the verdict by inches from Lawson, while Lawson beat Taylor by inches for second. Time, :56 4/5."

I quote the following paragraphs concerning the First Class Handicap (one-mile) which was featured at the Major Taylor Cycling Carnival and in which twenty-one riders started in the various heats:

"In the final heat Taylor put in a terrific lap sprint, and notwithstanding the big gaps he had to bridge he caught the tail end of the field in three-quarters of a lap. At the bell Carter and King led Taylor by 15 yards, and Taylor was a bit distressed with his great effort in catching the field. Carter won easily by 25 yards. Taylor easily beating the others home for second. Time, 1:59 2/5. Taylor got a cramp in one of his legs in the last lap, otherwise he might have won."

One of the Melbourne dailies printed the following article relative to my being thrown from my wheel in the three-mile event of the Commonwealth Stakes:

"Major Taylor was heartily cheered on his first appearance in the Melbourne Bicycle Club's program yesterday. Unable to utilize his skill in holding his position, however, he was never near enough at the finish to execute one of his famous jumps, apparently the grass track bothered the champion a great deal.

"A regrettable incident took place in regard to Taylor. He appeared to be bored in during the race by Richard Cameron. After expostulating with him, Taylor at one stage shoved him off. Just as the riders were entering the last lap Taylor and Cameron were lying last. Cameron was on the outside, and bumped Taylor, who had a nasty fall just opposite the judges. He lay prone for a minute or so before he was raised. Beyond a rather deep cut on the arm he was not badly injured. The spectators loudly cheered Taylor and hooted Cameron. The stewards met in the evening and decided to disqualify Cameron for twelve months. There were other falls during the day, due to the machine skidding, but no one was seriously hurt.

"The official inquiry into the Taylor-Cameron affair was held by Mr. Joy, referee, and Messrs. Gleeson and Shore, stewards. Major Taylor made no charge and did not even enter a protest, giving as his reason that it was the duty of the officials to see that there was no unfairness. Cameron was called at the inquiry, but the conclusion was arrived at on the evidence of Umpires Fawkner and Middlemiss, who strongly asserted that Cameron wilfully interfered with Taylor in the second last lap.

"The fall of Taylor occurred right under the eyes of the stewards, and they did not attribute any blame to Cameron for the accident, but felt that Taylor was responsible for it in forcing himself into a place that was not there for him. With the experience that he had in riding it was considered that at the particular point referred to he should have retained the outside running and not endeavored to get on the inside of the track. Cameron was therefore exonerated as regards Taylor's fall; but he was disqualified for twelve months under rule 105 of the league rules for unfair and foul riding in elbowing and kneeing Taylor on three or four occasions.

"Cameron's contention was that the interference was due to his shifting in his saddle; but the stewards were satisfied that it was done to put Taylor out of the race. Cameron also said that Taylor had 'Taken him off someone's wheel,' and that he considered he was justified in endeavoring to get back to that position.   Cameron may appeal against the decision to the appeal board, but the present effect of the decision is that he will lose all his privileges as a member of the League for twelve months, which period covers the Sydney Thousand and the next Austrial meeting."

Referring to the McCullagh Plate, a five-mile scratch event, which was featured at the International Test Carnival in Sydney, one of the local dailies carried this paragraph:

"Eighteen started.   MacFarland retired in the twelfth lap.   At three laps to go Gudgeon, Taylor, and Farley rushed to the front, but they were headed again, and at the bell MacDonald went out, with Taylor on his wheel, and Taylor was left with the lead half a lap from home. . As they swung around into the straight, Lawson came at Taylor, and in a terrific finish he overhauled Taylor and won by a length, with Mutton a close third.   Time, 10:37 2/5.   Last lap, :31 2/5.   This is the fastest five miles ever ridden in the world."

The following paragraph was printed in a Sydney newspaper concerning the final heat of the Melbourne Handicap, one mile, which was also held in connection with the International Cycling Carnival in that city on January 10:

"Taylor paced MacFarland for over half a lap, and the pair caught Mutton (50 yards) in that distance.   The trio paced alternatelv, Taylor doing magnificent work in this respect.   MacFarland was last at the bell.   He soon moved round the field, with Taylor following him.   As they swung into the straight the issue was between Mac-Farland and Taylor, and everyone was expecting to see Taylor fly around his great opponent, but he appeared to lack his usual finishing dash, and did not get near enough to fight it out with the winner, MacFarland winning by nearly two lengths.

"Taylor did more pacing than MacFarland, and this no doubt took a lot out of him.   Out of the three laps and a distance Taylor paced a lap and a half.   MacFarland's finishing effort was a magnificent one, and the time was again exceptionally fast, viz., 1:55."

# CHAPTER LXXVI



With my second tour of Australia over I could not help but contrast the treatment accorded me by my rivals on the two occasions. Throughout my first invasion of that country I was given the most sportsmanlike treatment on the various tracks, but found conditions changed in a marked fashion in the course of my second trip.

I account for this turn-about through the presence of Floyd Mac-Farland and his retinue of American riders who had preceded me on my trip to that country. Instances of jealousy and bitterness showed themselves almost before I had lost my sea legs. In a short time I ascertained that the American and Australian riders were teamed up in a formidable combination to bring about my defeat in my tour of the country.

Floyd MacFarland, my arch enemy of many years standing, was the king-pin of·the schemers against me. He pointed out to them that while I received a bonus above my prize winnings, the other American riders were dependent entirely on their winnings as they received no guarantee. In other words, his plan was for them to pool their winnings and split them evenly at the end of the season, MacFarland, himself, being cashier. He further inflamed the minds of the riders particularly the Australians that while I was being well paid for my appearances in Australia, whether I won or lost, they were on their own, and were in a street-word "suckers." He told them that I would not split or team up with them in the various races, but that I would expect them to go out and do all the pacing or "donkey-work." MacFarland used a far more cowardly weapon in his efforts to bring about my defeat in my tour of the country by laying special emphasis on the color line.

It was a strange revelation for me to note how MacFarland's victorious propaganda had taken root among the Australian riders. On my first trip through that country I found my rivals to be straight shooters in every·sense of the word, but on the current (1904) trip things were quite the reverse. I might mention the complete turn-about of Don Walker, the champion rider of Australia, as an example of the about-face of the local riders in their dealings with me on the track. On my initial trip I was particularly impressed with the fairness of Walker. Regardless of the fact that we were keen rivals, he acted the part of a gentleman towards me at all times, not one unpleasant word having passed between us despite the fact that he was my greatest rival for the championship honors. While Walker was not outspoken in his feelings towards me on my second trip, I could see that his mind had been poisoned by MacFarland, Iver Lawson, Orlando Stevens, and Hardy Downing, my "fellow-Americans."

History repeated itself as far as I was concerned, and the ill feeling engendered against me by MacFarland and his gang only served to spur me to my greatest efforts on the track. The result was that I had one of my most successful seasons on the Australian Circuits that year.

While the press of Australia admitted without reserve that my riding in that country on my first visit there did much to regain much of the prestige that bicycle racing had lost for various reasons, the public again grew cold toward the sport as they noticed the combinations that were working in such an unfair manner to defeat me. I sympathized with the promoters of the meets as this state of affairs became plainly noticeable, but there was nothing I could do to prevent public opinion turning against the pastime. It was due solely to the underhanded warfare waged by my American rivals, by themselves, and through their efforts, by the Australian riders.

MacFarland drew a month's disqualification for riding unfairly against me in the International Test-Half-Mile at Sydney. He appealed this suspension, and the racing stewards withdrew the sentence and imposed a fine of $125.

It will be recalled that in this International Test Half-Mile MacFarland, Lawson, Walker, and myself, were the starters in the final. In the course of this race I was bumped off the track in the last 200 yards, MacFarland winning with Lawson second, myself third, and Walker fourth. The setting-down of MacFarland followed this incident as the crowd hooted MacFarland and Lawson vigorously for the rough tactics employed against me. In addition to suspending MacFarland, the League Officials ordered the final heat of the half mile re-run. Lawson and MacFarland refused to ride in the event in which I rode a tie with Don Walker.

I quote the following paragraph from one of the Sydney papers relative to MacFarland's disqualification:

"Floyd MacFarland's appeal against a month's disqualification imposed on Monday last week was heard before a special meeting of the New South Wales League Council on Monday night. The allegation was that MacFarland's story was that Taylor went on the grass on his own accord; at any rate he did not deliberately 'cut down' on him; if he (MacFarland) did so, it was unwittingly. He called Mutton and Downing to support his case, their story being that Taylor went on the grass through trying to take Lawson's position behind MacFarland. Lawson declared that it was Taylor's well-known wobble that sent him to the grass. He admitted that he and Taylor bumped, but that was because Taylor was trying to take MacFarland's wheel from him. The council decided that the stewards and referee were quite right in imposing the disqualification, but as the incident would be a warning to the riders in the future, as MacFarland had already been punished by being barred from two important races here, they would give him the option of paying a fine of twenty-five pounds ($125)."

I next encountered rough tactics in the Austrial Meet in Melbourne. On this occasion Cameron, an Australian, put me down in the first heat of the three-mile race, after he had elbowed and kneed me on three or four occasions. Cameron was disqualified for twelve months for unfair and foul riding in this race.

In addition to the disqualifications of MacFarland and Cameron for foul tactics employed against me in the races mentioned, I saw many other unmistakable signs of feeling against me in practically all of my races in Australia in 1904. These conspiracies all centered about my color and possibly because of the success that I had met with in Australia in the preceding year. Besides the rough work of MacFarland and Cameron I encountered many pre-arranged pockets and other unsportsmanlike tactics that are never thought of in the same breath with good sportsmanship anywhere.

Relative to the suspension of MacFarland for his unfair riding against me in the International Test Half-mile event I quote the following self-explanatory letters which were printed in a Sydney newspaper within a day or two after the race was held:

"To the Editor of the *Herald*:

"Sir: As a British sportsman of many years' standing, with a lengthy experience of cycle racing throughout Australasia, America, England, and the Continent, I wish to enter a strong protest against the unfair treatment meted out to MacFarland, whose only crime was in downing the 2,000-pound sprinter in the mile final of last night. Disqualifying the man is absurd. He has not done anything to merit such disgrace. The real fact of the matter is the 2,000-pound big gun, (in spite of his mile record of 1:53 3/5 on Saturday night, which certainly does not show want of form), has at last met his Waterloo, (at least, just now, and the present is all we have to do with); and to have him beaten in one or both of the finals on Wednesday night would also tend to remove a great deal of the glamour that has hung round him like a halo. Anyone with but slight experience of cycling must see that Taylor, by always hugging the inside, displays shocking want of judgment; while the other Americans, to give them their due, have reduced riding to a fine art.

"Thousands believe MacFarland has been disqualified so that Taylor may have a better chance of regaining lost laurels; but as he is now showing, what chance would he have with Lawson, who did his mile, three weeks after landing, in 1:55, from fifteen yards behind scratch? And who would believe it! even the great 'Mac' was not pacing. I am, etc. British Sportsman."

"To the Editor of the *Herald:*

"Sir: 'British Sportsman' has been permitted in your issue of today to defend the grossly un-British conduct of the American riders. I was close to the spot where the 'accident' happened on Monday evening. Half a lap from the finish Taylor led, riding next to the grass. 'British Sportsman' objects to his retaining this position even when leading. Then alongside drew MacFarland and Lawson as usual. To defend himself from being pocketed, by this ambition, as before, Taylor raced MacFarland for the lead, whereupon I saw this superior American man look around at Taylor and most deliberately cut in on him, putting him on to the grass. It seems to me that as many riders have been killed on the track, any wanton offense such as this should be met by severe and deterring punishment.

"I daresay by the time this appears MacFarland's suspension will have been removed, as was customary in the case of that other American, 'Plugger Bill' Martin, to the frantic delight of the blind populace. If we have any doubt regarding the guilt of MacFarland and Lawson, we find on inquiring that there are prior convictions. Lawson was punished by the American cycling authorities quite recently for interference with the same hated colored rival, who is objected to apparently on account of his inoffensive prosperity. I am, etc., Geebung."

"To the Editor of the *Herald:*

"Sir: Referring to 'British Sportsman's letter, appearing in your today's issue, I cannot, as a sportsman, allow the matter to pass without comment, seeing, as I did, what took place on Monday night and other nights of the cycling carnival in the way of gross interference to Major Taylor. On every possible occasion he was interfered with. I certainly think 'British Sportsman' narrow when he talks of MacFarland's only crime being the downing of the 2,000-pound sprinter in the half-mile final on Monday night, and that he has been removed to allow Taylor a better chance of regaining his lost laurels. Most spectators who witnessed the sports saw how Taylor was treated at the finish of the big race.

"What chance he had of winning was nullified by MacFarland's crossing him and forcing him (to avert accident) on to the grass, and had Taylor had a clear run the result may have been reversed. The committee of the League are to be complimented on the stand they took, by promptly disqualifying a 'top-notcher,' as in most cases it is generally the small fry that are peppered, and it is high time for the sake of the sport, and the public who keep it going, that such riders should be asked to stand down.

"While agreeing with 'British Sportsman' that Taylor hugs the rails there is no reason why he should be interfered with. A sportsman of Taylor's calibre does not merit such treatment; and I hardly think such a successful, brilliant cyclist as Major Taylor requires any hints as to how to ride his race. I am, etc., Gowrie Ruthven." These are only a few of many similar letters from enthusiastic sport lovers of Australia concerning the unfairness and poor sportsmanship the riders employed against me.

Some time after this incident one of the newspapers carried the following amusing story. "Major Taylor hasn't got the huge picnic on that many people imagine. His legs and riding capabilities are sold to a syndicate which negotiates for him,—and he cannot compete in a race without the sanction of this syndicate, but therein he has a great pull over the Yankee visitors, Lawson, MacFarland, and Downing. It doesn't matter so much to Taylor whether he is defeated or not in bike races, he scoops in the appearance money, while the other Yankees have to depend mainly on the prizes. By the way, Major Taylor being a 'colored' person should be doubly challenged by the Australian Government laws—as a colored alien and an immigrant under contract.

" 'Hello, Exchange! Federal Government, please. What number? Mr. Atlee Hunt, of course.'

" 'Oh! you haven't a possible chance. He's too busy guarding our shores from foreign invasion, as it were.'

" 'Well, give me some of the smaller fry. The prime minister will do.'

" 'Yes, Sunday Times.'

" 'That Mr. Deakin? We regret to be the bearer of an unpleasant message, sir, but duty is duty.'

" 'Say it quickly,—that Reid again, I suppose?'

" 'No, worse than that—a terrible dereliction of duty on the part of the Government's chief executive.'

" 'Mr. Hunt?'

" 'No less.'

" 'I cannot credit it. What are the facts?'

" 'Well, there is an immigrant at large who is a citizen of another country and was not given the Greek Test.'

" 'Perhaps he was of Greek nationality. In that case, of course, we would have to examine him in Choktaw. We have a language to fit every case.'

" 'But this unprohibited prohibited alien is an American citizen and came out here under contract.'

" 'Phew!  This is serious.'

" 'But we have not finished yet.  He is not only an alien, and a contract alien, but he is a colored alien, uniting in his own person all the dire things that the Act was intended to save this new country from.'

" 'You must really pardon me, but I can scarcely credit it.  How is it that we have heard nothing of this man?'

" 'Now that shows what an unpractical, mentally-detached dreamer you are, Mr. Deakin.  The papers have been full of the case for months past.'

" 'Oh well, he will have to serve a term of imprisonment for being illegally at large.  That will be pleasant news for him.  He cannot possibly escape.  But really, 'Sunday Times,' someone must surely have been jollying you.'

" 'Quite the contrary, Mr. Deakin, quite the contrary.  May we further inform you that this colored contract-alien expects to escape with a creditable haul of some thousands of pounds?'

" 'Impossible!  Is he a mental or manual worker?'

" 'Neither, he is a pedal worker—Major Taylor!'

" 'Ah, now I perceive that it was I that was being jollied.  You know quite well that the Act was made both rigid and elastic.  It has to be stretched sometimes?'

" 'Rather!  The public would sacrifice the Act.  And the Government.'

" 'Yes and the Government, before they would forego Major Taylor.'—Ting-Ting!"

# CHAPTER LXXVII

### DEFEATING LAWSON AND MACFARLAND IN MELBOURNE

Leaving Sydney I went to Melbourne to participate in the National Fete which marked the 16th anniversary of Australian Colonization. The feature event of this meet which extended over two days, the riding being done on the afternoon and evening of each occasion, was the Australian Natives' Association Gold Stakes, a scratch event. This race consisted of four separate events. Three of them were known as qualifying events, the distances of which were one, three and ten-miles, and the grand finale of five-miles.

The one-mile race found MacFarland and myself in the first heat with Forbes, Burton and Gudgeon. I won from MacFarland. The final was won by Lawson and I was second. In the ten-mile event Lawson was first, MacFarland second, and myself third. Lawson won the three-mile race in which I finished second.· In the grand finale of the program, the five-mile race, I won with MacDonald second, Lawson third and Walker fourth.

I quote the following account of the Gold Stakes races from a Melbourne newspaper:

"A crowd of 25,000 persons saw the Australian Natives' Association Gold Stakes events run at the Exhibition Oval yesterday afternoon and last night. The first race on the program was over the one-mile distance, the outstanding heat of this feature bringing together Major Taylor and Floyd MacFarland. They met in the first heat in which Gudgeon, Forbes and Burton also started. However, the last three named were never in it.

"Down the back stretch on the last lap MacFarland was right in front of Taylor and going for all he knew. The throng was satisfied that MacFarland could not be beaten. At the turn into the stretch the positions were unchanged. At this point Taylor removed one hand from his handle bars, wiped his mouth, put his hand back, and streaked right past MacFarland. It was a magnificent finish and Taylor's riding set the big crowd half wild.

"The final was run at night, and when the men came out there was great excitement. Early it could be seen that Taylor had to beat a combination in which one man was nursed to make the deciding sprint. Although he had a fair run, Taylor could not live it out with Lawson at the finish, and Lawson won an exciting race by a wheel.

"The ten-mile event was a revelation in 'teaming.' The Americans, MacFarland, Stevens, and Downing, all rode in the interest of their teammate, Lawson. This was as plain as a pike-staff even to the palest-faced laymen. It was a blood-thirsty looking race, and a red hot pace was kept up right through. With a mile left to go, the Americans moved to the front, the four trailing with Lawson, nicely nursed. The finish was terrific, Lawson winning by two lengths. MacFarland, who had done more work than any other man in the race was second, and Major Taylor, run off his legs, finished third.

"I hold no brief for Major Taylor, while admitting that he is wet nursed a good deal on the Sydney side. But no man in the world can have a chance against Iver Lawson, when he has MacFarland working in his interest. In both races yesterday Taylor was not interfered with, and had a clear run. But he can't compete against one who has another man to do all the head work for him. This takes it out of a man physically in securing his position, and takes him away at the right moment. Shouldn't MacFarland be made to try when he gets up in a race. If not, then no Australian rider should be questioned for non-trying.

"The three-mile and five-mile events on the closing day of the Gold Stakes feature of the National Fete were better contested than the mile and ten-mile events. In the three-mile final Lawson defeated Major Taylor in a great race. Lawson did not have all the advantage in the pacing. True he had MacFarland, without whom he seems to be useless, but Taylor was just as fortunate, as it was quite evident that at least two men in the race were nursing him. At the bell it was MacFarland, Lawson and Taylor. MacFarland made the pace very hot. At the turn into the stretch, Taylor made an effort to pass Lawson, but he was beaten. Lawson drew away and won an absolutely fair race, beating Taylor decisively.

"In the grand final, the five-mile event, things were altogether different, Taylor defeating Lawson just as decisively as he had been beaten by Lawson. It was a very fine race.

"The four Americans, Lawson, MacFarland, Stevens and Taylor, rode together for the greater part of the journey. At the end of the third-mile, Stevens ran right down onto Taylor. It looked deliberate too. Major Taylor's blood was up now, and a mile further Stevens was run up to the fence through Taylor's wobbling. That looked deliberate too, anyhow they were now even. Taylor perhaps having the best of the deal.

"Then MacFarland's tire went wrong and he retired. The last mile was beautiful with MacFarland out of it, Lawson's feeding bottle was dry, and when the bell rang for the last lap, the race got desperate, but Taylor simply played with the others when sprinting time came, and won by a couple of yards. MacDonald beating Lawson out for second place, while Don Walker finished fourth. Taylor was given a great ovation."

# CHAPTER LXXVIII



At the close of the National Fete in Melbourne a series of three match races to decide the championship of the world were arranged between Iver Lawson and myself, and Floyd MacFarland and myself, Lawson and I being scheduled to ride in two of these International Tests. It was stipulated that the winner of two of three heats in each race would be acknowledged the champion. The first heat in my match with Lawson was to be over the half-mile distance, the second heat was to be one-mile, the toss of a coin to determine the distance for the third and deciding heat.

A crowd of 20,000 were on hand to witness my first match race with Lawson on the Exhibition Oval. I won the opening heat, one-half mile, from Lawson by six lengths. I also won the second heat, the one-mile distance, from him by half a length, and by virtue of these two straight victories in the heats there was no occasion to hold the third brush between us.

I quote the following account of this match race from one of the Melbourne newspapers:

"On Monday evening the wind was bitterly cold and interfered with the several events which were built around the widely heralded world's championship match race between Major Taylor and Iver Lawson for a purse of $500, winner take all. However, an immense crowd estimated at fully 20,000 assembled for the program and the tumultuous applause with which the match contest was received, gave the lie direct to those who assert that cycle-racing is dead. Such shouting and delirious excitement has never before been seen in Australia. If the crowd was demonstrative at the Australian Natives' Association gathering, it was doubly so on this occasion.

"The issue lay between man and man. It was to be a straight outgo, separated distinctly from anything approaching trade influences. There was no nursing and no advantages on either side, and the crowd was not slow to recognize it. As the thousands of people flocked in, the great question was on every mouth: which would prove to be the better man? And the answer was, the issue will decide. And it did decide unquestionably, and beyond a shadow of doubt. As usual there were the malcontent. Some wanted this, and some wanted that. At the conclusion of the meeting the spectators were heard on tram and train eagerly discussing the affair. 'I would have preferred to have seen them together in the straight,' (home stretch) said one, 'Lawson was going faster at the finishing post,' said another, and so on.

(345)

"No doubt, but Major Taylor 'got there' first. His marvelous jump carried him to victory. No other rider in the world can shoot away like a bolt from the blue, as Taylor did on Monday night. He was lengths ahead before his opponent realized the fact. How he does it, no one knows. It is magnetism. He has his rivals at his mercy, but it is grand to watch. Those two jumps, one on the inside, and one on the outside, fairly appealed to the crowd, and had Gabriel sounded his trumpet, at that moment, they would not have heard. Never before has so vast an assemblage been lifted out of itself. Sitting in the arena, watching with all eyes the flying foemen, and listening to the earsplitting yells which rang in all keys from every part of the grounds, was indeed an education. The truth was driven home to us that if all cycle racing was imbued with the same desire to conquer, if only the competitors raced with that same fixity of purpose, to win, to what possibilities might cycle-racing not be brought? But alas! a genuine struggle is of rare occurrence, and when it does come, to break the monotony, the result is electrical.

"The first heat, which was the half-mile distance, was, of course, full of finessing, and here Taylor's superiority was at once apparent. He got his opponent into the lead and kept him there. The pace was slow, but a section of the crowd and others who ought to know better, failed to grasp the fact that the men did not ride themselves out, there was racing, not with limbs, but with brains and cycle-racing strategy. Lawson hugged the outer railings, prepared for a swift descent of the banking, but the Major's sudden spring put several lengths between them in a twinkling of an eye, and in his great effort to catch him Lawson did not gain any appreciable extent, and was six lengths behind at the tape.

"The second heat, the one-mile distance, was paced by Burton and Don Walker. An Indian file was at once formed, Lawson taking the lead behind the pacers. Four laps were taken at ordinary speed without any change taking place. Then at the bell the pacers dropped out, and the real race began. Again Taylor forced his man to the front, and at the self-same spot where the Major ran down the banking, but on the inside, but this time Lawson was better prepared. Although a few lengths separated him from the negro, he pulled up magnificently and in the finishing straight was travelling considerably faster, but he was barely fast enough for the victorious champion, who won by half a length."

Still another Melbourne daily carried the following account of this big match race between Iver Lawson and myself:

"Residents of Victoria witnessed the greatest cycling race that we have ever seen on the Exhibition Oval last evening. The contestants were Major Taylor, the champion of the world, and Iver Lawson the spectacular American sprinter, who is undoubtedly Major Taylor's closest rival for the international honors.

"The 20,000 who attended the race knew full well that they were going to watch two of the finest riders in the world, match skill, brain and muscle, in the match race for a purse of $500, winner take all. Not one of them was disappointed in the race. It was simply lovely. Last week's monster gathering for the races at the Oval was attributed in part, at least, to the industrial exhibitions, which form no small part of the racing program.

"Yet a purely cycling meeting drew such a large attendance. Astonishing. No. People here like sport. And to the everlasting credit of Major Taylor, the negro, who is as white as the best Australian born. People know that when he is there they get it. Say, Taylor has made a special study of match racing. He has never been beaten at the game. Every known point is in Taylor's grasp. If necessary to ride backwards or stop dead still for thirty seconds, Major can do it. Last night it was an awfully cold night, and most of the crowd brought overcoats and wrappers. Taylor hates the cold, but Lawson doesn't give a continental, so before the end of each heat of the match Major Taylor did a couple of miles to get warmed up. Just a few minutes before the program started, the Massey Harris pacing motor, driven by Bill Lewis, gave Taylor a few preliminary laps. As the clock pointed to the starting-time, the motor drew off and Taylor pedalled slowly around.

"Every eye was now turned in the direction of the dressing room. Had Lawson flunked out of it? The crowd waited in dead silence, and from the press table anxious glances were cast at the more convenient electric-light posts up which to swarm in case the crowd rushed the grounds. At last Lawson appeared, amid a wild storm of cheering, and without preliminary rode to the starting point. Taylor took a position on the outside, and at the start forced Lawson to the front, taking his wheel. The crowd roared themselves hoarse with excitement. The grand stand spectators rose to their feet, and people went almost delirious.

"The first lap was easy, the riders keeping in the middle of the track, but in the second lap Lawson edged towards the fence in the endeavor to make his adversary take the inside running. Taylor drew back and watched his opportunity and on the westward turn it came. Lawson left the outside unguarded for a second, and like a shooting star, the negro was through and away. Twenty thousand throats raised a shout which could have been heard for miles, and the scene was indescribable. Hats, handkerchiefs, programs, wooden legs, or whatever came handy, were waved in the air, as Major Taylor, leading by five or six lengths, flicked across the tape. As he pedalled his lap of honor it is safe to say that a more flattering reception has never been vouchsafed to any cyclist in the history of man. Amid the tumultuous cheering a few groans were heard for Lawson, but this was manifestly unfair, for he had ridden an undoubtedly fine race and his final sprint was fully equal to his rival's. The time was 1:50.

"The second heat was paced by C. E. Burton and Don Walker. The distance was one-mile. At the pistol fire Lawson was so slow getting under way that Mr. Gleason called for a second start. Getting under way again Burton took the lead and in Indian file came Walker, Lawson and Taylor, and so ended the first lap. In the second lap Burton got away a few lengths, but dropped back into file on entering the third lap, when he retired.

"The fourth lap was paced by Walker, with Taylor the whipper up. At the bell Walker then retired, and the men finessed, and slackened speed, Lawson running up the banking close to the railing determined not to be caught in that quarter again. Honors were evenly bestowed by the big crowd, and the 'color line' never troubled it. It was a battle between champions—white, black, yellow, or red, never mattered a snuff of a candle to it. Lawson rode watchfully at the very top of the banking, Taylor lying behind. Thus they reached the grandstand corner, when Taylor, making a superhuman bound, dashed down the banking on the inside, and Lawson set off in full cry. Again the uproar arose, but even louder than before. Pandemonium reigned. The shouts fairly rent the air. 'Taylor! Taylor! He wins!' And so it was. Like an express train he flew for the tape.

"In the meantime Lawson had made up some of the distance which Taylor's great jump had put between them. Quick as a flash he gained on the flying negro, and in the straight, by a phenomenal sprint, gained rapidly on the Major, who was palpably laboring hard. But the end came and Taylor's wheel shot over the line two yards ahead, and if plaudits count for anything he must have been a proud man. He rode the last 230 yards in :15 from a slow start. Having won the first two heats, the third heat was abandoned. The time was 2:30 2/5"

In the last-mentioned daily the following letter was prominently displayed on the sporting page next to the story concerning the race itself:

"To the Editor—When Major Taylor and Iver Lawson were racing it out in the last lap of the match race last night I distinctly heard Lawson calling out for MacFarland! MacFarland!! He evidently needed MacFarland. What do you think about it ? Yours, etc., The Liar."

# CHAPTER LXXIX

With mv victory over Iver Lawson in our world's championship match race still fresh in the minds of the Australian lovers of bicycle racing, I was challenged to meet Floyd MacFarland in a similar race for a purse of $375. This match was to be decided over three distances of one-mile each, and all of the events were specially paced by the fastest riders in Australia, aided by Downing and Stevens, the Americans.

This match race was held on the Exhibition Oval in Melbourne, Australia, February 13, 1904, and was attended by 20,000 people. MacFarland won the first heat, but the race fell through after MacFarland and I had ridden a dead heat which he refused to ride off. Later it was arranged that MacFarland and I would settle that dead heat after Lawson and I had ridden our return championship match race a week later. However, I was injured in the course of this last mentioned event, preventing my starting against MacFarland, so the dead heat has never been run off.

I quote the following account of my match race with MacFarland from one of the Melbourne newspapers:

"Major Taylor was first to make his appearance, and put in a few laps behind the motor. MacFarland came out almost simultaneously and trailed behind for some distance. The crowd cheered both men, but it was evident that the grandstand spectators plumped for the Major, but those on the ground were solid for the big man.

"The first heat was paced by Corbett and Burton. Taylor started on the inside, and went to the front immediately after the pistol shot, with MacFarland hugging his rear wheel. A fairly good pace was maintained. At the end of the first lap MacFarland crept steadily up by inches. Corbett then dropped out, and the same positions were maintained for another lap. At the dressing shed in the fourth lap Burton dropped out, and at that moment, Taylor who was slightly ahead on the inside, ran MacFarland up the bank almost to the fence, a maneuver which was greeted with boos from the crowd. At the bell, MacFarland shot past the post with a terrific rush nearly a length ahead of his opponent.

"Then amid wild cheering Taylor performed several of his famous 'jumps' and at the pavilion the two machines were wheel to wheel, and from this point on, the pace was tremendous, with each man straining every nerve, and each alternately gaining and losing inches. At the dressing-shed MacFarland was ahead, and a splendid race home resulted in his passing the winning post about a wheel ahead of Taylor. Time 2:09. The result was greeted with enthusiastic and prolonged cheering.

"The second heat furnished the sensation of the evening. There was no pacing. MacFarland started on the inside and immediately went to the front with Taylor a length behind, the pace being moderate. The position remained the same for a lap, then MacFarland slowed down, and Taylor persistently stayed on his back wheel. The pace became slower and slower, and just near the grandstand the assemblage witnessed the unique spectacle of two racing champions coming to a dead standstill with about a fourth of the distance covered. MacFarland slowly crept up the bank and holding onto the fence deliberately stopped his machine. Major Taylor followed his example.

"A great roar of derision rose from the crowd, and the stewards immediately declared 'no race.' As the competitors rode back to the starting post Taylor's tire blew out, and after some delay a second start was effected. Taylor, riding on the inside, went to the front at the pistol shot with his opponent a length behind. The pace was now much better. MacFarland passed Taylor on the inside at the end of the first lap, but Taylor again overtook him at the beginning of the next lap. The two had evidently agreed to pace alternately. MacFarland went ahead again and at the end of the second lap was leading by a good length. The third lap was like the two previous ones. Taylor going to the front at the grandstand and falling back behind again when approaching the dressing shed.

"In the fourth lap the racing really commenced, Taylor getting to the front at the grandstand and keeping his lead for a length until the bell sounded. Then MacFarland made a dash and a very fine contest ensued. Half-way around, the competitors seemed as if locked together for some moments, but before the dressing room was reached, MacFarland had gained nearly a length, but a series of jumps by Taylor brought the men almost level. But the colored man skidded badly twice, just when turning into the home straight, and another dash brought him up to MacFarland and amid frantic cheering the two passed the winning post simultaneously. Time, 2:35.

"A dead heat was shown on the scoring board, whereupon the crowd made an angry demonstration, being evidently of the opinion that MacFarland had won. The two competitors afford a contrast in physique, MacFarland being tall, while his opponent is somewhat short of stature, and this explains the difference of opinion between the crowd and the officials. Several of the officials considered that MacFarland's head actually passed the post in front of Taylor's head, but it was the duty of the officials to watch the wheels only.

"It now remained for Taylor and MacFarland to meet in the final of the one-mile. This heat was to be paced or unpaced according to the winner of the toss of a coin. MacFarland, however, left the ground at the conclusion of the second heat, and when the time for starting the final came and there was no appearance of MacFarland, the impatience of the crowd was again manifested by hooting and booing, and the officials fearing that the grounds would be rushed, called a body of police on the Oval. Happily their services were not required, for though there was a rush across the grass, the crowd contented themselves with freely expressed and vigorous comments on the decision.

"At the conclusion of the racing Mr. Gleason, the referee, made the following statement: 'The first heat of the grand challenge match having been won by MacFarland and the second being a dead heat, the second heat will have to be run over again. MacFarland left without notifying anyone at all. It was his duty before leaving to see the board which decides who are the winners of dead heats. The officials sent into the dressing room five minutes after the race had been decided a dead heat, so that there would be no misunderstanding. I also told Taylor so that he might know the position, but MacFarland had left. The second heat will be run off on the Oval Wednesday evening. In event of MacFarland's winning the second heat, there will be no necessity of a third, and whereas, if Taylor wins the second there will still remain the third to be run. In the event of either Taylor's or MacFarland's not appearing, the race will be awarded to the man who rides over the distance.'

"MacFarland next day made a statement in regard to his action. He said he had left the ground because he had won the match; 20,000 people had seen him do so. 'I won with plenty to spare,' he continued, 'what did Taylor say?' 'He rode up to me on the back stretch and took my hand and said, "It was a good race, you beat me." There was a gross injustice done me last night. I beat him fully two feet and a half. I want to say this about Taylor, he is a good sportsman, there are not many riders who would do that. It was a big event in my life to beat Major Taylor, and it knocks out the idea that we have no chance against him alone. As far as running the match off is concerned, what assurance have I that they will not call it a dead heat again?'

"Major Taylor said when questioned that he could not say anything against the decision of the judges. MacFarland was a good sportsman, and a good rider, and if he won from him on Saturday evening he could win again. In his own career he (Taylor) had had many races given against him which he thought he had won, but he always endeavored to take it in the best spirit, knowing that if he had won once he could do it again. However, when it was a close finish the judges could tell better than the riders, and in any case the rider could not be his own judge. He felt confident that the merits of the case would be demonstrated at the meeting on Wednesday night."

Another Melbourne writer commented as follows on my match with MacFarland:

"In the second test referring to the Taylor-MacFarland race on Saturday night, with the same conditions as in the former trial, before the bell, Taylor was quite content to let the long fellow go by, reserving himself for his dash up the home stretch, but he reckoned without the track. MacFarland's pace on the home turn was tremendous, but Taylor when he jumped more than held him, and his series of skids and recoveries up to the tape was a masterpiece of riding. There was no question as to who was the faster man. Had the track been safe, Taylor would have passed the line a length ahead. MacFarland, however, rode gamely throughout and was greatly applauded on his victory in the first place which was repeated for his plucky fight in the second one."

Still another Melbourne newspaper carried the following account of the dead heat:

"After some delay the men were sent away again with the explicit instructions to alternate the pace every half lap. This was followed out. Just before the bell, MacFarland got going and challenging the Major went past him at a good clip. Taylor, however, let him go and jumped in behind him, until entering the finishing stretch, when he came along with an irresistible rush, and gained hand over fist on his opponent. It was a lightning-like jump, such as has never been seen before, but directly he struck the level straight, his wheels failed to hold the track and skidded badly. His recovery was rapid and wonderful, but directly he essayed again the same thing occurred about half way up the stretch. The negro pulled himself together and with a great effort managed to just land his front wheel on the tape with MacFarland's wheel.

"In this case we had an inferior track and a bitter rivalry, the latter being calculated to increase the danger, with each rider straining every nerve to win. Supposing that all was fair, and as we write the blame if any has been decided, the track as we said is not fit for up-to-date racing. In almost every contest in which Major Taylor rode mention was made of his wheels skidding when sprinting at full speed.

"MacFarland, while a splendid rider, is lacking in discretion. One of his experience ought to be able to control himself better, particularly after the lesson in Sydney, when he said he was not going to open his mouth again. Even champions must abide by the rules, as is shown in all kinds of sports every day. He may have won or he may not have won, when the officials made it a dead heat, on Saturday night. If he thought he did, he had no right to take the law into his own hands, and also attack the officials with his tongue. How would a jockey get on if he thought he had won (and there are often differences of opinion) and abused the judge and stewards? Disqualification would certainly follow, and MacFarland may count himself lucky to get off with a reprimand."

# CHAPTER LXXX



Following my unsatisfactory World's Championship Match race with MacFarland at Melbourne, February 13, 1904, I was matched to ride a return world's championship match with Iver Lawson in Melbourne, Australia, one week later. Most of the Melbourne newspapers referred to this return match as a "revenge" match and subsequent developments proved the reporters were good prophets. The distances in this match were one, two, and five miles—all paced.

I won the first heat and was deliberately thrown by Lawson as we squared into the back stretch in the second heat. I was so badly injured in this spill that I was unable to re-ride the race which was ordered by the officials and it has never been finished. Thus a fiasco marks the finish of this big match race with Lawson as it did my match race with MacFarland.

As a result of this foul riding against me on this occasion Lawson was suspended for one year by Australian League officials. Later he pleaded with that group to reduce the period of suspension that he might participate in the World's Championship events in England, and the sentence was cut to three months, but he was never allowed to ride in Australia again that season.

I quote the following account of the "revenge" match for the world's title with Lawson:

"Twenty thousand people again were disappointed at the cycling carnival last night, for the chief attraction, the challenge matches between Major Taylor and his two American rivals, MacFarland and Lawson, came to a most unsatisfactory end. The weather was perfect, and the program of the evening's sport opened auspiciously with the preliminary heats of the MacFarland Handicap and Class Handicap, as well as the first heat of the Taylor-Lawson contest.

The last-named event took pace at 8:30, and passed off without mishap. The competitors were paced by Scheps and Morgan, and the race was a straight out-go, with little to be described. There was an utter absence of what cyclists call "tactics." Taylor was on the inside, and following the pacers closely, gave Lawson his wheel, throughout the race. After the pacers had dropped off at the bell, Taylor continued to lead, with Lawson at his wheel, until the half-distance, when the former made his dash, and although Lawson tried to overtake him, gradually increased his lead, and won by two lengths, amid enthusiastic cheering, which lasted several minutes. The time for the race was 2:03. Taylor's brilliant form indicated that it was his 'night out,' and the weather being cool and most suitable for him, there was a general expectation that he would win all along the line.

"When he came to the starting point for the second heat, with Lawson, he was warmly cheered. This event was over a distance of two miles, and was paced by Goodson, Gordon and Burton. Taylor had the inside position, hanging on to his wheel. The pace was good. The same positions were maintained lap after lap and even until after the last lap was begun, and the pacers had all dropped off. Half-way round Lawson made a jump, got about a length ahead, and the racing began. Round they flashed, and at the corner, opposite the eastern annex, amid great excitement, Taylor had drawn up almost level. The pace was tremendous, but suddenly Taylor and his machine fell with a crash. Lawson shot into the straight and passed the winning post, while the cry went round the ground—'The Major's down! The Major's down!' they screamed.

"The Major was down and lay motionless on the track until those who had run to his rescue carried him on to the grass, and chafed his limbs. In a few minutes he revived, and it was found that he had sustained no broken bones, although he was severely bruised, and his shoulder and thigh were badly lacerated. With assistance he limped off the ground.

"There was much hooting from the onlookers at the part of the track where the fall occurred, this demonstration being apparently directed against Lawson. The number of Lawson was posted as the winner, and the time was announced as 4:20 2/5.

"There was a brief interval in the events, and then the notice 'no race' was posted, the stewards having that power under the agreement. This decision was accorded a mixed reception, the spectators in the grandstand cheering while those on the hill groaned, and called out, 'Give us God Save the King, and our money back.' Within a few minutes serious statements were in circulation, but nothing definite was known as to the cause of the fall. Taylor sent word that he would endeavor to take to the track again after a rest, and other races were gone on with in the meantime.

"Another complication arose when the match between MacFarland and Taylor was reached. Owing to the difficulty that arose on Saturday night, it had been announced that if either party did not appear at the starting-post, the race would be awarded to the one who did. Now MacFarland came to the post with his machine, and Taylor was lving helpless in the dressing room. In the circumstances, however, the stewards put the event back to a later hour in the evening. It was not till nearly eleven o'clock when it became known that Taylor could not possibly ride again that night. The stewards held a consultation, and decided that all matches should be postponed indefinitely, and that the prize money should be held by the League of Victorian Wheelmen. It was also announced that Taylor had made a charge against Lawson of having interfered with him. The stewards took some evidence, as a result of which they decided to adjourn the inquiry until the following day, when they would go most carefully and thoroughly into the circumstances of the affair.

"It is a bit strong on MacFarland's part to claim the prize-money because Taylor is unable to go on with the race. In the strict letter of the law he may be right, but what would he say were the positions reversed, and Taylor claimed the money, while he was disabled by accident. The League will be foolish under the circumstances to pay the stake over.

"MacFarland, the American, gave the management and officials of the recent meetings no little trouble last week. It was known that he felt the keenest disappointment at being dead-heated with Taylor, when he was of the opinion that he won, and when the officials decided that his match with Taylor was to be decided on the last day of the series (Wednesday, the 17th instant) he, almost at the eleventh hour, intimated that he would not be able to compete, as he was sick—physically unfit, and produced a doctor's certificate to that effect. Post-haste the stewards engaged a cab and a couple of independent doctors, and drove down to this hotel, and found the patient at a substantial dinner. He submitted at once to an examination, the result of which was that the medical men pronounced him to be in perfect health, and fit to ride for his life, if necessary. He was then quietly told that he was expected to compete at the meeting, and he complied.

"Those who witnessed his ride in the five-mile scratch race were unanimous in saying that it was one of the finest seen. At one point he simply left the field, looked back, and smiled, then pedalled more easily until the gap was bridged. His brilliant fight with Lawson in the last lap was another example of his condition, and it was admitted that for a 'sick man' his effort rivalled the best we have seen on that track."

Another Melbourne daily commented on my accident in my "revenge" match race as follows:

"It was no surprise that Taylor met with an accident in Melbourne. Apart from any other consideration the Exhibition Track is unfit for up-to-date cycle racing, and it seemed to me that the syndicate was taking a big risk in allowing him to race there at the A. N. A. meeting, and again in this series of match races. Almost any rider is liable to fall at any time through a fault to his machine of the action, intentional or accidental of another, and knowing the animosity that existed against Major Taylor in some quarters owing to his color, (which exists more or less in America, and everywhere he races) the risk was even greater in his case. However, while all lovers of a great athlete will be sorry for him, they will also rejoice that it was not even more serious.

"Like Peter Jackson, who gained universal respect, Major Taylor is a white man, and much whiter in fact than some others who have paler skins, and who think themselves superior. As, after inquiry, the Victorian League Officials found Lawson guilty of unfair riding, and imposed a severe penalty, it is fair to assume that he was guilty of misconduct, and it is a bad feature of the sport, that, because he is wanted in Adelaide to make the meetings more attractive, efforts are being made, it is reported, to have the ban removed. What inducement is there for officials to do their duty if their action is to be set at naught on such considerations? Of course, if on appeal it could be shown that Lawson was not fairly treated, that is another matter, and he is entitled to all he can get in that direction.

"The accident which brought the Taylor-Lawson-MacFarland match in Melbourne to such a sudden stop on Wednesday night was no more than those who follow the game expected. Cycle racing is dangerous enough even under the best conditions and on the most up-to-date tracks.

"It is remarkable how ill-fated these matches have been in Melbourne. Nothing but trouble from start to finish. First the League was not going to sanction them, and it is a pity now that they did. Certainly they drew up some stringent rules, but for some unexplained reason hardly ever a match race has been run in Melbourne, which has not ended in a fiasco. Here where matches are rarer, the opposite is the case, but the way the *Arrow* pointed out days ago that it was a foolish thing to allow an unpaced event, which would only provide the Continental 'Crawl' which reduces racing to the broadest farce.

"Cyclist Major Taylor is recovering from injuries, and when seen today he was still suffering from the effects of his fall at the Exhibition Track. At noon he was reclining on a settee in his room nursing his injuries, which consist of painful-looking flesh wounds on the fleshy part of the forearm and thigh. Taylor asserted that he had been interfered with, and expressed himself as confident of having been able to win the second heat also.

"As he takes great care of himself, he hopes with the assistance of Dr. MacGillicuddy, who is attending him, to be soon well enough to mount the saddle again. The Champion will, however, be compelled to forego his trip to take part in the Adelaide meeting, although he hopes that by the end of next week he may be able to ride in the following Saturday's races in Adelaide.

"A meeting of the stewards of the championship cycling contests took place last evening, and after hearing further evidence, they decided to disqualify Lawson for twelve months for foul riding on Wednesday night last. The decision was not arrived at till after one o'clock this morning.

"Iver Lawson's twelve month's disqualification has been much discussed in cycling circles. Lawson has announced from Adelaide that he intends appealing against the L. V. W.'s disqualification, which is a serious matter, as it will prevent him from racing in any part of the world for twelve months. He will not only miss the big Sydney Thousand Handicap, to be decided in Sydney this month, but also the world's championship contests, which are to be decided in London a few months hence, and he is also precluded from racing on the American circuit. Altogether Lawson's retirement will mean a loss of 1,500 pounds to him, consequently it is no wonder he intends appealing.

"The Appeal Board of the League of Victorian Wheelmen gave its decision in the case of Iver Lawson, the American cyclist who had been disqualified for twelve months by the stewards at the recent International Cycling Meeting, held at the Exhibition Oval, for having interfered with Major Taylor, and caused that rider a severe fall.

"The appeal board consisted of Mr. J. M. A. Callaghan (chairman), Messrs. W. Bruse, J. E. Lipscomb, L. Southern, J. Morris, the two stewards, Messrs. E. Shaw and A. Joy, and the referee at the meeting Mr. W. Gleason. About twenty witnesses were examined during the two sittings of the board, and at 10:30 last night, at the Port Phillip Club Hotel, the members began the consideration of their finding. After an hour's deliberation Lawson was called in, and the following decision was read to him:

" 'The board, not being fully satisfied, after hearing all the evidence on both sides, that the fall of Taylor was brought about by the deliberate intention of Lawson, still considers that the latter was guilty of unfair and careless riding, and in the circumstances have determined that a disqualification of three months will meet the case, and, therefore, reduces the term fixed by the stewards to the said period. The disqualification dates from the 17th of February, 1904.'

"All things considered Lawson may consider himself lucky in having had the twelve month's disqualification reduced by three-quarters. As it will stop him from racing here any more this season, the officials have virtually said to him, that while he is not wanted in Australia, he is at liberty to race in France, England, or America as soon as he gets there.

"The action of the racing officials and the League in cases like the Taylor-Lawson affair means a great deal for the sport, and may either make or break it. The advent of Lawson-MacFarland & Company, no doubt, did a great deal to liven up the public interest in cycle-racing, but there are other considerations.

"The only ground on which Lawson was given more lenient treatment on appeal was, that it was not proven that he deliberately fouled Taylor. In nine cases out of ten of the kind it was almost impossible to prove deliberate intent. But when a rider of Lawson's experience takes the risk of cutting across another rider, and so brings about an accident, he is almost as guilty as if he acted with malice. Experienced riders know exactly the danger of this reckless practice, and also how much room to allow, and if they take the risk, and trouble occurs, they should be made to pay the full penalty for the effects of their misdeeds. Had Major Taylor been killed or permanently incapacitated, which might easily have happened, it would have been no consolation to him, or the followers of the sport to know that Lawson did not mean it. The fool with a gun who shoots some innocent person does not mean it, but where that was caused by inexcusable carelessness it is nearly as bad as premeditated murder.

"It is to be hoped, however, that the Lawson case will be a warning not only to that rider but to everyone else who races be he an Australian or American. And if another of the kind occurs, a sentence of life will be about fit for the occasion. There was far too much unfair riding before this accident, and an example of official severity with no unwise wavering was badly needed.

"The bad fall which Major Taylor suffered has been alleged to have been caused by Lawson's interference with him. The stewards of the meeting, after taking evidence, which included a specific charge from Taylor that Lawson did interfere with him, discussed the affair at length, and taking everything into consideration, determine to disqualify him for a period of twelve months. When it is understood that this penalty takes effect throughout the Commonwealth, in Europe and America, the severity of the punishment will be better understood. Still, if the officials had no doubts on the matter, the punishment is merited, for thousands of people were disappointed, and the sport suffered materially.

"The proposal of the S. A. League that the Victorian League should remit or suspend the twelve month's disqualification of Lawson so that he could compete at the Adelaide meeting, is one of the coolest things the *Arrow* ever heard of. A Melbourne contemporary thus refers to it:

" 'The very bad precedent set by the N. S. W. League of Wheelmen is already bearing fruit. It will be remembered that the New South Wales body remitted a term of disqualification imposed on MacFarland, and inflicted a fine of 25 pounds instead, in order that he might take part in the A. N. A. and other important cycling meetings.

" 'Now, I see that Mr. George Ruthven, secretary of the South Australian League of Wheelmen, has arrived in Melbourne to consult with the Victorian League of Wheelmen, regarding the disqualification of Lawson.

" 'The South Australian League is anxious to secure Lawson's presence at the remaining days of their current meeting, and with that object Mr. Ruthven had come to Melbourne to, in plain language, ask the Victorian League to stultify themselves by removing Lawson's disqualification. Could impudence go farther? Because, forsooth, the South Australian League want Lawson to act as a draw at their meeting they ask the victorian body to whitewash him. Unless I am much mistaken in the Victorian League, Mr. Ruthven will find he has come to the wrong shop with such an outrageous request.

" 'Major Taylor is really more seriously injured than was at first supposed, and it may be at least three weeks before he will have recovered sufficiently to enable him to sit on a bicycle.' "

"To the Editor:

" 'Sir, in the interview with Mr. MacFarland in your issue of the 20th instant, I notice some misleading remarks which are altogether inaccurate and unfair. It is not true that Mr. MacFarland holds the world's competition record of 1:54 2/5 at Sydney. That is held by Major Taylor, in 1:53 3/5. I also notice that when asked about the unfortunate accident which happened to Major Taylor, Mr. MacFarland had the impertinence to state that Taylor, when going at an enormous speed, deliberately put out his arm to push Lawson, thereby causing himself to fall. What rubbish the public is asked to swallow! The statement that Taylor took the risk and trouble of doing such a thing shows that Mr. MacFarland is only trying to injure his rival in the eyes of the people. The judges could not help noticing that Lawson was the man who caused the fall; and in their opinion it was done deliberately. They very properly gave Mr. Lawson twelve months' disqualification. Now, the facts are these, Lawson is the man who caused the trouble, and to shield himself, and of course MacFarland, now turns round and tries to make out that Taylor would be fool enough to cause the injury to himself, when he had quite as much chance of winning the race as Lawson.

" 'Messrs. MacFarland & Co. know very well that Taylor is their master on the wheel, and that is the great reason why they do not like him. As to MacFarland's ability I consider he is a rider of the highest class, but he will find he will have to bow to Taylor in the match between them. (Taylor of course, being fit after his fall.) There is no doubt that Major Taylor, champion cyclist of the world, (a title which he so ably earned and keeps), is in a class by himself, facts having proven it, not only in Australia, but all over the world.

" 'Out of the 212 man-to-man contests in which Taylor has ridden he has won 200, exclusive of all competition races. On the list of the four best men in the world Mr. MacFarland places Taylor last, a fact which does not say much for the former's cycling experience. In conclusion, I might state that when in the return match Taylor beat the great French crack, Jacquelin, Le Velo, writing on the match, stated that in his opinion Taylor was even a class above Jacquelin. I am, etc., One Who Knows.'

"MacFarland has been riding for about twelve years and has won between 600 and 700 races in his career. His forte is handicap racing, ten years he has been riding from scratch in America, and over the rest of the cycling world. He holds the world's record for one-mile of 1:55 which he established in America, and in Sydney a few weeks ago he did the same distance from scratch in 1:54, but it is only a chance whether it will officially be recognized by the International Unions.

" 'What do you think of Australian racing?' asked the interviewer. 'It is the best kind of racing so far as the interests of the public are concerned. Our racing in America and that on the Continent is fairly slow, but the American takes more after your Australian. Over there we have no pacing as you have here!'

" 'What was the cause of Taylor's fall on Wednesday night?' 'Look here, if any other rider had done what Taylor did he would have to go under for a year, sure, and at the time he fell he was beaten. Lawson was about three-quarters of a length past him and Taylor reached out his hand and pushed Lawson up the bank so that he could get through on the pole, then he struck his pedal on the bank and dropped.' 'Can he ride· here on Saturday?' 'It is almost impossible. All the skin is off his thigh, and he can't sit on his saddle. He may come over, but what will be the use?' "

# CHAPTER LXXXI



Two weeks after I had been deliberately thrown by Iver Lawson in the second heat of our match race at Melbourne (I had won the first) I was called upon to compete in the International One-mile Championship in the South Australian Carnival at Adelaide. Realizing that all of the star riders with the exception of Lawson, who had been suspended for the above-mentioned foul riding, and could not compete in this event, I bent my energy to recuperating from injuries sustained in that mishap. Despite my best efforts, however, and those of several of the leading physicians of Melbourne I was unable to leave my bed for a fortnight.

That meant in order for me not to disappoint the promoters of the Adelaide meet, to say nothing of the thousands of bicycle enthusiasts in that city, I had to go direct to the track from my cot, a distance of 500 miles, to take part in the International One-mile Championship Event.

This I did, however, despite the fact that I had not sat upon my bicycle in the intervening two weeks. Notwithstanding that tremendous handicap, I went into the one-mile championship race, won my heat and then defeated MacFarland and Don Walker in the final, in 2:05. A wire from Mr. George Ruthven, secretary of the League of Wheelmen, implored me to go to Adelaide to take part in the first two day's racing of the meet there, but it was physically impossible for me to do so. In fact my doctors' informed me that I would be unable to sit in my saddle for three weeks. However, I stretched a point to participate in this feature event which is mentioned above.

Concerning that race I quote the following from one of the Adelaide newspapers:

"The surprise of the season was Major Taylor's defeat of Floyd MacFarland in the one-mile International Championship race at Adelaide. The dusky champion had only arrived by train the same day, and not having ridden since the accident, did not give himself a chance. But as the race was run fortune favored him at the psychological moment, and none being quicker to take advantage of an opportunity, he won in great style, giving a great shock to most of the riders in the race, who were in on the 'know' concerning the pre-arranged tactics of the contest.

"It is not uncommon for riders to arrange in their own minds beforehand how they will run a race, the ever-changing circumstances are liable to upset their plans, and new ones must be adopted on the spur of the moment. Taylor did not dream of winning when he started, and the charge of collusion alleged between himself and MacDonald, (which the officials paid no heed to) was therefore a poor one. He simply saw a chance and took it. The other riders who witnessed the race are not done talking about it yet, and won't be for a long time.

"The appearance of Major Taylor, who was tendered a magnificent reception, was largely if not wholly responsible for the improved financial position of the promoters of the meet. His brilliant performances at the Wheel Race meeting of 1903 had not been forgotten, and the absence of the great sprinter from the earlier meet had disappointed thousands. The decreased gate receipts told that. Prior to Saturday the profit and loss account revealed a deficiency of over 1,500, and the outlook a few days ago pointed to a further decrease. However, the surprise appearance of the injured Major Taylor put a new complexion on the box office end of the meeting, and drew an attendance that wiped out the deficiency and put the promoters on easy street."

Concerning the one-mile international championship race I quote the following article from an Adelaide newspaper:

"Twenty-five riders came out for the One-Mile International Championship race and the four heats were stubbornly contested. The final of this event was paced by Hunt and Gordon. Major Taylor quickly took up the pace early, and was followed by Downing, MacFarland, MacDonald, Scheps, Walker, Pye and Filsell, and the pace quickened. When the bell rang for the last lap the order was Hunt, Taylor, Scheps, MacDonald, Downing, MacFarland, Walker, Pye and Filsell. MacDonald shot out the eastern side and went to the front on the outside of Taylor. He was quickly followed by Downing, MacFarland, and Scheps, at this point Taylor seemed to be pocketed. At the northern turn MacDonald ran wide a little, and Taylor dashed through inside, and got the inside running and came into the home stretch as MacFarland dashed around MacDonald. Then there was a desperate contest between the two champions for the tape. Taylor had a length's advantage on entering the stretch and which he maintained to the end.

"A scene of great excitement followed, MacFarland put up his hand in protest immediately he crossed the tape, but the great majority of spectators failed to see that he had any cause to complain, and cheered Major Taylor vociferously, while MacFarland was hooted. He was not wildly excited and rode across the green to the referee and said he protested against MacDonald for running wide on purpose to let Taylor through. Then he withdrew the protest, because he saw if it were successful it would not alter the result of the race. He afterwards confided his troubles to the other officials, to the reporters, and even to the bandsmen, but to no avail."

The same writer wrote the following two paragraphs:

"Major Taylor may be a pointer, but all the same he is a wonderful cyclist.  Saturday saw him arrive in Adelaide just a few hours before the races started at the Oval and although he was said not to have been on a bicycle since the smash-up with Iver Lawson at Melbourne on the night of the 17th, he sailed right in and defeated Floyd Mac-Farland and Don Walker for the International Championship in good order.

"Must have been a lot of make-believe about Major Taylor's recent injuries.  The final tussle with MacFarland for the International Mile Championship was a very warm affair.  'Mac' was completely taken by surprise, and before he could recover himself the race was lost and won, amid indescribable applause."

Personally I got the greatest thrill of my life when I defeated Mac-Farland and the rest of that field in the International Championship race at Adelaide.  The event came two weeks after Lawson had thrown me on the Melbourne track and my injuries had confined me to my room throughout the fortnight.  Promoters of the Adelaide meet made a special trip to Melbourne to plead with me to compete in this event, telling me that they stood to lose a considerable sum of money unless something were done to attract more people to the races.

However, my physician objected to the plan as did my wife and the promoters left me feeling very much depressed.  After a brief period had elapsed I decided that I owed Adelaide something for the splendid reception its citizens had given me in the previous year.  Likewise I sympathized with the promoters and felt if there was anything I could do to help recupe their losses on the meet I should do so.  The result was that I got the next train for Adelaide.

After a sleepless night on the train during which I was bothered considerably by my injuries, I went direct to the track and received a tremendous ovation following the receipt of a telegraph which I had sent to the officials in the meantime.  There were 20,000 people on hand for the International One-mile Championship.

My trainer had bandaged me up so thoroughly that I could hardly get into my street clothes.  The skin which had formed over my bruises had to be broken before I could bend my right leg, arm and hip.  This painful operation was performed out behind the grand-stand before the race was called.  Then I was carefully lifted onto my bicycle and starting with the fight pedal down at the lowest point, my trainer slowly pushed me backward and forward, each time rolling me a trifle further, until a complete revolution of the pedal was made.

This operation caused me great pain, and also made me bleed profusely from the injuries I sustained when Lawson bumped me off my wheel in Melbourne. However, once the skin was broken on my cuts and bruises I could use my legs as freely as ever. Applying just enough cotton to absorb the blood I went on the track for a preliminary warm-up. I received such an ovation that I promptly forgot I was an invalid and after a few miles of easy work-out and fine rub-down on my good side, I felt quite fit and confident.

I rode in one or two races earlier in the program as a sort of try-out, and then qualified in my heat for the championship. Realizing the tremendous handicap under which I was working the audience gave me a rousing cheer when I crossed the finishing line to win a place in the final of the big race.

While being massaged in my dressing room just prior to the final of the feature event on the program, the mile championship, the blue ribbon classic that every rider on the track was out to win, this being especially true of MacFarland, in rushed Bill MacDonald. He was incensed over a plan he had heard MacFarland and his cohorts hatching up to bring about my defeat in the big race. MacDonald said he knew I could take care of myself when I was well and fit, but he said he could not remain idle when he heard them framing me up when I scarcely had a leg to stand on.

"I am in this final myself," declared MacDonald with much feeling, "and I am ready to offer my services to you to see that you get a square deal. I would like to see you beat that whole bunch of rotten sports today, and it would give me great pleasure to help you to do it." I thanked him very much for his display of sportsmanship, but added that I would much prefer to defeat the other starters single-handed.

"Well," said MacDonald, "if I see anybody attempting to put anything over on you, I'll break his miserable neck." However, I requested MacDonald not to do anything rash or get into any difficulties on my account.

As a parting shot to MacDonald I said, "Now if you really want to see me bring that bunch into camp, and if you would like to have a hand in it, I will give you your opportunity." MacDonald beamed as he said, "Certainly, I want to help you. What shall I do, you just say the word and it will be done." I replied, "All I want you to do is to go to the last lap at top speed, and be sure to hold the black line (the pole) all the way regardless of what position I am in. Take no notice of me whatsoever. I will be on the lookout for you nevertheless. But above everything else keep pedalling for all you are worth." MacDonald smiled knowingly as he stepped out of my quarters, saying, "I want to do more for you but if that's all you want to insure your winning the race, you can count it yours now. Count on me, Major, I'll take care of my assignment to the very best of my ability."

There was excitement aplenty as we lined up at the tape for the final. All got away to a perfect start, and things went along quite smoothly until that last hectic lap. I was sitting pretty in a handy position coming up to the tape in second place, on the bell lap, watching the other riders from under my arm. At this point who came bolting by, true to his word, but my big brave Bill MacDonald. The big Scotchman was tearing off speed at a relentless clip such as he had never before shown.

Downing, who was pacing for MacFarland, was on MacDonald's wheel with MacFarland tacked on to his rear wheel. I quickly dashed to the front as MacDonald rushed ahead of me giving me his rear wheel just as I had figured. At this tense moment, just as we were turning into the back stretch, Downing rushed up and undertook to wrest the lead from MacDonald, and it was a battle royal down that back stretch. On reaching the last turn MacDonald had a slight advantage over Downing, and this placed me in a very bad pocket. Seeing my predicament MacFarland made a terrific bolt for the tape. Simultaneously I shot through on the inside of MacDonald, inside the black line, on the pole snatching the lead by inches from MacFarland.

We tore around the turn into the home stretch. I was gaining on MacFarland with every kick of the pedals down that long home stretch, but it was a savage battle right on up to the tape, which I reached about a length ahead of the surprised and raging MacFarland. The furious finish of this sensational race threw the spectators into a frenzy, one of the wildest scenes that I have ever experienced at a sporting event. I received a thunderous ovation as I wheeled my triumphant lap of honor while the band played the Stars and Stripes Forever, and a huge bouquet of roses presented by the League officials rested on my handlebars. The tumultuous uproar and applause fairly rent the air, it seemed to cause Old Glory which hung out over the grandstand surrounded by the Australian and British flags to flutter with delight. This was the most dramatic and thrilling incident of my racing career, and as I dismounted from my wheel I fairly trembled with emotion. This was indeed the thrill of thrills for me.

It had been my experience that Australian audiences were very conservative as a rule, but whenever I put across one of those Newby Oval "jumps" or a Manhattan Beach thrill producer, as on this occasion when I won that big race at Adelaide, the 20,000 spectators threw their reserve to the wind, stood up on their chairs, and yelled as long and loud as any gathering of American bicycle fans I had ever heard.

My success in this race proved another great setback to MacFarland and to his combination of underhanded riders, both American and

Australian. MacFarland, the arch conspirator, was fit to be tied as he heard the splendid ovation accorded me. Hardly had he crossed the tape when he raised his hand indicating he wished to file a protest, and followed by Downing he rushed around the track, across the green to the judges' stand. MacFarland told the officials that he had a kick coming against me for collusion. However, the officials waived him aside and continued their celebration of my victory. Imagine a man of MacFarland's makeup charging anybody with collusion.

Utterly flabbergasted and keenly disappointed in my winning of that event and ignored by the track officials as he tried to lodge his grand protest, MacFarland saw that he was entirely out of order and left the track in a rage. He openly threatened "to get" me if I dared start in the next race, the five-mile scratch event. However, Mac-Farland's threat made no impression on me. Under the circumstance I had no intention of competing in the five-mile event. I felt that the honors I had won in that classic were sufficient for one occasion.

Turning to MacFarland my blood boiling, despite my outward calm, I said to him, "See here, MacFarland, ever since I started racing, I have been credited with being one of the gamest riders in the business. You have made this assertion more than once, yourself. Now if there is any merit in that allegation of yours, it still holds good, but I do not feel that I can do myself justice in the next race, a five-mile event. However, I hope to be in my best form for our coming match race during the Sydney Thousand. Then you shall have an opportunity to see for yourself whether I am still game or losing my nerve. It will be interesting to see which of us bites the dust first."

Two of the happiest men perhaps in that great joyous throng were Bill MacDonald, and my trainer Sid Melville. Melville's joy was without bonds and he fairly danced in his glee. Meantime MacFarland, Stevens, Downing and the Australian riders who were in on the frame-up were a very gloomy and crestfallen group of athletes.

This was the first and only time in my tour of Australia that I have entered into a scheme with any other rider to assist me in any way. I always fought out my own battles, single-handed, and I would have done so this time except for the fact that the Adelaide group of the fastest men who competed against me were bent upon injuring me again, let alone bring about my defeat by unfair methods. Their scheming against me when I was hardly physically able to sit on my saddle stirred me as I never had been before. The result was that I rode one of the greatest races in my life against them, this feeling being shared by the riders, managers, and trainers who were grouped about the track on this memorable occasion. It was by far the greatest personal victory of my life.

# CHAPTER LXXXII

## THE GREAT SYDNEY "THOUSAND" SCANDAL

Advertised as the bicycle classic carrying the largest purse ever offered, $5,000, the Sydney Thousand (one-mile handicap) of March 1904, provided a scandal which rocked the sporting world. A combination which was alleged to have been formed by MacFarland and other riders in the race dragged through the League officials and through the courts there, for almost one year before it was decided and the prize money awarded.

As a result of the deliberations of the officials of the League of New South Wales Wheelmen, Floyd MacFarland was disqualified for three years, Hardy Downing for one year, Larry Corbett two years, D. J. Plunkett one year, Gordon six months, Bathie one year and Kett one year. Gordon's sentence was curtailed because of the accident he met with in a subsequent race. That governing body decided that the riders so punished were in collusion to bring about my defeat. They further awarded first prize to O'Brien, and second place to me, despite the fact that as the race was run Corbett finished first, O'Brien second and Plunkett third and myself fourth. Then Larry Corbett who won the Sydney Thousand, and was afterwards disqualified by the League of New South Wales Wheelmen, on a protest filed by O'Brien charging collusion, dragged the case into court. There it was tried out at length and after almost a year of hearings and legal procedure the court decided that first prize would be awarded to Plunkett, while second money, $500, was awarded to me, the same reaching me on Christmas eve at my home in Worcester, Massachusetts.

In this Sydney Thousand which is the blue ribbon event in Australia, MacFarland, Lawson and myself were scheduled to ride from scratch until Lawson was disqualified for bumping me off my wheel in a race at Melbourne. This classic attracted all of the Americans who were touring Australia, and the cream of the Australasian riders, ninety competitors all told. The handicaps ranged from 10 yards to 250 yards. Handicaps for the more prominent of the riders were: Downing, 10, Stevens, 15, Don Walker, 20, MacDonald, 30, Mutton, 50, Gudgeon, 60, Megson and Carter, 80, Gee, 90, Corbett, 120, and O'Brien, 180.

MacFarland won his qualifying heat on the first night of the program and I won my heat also. MacFarland had Downing, Scheps, Farley, Gudgeon and others opposed to him in his heat. My closest rivals were Stevens, Pye, MacDonald and Palmer.

(368)

In the final of this blue ribbon event, which drew a crowd of 32,000 people, the field was reduced to the following eleven riders: MacFarland and myself scratch, Hardy Downing, U. S. A., 10 yards; Don Walker, Victoria, 20; Scheps, S. A., 30; Barney Kett, Victoria, 100; Larry Corbett, N. S. W., 120; D. J. Plunkett, N. S. W. 130; Gordon, N. S. W., 160; A. E. O'Brien, N. S. W., 180; Bathie, N. S. W., 200. Corbett won, O'Brien was second, Plunkett third, I was fourth, MacFarland fifth, and Walker sixth, the time was 1:54.

Relative to MacFarland and myself qualifying for the finals of the Sydney Thousand I quote the following paragraphs from a Sydney newspaper:

"In MacFarland's heat all paced in turn, but there was still a big gap to bridge when MacFarland headed the bunch. But he appears to revel in stiff tactics and he settled down to his work with a tremendous burst of speed. His companions had to pedal desperately to hold him, especially on the back stretch where a stiff wind blew in the face of the riders. The American, however, did not falter, and with a final effort carried the back-markers up to the men and sustaining his sprint carried them to the front. After this effort it would not have been surprising if one of them had beaten him in the sprint for home, but with extraordinary endurance he kept on going while his opponents with the exception of Farley were pumped out. There was a great cheer when Farley tackled him at the members' stand. Locked together they swept around the turn, MacFarland, however, notwithstanding his previous heavy work, sprinted again and won a great race by a length.

"Taylor won his heat because of a remarkable sprint, in the middle of the race, when he jumped away from the back bunch, and in the teeth of a strong breeze pedalled unaided up to the front division, whom in the final sprint he beat with great ease. Three of the limitmen followed him home, while Stevens was the only other rider of the back division to qualify. After Taylor cleared out from the back men, the bulk of the pacing fell upon MacDonald, and it was hard luck for him that he did not qualify, and but for his effort Stevens would not have finished fifth."

This same writer wrote the following account of the final of the Sydney Thousand:

"The race itself was full of incidents, but lacked the spectacular effect that was expected from the competition for such a large prize, particularly with two such world-famed cyclists as Taylor and MacFarland among the contestants. All the lights in the track with the exception of the lamps directly over the track were extinguished as the report of the starter's pistol struck the ear, and like a flash, Major Taylor had jumped onto Downing's wheel, leaving MacFarland almost standing.  Downing did not get going, however, until MacFarland was on Taylor's wheel.  Then the trio went after Walker, who was making a fine effort to catch Scheps.

"In the meantime, O'Brien had run up level with Bathie, while Corbett and Plunkett had caught Gordon, who was fast overhauling the pair on the limit.  Kett was making a brave effort to get in touch with the front bunch, but the hot pace set by Gordon forced him out of the race, and the back-markers, who had now caught Walker and Scheps, swept past him.  Taylor finding Downing too slow, set out after Walker, and they were soon onto Scheps who then paced the bunch, whipped in by MacFarland for a fine half lap.  Taylor again took up the pace, and then Walker made a fine effort.

"It now looked as if the flying front bunch would be overhauled. The leaders had dropped Bathie and Plunkett, taking them along at a merry pace, with O'Brien and a hot pace for the bell ensued between the two bunches, Walker pacing all out with Taylor on his wheel.

"At the bell Plunkett was pacing the leaders, and about thirty yards behind, Major Taylor was bringing up the back-markers in fine style. As they crossed the line for the last lap Taylor steadied his pace and opened out for MacFarland to take his share of the pacing, but the tall American ran up the bank and Taylor had again to take up the pacing, then at the scoring board Taylor again tried MacFarland who again refused, and it was seen that the back men had no chance, although when Major Taylor was pacing they had almost got within striking distance.

"MacFarland's refusal was right in the interest of the front bunch, for Plunkett racing all out brought Corbett and O'Brien down the back stretch at a hot pace, and it was then seen that the winner would be one of this trio.  Passing the roller gate Plunkett swung out and Corbett shot through on the inside with O'Brien trailing him, but Plunkett closed down again and O'Brien was in a pocket.  As Corbett raced for home O'Brien tried to get out, but it was not until they swung around the last turn that the ex-state champion could make his final effort.

"When he got clear he came at Corbett with a rush and gaining inch by inch looked a sure winner, but when they flashed across the line he was beaten by a narrow margin, although he was then traveling faster than the winner.  Plunkett was a good third, and Major Taylor, who made a final plucky effort when he found MacFarland would not take pacing, ran fourth.  MacFarland was fifth, while Walker, who had done some hard pacing, was sixth.  The remaining five did not finish.

"There was great excitement when the race was finished and the winner was heartily cheered, but the vast crowd was far from satisfied with the race as a whole, and showed their disapproval of Mac-Farland's tactics in it by some vigorous hooting."

However, there was great dissatisfaction on the part of the immense throng present for the event at the way the race terminated. No sooner had the Sydney Thousand final been completed than O'Brien lodged a protest against Corbett and Plunkett charging collusion. The stewards dismissed the protest and then O'Brien appealed to the Council of the League. The case was thrashed out at length on the same night, but no decision was reached. Evidence was submitted by Mac-Farland, Plunkett, Curly and myself among others. At a late hour the hearing was continued.

Upon being interviewed relative to his protest O'Brien was quoted as follows in a Sydney daily:

"My protest is against Corbett and Plunkett for collusion. I can assure you there will be some revelations at the inquiry which will startle the public. I ask you through your paper to invite anyone who saw or heard anything as Plunkett, Corbett and myself were passing from the northern end of the shilling portion of the ground to the members' stand, to come and give evidence at the inquiry, no matter whether their statements will be for me or against me, I want the whole matter thrashed out."

At this point the interviewer asked O'Brien, "What do you think of the race?" O'Brien answered, "Well, if MacFarland had done his share of the pacing, the winner would have come from the back men."

This same writer wrote the following paragraph under the caption of The Betting on the Big Race:

"As was expected Corbett was the favorite in the betting for the big race. It is said he was backed from 2 to 1 against to 2 to 1 on, with Taylor at 3 to 1 against, MacFarland 6 to 1, and 10 to 1 against the others."

Still another Sydney newspaper commented on the scandal that followed in the wake of the Sydney Thousand as follows:

"The Sydney Thousand agreed to make statutory declarations instead of the customary statements. They were sworn and their evidence was taken down in shorthand. O'Brien was examined at some length, he alleged collusion.

"Corbett who won the race, and Plunkett who finished third were examined in exhaustive fashion, the hearing of their evidence taking several hours. Both denied that any agreement had been come to prior to the race. Kett and Gordon, who were also competitors in the final, were also asked a few questions. The further hearing of the appeal will be continued tonight, but it is doubtful if the proceedings will have been concluded by that time."

I quote the following paragraph relative to the same scandal from another Sydney newspaper:

"The council of the League of Wheelmen has rigidly excluded the press from the hearing of O'Brien's appeal against Corbett, the victor in the Sydney Thousand. It is now commonly stated that O'Brien charges a considerable portion of the competitors with being parties to a conspiracy to cut up the prize among them.

"The exclusion of the press looks as if the League were frightened that some of the evidence is too smellful to be allowed to reach the public. Meantime Taylor and MacFarland, and some of the others are ill at ease at being detained at Sydney when they ought to be at Melbourne getting ready for the Easter Holiday races." Meanwhile all of the prize money was still tied up.

I quote the following paragraph from a Sydney newspaper in further reference to the Sydney Thousand scandal:

"Cycling Scandal. Sydney Thousand Winner Disqualified. Six Other Riders Involved. The investigation by the Council of the League of New South Wales Wheelmen into the protest entered by A. E. O'Brien, who was second in the Sydney Thousand final, against the winner, Larry Corbett (New South Wales) and D. J. Plunkett (New Zealand) has resulted in a decision affecting no fewer than seven riders in the final of the big handicap race. The evidence taken by the Council was not made public, but it is understood that there had been a large amount of betting on the part of some of the competitors, and on the ground that there had been collusion between Corbett and Plunkett, and that O'Brien alleged that near the end of the race he was forced on to the grass by Plunkett. O'Brien was second, Plunket, half a wheel behind was third, while Taylor, yards away, was fourth. The time was 1:54.

"Cycle racing is beginning to smell and the odor of a fish-market is eau de Cologne compared to it. There was a race worth about seventy pounds won by an Australian rider recently, and two days afterwards it was a matter of common report that the winner got only twelve pounds out of it. The rider who didn't win got forty odd, and the rest was split up among various competitors. The morning of the Sydney Thousand final, even the gamins at the street corner were prophesying and advising those whom they loved to place their little bit of stuff on Corbett.

"From the writer's observations, Major Taylor certainly rode to win, and Don Walker did the best that was in him, but it is an unfortunate fact for the popularity of cycle racing that so many people were suddenly so willing to bet their boots on Corbett to win. Rumor was babbling with a thousand tongues, and Corbett won.

"Had MacFarland done his share of pacing, barring accidents, either he or Major Taylor must have been in the front bunch. The time had been beaten by both of them over and over again. MacFarland had set up a new record of 1:49 for the distance himself. Truly there was a slight breeze, but all the same had MacFarland shared the pacing with Walker and Taylor, the front bunch almost certainly would have been overtaken at the ringing of the bell and left hopelessly in the rear before the straight was reached.

"To make money at cycle racing it is not necessary to win races, the rider who does that generally has to borrow money from his old man to pay his entry fees. What is required to win, or better still the ability to convince the other fellow that you can win his particular plan if you want to, is to call yourself the Sprint Emporer, or the Jump President, or the Mikado of the Wheel, or some other high sounding melodramatic designation; and bleed the fellows who want to get their names in the papers as first across the tape. Cycle racing is a lucrative business if you can put up a great sprint now and again, just to make the fellows who want to win understand the necessity of paying you not to.

"The beauty of being a record breaker, is that you can demand at least fifty per cent of the prize money; if there are no other competitors to square, even seventy-five per cent may be demanded with impunity. Always ask big as it is unworthy of a champion to ask small, and besides it doesn't pay.

"One of the most successful Australian riders of today, a man who will cut up a purse with a Chinaman, is dog-poor just because he hasn't the brains or cheek (they are the same thing in cycling) to ask big. He even allowed a man to bleed him for sixty-five per cent of a big prize. The most humorous news item appeared recently which mentions that the dashing young rider Jig Sprinter, won thirty-five races and 450 pounds at the meeting just concluded. No doubt he won the races and the money, but somewhere in the background you will find an unobtrusive cuss who calls himself the Cycling-Pie-Biter, who pocketed most of the 450 pounds to let Mr. Jig Sprinter have the honor and the glory. Cycling is much more lucrative than gold mining, if one has business acumen and a bit of speed."

# CHAPTER LXXXIII

FAIRLY DEFEATED BY MACFARLAND, HE REFUSES MATCH RACE

While the qualifying heats of the Sydney Thousand were being run off in a series of races on the Sydney Cricket Grounds Track in 1904 numerous other races were staged for the cracks entered in that blue ribbon event. One of them was the Kent Plate, a one-mile handicap event, which attracted a list of entrants hardly less imposing than that which lined up for the Sydney Thousand Mile which carried the $5,000 purse. After hotly contested qualifying heats MacFarland won the final, I was second and Don Walker was third, time 1:52 3/5. MacFarland, Walker and myself all started from scratch.

Concerning this race I quote as follows from the Sydney *Star:*

"The big race of the night was the Kent Plate, in which Mac-Farland and Major Taylor met. Don Walker and Downing supplied the rest of the field, but all the men had the benefit of pacers. This was a race of tactics.

"Taylor went to the front very quickly, but before going a furlong he was calling for more pace, his evident idea being to get a jump on his followers. He remained in that position until the bell went, when the pacers left the track. Taylor was then in front, a position he did not much care about. He stopped for a while to allow Downing to come up to him, but finding that Downing was going very strong he thought it necessary to keep him in check. While Taylor was dealing with Downing MacFarland made a brilliant run on the outside, and soon got to the front. Taylor then settled down to finish with Mac-Farland, but the 'Handicap King' carried too many guns, and he shook Taylor off at the members' stand. Taylor then got in one of his kicks, but could not overhaul the leader, who won by about half a length.

"MacFarland rode round a couple of times after finishing, and was loudly cheered for his victory.

"It was a great race. The pace was a cracker, but still Taylor was calling out for more. When the pacers left the track Taylor was in front, but Downing quickly went at him. Taylor had no sooner knocked him out than MacFarland came with a great run on the outside. MacFarland, however, was not to be denied, and in spite of a final kick by Taylor he won by half a length. Time, 1:52 3/5."

I was hardly satisfied with the form I showed in this Kent Plate race which was won by MacFarland and immediately expressed the desire to meet him in a series of man-to-man contests for a purse of $500. It was eventually agreed that we would ride a series of five races to settle the question of superiority, each of us choosing two of the distances, while the League officials picked the fifth. I chose the quarter and half-mile unpaced, while MacFarland selected the one-mile pursuit and the one-mile paced events with a time limit of 1:50 or better. Mr. Hugh McIntosh, the secretary of the League, chose the one-mile unpaced event for the fifth race. It was agreed that the rider securing three wins would be declared the winner, and take the entire purse.

Much space was devoted to the pending championship clash between MacFarland and myself, and the bicycle enthusiasts of Sydney were all worked up over the prospect of the races. However, they were doomed to bitter disappointment when MacFarland refused to ride against me, making known his decision on the eve of the day set for the first race. He refused to give any reason for his action. MacFarland also refused to see the League officials who sought to interview him in regard to the step he had taken.

Concerning MacFarland's backing down on this occasion I quote the following paragraphs from one of the Sydney dailies:

"MacFarland's latest move is to be deplored. There is no doubt that he is a very fine rider, in tip top form; every concession was extended to him in order to clinch the match; and it was on his own suggestion that the heats were arranged as they were. A prominent official of the League when informed of MacFarland's back down, said that he was not at all surprised. MacFarland had made every effort to avoid the acceptance of Taylor's challenge. He had set up many difficulties in the way of the match being brought about, and now after due consideration had come to the conclusion that defeat was inevitable. Rather than submit to a licking by Major Taylor, he has taken the rather undignified course of backing out of the match altogether. It is retreat without even a show of fight for he hasn't given a single reason for his action.

"When MacFarland came here first he soon established for himself a reputation for endurance and pluck of an unusual character. His fine performances have aroused admiration and enthusiasm, but recent events have begotten another feeling, and his latest move will accentuate it. The breach of agreement is MacFarland's own affair, but that will not stop the public from expressing opinions concerning a man who does things of that kind.

"The League announces that owing to the defection of MacFarland they are reluctantly compelled to abandon the Carnival scheduled for Saturday and Monday."

When asked to make a statement concerning MacFarland's refusal to ride a return match with me to which he had already agreed, to settle the question of supremacy, which was not determined in our match race in Melbourne, I said:

"Why can't he be compelled to stick to his agreement?  It isn't fair to the Sydney public who went out to the Cricket Ground to witness the final of the Thousand Wednesday night, expecting to see a battle royal between MacFarland and me.  Instead they saw something that disgusted them and caused them to say a lot of hard things. I don't blame them, it's spoiling the sport.  I agreed to this match with him to compensate for that disappointment, and considered it was due them.  All racing cyclists, especially the visitors, should do their very best in a country that puts up the biggest prize-money in the world, and gives everyone a square deal.

"One hundred pounds ($500) is not so much for a match upon which my reputation depends.  I consider it is a small amount to race for.  I had nothing to win and everything to lose and now he refuses to race.  Well, all I can say is that I am sorry the Sydney public are disappointed.  They certainly deserve better treatment."

Naturally I was keenly disappointed at MacFarland's refusal to ride me in our series of special match races in connection with the Sydney Thousand Carnival, especially as a decision in them would have definitely settled the question of superiority between us for all time

Four weeks after I was badly injured on the Melbourne Exhibition Oval I returned thereto to participate in the Druids' Gala. This program which followed the Sydney Thousand Carnival lasted two days and had events both in the afternoon and evening. While I had not entirely recovered from the effects of my bad fall on this same track I was beginning to feel more like myself again as I continued my serious training for the event.

Shortly before the opening feature of this program, the half-mile International Championship, which I won with Farley second, and Filsell third, the time being 1:00 1/5, Floyd MacFarland was disqualified for three years by the New South Wales League officials for his participation in the scheme aimed to bring about my defeat in the Sydney Thousand One-mile Handicap. I also won my two qualifying heats and the final of the Druids' Plate, a half-mile handicap event, Middleton being six lengths behind me with Harris and Walker finishing in that order.

Referring to this race the Melbourne *Herald* had this to say:

"Major Taylor gave some exhibitions of his form during the afternoon. He won his two heats in the Druids' Plate in a style which won the admiration of the crowd.

"The race for the final was not so closely contested. Brown, Harris and Middleton led half way round the first lap. Racing for the bell, Harris was in front, with Middleton close up. At the bell, Walker and Taylor caught the field. Half way round Taylor shot in front, and in the straight he was leading by two lengths. At the post he was half a dozen lengths from Middleton, who was a few inches in front of Harris. Walker was fourth. Middleton was posted for second place, but was afterwards disqualified for boring down on Walker."

I also qualified in my heat of the Druids' Wheel Race, a two-mile handicap event, but did not finish in the semi-final.

In connection with the Druids' Gala I was fined $10 for alleged interfering with a rider in the fourth heat of the Druids' Wheel Race. Relative thereto I quote the following paragraph from a Melbourne newspaper:

"Major Taylor was fined two pounds for interfering with Flack in the fourth heat of the Druids' wheel race last night. But his success was none-the-less popular for that. The International Half-mile Championship event, although by no means a soft thing, fell to Major

Taylor, and as a result in view of his previous performances that was not surprising.  In the final event he seemed to have the field well in hand from the sound of the starter's pistol.

"Although he won his heat in the International Scratch race after a game struggle, he was just beaten by Scheps in the final which was the last race of the evening."

Concerning the International Championship of Australasia, half-mile race (scratch), a Melbourne newspaper carried the following paragraph:

"Filsell led at the start from Taylor, followed by MacDonald. Farley was ahead at the second lap, but Taylor spurted 100 yards from home, winning by a length and a quarter from Farley; Filsell a good third.  Time, 1:00 1/5."

On the second day of the Druids' Gala I finished second in the International One-Mile Scratch race which was won by Scheps with Farley third, the time 2:08 1/5.

The following paragraph from the Melbourne *Argus* concerns the final of this race:

"Shortly after the start the field began to string out, and Murphy led for three laps, followed by MacDonald, Taylor, Filsell, Scheps, and Farley.  A slight change of the relative positions of the riders followed by Taylor and Farley, with Scheps fourth.  Scheps improved his position with a sudden spurt, and Scheps, Taylor and Farley flashed past the post in a bunch.

"The posting of the numbers, which awarded the victory to Scheps, was greeted with loud hooting by a section of the crowd."

Another Melbourne newspaper printed the following story concerning the Druids' Gala meet:

"The cycling sports were resumed this afternoon (the second day) on the Exhibition Oval in the presence of a large crowd.  The principal events of the program were the two International Scratch races, both of which were won by Major Taylor.  The final of the Half-Mile International Scratch Race was a very interesting event, though the heats were disappointing.  One was a walk over, and in each of the other three there were only two starters.  This state of things being due principally to recent disqualifications in Sydney.  The starters in the final were Major Taylor, Farley, Filsell, Scheps, and Gordon, who was the only starter in the second heat, paced the final.

"At the bell Filsell went to the front, but Taylor warily held his rear wheel with Farley close by.  Half way round Taylor overtook Filsell, and led into the straight, Farley came up with a rush and made a gallant fight to the finish.  Major Taylor won by about a length. Farley, passing Filsell and Scheps, running into second place only a few yards from home.  Time, 1:10 2/5.

"The starters in the final of the International One-Mile Scratch race (afternoon program) were Major Taylor, Don Walker, Farley, Burton, MacDonald and Symonds. The result was a foregone conclusion for Major Taylor, but some good riding on the part of the other competitors was witnessed. At the bell the order was Mac-Donald, Taylor, Burton, the last named made a fine sprint, Taylor and Walker then came up with a rush, closely followed by Farley, followed by Burton and beat him home by a few yards. A splendid finish was made by Major Taylor, by a length from Don Walker and Farley was a close third. Time, 2:09 2/5."

My success at the Druids' Gala had included the Half-Mile International Championship of Australasia which I was particularly anxious to win, since I had won the mile a few weeks before against MacFarland in Adelaide. Now I was more anxious than ever to win the last of the championship series, the Ten-Mile International Championship, to be run off in the Adelaide meet, where I was scheduled to ride the next week.

# CHAPTER LXXXV

AUSTRALIAN RIDERS, PEEVED OVER AMERICAN SUSPENSIONS,
SEEK REVENGE

With two of the American riders, Lawson and MacFarland, disqualified for long periods for unfair riding against me, I felt that my worries against combinations were over, as I repaired to Adelaide for the cycling carnival there. However, I was doomed to disappointment and before this program was finished Scheps and Pye were disqualified for employing unfair tactics towards me in a race, and the only American besides myself, Orlando Stevens, received a silent rebuke from the officials when he said that I had elbowed him in a heat.

My first appearance in the carnival conducted by the League of Wheelman on the Adelaide Oval, April 9, 1904, was in the fifth heat of the Norwood Handicap, a first-class half mile race. It was in this event that the collusion between Scheps and Pye and the balance of the field against me made its appearance. This heat was won by Sawyer (70 yards), Thomas (80) second, time, 58 3/5. I started from scratch, Scheps had 10 yards, Pye 15 yards, Murphy 30 yards, and Rolfe 40 yards.

Ridiculous as it may seem the officials took me to task for my efforts in this race and they seemed greatly surprised when I explained to them calmly just what had happened. Although they saw light apparently, they did not take action against Scheps and Pye or any other of the riders at this time. However, they were on the alert when the riders including myself were called out for the second heat of the Easter Wheel Race, a two-mile handicap event, in which I had nine opponents. I rode from scratch. This heat was won by Waldi (160 yards), Farley (80) second, Houston (220) third, Palmer (70) fourth. The time was 4:10. Other riders besides myself included Scheps (30), Pyne (150), Fitzgerald (200), Pye (40), and Ben Goodson (120).

At the conclusion of this race the officials called Scheps and Pye to the judges' stand and asked them for an explanation of their unsportsmanlike conduct towards me in the course of the race. At the conclusion of their statements the officials disqualified Scheps and Pye for six months.

Then came the final event of the day, the Goodwood Stakes, a first class one-mile handicap event. MacDonald won this event over me, Farley was second, I was third, and Stevens fourth.

One of the Adelaide newspapers commented on the day's racing as follows:

(380)

"Cycling Carnival. Races on the Adelaide Oval. Scheps and Pye Disqualified for Six Months. To those who followed closely the proceedings in the bicycle races on the Adelaide Oval yesterday it was early apparent that there was a strong combination out against Major Taylor. The trouble began in the Norwood handicap, a first-class half-mile race. Here the visitor had to bridge a gap of 80 yards, to catch the limit-man.

"He got going splendidly, caught his nearest antagonists, Pye, Murphy, and Rolfe, in a few kicks and paced them to the bell. Considering that he had done his share of pacing Taylor then swung out to allow his colleagues to lead, but apparently they were not disposed to do so. The dusky sprinter 'sat up and waited.' Meanwhile the front-markers were taking advantage of the hitch, and were pedalling vigorously, but the Victorians maintained a stolid demeanor, and what little pace they did reluctantly supply was spasmodic and ineffective. Taylor then made another effort, and a moment or two later sat up and watched the leaders flash over the tape. Spectators who did not understand the technicalities of the sport and thought the champion should have won with ridiculous ease, appeared hostile towards him, and they felt strengthened in their belief when Taylor was called before the coterie of referees on the green. There was a flash of comedy then.

"Taylor with much dramatic gesture rode the race over again for the officials, and asked if he hadn't a perfect right to sit up after he had done his share of pacing, and hinted that they were cross-examining the wrong party. The referees weighed the pros and cons of the case, and resolved that there was no evidence of 'stiff riding' against the American who walked to his dressing room with quiet dignity. In the second heat of the Easter wheel race, two miles, Taylor had nine opponents. Prior to mounting his machine he requested the referees to 'keep their eyes open' as he believed there was a plan against him.

"Subsequent proceedings indicated that Major Taylor knew something, for Scheps and Pye, consequent upon alleged conduct during the event were disqualified for six months. These riders formed the back trio with Taylor, who starting from scratch picked up the forty separating yards in a twinkling. He took them along at merry bat, then waited for Pye and Scheps to take command. Neither of them seemed in a hurry about it, and they were evidently content to see the front-markers increase their advantage. Despite Taylor's attempt to force them into the lead for a fair distance, they hung back, going out for a few yards at only moderate speed and then retiring.

"The American's perplexity did not escape official attention and repeated warnings to Scheps and Pye to take their fair share of pacing were shouted to them as the trio swept around the track.  The spectators were now beginning to see the unfairness of it and hooting began.  'Buck up, you cowards.  Go to the front there, Scheps.  What are you playing Pye?'  Remarks of this character were heard from all parts of the Oval but without avail.  With demonstrations of disgust Taylor sat up at the bell, to the appreciative applause of the crowd, and his rivals were vigorously hooted when they followed suit a quarter of a mile later.  'They're satisfied.  They played their game,' remarked an indignant official in the arena.  'It is the most disgraceful thing I have ever seen.'  Scheps and Pye were promptly carpeted, and it did not take the referee very long to inflict the penalties.

"Someone carried the news of the disqualifications to Taylor, and he was anything else but surprised.  'Well, I guess the officials did quite right,' he said of the referee's verdict, 'their tactics were patent to anybody.  Six months, well, I should think so.'

"The best event of the quartet was that in which MacDonald raced Taylor over the tape and beat him by inches.  In the final the American was again placed in difficulties.  The champion, however, made the best of a bad job, and with a characteristic duck of the head, he pedalled with the tireless consistency of a steam engine.  Although he made a marvelous recovery, Taylor could not displace either MacDonald or Farley, but it was only his superior strategy that enabled him to beat six other riders for third place.  Stevens complained that Taylor elbowed him up the straight.  Subsequently the referees went fully into the question of elbowing which Stevens raised in his allegations against his own countryman, Major Taylor.  They found that Stevens and his witnesses alleged that he was elbowed on the left side.  The evidence of the League officials showed that at the spot where the elbowing is alleged to have taken place, Taylor was on the right side of Stevens.  The referees promptly dismissed the protest.

"The present cycling season in Australia has afforded numerous illustrations of how bitter the feeling in America must be on the color question.  The enterprise of a Sydney syndicate, the rich prizes offered in Sydney, Melbourne and Adelaide induced five of the best American cyclists—Taylor, Lawson, MacFarland, Stevens, and Downing—to visit Australia this year.  Taylor is black and the others are white, and this difference it is understood, is largely responsible for the frequent collisions that have occurred between the riders.  Lawson has gone back to America, disqualified for three months; MacFarland has departed with a sentence of three years, Downing for one year, and Taylor and Stevens are left to squabble.

"They fell foul of one another at this meeting Saturday, the result being that Stevens lodged a protest against his dark compatriot for elbowing."

One of the spectators at the Adelaide Oval Carnival wrote the following self-explanatory letter to one of the local papers following the above mentioned races:

"Sir: Such a miserable exhibition of palpable 'jobbery' was witnessed at the Oval this Saturday afternoon at the League of South Australian Wheelmen's cycle meeting that I think all fair sportsmen will agree with me, it is about time professional cycle races (so-called) were abolished in Australia, and tracks closed to all but amateur cyclists. The public pays to see fair racing, but all it gets for its money is sundry, long, dull, and uninteresting processions of cyclists, of whom seldom the best man passes the judge first.

" 'Jobbery' and flagrant unfairness are rampant; prejudice seems to run riot; and so seldom is a race won by a man on his merits that the proceedings degenerate into a farce. The riders, with few and notable exceptions, are apparently corrupt, and ready to league together against any man whom they dislike, either on account of his refusal to join in their crooked practices, he being able to beat them on the track or the color of his skin. A certain few of the riders are richly deserving of the most hearty and wholesale condemnation in regard to their despicable and crooked maneuvers on the track this afternoon; and those who did come in first (in all except one or two races) merited no applause, nor did they get any.

"It is extremely significant of the nature of the proceedings, and illustrative of my remarks that the acknowledged champion cyclists of the world should have ridden in several races and not come in first once! Disqualifications and fines seem to be of very little avail to free the sport of this great reproach, as witness the numerous and heavy ones meted out lately in Sydney, Melbourne and Adelaide. And, anyway, if these be carried much further, nearly all riders will be debarred from the track.

"Certain it is, however, that people are getting thoroughly disgusted, and tired of such disgraceful spectacles as that of this afternoon; and if cycle races cannot be put on a different basis, or something done in the direction of fairness, public patronage will be withdrawn, and the sport will become a thing of the past. I am, etc.,   Englishman."

An appeal by Scheps and Pye to the Appeal Board of the League of Wheelmen resulted in the reinstatement of those two riders after a spirited discussion. Concerning this turn of affairs I quote as follows from one of the Adelaide newspapers :

"The inquiry by the Appeal Board by the League of Wheelmen into certain matters connected with the cycling meeting on Saturday last was opened at the League rooms on Monday night. The Board took evidence in regard to the charge of 'not trying' in which Scheps and Pye had been disqualified by the referees for six months.

"They also inquired into the alleged elbowing of Major Taylor in the final of the Goodwood Stakes. They then reversed their decision until today when Mr. J. R. Anderson, the absent member of the Appeal Board had an opportunity of reviewing the evidence. The desire of the Appeal Board is that their decision should be unanimous.

"The Appeal Board of the South Australian League then removed the disqualification of six months imposed upon Pye and Scheps and substituted a fine of five pounds ($25). The Board expressed the opinion that Taylor was equally to blame with Pye and Scheps for not pacing. This seems silly on the face of it. If Major Taylor was guilty (which judging by the report of the race and knowing his readiness to do his share, I doubt), he should have been punished also, still it was no reason for excusing the others."

# CHAPTER LXXXVI



Relative to the reinstatement of Scheps and Pye I quote the following letter which was printed in one of the Adelaide newspapers:

"Sir, I was disgusted to see that the Appeal Board of the League of Wheelmen had removed the six months' disqualification imposed on Scheps and Pye and inflicted instead a fine of five pounds each. I think I claim to be an enthusiastic follower of cycle-racing, as for the past six or eight years I have attended every meeting held in this city and have followed by means of the cycling press the sport in the other states, England, and the Continent. The way in which the sport has degenerated in Australia through gambling and splitting up of prizes, with consequent unfair riding, has been a matter of regret to me and to many others.

"When the Sydney officials recently disqualified some of the best-known riders, many of us thought that a firm stand was to be made to put down 'cronk' riding. Unfortunately the Adelaide officials do not seem disposed to help in the attainment of this desirable end, as the riding of Scheps and Pye appeared to me to correspond in nearly every way to that of the delinquents in the Sydney Thousand. The riding of these two men appeared so palpably unfair that when it became known that they had been disqualified for six months the only surprise shown by the public was that a heavier sentence had not been imposed.

"The officials must also have a certain bias against the color of Taylor, as otherwise they could hardly state that Taylor was to blame for not pacing more than he did. Your report of the meeting will bear me out in this, as it states that those who had no experience of the sport showed signs of disapproval of Taylor's riding, but all who had any knowledge of cycle-racing knew that the mode of riding adopted by him was the proper one under the circumstances.

"I sympathized with the League in the many unfortunate occurrances that have taken place to spoil the success of the meeting, but now that they do not seem disposed to keep the sport pure I shall certainly withdraw my patronage, for this meeting at any rate, and I can confidently say that I am not alone in this. Saturday's sport made me nauseous."

Still another letter bearing on the same case was printed in the same newspaper. It read as follows:

"Sir: I was amused at Onlooker's description of Scheps and Pye as 'boys.' If that is right, then Taylor is a boy, for I do not think there is twelve months' difference in their ages. Scheps and Pye have won respectively about 500 and 200 pounds this season, and considering that the former beat Taylor in a recent scratch race, he could easily do his share, and not expect the colored champion to put in all the work. Sometimes it looks as though the front-markers pay one or two back men not to pace, thereby keeping a dangerous sprinter back. It looked like this in the recent Sydney Thousand.

"I think the only remedy is to disqualify cronk riders for life. I am, etc., Cyclist."

Here is still another letter relative to the same topic:

"Sir: The recent action of the Board of Appeal in connection with the League of S. A. Wheelman in disregarding the referee's disqualification of Scheps and Pye, and substituting therefore a paltry fine of five pounds each, will meet, I am sure, with general and hearty disapproval. There must be a great want of confidence in the referees appointed, or the original penalties (in themselves light enough) would have been uncompromisingly upheld; but it is such a palpably inadequate penalty, and so manifestly unfair to Major Taylor, that sportsmen will be universally disgusted at it.

"Taylor was the only rider in the rear trio that did any pacing at all in the race in which the trouble occurred, and it was but natural for him to slow down and relinquish his efforts when he found that the other two riders did not intend to take their share of the pacing, and so spoiled his chances.

"To impose such a ridiculously small penalty as five pounds will be useless to stop the present system of 'jobbery' carried on by professional cyclists. Examples of all unfair riders should be made, and heavy disqualifications and fines inflicted. Cycling can never be expected to regain its lost prestige while flagrant offenses against common fairness are thus lightly passed over. I am, etc., Englishman."

Then came the following letter, which was printed in the Adelaide dailies, from the pen of Scheps:

"Sir: As I did not ride in any of the events promoted by the League of S. A. Wheelmen today, and as my friends will be anxious to know the reason, I feel that I should give some explanation.

"I feel that I have been badly treated by the League. If guilty of the offense accused of, why should I be imposed upon any more than Taylor, who was found guilty of the same offense, and so published by the S. A. W.? Taylor poses as champion of the world. Why should he expect men who are not in his class to set equal pace with him? MacFarland does not.

"In this particular race I took my equal share of the pace, and as fast as Taylor took his. This I leave to the judgment of those who witnessed the race. This being my home, and as I have a great many friends who are anxious as to my success, I felt obliged to ride at this meeting, but to the best of my belief I have been done a great injustice, and I refuse to ride in any more events during this meeting.

"I lay as little blame as possible on the League, as I am of the opinion that they have been misled through the sympathy played for by Taylor. In an interview he asked the question, 'What will the general public think of me, recognized as the champion of the world, not winning an event today?'

"Speaking of last Saturday's races, I wish to ask why did he not win his heat of the one-mile scratch race, where he let MacDonald go, and held Filsell back? I compare his riding in the heat of the half-mile handicap in Melbourne, run by the Druids, which he won in :57, entirely unassisted. Comparing the two tracks, the Adelaide is from three to five seconds faster in the mile than the Exhibition in Melbourne track. This is admitted by all racing cyclists.

"MacFarland and Lawson have gone through as many difficulties as Taylor, yet none of the racing cyclists have got into difficulties through riding against them, because they have taken their defeats as cheerfully as their wins. I defeated Taylor in the final of the One-Mile International Scratch Race given by the Druids on Easter Monday for which he protested me without the least provocation. This bears out my argument that he cannot get beaten without having an excuse. His protest was dismissed immediately. I am, etc., F. H. Scheps."

In reply to the above letter from Scheps came the following:

"To the Editor: Dear Sir: The letter signed F. H. Scheps in your issue of April 14th may be compared with the whine of a child, who having been chastised by his father for playing unfairly says, 'I sha'n't play any more.' He complains that he has been badly treated, and a great injustice and so on. I suppose he considers it the proper thing to start out in a race with the intention of spoiling at all costs another man's chances of winning, and it follows naturally, I take it, when found out and punished, he should publicly cry out about injustice and bad treatment.

"He states in his letter also that he took equal share of pace and just as fast as Taylor took his, in the race in which the trouble occurred, and also that he leaves this to the judgment of those who witnessed the race. As I witnessed the race, I suppose I am included, and I must say that the tactics of Scheps and Pye in that race were absolutely disgraceful. So far from taking their equal share of pace and as fast as Taylor, they paced in little more than forty or fifty yards and except when Taylor was pacing the speed of the trio was a mere crawl.

"When the spectators heard of the disqualification for six months, the only feeling evinced by the majority was one of disappointment at the lightness of the penalty inflicted, and I personally was surprised that they had not been disqualified like MacFarland in the Sydney Thousand for three years.

"When, however, it was announced that the penalty was reduced to a small fine of five pounds each, astonishment gave way to disgust. The acrimonious remark of Scheps in reference to Major Taylor which made up the bulk. of his letter can only be regarded as the outcome of a spleen at being prevented from trying to be beaten by unfair means, a man who, although an American negro, can show Scheps and his class the way around in regard to speed, as well as fair riding.  I am, etc., Englishman."

In the weekly magazine devoted to cycling which is printed in Adelaide the sporting editor writing under the nom de plume 'referee' wrote the following article about the combinations against me in my races there:

"While it has to be admitted that a solution of the pacing trouble in handicaps so far as officialdom and the racing men are concerned is a long way off, the latter, as things are, appear to be bent upon killing the game of cycling as fast as they can.  On top of all that had previously happened detrimental to the sport, the riders at Adelaide seem to have been as determined as ever to prevent Taylor from winning, thus cutting off their noses to spite their faces, as they threw away their own chances, though no doubt some of their 'pals' were assisted. As a result Scheps and Pye, leading cyclists, were disqualified for six months.

"Only that the season is nearly closed, the sport would soon, at the next season.  While admitting that the present position in regard to pacing is most unsatisfactory (and the officials will have to try and evolve better methods next season), the riders, if they were not very foolish, would not be running their heads against a stone wall in the way they are doing.  With Taylor absent an arrangement to pace turn in turn can generally be come to in mutual interests.

"But there is a prejudice against Taylor both for his color and (more particularly) because he will not cut up the prize with those who assist him, or pay for assistance.  In the past, leading riders (local and imported) have been known to frequently lose over a victory in a big race, because they parted with the stake to the other riders.  But indirectly they gained and they had the honor of the thing.  Taylor will have none of that; he will win all or nothing.  This mutual pacing while almost a necessity is not strictly fair racing for the best man may not win; but the officials have countenanced it for some time, and the day has not arrived when every rider can be got to race on his own all he can from pistol shot to winning post.

"Another view is that, even with an understanding about pacing, the rider who takes the last part of it is at a disadvantage in the finish, as he is winded, while the others are comparatively fresh, and with such a rider as Taylor they all know that he had only to get up to the front bunch to win. The same applies to MacFarland and other good riders; but in their case the 'consideration' for assistance received is satisfactory. The riders ought to make the best of the conditions which exist or stay out of the races. If they can suggest better methods no doubt the officials would adopt them."

This letter is quoted from an Adelaide daily:

"To the Editor:

"Dear Sir: I am in no way connected with any competitor and it makes no difference to me who wins or who is disqualified, but I believe in treating all men, be they champions or novices, alike. This crawling to Major Taylor on the part of the Australian League officials makes me tired. They have made a god of him and consequently he can do no wrong. Last Saturday Taylor met his match in Pye and Scheps who made him do his share of pacing instead of as he desires, taking him up and leaving him quite fresh for the final sprint.

"MacFarland at our last meet did the Lot's wife act and was fined. Yet in the last race on Saturday Taylor was looking everywhere but in front of him at the bell, and his case was overlooked entirely. Iver Lawson fouled Taylor in Melbourne and was rubbed out for three months, Taylor did the same thing to MacFarland in Sydney, and his punishment was only a five-pound fine.

"Of course it is folly to expect the Leagues to wipe up their 'magnet,' notwithstanding that one of our referees last Saturday said that he would deal with Major Taylor if he did wrong, but that statement has proved to be worthless, as the glaring, glossing-over of Taylor's shortcomings and the punishment meted out to other racing men clearly shows. I am, etc., Felix Austed."

Still another letter bearing on this same subject appeared in the last-mentioned paper on a subsequent date:

"To the Editor:

"Sir: What kind of spineless jelly-fish officials have we got in South Australia to carry on the work of the League of Wheelmen? They dismissed Stevens' complaint against Major Taylor on account of contradictory evidence of the witnesses. Do they want any more evidence than their own eyesight to disqualify a man for such a gross piece of unfair riding as Taylor was guilty of Saturday.

"The incident occurred right in front of the main pavilion and before all the officials grouped around that quarter. I was in direct line facing the men as they came up the stretch in the final lap and I and others near me saw Taylor deliberately elbow Stevens with his left elbow onto the grass, thus spoiling all chances he had of winning, besides endangering his life and limbs.

"How there could be any doubt as to which arm Taylor used in this act I am at a loss to conceive, as Stevens was on the inside and was pushed off the track onto the grass. In my opinion the finding of the referees is absurd, and shows a lack of fair play.

"In the other instance in which Scheps and Pye have been fined for not trying to win their heat in the Easter Handicap, while they were not acting advisedly in what they did, I think they did it in order to make Taylor do his fair share of pacing. Where they made the mistake was in carrying it to extremes. I have seen Taylor race a good many times, and it has always seemed to me that he expected everyone in the race to pace him right and let him win with his great sprint at the end. Pye and Scheps evidently determined that they would not do this and they have been penalized in consequence.

"But what of the action of the Appeal Board in fining those two riders and letting Taylor off, while in the same breath they say that Taylor was equally to blame? I believe the whole trouble arises from favoritism shown towards Taylor. His color is nothing to me. I do not care whether his color is black, blue, yellow, or white, but I do like to see fair play and even-handed justice.

"I am told on good authority that the following is a very fair sample of the comparative way in which Taylor and the other riders are treated. There is a rule that competitors in their racing clothes shall not be allowed on the grass except immediately before the race in which they are engaged. An official goes up to Taylor and says, 'Mr. Taylor, the riders are not allowed to remain in the arena unless they are racing, will you kindly leave please?' Then they go to the other riders and say, 'Now then, get out of this, you know well enough you've got no right here, clear out!'

"Of course this sort of thing gets a man's back up. As one of the public I go down to the Oval to see fair and square racing and I do not care if the League has been put to great expense or not to bring over certain men to race. If a man does unfair things, I say punish him for it, and stand the consequences. If the League once allows the public to get the impression that certain riders are to be favored unduly, it is goodby to cycle racing in South Australia. I am, etc., Scott."

As a result of the scandal centering about Scheps and Pye in the opening day's races of the Carnival at Adelaide Oval the entire field was pitted against me in the second day's races. I had often contended against the entire field in my races, both in this country and abroad, so I made light of the matter, relatively speaking, until I was informed that some of the officials had grown quite cold towards me because of the criticism they had drawn upon themselves through their tactics in the opening day's races at Adelaide. Nevertheless with that powerful combination of officials and the entire field of riders against me I won the Fitzroy stakes, a one-mile scratch event, in 2.04 3/5. Walker was second, and Pye third.

I won the first heat with Filsell, Goodson and Fisher in that order in 2.13 2/5. Nine men qualified for the final of the race, the others in addition to the above mentioned being MacDonald, Stevens, Murphy, Walker, Gordon and Pye.

Later in the afternoon I won the Medindie Handicap, one and one-half mile handicap, in 3.32 2/5. Don Walker, 15 yards, finished in second place, and Filsell, 45 yards, third.

Concerning the riding of the Fitzroy Stakes the Adelaide *Advertiser* printed the following paragraph:

"Taylor's second appearance was in the Fitzroy Stakes, a mile scratch event, in which in Taylor's heat only three riders competed for the three places. Nine of the best men qualified for the final, which was a fast and exciting race.

"Murphy was in command at the bell, but MacDonald, with Taylor on his wheel, rushed to the front at the southern end, and shortly Stevens shot up in dangerous proximity to Taylor. MacDonald, however, was making such splendid pace that Stevens was left behind at the scoring board. Once into the straight Taylor came away with one of his best sprints from Walker, who finished second. Pye was third, MacDonald fourth, and Filsell fifth. Previous to this the racing had been dull and uninteresting, but afterwards it was as keen as could be desired."

The same newspaper carried the following story concerning the Medindie Handicap which I also won:

"The Medindie Handicap, a mile and a half race, run in two heats and a final, provided three of the best races of the day, two of them being won brilliantly by Taylor. In his heat Taylor took up a good position, and watching for a clear run in the last half-lap, he sprinted home a winner by lengths.

"Walker similarly demonstrated his superiority in the second heat, but in the final he had to be content with second place to the more brilliant American. The men were all together in the first half-lap, and as the bell rang the first five men were Farley, Palmer, Filsell, Taylor and Walker. Taylor moved up at the scoring board, and led into the straight, with Walker on his wheel. Settling himself down for one of his best sprints, he ran away from the Australian champion, and won by lengths. "

Another Adelaide newspaper printed the following story relative to the second day's races of the Carnival:

"Races on the Adelaide Oval. Fine riding by Major Taylor. The league of Australian Wheelmen made some amends to the public on Wednesday for the sorry exhibition of cycling with which the Major Taylor Farewell Meeting opened on Saturday. Unfortunately, there were not many of the public present to receive the better return for their admission money. The bad advertisement for the poor racing on the first day had done its work, and for the sake of the League it can only be hoped that such keen and honest racing as was witnessed on Wednesday will have a contrary effect on Saturday next, but it takes much to rehabilitate a sport once it falls into dispute.

"Fortunately the League in Southern Australia has, ever since the boom days of ten years ago, had the confidence of the public, and this confidence may be maintained by a strict observance of the conditions which made for success in the past. First of all the League must have men at its head who personally inspire confidence, the chief executive officer must be a fine business man, who is full of enthusiasm for the sport, and who must give practically all of his time to the interests of the League when a race meeting is being promoted; the tastes of the public must be fully considered in the preparation of race programs, novelties, such as the musical chairs' competition, being preferable to second and third-class races; and finally the racing rules must be strictly enforced.

"The future of the sport depends almost as much on the riders as on the management. Dishonest practices will ruin the sport; with honest racing it will live, and with good management as well it will flourish.

"The chief feature of Wednesday's racing was the success of Major Taylor, who on each appearance roused the spectators to a high pitch of enthusiasm. The American did not start in his heat of the Lap Dash. It appears to be the rule 'among handicappers to handicap the back men out of these races; and it is very rarely indeed that a scratch man wins. Most of the back men did not start in their heats, and the scoring-board did not indicate all who scratched themselves."

On the final day of the Cycling Carnival at Adelaide I was scheduled to participate in the Hawthorne Stakes, a one-mile handicap event, but my front tire blew out. I refused to ride in the five-miles scratch event because I feared I would be disqualified by the referee. On top of that I had been tipped off just before the race was to be run that the entire field was going after me with a vengeance in this event, and I felt that with the riders feeling as they did towards me, and knowing that the officials were not friendly either, I felt that it would be useless for me to compete in the race.

Feeling that the 30,000 sport lovers who had paid in to see the racing on this occasion would be disappointed at my refusal to ride in the five-mile event I volunteered to try to put up a new record behind pace. The motor failed me, however, and the best I could do was 1.37 4/5 which was 4/5 of a second above the time made by A. E. Pye recently. In the home stretch in this effort of mine to set up a new record for a paced mile I got the jump on the motor and beat it across the line.

# CHAPTER LXXXVII



A few days after the wind up of the Adelaide Carnival the sporting editor of the Adelaide *Register* wrote the following article which, I believe, is self explanatory:

"Cycle racing as a sport is distinctly on the down grade in South Australia. In many respects the three days Cycling Carnival which was concluded on the Adelaide Oval on Saturday afternoon was the most unsatisfactory one in the history of the League of Wheelmen. The racing probably did more to injure the post in the eyes of the South Australian public than any since the establishment of the controlling organization.

"Some of the competitors were partly responsible for this, owing to the tactics which they adopted, but there were other causes. Want of efficient organization was one, and want of official harmony was another. From start to finish, according to persistent rumors, the gathering was characterized by regrettable dissension. The statement was frequently made that the executive was at 'sixes and sevens', to use the expression used by one speaker. Major Taylor, the star attraction, was the bone of contention. The crack American sprinter did not attempt to hide the dissatisfaction he felt at what he described as 'disgusting prejudice entertained against him by certain of the officials.'

"Major Taylor has not enjoyed his present visit. He told me that if he had not been bound by the agreement to appear on the three days, he would have returned to the eastern states early in the week. He likes the public, he said, and could see that they were quick to appreciate honest racing methods. It was apparent to him too that there was no color prejudice about the local spectators, and that he was sorry for their sake that such unhappy developments had occurred. 'I have some good supporters in the League,' he remarked, 'but they constitute only a small section, you can count them on the fingers of one hand.'

"It has been common talk in cycling circles that the action of the Board of Appeals in reducing the punishment inflicted on two competitors, for alleged interference with Taylor, from a term of disqualification to a nominal fine, has intensified the trouble. There were threats of resignation on the part of veteran officials who were tired of the whole thing, and although a lull followed the storm it was hinted on Saturday that these might yet be submitted.

"In other directions difficulties arose during the week, and it is not improbable that certain matters will form subjects of thorough investigation. To those just outside the circle of officialdom, it was evident throughout that there was an absence of that complete harmony which had made previous carnivals most enjoyable, even to the officials who metaphorically have to take off their coats. 'I am full of it, but shall see the League through this meeting.' This in effect was the remark frequently made in the course of the meeting.

"There was a fresh development on Saturday afternoon when official instructions were issued to the representatives of the press that they were to keep within the ridiculously small enclosure set apart for them on the arena. Hitherto, like their colleagues in other states, they have enjoyed access to the whole of the grounds and authorities in the past have presumably recognized that this is necessary to facilitate the carrying out of duty.

"Notwithstanding the fact that the arena is extensive, the reporters were tethered to a small patch of grass, and were granted a minimum writing and standing accommodation. A table which might possibly offer convenience to half a dozen writers had to do duty for double that number. The band engaged for the afternoon was located a few feet away, and the big drum and one or two performers successfully blocked the view of the finishes of the races. And a little distance further on the starting movements were obliterated by another coterie of officials. Evidently it was not thought advisable to allow the press men to see too much in these days of questionable tactics.

"While a reporter was chatting with Major Taylor prior to a race he was bluntly told to keep to his quarters, and the visiting champion was ordered to his dressing-room, it was somewhat inconsistent of the responsible official to subsequently allow a number of his colleagues to inspect the racing-motor in the arena, especially when it is remembered that the interested spectators included several track stewards who ought to have been watching the competitors in the five-mile scratch race."

Concerning the treatment accorded me on my second trip through Australia one of the Melbourne newspapers printed the following article:

"A message from Adelaide published on Monday, states that Major Taylor had declined to start. He only rode half a lap in the event when his tire blew out. His excuse for refraining from riding afterwards was that the referees were evidently determined to penalize him for the slightest fault, and he would not risk disqualification. He said, 'I am too frightened to race.' This latter remark does not make it quite clear whether the fear is on the part of the riders or the officials, but from what I know of his experiences in Australia, I should say it was a little of both.

"However, apart from this incident, and leaving out the question whether the riders or the officials were to blame at Adelaide, there is not a shadow of doubt that Major Taylor has not had fair play in Australia. It used to be our proud boast that an athlete, no matter what his color or nationality, could depend upon a fair field and no favor, and in the old days (making allowances, of course, for exceptional cases, which will occur under any circumstances), it was true.

"In Major Taylor's case he has had to put up with generally unsportsmanlike treatment from the majority of his opponents, (not to use a stronger term), and unfairness from some of the officials. Those who did not treat him unfairly directly, have done so indirectly by neglecting to properly punish those who have not given him a fair deal.

"After what has happened at various times it is no wonder that Taylor is scared. I have heard ex-racing men say and those who know the whole game from A to Z remark that they would not ride under similar circumstances to Major Taylor for a fortune, and I quite agree with them.

"Apart from the chances of accident, and only his phenomenal cleverness has saved him from worse than has happened, the combinations and tricks employed in order to prevent him from winning has been heartbreaking. Of course, as I have said before, the pacing question is at the bottom of some of the trouble and it is hard to regulate, but that does not alter the fact that as far as Major Taylor is concerned he has had an almost hopeless task—although the superior man—in attempting anything. Nine-tenths of the Australian riders, for divers reasons—cash, color, and otherwise, have been out of sympathy with Taylor, and the antagonism has grown with each meeting.

"It is a laudable ambition up to a certain point, but beyond that only defeats its own ends, and kills the sport. Sport of many kinds today is about as rotten as politics, the goal is always pounds—money. There is no question of the best and fittest man, but get there first by the straight road, if you can, if not by any road.

"While it is a disgrace to us as a sporting community it is not surprising as things are that Major Taylor, who, I affirm here, is one of the most genuine athletes that ever strove for victory in any country, should meet with the treatment he has done. Bad as we are, we are perhaps no worse than America, (if that be any consolation), where a man's color alone is enough to damn him. Indeed, I think it can be safely said that a good deal of our corruption in sport has come out from the land of the Stars and Stripes, where in boxing and other lines 'fake' and 'hippodrome' have long been recognized as a matter of course."

Just before I left Adelaide for Melbourne in reply to a request for a statement by a local newspaper man I said:—"Don't make any mistake about it. I shall never ride in South Australia again so long as the management of the sport is in the hands of the present officials."

"Major Taylor, the champion cyclist of the world, was sincerely indignant when he made these remarks at the South Australian Hotel on Monday afternoon. The crack sprinter thumped the reporter's knee with almost painful emphasis, and simultaneously stamped the floor with his feet. There was a suggestion of vigorous contempt in his demeanor.

" 'The only condition which would secure my reappearance on your track,' he continued, 'would be a change in the personnel of the executive. That's the secret of the whole thing. Some of your officials have all along entertained a disgusting prejudice against me, and I can assure you that I am anything but satisfied with their conduct. There is no tactful sympathy about them. They have regarded me merely as a revenue-earning machine, nothing more. My, I could fill your paper with incidents of how this bias has been displayed. There are a few gentlemen in the League for whom I have the highest respect, and I believe I have had their support, but I guess I've had to contend with more from the others.

" 'Spectators at the recent carnival wondered why I scratched for so many events. Look here! you can tell them through your paper what the reason was. I feared disqualification. Yes sir! Absolutely afraid of being dealt with. Last year I rode in every event, and I came here this time with the intention of doing so again. Now you know why I didn't. I believe the League here would have been tickled to death if they had got the opportunity of keeping me off the track for a few months. You see, the Victorian League disqualified Lawson, and sent him home for a rest, and then MacFarland was compelled to retire by the New South Wales League. Taylor disqualified by the South Australian League! Whew! What a grand advertisement it would have been!

" 'I would swear on a stack of Bibles as high as this ceiling that I have been innocent of certain actions attributed to me by some of the officials here. They evidently forget that I did not begin bicycle riding yesterday, and that I have raced on the principal tracks of the world. Perhaps it will be news to many to hear it was persistently rumored that I would be 'dealt with' at the first opportunity. I have important engagements to keep, and I was not taking any risks.

" 'My experience has been that some of your Australian riders are pretty good at the manufacturing process. It is not generally known that my contract with the League is for only one race a day. Call it silly superstition, if you like, but since Saturday I have felt somehow that the accident to my machine in the mile scratch race was an act of providence. I really believe that a deliberate attempt to slow me was in progress. One of the officials questioned me afterwards about the incident, and this is what I told him. "When you heard the explosion of my tire, it was an indication that the South Australian League's last chance to deal with me had vanished." He laughed, but I was serious.

" 'I cannot exaggerate how sorry I am if the public have been disappointed. Without being egotistical I think they were. Your people are generous in their enthusiasm, and they appreciate good, honest sport. I would like to have gone away with the reputation of having demonstrated my ability, but I have not had the chance to appear at my best this time, and, what's more, I've not felt like it. Do you know, I came here feeling that in certain quarters there was a set against me and I am sorry to say that events have justified that feeling. Yes, and justified it to a disgusting extent. In my journey over to Australia from America this time, I felt almost impatient to get on to your track. The people gave me a splendid reception last year, and I was looking forward to my appearance with the keenest anticipation. And when I think of the result, well,—I like the climate here, the track is easily the best in Australia, and the people are grand. But you must put your full stop there.' "

Still another Adelaide newspaper printed the following article:

"Major Taylor left Adelaide for Melbourne on Thursday afternoon, taking with him a poor opinion of the South Australian League of Wheelmen. So incensed is he with some of the officials that he declared to a representative of the *Advertiser* that he would not ride in Adelaide again with the same officials in charge of the affairs of the League, and he came to this decision notwithstanding a desire to please the public, whom he says are most appreciative of clean, honest racing, and allowing a preference for the track as the best in Australia, and for the climate of Adelaide which thoroughly agrees with him.

"Major Taylor alleges that a feeling against him has been worked up in the League and that there was a desire amongst most of the officials to find some pretext at the recent race meetings, especially on the last day for disqualifying him. The champion became aware of this and fulfilled his agreement with the League on the last day by starting in only one race. Fortunately, he declares, his tire blew out, and the League's last chance of dealing with him vanished. He pointed out that all the officials were not prejudiced against him, and one who would deal fairly with him was Mr. J. Bond, the chairman of the referees, and there were one or two others.

"Inquiries among the League officials showed that there is some ground for the statements Major Taylor has made. Several of the officials having an animus against him. The cause of this feeling is more difficult to determine. Some frequenters of the League rooms and followers of the cycle racing consider it is the outcome of the demonstration made against Taylor by Lawson in Melbourne, and MacFarland in Sydney, and at the Adelaide meeting.

"It is said that other riders with whom MacFarland and Lawson were very intimate, have taken up their quarrel, and it is thought that in this way the sympathy of the League officials has been gained. If there is any truth in the rumors that are current, and good cause for the allegations of Major Taylor, the League for the credit of the sport should have the matter fully inquired into.

"Major Taylor, who was induced to come to Australia by a Sydney syndicate which hires him out to promoters of race meetings, has two more engagements to fill in Australia, one at Melbourne, and the other at Wagga, New South Wales."

## CHAPTER LXXXVIII



I next participated in the Eight Hours' Anniversary on the Exhibition Oval, Melbourne. The first of these races was the Autumn Handicap, one mile event. I rode into a pocket in my heat and was unable to place. In the ten-mile International Scratch Race, a championship event, I got going and won with Farley second, and Sheps third.

Concerning this Carnival I quote the following paragraphs from one of the Melbourne newspapers:—"The greatest interest naturally attached to the riding of the champion, Major Taylor. The speedy Negro made his appearance twice. On the first occasion he rode in the second heat of the Eight Hours Autumn Handicap, and occupied a good position until two laps from home, when Forbes and Rolfe dashed out in front as the rest of the field apparently made an endeavor to slow the pace.

"But Taylor noticed the ruse, and, running out alone, caught the front men. At the bell he was riding third to Murphy and Payne, with Pye close up, and, by an unexpected act of carelessness, allowed himself to get into a pocket, from which the other competitors took good care he did not escape. The result was that Taylor had no chance of showing his pace in the final sprint, and while Farley, Pye, Rolphe, and Payne qualified for the semi-final he was compelled to ride in with the field.

"The spectators manifested their disapproval of the manner in which the race was run by hooting some of the competitors, and waited vainly for the stewards to take action.

"Taylor's second appearance was in the Ten-mile Championship, with which the meeting closed. In this he made no mistakes. He rode in the middle of the field until the pace quickened at the last mile, when he gradually moved up to where Gee, Pye, MacDonald, and Walker were leading the field.

"At the bell Filsell made a run past, but Taylor was behind him, with Farley and Walker following. In the last half-lap the issue was not in doubt. Taylor waited until the final turn, and then swept past the others, and won by two lengths. Farley was second, and Scheps third, Walker and MacDonald being 30 yards in the rear. No time taken."

On this my second visit to Australia I won all three championship events, duplicating my feat of the preceding season. However, while

I won the quarter, half, and the mile events in my 1903 tour, I was successful in the half, one, and ten-mile events in the 1904 trip.

In the course of my second tour of Australia despite the additional opposition of the American riders against me I succeeded in winning 12 first places, 11 second's, 3 thirds, 2 fourths, and rode two dead heats. I also received three championship medals.

Upon being presented the championship emblems I remarked to the officials on the similarity of the design of each of them. In this country and in Europe one would seldom find a duplication of championship medals or other prizes awarded for sporting events. I was informed, however, that in Australia all the championship medals were struck off from the same dye, in other words, the design for them was standardized. Moreover it was brought to my attention after the presentation had been made that never before had any one bicycle rider been able to win more than one of these championship medals in a single season.

As I look back over my last season's work in Australia I was highly pleased with my accomplishments. Shortly after I arrived there and learned that several American riders had preceded me I realized that they were in a combination to prevent my winning a race. Not satisfied with that underhanded procedure they enlisted all of the Australian riders to help them put the program over, coupled with that all of the other riders had the advantage over me of having been in training for several months before I left the ship. As a result I was beaten several times before I reached my best sprinting form, but I quickly found myself and swept my way to a number of victories in spite of the powerful combinations against me. Incidentally on my last visit to Adelaide I found that several of the officials were in league to bring about my suspension.

As I recall my last trip to Australia, the 1904 season, my thoughts center on my first success over the MacFarland combination which I consider one of my greatest personal triumphs. It came in the final of the International Test Race on the famous Sydney Cricket Grounds Track, in which both MacFarland and his *protégé*, Lawson, among others competed. I won over Lawson after having tried him out carefully throughout the race. The final of this event developed into a team match with Lawson, Downing, MacDonald and myself seeking the honors. Things worked smoothly for the first two laps and I managed to have MacDonald's rear wheel when the pacemakers drew out and the bell sounded for the last torrid lap. Lawson was sitting in behind his team-mate, Downing, at the moment, MacFarland having failed to qualify. I retained my position until Downing rushed up with Lawson, and headed for the tape. Then I jumped into the lead and stalled for Lawson's attack in the home stretch about 250 yards from the tape.

Anxious to get a real line for myself on Lawson's ability I actually allowed him to pull up on even terms with me to determine the question of superiority between us to my own satisfaction.   Then I made my bolt for the tape and reached it with a length's advantage over Lawson.   I was satisfied thereafter that I had Lawson's measure and while I did not lack confidence when I started in this International Test Race I felt doubly sure now that I could defeat Lawson on even terms every time we started.   My theory was correct as Lawson never defeated me again in a man-to-man match race.

My next victory over Lawson came in a series of man to man contests in Melbourne against him and MacFarland.   I won the first match from Lawson defeating him decisively in two straight, hard-fought, heats.   Then came my match race with MacFarland.   In the first heat of this terrific struggle he defeated me fairly and squarely. ·In the second race of this series all went well until we reached the last desperate lap.   MacFarland took the last turn at a terrific rate of speed.   In order to pass him I would naturally be obliged to travel at a much faster speed than the banking would allow.   I made two desperate attempts to do so, but my machine skidded badly, causing me to lose a length or more.

Entering the home stretch with MacFarland in the lead, I made a frantic effort to overtake him, and was positive I had turned the trick just before we reached the tape.   Tremendous cheers greeted our efforts and I thought I heard one of the officials call out "MacFarland."   As we circled the track after crossing the finish line MacFarland rode alongside of me and extended his hand indicating I had won.   As a matter of sportsmanship I congratulated him, but upon returning to the judges' stand I discovered the judges had declared the heat a tie.   MacFarland refused to ride the heat over and was hooted by the gathering as he left the track in a huff.

I cannot help but recall the number of close decisions that I had lost through the ruling of officials in races in this country, on the Continent and in Australia.   Not once had I complained about the officials' decisions on these occasions, feeling that they were in a better position to judge than I was.   Only a few weeks before my race with MacFarland the referee decided the final of the Kent Plate, a big race, was a tie between Don Walker and myself.

Later MacFarland had a change of heart and agreed to ride the tie-off with me the following week.   On the same evening I was scheduled to ride a return championship match race with Lawson. However, after I had defeated Lawson by three lengths in the first heat, he threw me in the second heat and I was so badly injured that I could not ride for the next fortnight.

For foul riding against me on that occasion Lawson was disqualified by the League officials. Shortly MacFarland agreed to ride me in a series of races during the Sydney Thousand Carnival, but he backed out and we never settled who was who in the man-to-man match race.

After my unfinished match race with MacFarland on the above mentioned occasion, Lawson challenged me for a revenge match. I accepted the defy in good faith, but afterwards learned that MacFarland and his gang were scheming to bring about my defeat at the hands of Lawson even to the extent of bringing me down, if necessary, in order that they would not lose their money with which they backed Lawson heavily.

After I defeated Lawson by several lengths in the first heat one of the Australian trainers got word to me, through my trainer Sid Melville, to be on my guard for some dirty-work in the next heat. He informed me that MacFarland had threatened Lawson with an oath, telling him that providing he could not lead me home he must throw me in order to save the money they had placed on him.

Being thus forewarned and on my guard, I intended to go to the front coming up to the bell lap, in order to have the lead in the last lap. He would then have no chance of cutting in on me when he attempted to pass. No pacemakers being employed, I took a position on his rear wheel at the start, as a matter of tactics, which I held until just entering the back stretch on the last lap. Lawson was holding the inside, and in order to avoid any possible chance of interference or collision, in making my jump I gave him a wide berth in passing by pulling to the center of the track. But before I could get quite past, he deliberately swung to the center of the track and dashed into me bringing me down with a terrible crash. It looked like murder, but fortunately it was not, and although no bones were broken I suffered the worst fall I ever had and was unable to ride for the next fortnight.

The two track officials who helped gather me up were horrified. One of them said that it was one of the most treacherous things he had ever seen. "Just look at those deep pedal marks on the surface of the cement. That shows that he deliberately came from the pole to the center of the track to carry out his malicious deed. He will go out for life for this," said another.

The spot where I hit the track was examined by officials, trainers, riders and the public, and the heavy marks left for a distance of fifteen feet or more were mute evidence against Lawson.

Just prior to the Sydney Thousand Carnival MacFarland approached me for the third time to see if I would enter a combination with him for the big event.

"Of course, I know you wouldn't agree to lay down," he said, "but I can fix things for you to win, providing, of course, that you will agree to split the purse."

But I steadfastly refused to be a party to anything that even looked suspicious, and answered, "I will agree to anything that is fair and above-board, and nothing else. But listen Mac, I'm at the height of my form, and take it that you are in fine condition also. This is what I will do. Barring accidents, you and I alone can catch the limit-men by alternating the pace. Then each take his chance and fight it out, and may the best man win. Otherwise you are only wasting your time here."

"Well, I might as well tell you now that unless you change your mind you haven't one chance in a thousand to win this race on your own."

"Yes, I appreciate what I am going to be up against, but I've always enjoyed the reputation of playing the game fair and square, win, lose or draw, and I do not intend to have my name smeared up with anything crooked now."

As he left my room he remarked that if I did not accept his proposal I would regret it.

I knew full well that I hadn't a chance to win on my own, but I stuck to my resolution and went out with a licking staring me in the face. I was trimmed all right, but took my medicine like a good loser, though only after the most desperate fight imaginable. Even though I lost I was not sorry for it afterwards, and under similar circumstances I would take the same course today.

For the second time the public was greatly disappointed at the way the big contest was run, not necessarily because I did not win, but because they knew that the best man had not won. The main trouble was what I had pointed out from the first—the mistake of featuring handicap races as the blue ribbon, or "classic" events, and giving all the big purses for this style of racing. There is positively no just and equal basis on which to run off a handicap race so that it shall really test one rider's true ability over another's. All sorts of experiments have been tried to make handicap racing a satisfactory test, but without success, and the only thing that it has proven is that it always caused a lot of scheming and crookedness which was inevitable where so much money was involved under such conditions.

The inferior riders scheme how to figure in on a slice of the big purse and gain an equal share with the winner. Many times when they were supposed to be in a combination to help a certain rider win they would double-cross him and win themselves, if they got a chance, and so get all the prize. I have always maintained that the big prizes should be given for scratch events, championship events or match races.

Then the best man, barring accidents, must invariably win and no one would begrudge him carrying off the big purse and the honors. This is the way it is done on the Continent where bicycle racing is always so popular and where the public patronize them so extensively. Thus they are always assured of seeing the best man win.

The greatest handicap races I ever saw were those in which the prizes were the smallest, although big handicap events always make betting excellent. However, I could not argue too strongly at that time, because it might appear that I simply wanted to feather my own nest. Some people would argue that the Australian riders would stand no show whatever in scratch events, which was possibly true, but I contend that they would soon develop into topnotch sprinters of this class.

Although I did not go to Australia the next season I later learned that the big race resulted in another disappointment. Elleggarde, champion of Denmark, who started from scratch and was paced all the way by the back-markers, finished only a poor third. Now, had it been a scratch event, it is a safe bet that the big prize would surely have been his.

# CHAPTER LXXXIX



The Melbourne engagement was my last in Australia. All in all this 1904 tour of that country was the most strenuous as well as the most eventful period in my entire career.

Mrs. Taylor had been awaiting certain interesting developments in Melbourne that would make me the proud recipient of the greatest prize of all, one even greater than the Sydney Thousand many times over.

Of course, he was going to be a champion bicycle rider, so the happy thought occurred to me that aside from those inherent sprinting qualities, perhaps his next biggest asset, to start him on his fast career to championship fame and glory, would be a fast name. Naturally the most suitable one would be "Major," not merely as a nickname either such as was wished upon me. For a middle name an idea struck me., I suggested to my wife that we leave at once for Sydney, then we could christen him Major Sydney Taylor, in memory of our wonderful Australian visits.

On May 11, 1904, this wonderful little stranger made appearance. When I inquired of the doctor if the baby was perfectly developed, he informed me that it was, but said quite soberly, "This child can never be the great sprinter that you are."

"Why, Doctor?" I demanded breathlessly.

"Because it's a girl," he replied.

This was true, she could never be a champion sprinter, but proved to be a champion good baby. We christened her Rita Sydney, but she has been Sydney to us, and is so known by all of her many friends and acquaintances. I made many true friends and admirers in the land of the kangaroo and always felt that some day I would like to return on a visit, but not to race. I should like very much for our Australian friends to see our prize baby girl now, more than twenty years later.

She has fully come up to all of our expectations especially in athletics. She is a graduate of the Sargent School of Physical Culture of Cambridge, Massachusetts, and is now a teacher of physical culture.

We· sailed for America with our little prize baby girl on June 6, 1904, on the S. S. Samoa, accompanied by the Australian champion, Don Walker. We were given a wonderful send-off. Although I lost two Sydney Thousand events and was somewhat disappointed, I was grateful indeed when we arrived home in Worcester safe with our little baby girl after a 12,000 mile voyage. We realized it even more when we later heard of the tragedy that overtook my great rival Thorwald Elleggarde, the champion Danish rider.

He succeeded me to Australia the next season accompanied by his wife and their beautiful little baby boy of about four years. The child tumbled from a third story window and was killed. I have often thought of what a long, dreary voyage they must have experienced on their return voyage to Denmark, leaving their dear little one sleeping in far off Australia.

# CHAPTER XC



Leaving Australia for my home in Worcester, Massachusetts, I was accompanied by Don Walker, the Australian Champion. He had decided to compete for the World's Championship at London, England, in the fall.

Upon our arrival in San Francisco we decided to rest up for a few days before starting the long trip to my home town. However, we encountered a new epidemic of Colorphobia which made me completely revamp my plans and leave California at the earliest possible moment. Don Walker was completely nonplussed as he observed the treatment accorded to Mrs. Taylor and myself and our infant baby. We found it impossible to dine in the restaurants because the management drew the color line, and the same condition confronted us at the hotels.

We made the rounds of the city, only to be refused shelter and in many cases to be actually insulted. After having been refused service in one of the largest cafés in the city we drove vainly for hours to the different restaurants, and it was late in the afternoon before we could get any lunch. Walker was still game, however, ("as only bicycle riders can be,") and positively refused to eat unless we could all dine together.

As a last resort, I suggested a plan whereby we might be served. We drove to one of the big restaurants where we had been denied earlier in the day. My wife and baby and I remained in the carriage outside. Walker went inside, seated himself, and ordered lunch for three, saying that the others would be along shortly. When it was served he paid the check, stepped out, and brought us in. The waitresses were shocked, the manager was nonplussed; but he did not molest us. So we did have at least one square meal in San Francisco, but we left for the east on the midnight sleeper.

This was our greeting upon our arrival in America after the rousing send-off three weeks before in Australia. I could hardly blame Walker when he broke out indignantly in this fashion after seeing the treatment of Negroes as practiced in this country:—"So this is America about which you have been boasting in Australia. From what I have seen of it in the past few days, I cannot understand why you were in such a hurry to get back home here. Do you prefer to live in a country where you are treated like this than to live in my country where you are so well thought of, and where you are treated like a white man, and where many inducements were made you to return to live? I can't understand this kind of a thing." I was unable to explain conditions satisfactorily to him, the more I tried to smooth matters over the more incensed he became.

Floyd MacFarland's attitude toward me, both on and off the track, was one of genuine hatred and bitter prejudice. I found that he reflected the attitude of the people of California, his native state, whom I encountered. While I thought of a time a few years later when the opportunity presented itself for my wife and me to contribute our bit toward a fund for the suffering people of San Francisco following the dreadful earthquake and fire there. When the city lay in waste and ruins, and thousands of souls were suffering, our hearts were touched and we gave liberally to that same city where we were actually denied the privilege to buy and pay for food and hotel accommodations. The contrast was indeed great.

Notwithstanding these indignities, however, I bear no animosity toward the people of that state, nor toward Floyd MacFarland a native son, Orlando Stevens, Hardy Downing or any rider from that State or elsewhere. In fact I have never hated any rider that I ever competed against. As the late Booker T. Washington, the great Negro educator, so beautifully expressed it, "I shall allow no man to narrow my soul and drag me down, by making me hate him." In these well-chosen words, he voiced the true sentiment of the entire Negro race. We Negroes have our likes and dislikes, of course, but literally speaking, Negroes as a race do not hate white people or others, but white people as a race do hate Negroes because of color.

I am a Negro in every sense of the word and I am not sorry that I am. Personally, however, I have no great admiration for white people as a whole, because I am satisfied that they have no great admiration for me or my group as a whole.

We do have numerous white friends and sympathizers, however, such sterling characters as the world famed Rev. Dr. S. Parkes Cadman of Brooklyn, N. Y., and Mr. Julius Rosenwald of Chicago, Illinois, who have sacrificed everything for Negroes, and who are still doing all in their power to bring about a new era with regard to equal rights and the brotherhood of all mankind regardless of creed, race or color.

There are still thousands of white friends who have the utmost admiration and affection for certain colored people and who have laid the foundation stones for many successful and prosperous Negroes just as my friend Mr. Munger did for me. Without such sympathy and support America would be a far worse place for Negroes to live in than it is at the present time.

Mr. Munger by the way would never accept one single dollar of my prize winnings.

Not long after I reached my home in Worcester I suffered a collapse and narrowly averted a nervous breakdown. This was caused by my recent strenuous campaign in Australia augmented by the incidental worries of life. Upon the advice of my physician I cancelled my European engagement and sent word by Don Walker to my friends whom I felt he would meet on his trip to London, that I hoped to be back racing with them. Later I confirmed my cable to my agents on the Continent relative to the cancellation of my tour with a letter which contained my doctor's certificate, explaining my physical condition.

However, they insisted that I fulfill my contract with them, and interested the N. C. A. of this country in my case. Since I had been at odds with the last named organization on several occasions it naturally welcomed a chance to get back at me. Not many days elapsed before the N. C. A. had brought my suspension for failure to fulfill my agreement to ride in Europe.

Noting my indifference to the suspension the Continental promoters, who had arranged another racing tour for me, brought suit against me for breach of·contract in the sum of $10,000. This action dragged through the courts for three years. Then Mr. Robert Coquelle, the French promoter, came over to see·me personally. We got together settling the dispute in short order. It was a compromise arrangement, my part in it calling for my participating in a stipulated number of races on the Continent. The agreement was entirely satisfactory to me with one exception—Mr. Coquelle insisted that I break my hard fast rule by riding on Sundays on this tour. Feeling that had I not consented to ride on Sundays the suit against me would have been continued through court action as previously, I reluctantly and sorrowfully too, I confess, was obliged to break my rule "never to ride on the Sabbath." However, like many other men I felt I was caught in a "jam." I wanted the worry of the suit ended, and to be free from the chance of losing such a sum of money. It would be a big slice of my savings and when I thought of my wife and child I weakened, as better men have done, and signed the agreement that demanded my racing on Sunday.

# CHAPTER XCI

## MY GREAT COMEBACK

Following a three-year lay-off I resumed riding on the European tracks in 1908, staging a great comeback, and establishing two world's records which still stand.

I was accompanied on this trip by Mrs. Taylor and little Sydney who was now about four years old. Following my three-year lay-off

Serious Faithful Training Brought Perfect Results

after my collapse upon my return to my home in Worcester, Massachusetts, due to my strenuous 1904 tour of Australia, I resumed racing in Europe. In that space of time I had acquired thirty pounds, tipping the scales at exactly 198. For six weeks after my arrival in Paris I followed a systematic course of training which brought my weight down to my former sprinting figure. I felt I was in fairly good shape but later developments proved that I had taken weight off too quickly. The result was I rode poorly in my first six races, failing to win one.

Undismayed, however, at my failure to regain my wanted form, I continued my serious training routine, and in the last race of my first series I was moving along in fine style.  In fact I was so pleased with my condition that I signed up for another series of races.  I told my wife that I had fulfilled my obligation to the race promoters and would return to Worcester any time she said the word.  However, I informed her also that I was just striking my winning form and felt if she would remain a while longer I would sign up for more races.

Physically Fit and "Rearing to Go"

I did not want to leave Europe until I had made a creditable showing against the new field of riders over there.

Time proved that I had sized my condition up accurately.  After the talk with my wife I signed up for a half dozen more races winning all but one of them.  Among those whom I turned back after I arrived at my best form on this tour, which was my fourth to the Continent, were Elleggarde, Jacquelin, Poulain, Friol, Dupre, Verri and Van den Born, all top-notchers, in fact I defeated several of them on a number of occasions.

In the meantime, I established two world's records on the Veledrome Buffalo Track, Paris, which have withstood the assault of crack riders of the world in the intervening score of years. One of them was :25 2/5 for the quarter mile, while the second was :42 1/5

Winning International Scratch Race, Paris

Winning the Race of Nations
Taylor   Dupre   Schilling
America   France   Holland

for the half mile. In both of these events I rode from a standing start.

On this same track I won the "Race of Nations," one lap of the track, establishing a record of 18, the fastest ever ridden on that track. Others entered in that race were Rutt, Dupre, Jacquelin, Schilling and Friol. I also won a three-cornered match race with Friol and Elleggarde here.

I recall a three-cornered match race between Elleggarde, Verri and I at Marsailles which was perhaps the greatest three-cornered match

race that I ever won.  In this race I won in straight heats, my margin
of victory varying from three to four lengths on each occasion.  In
them I shook off my opponents in the last 200 yards, Elleggarde ad-
mitting later that in all our great match races he had never seen me
display the form I showed in this event.

In a match race with Verri, who at the time was champion of Italy,
I was at top form when we were called to the scratch for this feature

THE TAYLORS

number in a carnival in Milan.  Although an excellent rider I man-
aged to defeat him in the first heat by a full length before a tremendous
gathering.  I was given a splendid ovation when we came out for the
second heat.  I allowed Verri to lead until the bell lap, and did not
attempt to pass him until we were entering the back stretch.  As I
started to jump past him, Verri deliberately brought me down with a
crash.  I had to be carried to my dressing-room, and while I escaped
serious injury I was badly bruised and cut by the malicious act.  The
track officials immediately disqualified Verri for one year.

Still another of my come-back races that season was with Friol, who
was then champion of France.  The match took place on the famous
Parc des Princess track in Paris and I won in two straight heats.  This
proved to be a great race.  I found Friol a thorough sportsman with a
charming personality both on and off the track.  Despite the fact that
I defeated him a number of times we remained the best of friends.

My last race of the season was the match with Poulain which I won. The next week Mrs. Taylor and myself and little daughter, Sydney, sailed for home.

As we pulled out of Cherbourg I could not help but reflect on the

Sydney on her Peugot, French Bike

great comeback I had staged on this trip after my enforced lay-off of three years. Most riders would have been discouraged and withdrawn from racing had they encountered the set backs that met my first half dozen efforts on this trip. However, I refused to be disheartened and kept on my serious training stunts until I showed a complete recovery of form before my schedule was completed.

Before I hit my stride on this trip the French sporting papers berated the promoters of the races which featured me, saying the public had rather remember me as I was in 1903 instead of the slowed-up rider I appeared in my first few starts this year. However, my managers had the last laugh when I finally arrived at my best form, and the newspapers were profuse in their apologies for rushing at their hasty conclusions.

On this, my last European tour, I won thirty-two first places, thirty second places, four third places and four fourth places in my four months' racing there.

### IT WAS AN AWFUL RAW DEAL

Arriving at my home in Worcester in the fall of 1908 I continued my training stunts and kept in splendid physical condition by riding at indoor meets that winter. I was successful in numerous match races, the most important of which was the memorable battle with Jackie Clark, who had become champion of Australia since my last trip there. This championship match took place in the old Park Square Garden track in Boston.

I won the first heat, Clark landed the second, while I won the third and deciding heat handily. Clark was the only Australian I had ever competed against who had anything like a real "jump" in his bag of tricks. He had a great future before him, but unfortunately retired from the track just when his future seemed assured and entered business.

I can still see Clark waiting to congratulate me as I finished my lap of honor, which was an outstanding demonstration of good sportsmanship. This act by Clark brought a roof-lifting round of applause which was second only to that which greeted my victory over him a few minutes before.

After the announcer had broadcast the fact that I had won the race and the crowd had filed out of the building a conspiracy charging foul riding was quickly hatched by some of the riders to bring about my disqualification. This group pressed Clark to protest the race on the grounds that I had ridden him too close. They evidently felt that if Clark, who was to sail shortly for Paris, under the management of Floyd MacFarland, had defeated me it would add considerably to his prestige overseas, and get him some very fine contracts.

The referee came to my dressing-room when I was fully dressed and told me that I would have to ride the race over again. He also said that if I refused that he would award the race to Clark. I told him that I would not ride again that night under any circumstances as I had won the race fairly and decisively. However, I offered to ride Clark another race for another winner-take-all purse at any time and in any place agreeable to him. Clark reluctantly accepted the race from the hands of the referee only after persuasion on the part of the clique, that forced him against his better judgment to protest our race and I was fleeced out of a $500 purse, winner's end.

I vowed I would never ride in the Park Square Garden again, and ordered my trainer to remove my bicycle trunk and all my racing outfit immediately. This proved to be a very wise move as the old Garden was reduced to a mass of ruins by a fire early the next day, and all of the other riders lost everything they had in the dressing-room—bicycles and all.

In the spring of 1909 I returned to Paris and was even more successful on this occasion than I was in the year before when I staged my great comeback. To enumerate my successes would be a matter of repetition.

Then I returned to this country and brought my racing career to a close in Salt Lake City in the fall of 1910, after a summer season that was not entirely satisfactory to me. While there I lost match races to Lawson and Clark and although I made a good impression I failed to make good before the fine sporting public of that city, which was Lawson's home town. Incidentally I felt this was the only city in this country where I failed to ride in my top form. Before this program was concluded, however, I got going in good shape and was sprinting as fast as ever before, but my decision to step down was made.

I recalled what the great Arthur A. Zimmerman, the former world's champion of several seasons had told me after he had retired from the bicycle track. In answer to my questions as to why he was unable to ride as fast as ever in spite of the fact that he had not taken on any surplus flesh, and looked as fit as I had ever seen him in his heyday he said: "My boy, when you have reached your zenith as a rider and have defeated every rider in the world, as I did, and when you have achieved all the success the racing game has to offer, then your enthusiasm will begin to wane and your star will begin to set. When you begin to dislike the game, and your enthusiasm for everything connected with it, then you will know that your racing career is just about finished. One thing I would advise you—when you succeed in winning the world's championship and honors, do not stay in the game so long that you become a second or third rater, and must allow every rider in the world to beat you. Nothing is more pathetic in the sporting world than to see the once brilliant athlete or world's champion walloped repeatedly by inferior riders." So remembering Mr. Zimmerman's advice I decided to bring my racing days to a close.

One mile International
Championship, Adelaide, 1903

One Mile International
Championship, Adelaide, 1904

One Mile World's Professional
Championship, Montreal, 1899

Quarter Mile International
Championship, Sydney, 1903

Five Mile International
Championship, Melbourne, 1903

First Place, Old
Timers' Race, September, 1917

Half Mile International
Championship, Melbourne, 1904

Grand Circuit Champion, also Quarter, Half,
Third, and Two Mile Championships, 1900

European Racing Tour
April, May, June, 1901

Ten Mile International
Championship, Melbourne, 1904

# CHAPTER XCIII



### I RETIRE AFTER SIXTEEN YEARS' RACING

After the season of 1910 I hung up my racing equipment. I felt that in my sixteen years of riding I had given my very best in every race that I started and that I was, therefore, entitled to a rest. I made this step despite the fact that in the closing days of that season I felt I was riding as fast as I ever had before. Recalling the great Zimmerman's advice to me as quoted in the preceding chapter, however, I decided to quit racing before second and third raters started to defeat me. During my heyday I defeated more than once every bicycle rider in this country in match races who was game enough to take me on including Butler, Bedell, Clark, Cooper, Elks, Eaton, Fenn, Fogler, Freeman, Lawson, Kimble and Kramer. Bald, Gardiner and Kiser drew the "color line."

I have been asked many times why I quit racing so early. Many of my friends criticized me for taking this step. Many of them felt that I should have remained in the sport until forced out, after the second and third raters had led me home time and again. They could not understand why I should retire from racing as physically fit as when I started.

Little did they realize the great physical strain I labored under while I was competing in these sixteen years of trying campaigns. Nor did they seem to realize the great mental strain that beset me in those races, and the utter exhaustion which I felt on the many occasions after I had battled under bitter odds against the monster prejudice, both on and off the track. In most of my races I not only struggled for victory, but also for my very life and limb. Only my dauntless courage and the indomitable fighting spirit I possessed allowed me to carry on in the face of tremendous odds. My trying experience on the tracks had exacted their toll from me, and I was certain the day had come for me to step out of the sporting limelight. Father Time was gaining on me.

I felt I had my day, and a wonderful day it was too. As I think back over those old days I have no retrospective regrets. Many of my good friends ask me if I would like to live the old days again. My answer in each case is "positively no." I have often wondered how long some of these friends would have carried on had they been in my place.

I was thirty-two years old when I retired having at that time spent more than half my life battling on the bicycle tracks. I cannot help but recall the many narrow escapes I had in my races, and shudder as I think of the many brave and outstanding riders who were killed or maimed for life in the pursuit of success on the track. I am grateful for having escaped serious injury in my races, and that I was able to leave the track in perfect physical condition.

I recollect that my good friend and team-mate, Harry D. Elkes of Little Falls, New York, as fine a motor paced rider as ever sat in a saddle, and the king of them all in his day, was instantly killed during a race on the Charles River Track, Cambridge, Massachusetts. Among other brave riders who lost their lives on the track were Joe Greibler, Myles, Aronson, Stafford, Nelson, McEchren, Leander, McLean, Mettling and the great Jimmie Michaels.

Floyd MacFarland was instantly killed in a quarrel over some trifling matter at the Vailesburg track where he had become manager after retiring from racing.

These athletes were killed on American tracks and I could recount a number of others who met a similar fate overseas. And still my friends wonder why I quit the game when I did!

Anybody that has followed bicycle racing knows that it is a hazardous pastime even when played fair. In my day I saw chances for fatal accidents, especially among followers of motor pacing, materially reduced through changes in the racing rules. One of the most notable of these common sense changes in the code book was the placing of the rollers on the motors back farther from the rear tire of motor pacing machines. This idea was adopted in order to place the rider so far back from the machine that he would have to combat greater wind resistance. Thus while he would be compelled to ride harder behind pace, his speed would also be retarded. Before the rollers were pushed back it was not an uncommon thing for a rider to be up so close to the motor that his head touched the back of the pacemaker. In another day I saw many other bad smash-ups on the track caused by the high speed of a rider. Friction caused the air in the tire to expand to such an extent that it burst, throwing the rider to serious injury or even death.

Upon being introduced to the late ex-President Roosevelt several years ago he grasped my hand with a hearty grip as he said:

"Major Taylor, I am always delighted to shake the hand of any man who has accomplished something worth while in life, and particularly a champion. I know you have done big things in your profession because I have followed your racing through the press for years with great pleasure. I was especially pleased and interested while you were racing abroad, defeating all the foreign champions, and carrying the Stars and Stripes to victory. Taking into consideration all the millions of human beings on the face of the earth, whenever I run across an individual who stands out as peer over all others in any profession or vocation, it is indeed a wonderful distinction, and honor and pleasure enough for me." It certainly was a distinction and a pleasure for me to hear such words from the great Colonel Roosevelt himself.

Notwithstanding the bitterness and cruel practices of the white bicycle riders, their friends and sympathizers, against me I hold no animosity toward any man. This includes those who so bitterly opposed me and did everything possible to injure me and prevent my success. Many of them have died and when I am called home I shall rest easy, knowing that I always played the game fairly and tried my hardest, although I was not always given a square deal or anything like it. When I am finally run off my feet and flattened by that mighty champion Father Time, the last thought to remain in my mind will be that throughout life's great race I always gave the best that was in me. Life is too short for a man to hold bitterness in his heart, and that is why I have no feeling against anybody.

Concerning my retirement from the track a New York newspaper printed the following paragraphs among others:

"A Picturesque Champion. Peculiar Traits and Career of Major Taylor Who Quits a Winner. The retirement of Marshall W. Taylor, better known as 'Major' Taylor, from cycle racing, removes one of the most striking and picturesque figures from that field of sport. Taylor who announced his retirement last week after his return from Europe, is the only Negro champion that cycle-racing has ever had, in spite of the fact that there have been many colored riders. But Major Taylor is a true champion and has proven himself on the track to be the peer, if not the master, of every white rider in the world.

"In 1897 Taylor, who was a professional at the outset, raced occasionally and gained some distinction. He was rounding into form, but on July 16 the following year, he shot to the fore in front of all the big racing men, by winning the One-Mile National Championship event at Philadelphia, defeating the great Eddie Bald, who was champion at the time, also Tom Cooper, who stood second to Bald, and the whole field of professional cracks, the best in America. Ever since he has been quite conspicuous.

"He won the championship of America for the first time in 1898. In 1899 he took the pace-following and proved himself as great at middle distances as in sprinting. He also won the sprint championship again that season and again in 1900. His ability to win at long or short distances is the one great distinguishing trait of Taylor's prowess. It is unusual and stamps him an exceptional rider.

"His physique from the points of symmetry and muscular development is one of the very best. Perfectly proportioned, he has a figure that excites unfailing admiration, though his skin is as black as ebony. In 1901 Major Taylor was beaten for the championship title by Frank

Kramer, but there was much complaint of unfair treatment that he received on the track, as all the other men being opposed to him were practically combined against him in every race.

"Last year Taylor returned late from abroad and entered the championships on the circuit when Frank Kramer had a lead of 31 points to his credit. Taylor scored a number of victories over him, but his unpopularity with the other riders was such that he lost heart and fre-

Bell Lap, Old Timers' Race—Won by Major Taylor, Vailesburg, 1917

quently failed to compete, and finally resolved to compete for the title no more. He went abroad last fall and remained in Australia all winter proving himself the best of all there. He went to Europe again in the spring where he again defeated all the best riders in Europe including Elleggarde, the great Danish rider, who held the World's Championship title. A couple of years ago Major Taylor held many American records, and his mile record of 1:19 stood for several years, but the figures have all been changed since he quit riding in this country."

The sporting editor of a newspaper in Sydney, Australia, published the following article relative to my retirement:

"Great Praise for Major Taylor. Sydney, New South Wales Paper Credits Him With Being Wonder of the World.

"Major Taylor recently received a copy of the 'Referee,' a Sydney, Australia paper which gives the former World's champion a measure of praise not often dealt out to an athlete. The 'Referee' in speaking of Taylor's retirement says:

" 'The retirement of Major Taylor is quite an event in the cycling world, that is, presuming the report is correct, for it is no uncommon thing for a star to be retiring annually.

" 'But in Major Taylor's case the probabilities are that he has really had enough of the racing game. No doubt he could keep on successfully for another year or two longer but his retirement would be compulsory in the near future, and as he had made considerable money, and has had the good sense to take care of it, he can well afford to leave the dangerous game of racing alone.

" 'It is not likely, however, that we shall look on his like again for some time. In my opinion he was the greatest racing cyclist the world has ever seen, and, as I pointed out only recently, that his wonderful record was gained under very often the most adverse conditions; for he was hustled and hated as only a colored person can be by the superior men in God's country; and he did not always receive fair play on the Continent, or even here in Australia.

" 'Had he not been a marvel of pluck, speed, and skill, he would not only have been the world's very best, but he would have either been killed outright or disabled years ago. Cycle-racing is a very dangerous game, even under ordinary conditions, but when deliberate fouling is introduced, it is then too risky for even the most daring, yet Major Taylor often had to chance it.

" 'Like all other mortals, however, he had his failings, but he was one of the straightest athletes that ever entered the arena. Although his absence will be a great loss to the sport, all admirers of a great cyclist and an honorable one will wish him the very best of luck for the future.' "

The world's fastest bicycle riders whom I met and defeated in my heyday rank as follows:

## AMERICAN

E. C. (CANNON) BALD, Buffalo, N. Y.
TOM BUTLER, Cambridge, Mass.
TOM COOPER, Detroit, Mich.
IVER LAWSON, Salt Lake City, Utah.
FRANK L. KRAMER, East Orange, N. J.
OWEN S. KIMBLE, Louisville, Ky.
EARL KISER, Dayton, Ohio.
WILLIE FENN, Waterbury, Ct.
FLOYD MacFARLAND, San Jose, Cal.
NAT BUTLER, Cambridge, Mass.

## EUROPEAN

THORWALD ELLEGGARDE, Denmark.
EDMOND JACQUELIN, France.
HARRI MEYERS, Holland.
WILLIE AREND, Germany.
LOUIS GROGNIA, Belgium.
PALO MOMO, Italy.
WALTER RUTT, Germany.
EMIL FRIOL, France.
DON WALKER, Australia.
GEORGE MORGAN

## MOTOR PACED

JIMMY MICHAELS, Wales.
HARRY ELKES, Glen Falls, N. Y.
EDDIE McDUFFEE, Boston, Mass.
TOM LINTON, Wales.

## A Tribute to my Silent Steed

I now hang up my silent steed
That served my purpose well indeed
Just like a true and faithful friend
It stuck right by me to the end

Whenever I called on it for speed
With a furious sprint we took the lead
Down the stretch and around the curve
Each rider straining every nerve

On we dashed at a reckless pace
A grim expression on each face
Into the home stretch, then the bell
A smash, a crash, and someone fell

The tumultuous fans how they roared
They knew the record would be lowered
Out of a pocket we would slip
To win the purse and championship

This was a thriller for the crowd
Which made us both feel very proud
We toured the world and beat the best
In many such exciting tests.

Now as a reward for faithfulness
My trusty bike has earned its rest
But not in the attic all covered with dust
Nor in the cellar to get all rust

But in my den on a pedestal tall
Or better still upon the wall
Where I can see it every day
And it will keep the blues away

We rode to win in every race
Fairly we played in every case
If life grows dull and things break bad
Just think of the wonderful days we've had.

# CHAPTER XCIV



### THE VALUE OF GOOD HABITS AND CLEAN LIVING

In closing I wish to say that while I was sorely beset by a number of white riders in my racing days, I have also enjoyed the friendship of countless thousands of white men whom I class as among my closest friends. I made them in this country and all the foreign countries in which I competed. My personal observation and experiences indicate to me that while the majority of white people are considerate of my people, the minority are so bitter in their race prejudice that they actually overshadow the goodwill entertained for us by the majority.

Now a few words of advice to boys, and especially to those of my own race, my heart goes out to them as they face life's struggles. I can hardly express in words my deep feeling and sympathy for them, knowing as I do, the many serious handicaps and obstacles that will confront them in almost every walk of life. However, I pray they will carry on in spite of that dreadful monster prejudice, and with patience, courage, fortitude and perseverance achieve success for themselves. I trust they will use that terrible prejudice as an inspiration to struggle on to the heights in their chosen vocations. There will always be that dreadful monster prejudice to do extra battle against because of their color.

It is my thought to present the facts to the rising generation of my people without coloring or shading them in the least. In a word I do not want to make their futures appear more rosy than they will be, nor do I wish to discourage them in the slightest degree as they face life and its vicissitudes. My idea in giving this word to the boys and girls of my race is that they may be better prepared than I was to overcome these sinister conditions.

I might go on discussing this subject at great length, but after all is said, done, and written, my own book of experiences will best show what these obstacles are, and how I managed to overcome them to some extent. I would advise all youths aspiring to athletic fame or a professional career to practice clean living, fair play and good sportsmanship. These rules may seem simple enough, but it will require great morale and physical courage to adhere to them. But if carried out in the strict sense of the word it will surely lead to a greater success than could otherwise be attained. Any boy can do so who has will power and force of character, even as I did, despite the fact that no one of my color was able to offer me advice gained through experience as I started up the ladder to success. In a word I was a pioneer, and therefore had to blaze my own trail.

(427)

I would like to cite an instance which proves the efficacy of clean living on the part of an athlete coupled with the inspiration received from a champion which go a long way to making a champion. Realizing full well that fine condition and confidence will not in themselves make a champion, it is my belief, however, that they are essential factors. Of course an athlete must have ability to reach the top, but many who have ability and who do not live clean lives never have and never will be champions for obvious reasons.

I recall that on my first trip to Europe in 1901 I saw a French youth, whose name was Poulain, ride in an amateur event at Nantes, France. He was very awkward as he rode about the track, but something about him caught my eye, and I became interested in him at once. At the close of the race I made several suggestions to him, adjusting his pedals, and handle bars, and giving him some advice on how to train. I stressed clean living upon him, and told him in conclusion that if he trained carefully and lived a clean life, I would predict that some day he would beat all the amateurs of Europe and the professionals as well.

When I returned to France in 1908 this same Poulain, who in the meantime had won the amateur and professional championships of France, defeated me in a special match race. Imagine my surprise at the conclusion of this event when my conqueror told me who he was. The laugh certainly was on me. I did manage to bring him into camp, however, after I reached by best form.

I know that a good many champions have entertained the thought that the more they discourage youngsters, the longer they would reign. However, this theory never impressed me, and I always made it a point to give youths the benefit of my experience in bicycle racing. I do this for a two-fold reason. First of all it was through the kindness of Louis D. (Birdie) Munger, now of Springfield, Massachusetts, that I became inspired and rode to American and world's championships. Secondly I always felt that good sportsmanship demanded that a champion in any line of sport should always be willing to give a helping hand to all worthy boys who aspire to succeed him.

When I was enjoying my heyday on the track I received hundreds of letters from youths asking for suggestions as to how to become a bicycle champion. As far as was practical I answered them personally, but as I was campaigning at the time it was physically impossible for me to pen notes to all of them. Naturally this procedure took considerable of my spare time, but I willingly did it as I realized and appreciated the kindness extended to me by Mr. Munger and many other good friends, which made it possible for me to lay the foundation for my remarkable career covering sixteen years on the track.

Modesty should be typical of the success of a champion. It always seemed to me that a real champion while possessing self-confidence on the eve of a race never became conceited. On the other hand I have seen mediocre riders who fairly breathed conceit in advance of the race in which they were entered. I have also noticed that when a rider who had confidence in his ability was defeated, after doing his level best to win, always received an ovation from the gathering. The reverse was true in regard to the conceited rider, regardless of how hard he tried in a race. The public has long since drawn a fine line between self-confidence and conceit. Sport lovers know that when they see a real champion he is going about his work in a businesslike manner. He does not have time nor the inclination to scorn his competitors, but rides against everyone of them as though he were his superior, with the result that the public is sure to witness a fine performance every time he starts.

Countless athletes have written articles relative to physical training which they deem essential to championship form. Many of them have dealt with the subject in a scientific manner, some foisted pet theories on their readers, while others advocated practical methods. I do not believe there is any royal road to success as an athlete any more than there is to others in everyday life. It is my thought that clean living and a strict observance of the golden rule of true sportsmanship are foundation stones without which a championship structure cannot be built. In a word I believe physical fitness the keynote of success in all athletic undertakings. Fair play comes second only to that factor, and I believe it should be impressed upon all boys from their marble-playing days.

Last, but not least, I would urge all boys aspiring to an athletic career to strictly observe the rules of the game, to practice good sportsmanship and fair-play, and also to be able to abide by an unfavorable decision with the same grace that they accept a victory. To these ideals which were instilled in me when I was a youth, I attribute in a large degree the success that was mine on the bicycle tracks of the world.

The moral turpitude of the boys of today appears to center in their failure to concentrate on any particular objective long enough to obtain their maximum results.

Clean living is the cardinal principle in the lives of the world's greatest athletes, as the phenomenal performances of these outstanding characters will obviously show.

In marathon running the marvelous Clarence Demar is a model in this respect. As a jockey the famous Earl Sande is another, in tennis the redoubtable William ("Bill") Tilden and the brilliant Helen Wills excel; while in golf Bobby Jones, the greatest golfer of all time, and the invincible Glenna Collette, the peer of women golfers, are exemplary; in wrestling the mighty Zybesco, Joe Stecher, and Ed. Lewis, the present champion, rule.

In baseball the late Christy Mathewson, Walter Johnson, Tyrus Cobb, and the "King of Swat" Babe Ruth, are splendid examples, and in prize fighting the late champion "Tiger" Flowers, Benny Leonard, the erstwhile champion Jack Dempsey, and the present champion Gene Tunney are exponents. In bicycle racing the former champion Frank Kramer, and Willie Spencer, the present title holder, lead all others. As an aviator the celebrated Col. Charles Lindberg is the shining example.

As a reward of their clean living and good habits these great stars have been able to withstand the rigorous test of stamina and physical exertion and have thus successfully extended their most remarkable careers over a period of many strenuous years.

Notwithstanding these facts, however, they must some day fade out of the picture altogether, even as I. They must some day bow to that perennial old champion, Father Time, even as I, for *Time* eventually wins.

## A DOZEN DON'TS

Don't try to "gyp."
Don't be a pie biter.
Don't keep late hours.
Don't use intoxicants.
Don't be a big bluffer.
Don't eat cheap candies.
Don't get a swelled head.
Don't use tobacco in any form.
Don't fail to live a clean life.
Don't forget to play the game fair.
Don't take an unfair advantage of an opponent.
Don't forget the practice of good sportsmanship.

## FINIS

9 798985 119404